The British General Election of 2005

The British General Election of 2005

Dennis Kavanagh
Professor of Politics, University of Liverpool, UK

David Butler
Emeritus Fellow of Nuffield College, Oxford, UK

First published 2005 by
PALGRAVE MACMILLAN
Houndmills, Basingstoke, Hampshire RG21 6XS and
175 Fifth Avenue, New York, N.Y. 10010
Companies and representatives throughout the world

PALGRAVE MACMILLAN is the global academic imprint of the Palgrave Macmillan division of St Martin's Press LLC and of Palgrave Macmillan Ltd.
Macmillan® is a registered trademark in the United States, United Kingdom and other countries. Palgrave is a registered trademark in the European Union and other countries.

ISBN-13: 978–1–4039–4252–4 hardback
ISBN-10: 1–4039–4252–8 hardback
ISBN-13: 978–1–4039–4426–9 paperback
ISBN-10: 1–4039–4426–1 paperback

This book is printed on paper suitable for recycling and made from fully managed and sustained forest sources.

A catalogue record for this book is available from the British Library.

A catalogue record for this book is available from the Library of Congress

10   9   8   7   6   5   4   3   2   1
14   13   12   11   10   09   08   07   06   05

Printed and bound in Great Britain by
Antony Rowe Ltd, Chippenham and Eastbourne

Contents

List of Tables

List of Illustrations

Figures

Party Advertisements

Cartoons

List of Plates

Preface

This is the seventeenth in a series of British general election studies sponsored by Nuffield College since 1945. With the help of many participants and many observers, we were fascinated observers of the latest evolution of campaigning techniques; in changed circumstances, each of the participants sought to exploit the new thinking about strategy and the new methods of communication which made the 2005 contest different from its predecessors a generation ago.

In the pages that follow we describe how Labour sought to secure a third term and how it was knocked off course by the Iraq war and for a time by the tensions between Tony Blair and Gordon Brown. We explore how the Conservatives sought to come to terms with their second consecutive defeat, in 2001, as well as the efforts of the Liberal Democrats to expand their bridgehead. The national campaign, its handling by the media and its reflection in the polls, are analysed as well as the new focus on a more intense but less visible struggle in the target seats. The way the parties played their hands is critically assessed and the statistical and electoral implications of the results are fully discussed.

We have to express our institutional, and still more our personal, gratitude to our colleagues in Nuffield College and Liverpool University for all the support they have given. We have to thank the Leverhulme Foundation for again so generously financing our operations and for imposing so little in the way of bureaucratic restraints. Our friends in each of the party headquarters and in the media know how much we owe to them – although they might not thank us for naming them.

We have particular debts to all our contributors whose names appear in the table of contents and who met our demanding deadlines. Among the many who have provided helpful comments on our repeated drafts we should particularly thank Chris Ballinger, Hugh Berrington and Vernon Bogdanor. Claire House at Liverpool did much more, over longer hours, than could be expected of any research assistant. We are also grateful to Geoff House's assistance in providing photographs. Lastly we must once again thank our long-suffering wives for bearing up with our electoral enthusiasms.

For 30 years these works have been published under the alphabetical label, David Butler and Dennis Kavanagh. It has been a very equal and congenial partnership. In 2005 we once again worked very hard together, but the burden fell more heavily on Dennis Kavanagh. It therefore seems appropriate, as David Butler bids farewell to the chronicling of general elections, that this final joint venture should be marked by a reversal of names.

Dennis Kavanagh
David Butler
August 2005

1
The Political Scene, 2001–04

The scale of its general election victory on 7 June 2001 surprised Labour. The Government had achieved another record majority – 167 over all other parties. The net loss was only six seats. But what were they to do with this commanding position? Their very long manifesto had, in essence, merely offered more of the same, even though it had included two promises which were to haunt them. The pledge not to increase taxes was followed in the next budget by an increase in National Insurance contributions which was widely seen as an increase in taxation. The pledge not to introduce top-up fees for university education in the lifetime of the Parliament was followed in 2004 by their imposition (the fact that the fees would not come into effect until the following Parliament did not quell the sense of betrayal).

In any case, such grand plans for public service reform as Tony Blair may have had were knocked off course by the event that shaped the political scene for the next four years. On September 11, 2001, al-Qaeda launched hijackers on an aerial attack on the World Trade Center in New York and on the Pentagon, causing 3,000 deaths and a fundamental shock to American attitudes. Tony Blair then led Britain in support of the US in two wars, in Afghanistan and later in Iraq, which were to dominate the headlines, year after year. The war produced deep divisions in Parliament, in the Labour Party and in the nation, and ultimately it became a key factor in the 2005 general election. The glow of military victory in Iraq did not last long and for many the war and its aftermath scarred the Blair image. However, these developments joined with the politics of the economy and of relations with Europe in shaping public opinion about the Labour Government and about Tony Blair.

After the election Tony Blair reshuffled his Cabinet, moving Jack Straw from the Home Office to the Foreign Office, demoting Robin Cook to the

Table 1.1   Economic and political indicators, 2001–04

		— (1) Real housholds' disposable income (2000= 100)	— (2) Average earnings (2001= 100)	↓ (3) Value of retail sales per week (2000 =100)	(4) Year on year inflation (%)	— (5) Unem- ployment (%)	▬(6) Days lost in strike (000s)	— (7) Gross domestic product (2001 =100)
2001	1	99.1	103.5	102.9	0.9	5.1	133.9	98.4
	2	98.6	104.0	105.6	1.5	5.0	121.2	99.5
	3	100.0	104.7	107.2	1.5	5.1	65.0	100.2
	4	102.5	105.5	108.1	1.0	5.2	203.1	101.9
2002	1	100.2	106.5	110.1	1.5	5.1	197.4	102.7
	2	102.0	108.0	111.3	0.9	5.2	158.1	104.2
	3	101.8	108.6	112.1	1.1	5.3	544.5	106.2
	4	101.6	109.6	113.7	1.6	5.1	423.6	106.9
2003	1	101.9	110.2	112.5	1.5	5.1	119.1	108.6
	2	104.6	111.2	113.3	1.3	5.0	69.0	109.6
	3	104.2	112.6	114.6	1.4	5.0	82.8	111.9
	4	105.2	113.5	116.3	1.3	4.9	228.3	113.0
2004	1	105.7	115.9	118.0	1.3	4.8	383.4	114.5
	2	106.5	115.8	119.7	1.4	4.8	281.1	116.2
	3	107.4	116.8	120.4	1.2	4.6	115.8	117.4
	4	106.9	118.4	120.2	1.4	4.7	123.9	118.6
2005	1	107.9	121.2	120.3	1.6	4.7	12.4	119.7

Sources: 1–5, 7–8, 10–12 *Economic Trends*; 6 *Labour Market Trends*; 9 *Financial Statistics*;
13 *Monthly Digest of Statistics;* 14–15 MORI.

Commons leadership and promoting David Blunkett to take over from ▪
Jack Straw. Further reshuffles followed so that by the end of the Parliament
only Gordon Brown and Tony Blair, together with John Prescott, Margaret
Beckett, Jack Straw and Alistair Darling, survived from the original 1997
Cabinet. Over the course of the Parliament Stephen Byers and David
Blunkett as well as Peter Mandelson were forced to resign. Estelle Morris,
Alan Milburn, Robin Cook and Clare Short chose to resign, while Lord
Irvine was *de facto* dismissed. But it could hardly be said that any great
new talents shone forth although John Reid and Charles Clarke came to
the fore as tough defenders of Government policy.

The economy continued to flourish. Tony Blair and Gordon Brown
could boast of the continuing increase in employment, of the lowest
rate of inflation in Western Europe and of the sustained growth in GDP.
Despite the unexpected costs of war and the rise in the price of oil,
Gordon Brown continued to refute the lugubrious forecasts of his critics
as he devoted increasing resources to the public services. Tony Blair,

(8) Balance of payments (£m)	(9) FTSE 100 share index (1 Jan 1984=1000)	(10) US$ to £	(11) Sterling exchange rate index (1990=100)	(12) Interest rates (%)	(13) House prices (1 Feb 2002 =100)	(14) MORI 'State of the economy poll': net optimists	(15) MORI polls (voting) intention) C L LD
−4756	5634	1.46	104.5	5.75	92.6	−13	31 50 14
−5467	5643	1.42	106.4	5.25	95.4	−13	29 51 15
−5686	4903	1.44	106.1	4.75	98.8	−34	26 53 16
−6276	5217	1.44	106.1	4.00	96.8	−36	25 57 14
−4702	5272	1.43	106.9	4.00	100.0	−21	28 50 17
−4988	4656	1.46	105.3	4.00	108.2	−15	29 48 17
−2287	3722	1.55	105.7	4.00	115.5	−25	27 53 16
−4510	3940	1.57	106.0	4.00	121.2	−32	31 41 21
−577	3613	1.60	102.3	3.75	123.4	−45	26 45 21
−4613	4031	1.62	99.1	3.75	127.2	−21	27 44 21
−5554	4091	1.61	99.2	3.50	130.7	−24	30 41 21
−6007	4477	1.71	100.2	3.75	133.4	−24	31 41 21
−4908	4386	1.84	104.1	4.00	136.4	−20	32 40 21
−5038	4464	1.81	105.2	4.50	142.5	−22	30 38 20
−8926	4571	1.82	104.8	4.75	148.8	−22	29 37 23
−4103	4820	1.86	102.4	4.75	149.8	−24	28 40 23
−5824	4894	1.89	102.9	4.75	448.3	−15	30 41 20

Note: C = Conservative, L = Labour, LD = Liberal Democrat

though sometimes through gritted teeth, could pay tribute to Gordon Brown as the most successful Chancellor ever. Nonetheless, economic commentators continued to point to the inevitability of the tax rises that would be needed to cover social outlays if Mr Brown's Golden Rule of fiscal prudence was to continue to be honoured.

Europe was never far from the news. In 2001 the Prime Minister announced that by mid-Parliament the Government would make available the Treasury assessment of the extent to which Gordon Brown's five conditions for joining the euro had been met. From the beginning it was plain that Mr Blair was more enthusiastic than Mr Brown and came to regret that he had conceded so much influence to Brown and his assessment over the decision. It was no surprise when, on 9 June 2003, the Chancellor reported that only one and a half of the five conditions had been satisfied. The promised referendum on joining the currency receded from the scene.

On 28 October 2002 the European Convention, under the former French President, Giscard d'Estaing, published its draft European Constitution. The document got a mixed reception in Britain. Its critics argued that it was a draft for a United States of Europe. Its defenders suggested that it represented only a tidying up of the complex and much amended Treaty of Rome, a necessary development to cope with the enlargement of the European Union from 15 members to 25. At first the Government argued that the changes involved were too minimal to need ratifying by referendum. But pressure grew from all sides, and, in a surprise move on 20 April 2004, Tony Blair announced that there would be a referendum after all.

The volte-face attracted some derision but it was of great tactical importance on the eve of the European Parliament elections. It saved the contest from being, as the Conservatives intended, a referendum about having a referendum. It also took the issue out of the general election, already universally expected for May 2005.

At the same time the Government also defended itself from the Eurosceptics by laying down 'red lines' beyond which it would not go when the Constitution came up for approval at a European Summit. Indeed, when that happened in Dublin on 20 June 2004, Tony Blair could boast that none of the red lines had been breached.

Chronology of events from June 2001 to December 2004

2001

7 Jun	General election: Lab 413 seats, Con 165, Lib Dem 52. Record low turnout
8 Jun	W. Hague announces resignation
	Reshuffle: J. Straw to Foreign O.; D. Blunkett to Home O.; R. Cook Commons leader
12 Jun	P. Hain appointed Minister for Europe
7 Jul	Bradford race riots
14 Jul	Stoke-on-Trent race riots
16 Jul	100 Labour MPs rebel over Whips' removal of two Select Committee Chairmen
19 Jul	Lord Archer found guilty of perjury and sentenced to two years in prison
2 Aug	Bank of England cuts interest rates by 0.25% to 5.00%
6 Aug	IRA agrees a means of decommissioning its weapons
11 Sep	Terrorist attacks on Twin Towers and the Pentagon
13 Sep	I. Duncan Smith elected Conservative leader

18 Sep	Bank of England cuts interest rates by 0.25% to 4.75%
1 Oct	War on Afghanistan declared
4 Oct	Bank of England cuts interest rates by 0.25% to 4.50%
8 Oct	H. McLeish resigns as Scottish First Minister
8 Nov	Bank of England cuts interest rates by 0.5% to 4.00%
13 Nov	Kabul captured
26 Nov	US economy declared to be in official recession
27 Nov	J. McConnell elected to succeed H. McLeish as Scottish First Minister
10 Dec	G. Marsden MP defects from Lab to Lib Dems
14–15 Dec	Laeken European Council meeting launches European Convention process

2002

1 Jan	Euro notes and coins begin circulating in 12 EU member states
14 Jan	Government declares that the UK is officially free of foot-and-mouth disease
29 Jan	President Bush labels Iran, Iraq and N. Korea as an 'axis of evil'
3 Feb	T. Blair pledges that 'wreckers' will not prevent public service reform
5 Feb	C. Kennedy calls for voting age to be reduced to 16
6 Feb	Queen Elizabeth II celebrates 50th anniversary of her accession
12 Feb	Colin Powell speaks of investigating how to topple Saddam Hussein
13 Feb	Scottish Parliament outlaws hunting with hounds in Scotland
14 Feb	President Bush announces his laxer alternative to the Kyoto protocol
28 Feb	G. d'Estaing opens the Convention on the Future of Europe in Brussels
5 Mar	R. Balfe MEP defects from Lab to Con
	President Bush imposes tariffs of up to 30% on European steel
30 Mar	Queen Mother dies
5 May	President Chirac wins second term, defeating le Pen 81%:18%
	A. Winterton sacked from Shadow Cabinet after making racist joke
10 May	Potters Bar rail crash kills seven

28 May	Transport Secretary S. Byers resigns. A. Darling succeeds him
	P. Boateng as Chief Sec. to Treasury is first black Cabinet minister
1 Jun	Four days of celebrations begin for the Queen's Golden Jubilee
11 Jul	Home Sec. D. Blunkett reclassifies cannabis from Class B to Class C drug
16 Jul	IRA publishes a full apology to families of all its victims
23 Jul	D. Davis replaced as Conservative Chairman by T. May
26 Aug	Ten-day UN Summit on Sustainable Development opens in Johannesburg
11 Sep	C. Kennedy becomes first Lib Dem Leader to address TUC annual conference
12 Sep	President Bush at UN General Assembly calls for rapid action on Iraq
22 Sep	Countryside Alliance protests at Westminster against banning fox hunting
24 Sep	In dossier on Iraq, T. Blair says that weapons of mass destruction (WMD) can be used in 45 minutes
7 Oct	Theresa May declares Conservatives are seen as 'the nasty party'
12 Oct	183 people killed in Bali bomb attacks
14 Oct	J. Reid suspends Northern Ireland Executive
24 Oct	Education Sec. Estelle Morris resigns. C. Clarke succeeds her. J. Reid becomes Party Chairman. P. Hain becomes Welsh Sec.
26 Oct	127 people killed when Russian troops storm hijackers in a Moscow theatre
28 Oct	European Convention publishes its draft Constitution
4 Nov	J. Bercow resigns from Con front bench over stand against adoption by gay and unmarried couples
8 Nov	Security Council passes Resolution 1441, returning weapons inspectors to Iraq
13 Nov	Firefighters commence 48 hours of strike action
7 Dec	Iraq publishes a 12,000-page denial of WMD
10 Dec	Cherie Blair apologises over lack of clarity about purchase of two flats in Bristol
12–13 Dec	Copenhagen European Council
14 Dec	Red Cross camp at Sangatte closes permanently
17 Dec	Polls show lowest Con ratings for four years

2003

3 Feb	Government publishes its second dossier on Iraqi WMD
6 Feb	Colin Powell says Iraq is in 'material breach' of UN resolutions
	Bank of England cuts interest rates by 0.25% to 3.75%
15 Feb	A million people march in London in protest against invading Iraq
17 Feb	Congestion charging scheme begins in London
24 Feb	Britain, US and Spain table Security Council resolution on Iraq
7 Mar	UK presents new draft resolution calling for Iraqi compliance by 17 March
12 Mar	Firefighters' union executive recommends rejection of employers' offer
17 Mar	UK, US and Spain attempt to get UN backing for invasion of Iraq
	R. Cook resigns from Government on point of principle
18 Mar	Commons passes resolution authorising use of British military in Iraq: 412:149
20 Mar	Bombing of Baghdad begins
20–21 Mar	Brussels European Council
6 Apr	British troops enter Basra
9 Apr	Statue of Saddam Hussein toppled in centre of Baghdad
2 May	C. Blunt calls for motion of no confidence in I. Duncan Smith; Cons advance in local elections
12 May	International Development Secretary Clare Short resigns
13 May	I. Duncan Smith pledges Cons will abolish tuition fees
20 May	Firefighters' union and employers reach agreement on staged pay offers
29 May	In BBC *Today* broadcast, A. Gilligan quotes anonymous source to claim government 'sexed up' its September 2002 dossier on Iraq's WMD
4 Jun	Israel and Palestine formally adopt the American 'roadmap' to peace
9 Jun	Treasury assessment of the five tests for joining euro says only one met so far
12 Jun	A. Milburn unexpectedly resigns as Health Secretary: J. Reid succeeds; Lord Falconer becomes Lord Chancellor; Peter Hain to Leader of Commons
10 Jul	Bank of England cuts interest rates by 0.25% to 3.50%

16 Jul	D. Kelly appears before Commons Intelligence and Security Committee
18 Jul	D. Kelly found dead near his Oxfordshire home
	T. Blair in Tokyo announces Hutton Inquiry
22 Jul	Saddam Hussein's two sons killed by US soldiers in northern Iraq
19 Aug	Massive truck bomb blows up UN HQ, killing top UN envoy S. de Mello
28 Aug	T. Blair appears before the Hutton Inquiry
30 Sep	Lib Dems win Brent East by-election
10 Oct	T. Blair admitted to hospital after suffering heart palpitations
13 Oct	Standards Commissioner to investigate I. Duncan Smith's office expenses
24 Oct	Concorde makes its last scheduled flight from New York to London
29 Oct	I. Duncan Smith loses confidence vote 75:90
6 Nov	M. Howard elected Conservative Party leader unopposed
	Bank of England raises interest rates by 0.25% to 3.75%
7 Nov	M. Portillo announces he will stand down as an MP at the next election
10 Nov	M. Howard announces first Shadow Cabinet reshuffle. D. Davis is Shadow Home Sec.; O. Letwin is Shadow Chancellor; L. Fox and C. Saatchi become Chairmen
23 Nov	England victory over Australia in Rugby World Cup Final
4 Dec	President Bush repeals US steel tariffs to prevent EU retaliation
14 Dec	S. Hussein captured by US soldiers
19 Dec	Libya renounces its WMD

2004

6 Jan	K. Livingstone readmitted to the Labour Party
9 Jan	BBC presenter R. Kilroy-Silk sacked for controversial comments on Arabs
23 Jan	Lib Dem spokeswoman J. Tonge sacked after comments on suicide bombers
27 Jan	T. Blair wins Commons vote on 'top-up' fees for university education 316:311
28 Jan	Hutton Report published
	G. Davies and G. Dyke resign from BBC
1 Feb	President Bush agrees to an independent inquiry on the use of intelligence

2 Feb	T. Blair sets up intelligence inquiry under Lord Butler
4 Feb	House of Commons debates the Hutton Report
5 Feb	Bank of England raises interest rates by 0.25% to 4.00%
16 Feb	Shadow Chancellor O. Letwin lays out plans on tax and spending
23 Feb	Blunkett says EU accession-country migrants free to work, but not to get benefits
25 Feb	M. Rifkind selected as prospective Con candidate for Kensington & Chelsea (Portillo's seat)
27 Feb	Widespread criticism of Clare Short after she reveals secret Cabinet papers and alleges UN Sec.-Gen. K. Annan was bugged
11 Mar	199 people killed in Madrid train bombings
15 Mar	V. Putin re-elected in Russia with 68% of the vote
	New Spanish PM J.L. Rodriguez Zapatero orders Spanish troops out of Iraq
17 Mar	G. Brown delivers eighth Budget
21 Mar	C. Kennedy dismisses attacks of poor health, but looks ill at party conference
31 Mar	Government wins further vote on tuition fee increases 316:288
1 Apr	Immigration minister Beverley Hughes resigns over 'dodgy visas'
	Bill on postal voting areas enacted after ping-pong with Lords
20 Apr	Blair promises referendum on EU Constitution
11 May	R. Kilroy Silk emerges as UKIP candidate
5 Jun	D-Day 60th anniversary commemorations
8 Jun	Euro-elections in UK
11 Jun	Con elect 28 MEPs; Lab 19; Lib Dem 12; UKIP 12; Others 6.
20 Jun	Blair agrees to EU Constitution at Dublin Summit
14 Jul	Butler Report largely clears Blair and MI6 over Iraq intelligence
15 Jul	Lib Dems win Leicester South by-election
21 Jul	T. Blair celebrates 10th anniversary as Lab leader
19 Aug	Iraq interim Assembly appointed
3 Sep	A. Salmond elected SNP Leader
15 Sep	Fox hunting bill passed again in Commons
16 Sep	K. Annan denounces invasion of Iraq as illegal
	T. Blair goes to hospital for heart treatment
6 Oct	Iraq Survey Group report says Iraq had no WMD

8 Oct	Confirmation that K. Bigley, an Iraq hostage, has been killed
3 Nov	G. Bush re-elected US President
11 Nov	Yasser Arafat dies
18 Nov	Parliament Act invoked to enact fox hunting bill
23 Nov	Queen's Speech
27 Nov	D. Blunkett denies that he 'fast-tracked' a visa application
2 Dec	G. Galloway wins libel case against *Daily Telegraph*
15 Dec	D. Blunkett resigns following Budd Inquiry
16 Dec	C. Clarke to Home Office, Ruth Kelly to Education
16 Dec	House of Lords rules against indefinite detention of foreign suspects
21 Dec	T. Blair visits Baghdad
26 Dec	Indian Ocean tsunami kills hundreds of thousands

(See p. 63 for continuation.)

The world reaction to the 9/11 attack was decisive. The Taliban government in Afghanistan refused to give up the al-Qaeda leaders and in December 2001, backed by UN resolutions, an attack, primarily by American forces, speedily destroyed the regime. Over the next few years a kind of democracy was established. But the US then turned its attention to the regime of Saddam Hussein in Iraq, demanding that it should comply with UN resolutions and get rid of its weapons of mass destruction. American and British forces began to assemble in the Middle East. Tony Blair presented to an emergency meeting of Parliament on 24 September 2002 an intelligence dossier claiming that Iraq had weapons of mass destruction ready for deployment in 45 minutes.

Fraught negotiations in the UN Security Council over how to react to Saddam Hussein's non-compliance with its edicts led to the unanimous approval on 8 November 2001 of Resolution 1441 with its reference to 'serious consequences' for further non-compliance. Since Saddam remained obdurate the US and Britain, aided by Spain, sought to get a further resolution passed explicitly authorising the use of force. A million people marched through London on 15 February 2003 to oppose military action. Negotiations continued at the Security Council, but the French made it plain that they would veto any ultimatum. The Americans and the British were advised by their lawyers that Resolution 1441 gave them sufficient legal authority to go to war, and on 20 March the bombing of Baghdad and other targets began. Two days before, the House of Commons had approved military action by a vote of 412:149; there had been a lot of heart-searching on all sides. The opposition front bench supported the Government while Kenneth Clarke was the most eminent of the 15 Conservative dissidents. On the Labour side, Robin Cook resigned from the Cabinet, together with two junior ministers and three Parliamentary Private Secretaries. There were strenuous efforts by the Whips, but 139 Labour MPs voted against – almost half of all the party's backbenchers. Clare Short, the International Development Secretary, wobbled for eight weeks before she resigned on 12 May.

After three weeks of fighting the Saddam Hussein regime was toppled but the victory proved somewhat hollow. In Baghdad and elsewhere resistance fighters and suicide bombers played havoc with the coalition's attempts at reconstruction, and an attritional form of guerrilla war set in, with regular loss of human life among the coalition's forces and still more among the Iraqis. There were scandals about the treatment of prisoners. Commentators increasingly drew parallels with Vietnam. Tony Blair found this all very depressing.

ALL BEHIND YOU, TONY

'All behind you, Tony' (l. to r.: Blair (chained to Bush), Prescott, Hoon, Straw, Cook and Brown).

(Martin Rowson, *Guardian*, 26 February 2003)

Meanwhile, on 29 May 2003 on a 6 a.m. radio news programme, Andrew Gilligan, a BBC journalist, reported allegations from a 'Government expert' that Downing Street had 'sexed up' the dossier that gave justification for the war. Mr Gilligan's story was vociferously disputed by the Government's press spokesman, Alastair Campbell. The Foreign Affairs Select Committee led a parliamentary inquiry in the course of which it robustly interrogated Dr David Kelly, the weapons expert who, it ultimately transpired, had been the source of Mr Gilligan's story. On 18 July 2003, Dr Kelly's body was discovered; he had committed suicide. Tony Blair immediately set up a judicial inquiry into the circumstances surrounding Dr Kelly's death, presided over by Lord Hutton, a retired Law Lord. The inquiry heard public evidence from everyone concerned, including the Prime Minister and the head of MI6, as well as Mr Campbell and Mr Gilligan, and in January 2004 published a report that cleared the Government and condemned the BBC in terms that led to the resignation of the Corporation's Chairman and its Director General.[1]

The whole episode put the credibility of the Government in doubt. Had Tony Blair led the country into an unnecessary and illegal war? Many in the Labour Party and the ethnic community were deeply disillusioned. The Muslim vote, for which the Labour Party was a natural repository, was seriously disaffected. The Liberal Democrats, on the other hand, could now expect to reap the benefits of their principled stand against military action. In January 2004, in a further reaction to complaints about the Dossier, the Government asked Lord Butler of Brockwell, the former Cabinet Secretary, to investigate the failures of the intelligence service in assessing the WMD situation. In July Lord Butler's report cleared Downing Street and MI6 of any deliberate deception, although it was critical of Mr Blair's informal 'sofa style' of running the Government, and of presenting 'sporadic and patchy' material as 'detailed, extensive and authoritative'.[2] It seemed that the war would not go away and soon led Blair to question himself and his colleagues, whether he should step down as Prime Minister at the October party conference (see Chapter 2).

Labour MPs acquired the habit of rebellion; and the large parliamentary majority allowed them to do so without threatening the government. The political scientist Philip Cowley has shown how the 2001 Parliament saw more revolts than any time since the arrival of party discipline in the 1890s. Iraq and top-up fees attracted most rebels. Ex-ministers who had resigned or been dismissed stiffened some of the revolts. Clare Short, Frank Dobson and Glenda Jackson were among the first to call publicly for Tony Blair to resign. But the government still did not lose a vote in the Commons, although it suffered twice as many defeats in the Lords as it had in the 1997–2001 Parliament.

Nonetheless, throughout the Parliament, Labour support, for a Government in its second term, held up relatively well in the polls (see Figure 1.1). Apart from a brief blip during the September 2000 fuel blockade, the Labour Party maintained the comfortable lead in the opinion polls it had enjoyed since 1992 and, even when the Conservatives came level briefly, Labour retained a position which, granted the bias in the electoral system, would ensure an adequate parliamentary majority. The Conservatives and the Liberal Democrats made advances in local council elections but Labour retained control of every big city except Liverpool (which the Liberal Democrats ran). Labour did not lose a parliamentary by-election until Brent East in September 2003 – and then it was to the Liberal Democrats. Despite their setback in the 1999 European elections, Labour had little reason to feel threatened by the Conservatives.

The main parties treated the European elections in June 2004 as a rehearsal for the general election, universally expected for May 2005. None of them fared well. The two biggest parties together won less than 50 per cent of the vote – 12 per cent less than ever before. Labour secured only 23 per cent, their lowest national vote since they first fought national elections in 1918, but the Conservatives, on 27 per cent, was also their lowest national vote for over a century. The Liberal Democrats were reduced to 15 per cent and fourth place. The only winners were UKIP who, with their simple slogan 'No', gained 16 per cent of the vote and 12 MEPs. Oddly, Labour and Blair emerged from this humiliation without serious damage. But as we show in Chapters 2 and 3, both the Labour and Conservative leaders, unhappy with their parties' campaigns, took the opportunity to change some key personnel for the general election. UKIP's triumph was short-lived, to the relief of the Conservative Party. The high-profile Robert Kilroy-Silk, who had contributed so much to the party's resurgence, left it in a huff to form his own party, Veritas (Latin for 'truth').

Another party to emerge in the 2004 European election was Respect, founded by the dissident Glasgow MP George Galloway after his expulsion from Labour in May 2003 for his stance over Iraq. Respect sought to win over the votes of old left, far left and anti-war protesters. But with 1.5 per cent of the vote it was not as successful as the 'racist' British National Party which secured 4.9 per cent, or the Greens who got 6.2 per cent and two MEPs.

Northern Ireland continued to offer a troubled backdrop to UK politics. The Northern Ireland Assembly elected in 1999 was suspended briefly

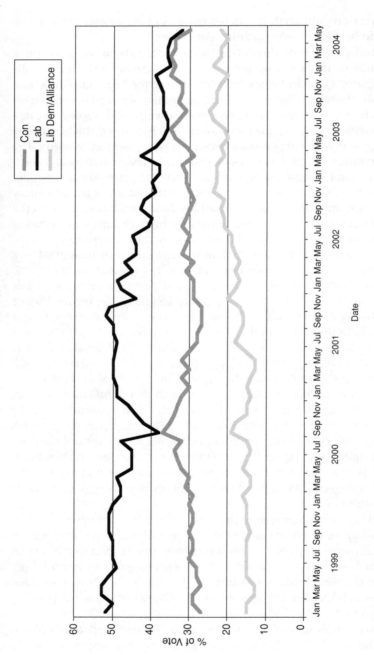

Figure 1.1 Three-party support, 1997–2004

Source: MORI.

twice in the summer of 2001 and then more permanently in October 2002. Hopes were raised that Sinn Fein would publicly decommission its weapons, but this was frustrated by the combined intransigence of Sinn Fein and Ian Paisley. Assembly elections took place on 26 November 2003, but the new Assembly never met. In 2004 Tony Blair had exploratory conversations with all the Northern Ireland leaders, but renewed prospects of an understanding were shattered when the IRA was implicated in a massive bank raid and, allegedly, in a much-publicised murder in a crowded Belfast pub. The Assembly election of 2003 and the European election of 2004 both confirmed the polarisation of the province, Sinn Fein overtook the peaceful SDLP and the DUP overtook David Trimble's UUP.

The Government suffered increasingly for its reputation for spinning news. Alastair Campbell, who had done so much to promote Tony Blair and the Labour Party's triumphs, excited more and more suspicion, and on 30 August 2003 he resigned his anomalous position at the head of Government communications as well as party spokesman, although it was plain that he continued as one of the Labour inner circle.

The Queen celebrated her Golden Jubilee in 2002, but it was not a very happy period for the monarchy. After the stalwart Queen Mother died in March 2003 (just after Princess Margaret), it became more common for republican views to be expressed and for royalty to be savagely cartooned, especially when the Charles and Camilla saga culminated in their marriage on 6 April 2005, just as the election was announced.

The Government was reluctantly dragged by its backbenchers in driving through a ban on fox hunting to take effect early in 2005. The attempts of a Commission under Lord Burns to find a compromise proved unacceptable to the House of Lords and to the anti-hunting enthusiasts.

The related questions of asylum and immigration reverberated throughout Parliament. The press, particularly the *Daily Mail* and the *Sun*, raised anxieties about infiltration through the Channel Tunnel or through heavy goods vehicles. The Sangatte camp at Calais was closed in December 2002 after long negotiations with the French. But scandals over holding camps and over the failure to remove unsuccessful claimants for asylum reverberated continually. As ten countries became new EU members in 2004, anxieties were raised about a flood of new migrants from Poland and the Baltic states. A scandal over casual administration of visas for Romanians led to the resignation of Beverley Hughes, a Home Office minister.

The Government were not very hard-pressed by the Conservatives. They seemed becalmed by their own troubles as they gradually discovered how unsuitable a figurehead they had chosen in 2001. Iain Duncan Smith came under increasing challenge from his own MPs until, on 29 October 2003, they passed a vote of no confidence by 90 to 75, making way for the unopposed succession of Michael Howard. Conservative disarray allowed the Liberal Democrats to claim that it was they who provided the real opposition, although there were those who made a similar claim for the media.

Efforts at constitutional reform embarrassed the Government. As part of a hasty reshuffle on 12 June 2003, the abolition of the office of Lord Chancellor and the establishment of a Supreme Court to replace the judicial role of the House of Lords was announced. But difficulties with the Law Lords and others prevented much happening beyond the renaming of the Lord Chancellor's Department as the Department of Constitutional Affairs. Efforts at Lords Reform were equally ineffective. On 5 February 2003, the House of Commons voted down each of seven alternative suggestions for a partially elected upper house. The Government did nothing to fulfil its 2001 promise of an assessment of the working of the various electoral systems installed since 1997.

It also faced civil libertarian objections to its proposals for identity cards and for penalising the stirring up of religious hatred as well as for the full application of the anti-terrorism legislation passed hastily in 2002. The Freedom of Information Act, implemented in January 2005, produced embarrassment for Governments present and past as journalists sought evidence of past scandals, ranging from the ending of Railtrack to the disposal of nuclear waste.

2004 did not end happily for the Government. David Blunkett, the tough-talking Home Secretary, became involved in a much-publicised paternity suit in the course of which it appeared that he might have fast-tracked a visa application for his mistress's nanny. After an inquiry by Sir Alan Budd, Mr Blunkett felt impelled on 15 December 2004 to resign. The equally robust Charles Clarke succeeded him, while the youthful Ruth Kelly took over his post as Education Secretary.

Notes

1. Lord Hutton, *Report of an Inquiry into the Circumstances Surrounding the Death of Dr David Kelly* CMG, HC 247.
2. *Review of Intelligence on Weapons of Mass Destruction. Report of a Committee of Privy Counsellors*, HC 898.

2
Labour in Government

At the beginning of the 2001 Parliament, Labour was in a historically unique position. It was enjoying a second consecutive full term and had every prospect of a third. Over the next four years, however, the fortunes of a number of the key players in the party's 1997 and 2001 election victories changed greatly. This was more true of Tony Blair than anyone else. During the Parliament he ceased to be the party's greatest electoral asset. The failure to find weapons of mass destruction in Iraq and his presentation of imperfect intelligence about the weapons had called his integrity and judgement into question.

A shrewd member of Tony Blair's Number 10 staff commented in March 2005: 'In 1997 Labour won a mandate for two terms. The Conservatives could never have won in 2001. Effectively our mandate has now run out and we are trying to renew it.' He thought that 2005 would be much harder to win than the earlier elections, partly because of Iraq, partly because of the breakdown in relations between Blair and Brown, partly because of the 24-hour media and partly because of the boredom factor. The list omitted any mention of Blair's declining popularity.

Blair had hoped that by the time of a 2005 general election he would be able to point to a massive improvement in the public services and appreciation of that among voters. It was not to be. The events of 9/11 ensured that the 'war on terrorism' became a major concern of government. The 2003–04 Parliament was dominated by the war with Iraq – the build-up to it and its fallout. The 139 Labour MPs who voted against the war on 18 March 2003, following Blair's failure to win support for military action from the UN Security Council, constituted the largest revolt on government benches in modern times, and one Cabinet minister resigned. Labour was the only social democratic party in Western Europe supporting the war. Blair was keeping close company with a right-wing

US Republican President and centre-left newspapers like the *Mirror*, the *Independent* and the *Guardian* were critical.[1]

The speedy victory in Iraq brought only brief political respite for Blair. The continued insurgency activities, the reports of the mistreatment of Iraqi prisoners, the rows with the BBC, the death of Dr David Kelly, the Hutton and Butler Reports and the increasing scepticism about the case for going to war all diminished his political capital and the Government's support. Before Iraq, Labour had enjoyed a commanding lead in the opinion polls; post-Iraq, its support fell by some 3–4 per cent. In spite of the Government's large majority in the Commons, the Whips struggled to pass contentious legislation, notably bills on foundation hospitals, funding higher education and combating terrorism, most of which went against the party's instinctive beliefs.[2]

There was discussion among Labour campaigners about the party's need to change its approach to the public. The low turnout in 2001 had come as a shock. Because the party had suffered most from the failure of its supporters to vote, it had an electoral interest in boosting turnout. Lord (Philip) Gould, the party's campaign strategist, and Douglas Alexander, campaign coordinator until September 2004, believed that the era of top-down permanent campaigns, so successful for the party in 1997 and 2001, had become less useful. New technology meant that voters were so inundated with messages, often commercial or personal, that political communicators had to struggle for attention. Politicians were talking to what Alexander and Gould called 'an empty stadium'. Research showed that voters were often satisfied consumers, but when it came to politics they felt impotent and ignored. Because voters were also looking for more engagement with politicians and engagement on their own terms, politicians, like successful companies, had to listen and to win their attention. With a less attentive audience, political parties had to move from *interruption* to *permission* marketing.[3]

Labour's reputation for spin (including economy with the truth and evasiveness) and control freakery was an additional problem. Its claims, even when backed by good evidence, were often not believed. A leaked memo from Gould to Blair in 2000 had already warned that the New Labour brand had become 'contaminated' and voters thought Blair all show and no substance. Revelations about the faulty intelligence on Iraq's weapons of mass destruction confirmed those suspicions. The departure of the Prime Minister's Press Secretary, Alastair Campbell, in September 2003 provided an opportunity to announce that the Government was moving to a new style of communication. As part of the fresh 'openness'

Blair held regular on the record press conferences and took questions from the Liaison Committee of the House of Commons.

The party also experimented with new methods of local campaigning, using more direct mail and email and promoting MPs as champions of the constituency. As we show in Chapter 11, Matt Carter, the party's General Secretary, decided that if local campaigning were to work, local party workers increasingly had to be helped by professionals employed at the centre, for example in preparing direct mail. The new 'professionalism' was most evident in the concentration of resources on key or target seats the party had to hold if it was to win a good majority in a general election. The party's communications centre in Gosforth employed over 120 staff and dealt with direct mail and the production of DVDs for candidates (usually sitting MPs) in the target seats. In late 2004, two recruits from the John Kerry presidential campaign arrived to help with the local campaigning: Karen Hicks advised on targeting messages in the key constituencies, and Zac Exley, who ran the 'Move On' project in the presidential election, helped with the e-campaign. In November 2003 the party launched the 'Big Conversation' to promote informal discussions between ministers and party members. The idea came from Geoff Mulgan and Matthew Taylor, two Number 10 advisers. 'There is a lack of engagement and we need to give more party people a sense of ownership of what we are doing.'

Approaching an election, Labour had a number of advantages. Its lead in seats was such that, even if turnout was low (and therefore hurting Labour most) and the Conservatives gained more votes, it was still very likely to win, given the bias in the electoral system. Labour's relative standing with voters at the mid-term point was still ahead of that for most governments at a similar stage in a Parliament. The opposition, under whichever leader, remained unimpressive, and surveys regularly showed that about a third of those dissatisfied with the Government would still vote Labour.

However, public and private polls reported that the Conservatives' supporters were more likely than Labour's to turn out; among those certain to vote, Conservative and Labour ran level. The party's problem was to mobilise the disillusioned supporters. It was difficult to replicate the same single-minded focus the party had for the 1997 general election because the leading figures were now distracted by the burdens of being in government.

Preparations for the election were also hindered by the continuing tensions over what was known as the 'succession question' between the Prime Minister and his Chancellor of the Exchequer, the two chief architects of the New Labour project and previous general election successes. The tension could be dated back to the lack of agreement between the two principals over the so-called 'Granita accord' in 1994. Gordon Brown, his friends claimed, had decided not to contest the election for the party leadership in return for Blair, if he became Prime Minister, granting Brown control over much of the domestic policy agenda and making way for Brown to become Prime Minister during a second term. Over time their relations deteriorated; they had been frosty during the 2001 general election campaign and were troublesome for much of the 2001 Parliament. The differences over approach were displayed at the party conference in 2003 and Brown's speech ('best when we are Labour') was seen as a challenge to Blair's programme of extending choice and diversity into the public services. On more than one occasion, the Chancellor confronted Blair and sometimes demanded a date for a handover of the premiership which Brown had understood would take place in the spring of 2003.

Brown was a huge asset to the Government and colleagues respected him because of his role as the campaign strategist in 1997 and 2001. But Blair looked back on the 2001 election campaign as one that had lacked vision and – thanks to Brown's command of the campaign – had concentrated too much on the economy. In late 2003 he refused Brown's appeals to be given a seat on the party's National Executive, a clear hint that Blair was not intending to appoint him to run the next general election campaign.

On 6 November 2003, the same day that Michael Howard was elected Conservative leader, John Prescott hosted a dinner for Brown and Blair in his grace-and-favour apartment in Admiralty Arch. The Deputy Prime Minister appealed for the two men to work together and warned that their rivalry risked destroying all that they had achieved so far. Blair indicated his willingness to resign the premiership before the next general election, but wanted Brown to help in promoting his public service reforms. The meeting was followed by the usual claims and counter-claims between the rival parties. Brownites claimed that there had been a breach of faith on Blair's part when he did not resign, and there were counter-claims that Brown had not been cooperative over public service reform, notably over foundation hospitals and top-up fees. Prescott commented that Blair worried over his legacy while Brown worried over his inheritance.

Much of the first half of 2004 was bleak for Blair – 'grim', said one of his staff. There were few signs of progress in Iraq, Labour MPs were unhappy about the war, health reforms and variable top-up fees in higher education, and Blair's poll ratings had tumbled. Iraq, and the related question of trust, would not go away, with the ample media coverage of the Hutton and Butler Reports. On 20 April Blair was forced to reverse his decision not to hold a referendum on the forthcoming European Constitution. The U-turn may have blunted a Conservative appeal at the forthcoming European Parliament elections, but it was not discussed in Cabinet and angered pro-European ministers.[4] Another Blair aide complained of a 'debilitating' atmosphere.

Blair felt under pressure because of worries over his own health (he had an irregular heartbeat, first diagnosed on 19 October 2003), and the loss of key aides in Number 10 (by early 2004, Alastair Campbell, Anji Hunter, Peter Hyman and his Principal Private Secretary Jeremy Heywood had all departed, while Peter Mandelson and Alan Milburn were no longer in the Cabinet), and fears that he had become an electoral liability. What he interpreted as pressure from Number 11 to stand down was also sapping his energy. 'They were trying to drive us out', said one of Blair's staff. He talked with friends about the possibility of announcing his resignation some months in advance. Some Cabinet colleagues, as well as Bill Clinton, pressed him to stay on to ensure that he leave a more substantial New Labour legacy.

Blair bounced back when the local and European election results in June 2004, and the report in July of the Butler Inquiry into the role of the intelligence services before the Iraq war, were not as bad as he had feared – although Lord Butler did criticise the Blair style of taking decisions and the glossing over of the Joint Intelligence Committee's caveats and qualifications of the intelligence. Moreover, Gordon Brown's behaviour was prompting doubts in Blair's mind about his suitability for the leadership: was he collegial enough? Was he New Labour enough? And was he willing to work with US and EU leaders?

Douglas Alexander, Minister for the Cabinet Office and Chancellor of the Duchy of Lancaster, prepared the European elections campaign and Gordon Brown took charge of strategy. Under Alexander the party established a call centre in the North East and an Attack Unit in Old Queen Street. He set in train plans for direct mail and the allocation of resources to key seats for the general election. Number 10, however, was not impressed when shortly before the European election Alexander took a month's paternity leave. Blair was also unhappy with the conduct of the campaign: aides told him that the committees were too large, people appeared to be working to different agendas, and there were unpleasant shouting matches between different factions. He did not want a general election to be run like this and looked for more progress on preparation of a manifesto, coordination of policy, selection of key seats, and a greater sense of unity. He may not, however, have appreciated the extent to which uncertainty over the leadership, in particular over who would be the leader at the next election, was a major handicap.

More unfortunately for Alexander, his close identification with Gordon Brown meant that he became a casualty of the worsening relations between the Prime Minister and the Chancellor during 2004. Although formal responsibility for the European election preparations lay with Ian McCartney as Party Chairman and a member of the Cabinet, Alexander did the work despite his lack of seniority and the inability of Number 11 and Number 10 to agree key decisions about the campaign. He was in the firing line when Blair decided to reassert himself on returning from his summer holiday at Cliff Richard's Sugar Hill mansion in Barbados.

By September 2004, Blair had decided that if he were to fight another general election campaign and serve a third term he wanted it to be on a New Labour manifesto – 'unremittingly' so, he liked to say. This would be his chance to create a legacy, one of reformed public services, involving greater diversity and choice among both service providers and consumers respectively. For some months he had encouraged two former Cabinet ministers, Alan Milburn and Stephen Byers, to act as outriders for a New Labour agenda. In speeches and newspaper articles they pressed for more radical reforms in the public services. Milburn had resigned, unexpectedly, as Secretary of Health in June 2003, after clashing repeatedly with Brown over his hospital reforms. Blair regarded him as a like-minded spirit and wanted him back in government; indeed Milburn probably took public service reform more seriously than Blair.

As so often with Blair's reshuffles, it did all not go to plan. Initially he had intended to replace McCartney with Milburn but, when Prescott objected, he decided to dispense with Alexander. Following discussions with a number of Blairite Cabinet ministers, Milburn accepted the post of Chancellor of the Duchy of Lancaster, with responsibilities for campaign coordination and policy development. He was assured that he would be in charge of the campaign and of the manifesto; he would have Blair's total support and a seat in Cabinet. For Milburn the post had the advantage that it was clearly time-limited – it would end with the general election. Perhaps Blair had not thought through the political consequences of giving Milburn such a wide remit. On the same day as Milburn told interviewers that he would be in charge of the election campaign, Blair replied to a Sky television interviewer that Gordon Brown would be in charge.

Ministers and commentators therefore regarded Blair's decision on 12 September to recall Milburn as campaign and policy coordinator as crucial. 'It's a big call, and has consequences for the government's immediate policy direction, Tony's relations with Gordon, and the policy agenda for the third term', said a confidant. Blair did not discuss the appointment with Brown. The 'spin' accompanying the announcement, never disowned by Number 10, seemed calculated to anger Brown, and it did so. A Treasury colleague of Brown commented: 'Gordon shrugged his shoulders. He had not been consulted, he thought it suggested that there would be a greater Presidentialism and saw it as having a one more heave campaign to keep Tony Blair in charge. His view was "Let them get on with it".'[5]

On 30 September, immediately after the party conference and with Brown in the United States, Blair announced that he would shortly be having a heart operation, that he would lead the party into the next general election and that, if Labour won, he would serve for a full third and final term. Blair's hand had been forced when he heard that the *Independent* newspaper was about to publish a story about his purchase of a house in Mayfair and that he was going to enter hospital. Brown – who had expected to be in Number 10 by this time – and his allies felt betrayed. To them, Blair's copper-bottomed promise had been reneged on, said a neutral figure.

From late 2004, regular members of the key campaign planning and strategy committees included Alan Milburn (in the chair), Philip Gould; David Hill (the Number 10 Press Secretary); Jonathan Powell, Pat McFadden and Baroness Morgan from Blair's staff; Alastair Campbell (who had returned to work a couple of days a week); the General Secretary, Matt Carter; Ian McCartney; a member of John Prescott's staff and, occasionally, Gordon Brown. But the all-important sessions between Blair and Brown were held only occasionally. One result was that the various campaign meetings lacked a sense of purpose; they were waiting for the key principals to decide some key issues, not least whether they would be working together and how they would promote the party's economic message. Blair therefore decided to chair a campaign strategy committee to take decisions.

The TBWA agency handled the advertising, as it had done in 2001. Trevor Beattie, the Chairman and Creative Director, took part in brainstorming sessions with Milburn's team, and the agency conducted regular focus groups for the party. Philip Gould drafted the election War Book, but what emerged was more a series of papers than a consolidated document. Although there was some talk of downgrading the role of the economy as the central election theme, all the research showed that that this was a key dividing line between the parties, a major advantage for

Labour over the Conservatives, and particularly attractive to the party's target voters. But all the talk of stressing the economy as an issue in turn raised the delicate question of the Chancellor's relations with the Prime Minister and his involvement in the campaign.

There was a change in the polling. Stan Greenberg had polled for the party in the two previous general elections, but Blair increasingly talked of the need for a fresh approach. Former US President Bill Clinton strongly recommended Mark Penn, who had polled for him in the 1996 presidential election. Greenberg, the campaign consultant for John Kerry, the defeated Democratic candidate in the 2004 presidential election, was identified with a strong anti-Bush and anti-Iraq war campaign, and his appointment as the chief pollster to the British Prime Minister might also be embarrassing for the UK Government's relations with the White House.

Penn's appointment was confirmed in September 2004 but was known to few. Greenberg however, continued to have a role. The polling budget was split between Greenberg, who conducted surveys in marginal seats, and Penn, who did national polls. Penn made monthly presentations to the party's strategy committee and had a monthly session with Blair. Because the party had decided to do half of its polling through cheaper internet-based surveys, it was able to increase the scale of polling compared to 2001.

Mark Penn addressed his first memo to Blair in September. He noted that 12 per cent of voters were now lapsed Labour; people who had voted for the party in 1997 or 2001 or identified with it, but were no longer prepared to support it. Many had moved to the Liberal Democrats, often because of Blair and Iraq; they complained that because of the war Blair had lost interested in their concerns, particularly on the NHS, education and the standard of living. Penn recommended that Blair apologise for the faulty intelligence about weapons of mass destruction, which meant that the public and Parliament were deprived of a full debate on the issues, and acknowledge that Iraq had created a division between him and the people. There was media speculation that he would do this in his conference speech, but what he said was less contrite: 'I can apologise for the information that turned out to be wrong, but I can't sincerely, at least, apologise for removing Saddam.' Reinforcing a theme of Greenberg's polls, Penn recommended that ministers take action to limit immigration and anti-social behaviour, as a way of assuring people that they would 'get a fair shake'. He also noted that lapsed Labour voters were twice as likely as party voters to read the *Daily Mail* and were predominantly middle aged and working class.

Blair was conscious that the preparatory work had not been done to make the 2001 Parliament one of achievement on public service reform. Indeed, the crucial and controversial legislation for introducing foundation hospitals and variable tuition fees in higher education had not been mentioned in the 2001 manifesto. Andrew Adonis, a policy adviser, sent Blair a memo in early 2003 arguing the case for a third-term agenda emphasising the themes of choice and empowerment. The Government had to show that it still had radical plans for the future. Mrs Thatcher had won a third successive election victory in 1987 after a successful party conference in 1986 organised around 'The Next Move Forward'. Labour should, Adonis argued, do the same – 'but on our own terms'.

In Downing Street, Lord Birt, operating privately, and Sir Andrew Turnbull, the Cabinet Secretary, also worked on policies for the third term. Birt claimed the credit for getting the departments to submit five-year plans and Turnbull played particular attention to the 20-odd public service targets on which the Prime Minister concentrated. Some of Blair's advisers argued for policies which would recapture the support and enthusiasm of disillusioned Labour voters. Blair, however, wanted to press on with radical reforms and looked to his Number 10 advisers for new ideas on health and transport. But, having earlier admitted in the Commons that '"policy first, explain later" was not the way to do things', he agreed to suggestions that he try to involve Cabinet colleagues and the party more fully in his plans. In late 2004, Blair took the departments' five-year plans to the full Cabinet rather than through Cabinet committees; he wanted ministers to be signed up for a radical third term.

Matthew Taylor, of the Institute for Public Policy Research, joined Number 10 in October 2004 with a remit to encourage new thinking, but also to draft the manifesto. In early 2004 he had drafted 'A Future Fair for All', and worked on the party's pledges. Labour had introduced the idea of pledges for the 1997 election and the Conservatives then followed. Campaigners believed that where pledges were modest and concrete they were more credible and had the advantage of encouraging message discipline. The pledges were tested in focus groups by TBWA (but, in the event, there was little enthusiasm for them among campaigners).

The party conference, largely due to the votes of trade unions, defeated the platform over the Private Finance Initiative in 2002 and foundation hospitals in 2003. There was a clear shift to the left reflected in the election of some new general secretaries, and the Fire Brigades Union and the RMT disaffiliated from the party. Prompted in large part by the need for union financial support for the general election, the party arrived at an 'accord' with the unions at the party's National Policy

Forum at Warwick in July 2004. The Government agreed to include in the manifesto proposals to provide longer periods of maternity pay, to protect Bank Holiday pay and to ensure that new contracts of employment for workers moving from local authority employment to the private sector would not be less favourable. The trade unions concentrated on the promised workplace reforms and acquiesced in proposals on ID cards, top-up fees and mixed public–private provision of public services. The unions continued to provide important financial backing for Labour. Over the lifetime of the Parliament they contributed over £40 million to party coffers, some two-thirds of total funding.

During August 2002, party headquarters were relocated from Millbank to less expensive and smaller premises in Old Queen Street in Westminster. Charles Clarke became Party Chairman with a seat in the Cabinet, and David Triesman, a former leader of the Association of University Teachers, succeeded Margaret McDonagh as General Secretary of the party in July 2001. Both Clarke and Triesman were insistent that the party must adopt a new style of communications and involve the grassroots more in policy-making and debate. They also wished to break with what, for shorthand purposes, was referred to as the Millbank model, associated with spin and central control; Millbank was, however, also identified with landslide election victories.

In October 2002, John Reid succeeded Clarke as Party Chairman, and Ian McCartney in turn replaced him in 2003. The latter's relations with Triesman were difficult, and after the depressing Brent East by-election result in September 2003, Blair was pressed to make changes. Forced to choose between Triesman and McCartney, who was backed by John Prescott and many trade union leaders, he chose McCartney. Triesman went to the House of Lords and served as a Whip. A worry for the party was that membership had slumped to 201,000 by the end of 2004, some 50,000 below the figure Blair had inherited in 1994.

The new General Secretary was Matt Carter, previously Assistant General Secretary in charge of policy. As a former organiser in the South West region, he had grassroots experience surpassing that of Triesman. Under Carter the 'ground war' and the concentration on the target seats proceeded without much regard to the tensions at the top of the party. 'We knew that the Tony–Gordon business would eventually be resolved, though we did not know how. We knew what we had to do and got on with it', said a senior organiser. Carter appointed over 100 local organisers on six- and 12-month contracts to work in the marginal seats.

By the end of 2004, Labour had a clear lead over the Conservatives in the opinion polls. But campaign planners were still uneasy over the continuing tensions between Numbers 10 and 11 and how this would affect their ability to mount a winning campaign.

Notes

1. See J. Kampfner, *Blair's Wars* (The Free Press, 2003) and P. Riddell, *Hug Them Close: Clinton, Blair and the Special Relationship* (Politico's, 2003).
2. On dissent among Labour MPs, see P. Cowley, *Revolts and Rebellions: Parliamentary Voting under Blair* (Politico's, 2002).
3. S. Godin, *Permission Marketing* (Simon & Schuster, 2002).
4. See A. Seldon, *Blair* (The Free Press, 2005).
5. On this see Seldon, *Blair*, and R. Peston, *Brown's Britain* (Short Books, 2005).

3
The Conservatives

During the twentieth century the Conservative Party had gained the reputation of being the natural party of government. When it lost general elections it was usually returned soon afterwards, thanks to a mix of new leadership and refreshed policies and organisation – as well as inept or divided opposition.

But the old formula had failed to work after the party's crushing defeats in 1997 and 2001. The elections were a nadir in terms of both seats and share of vote. Since the beginning of 1993 the party had trailed Labour in all but a handful of opinion polls, rarely gaining the support of more than a third of the electorate. Indeed, surveys showed that had turnout not fallen so sharply in the 2001 general election, the Conservatives would probably have suffered an even heavier defeat.

There was much debate about the causes of the sudden but apparently enduring Conservative decline.[1] Tony Blair had reinvented the Labour Party; it was no longer the unelectable opposition it had been in the 1980s; it now occupied the political middle ground, and it had succeeded in reassuring much of the middle class. Thanks to Gordon Brown's stewardship, it was regarded as the party of competent economic management, a mantle traditionally worn by the Conservative Party. Apart from politics there was an additional barrier. The first-past-the-post electoral system was heavily biased in favour of Labour because of that party's more efficient distribution of its vote across constituencies. By 2005, if Labour and the Conservatives were each to gain 36 per cent of the vote, Labour would still have a comfortable majority.

Although Margaret Thatcher was looked upon as a great Conservative leader, many of the party's troubles were already apparent by the end of her premiership. The party had little presence in Scotland, Wales or many of the northern cities in which the Liberal Democrats had emerged as challengers to Labour; the Conservative Party was increasingly a party of South East England and of the elderly. So-called modernisers complained that the party's language and culture too often resonated a tone of intolerance, social exclusiveness and xenophobia, all of which were ill-suited to Britain in the twenty-first century.[2]

Before the 2001 general election, a new division in the party had emerged between the social liberals, who organised around Michael Portillo (and became known as the 'Portillistas'), and defenders of traditional values. William Hague tried to steer a path between these rival views, but only at the cost of seeming to be opportunistic as he flip-flopped between them. His 2001 election campaign, with its message of income tax cuts, tighter controls over immigration, tackling crime and, primarily, saving the pound, was aimed squarely at the core vote. The party appeared to have little to say on the economy, health and education, largely because these were seen as strong Labour issues. Unfortunately, voters, according to opinion polls, ranked these the key issues.

On 8 June 2001, the day after the general election, William Hague resigned as soon as it was clear that Labour had won another landslide victory. Five candidates stood in the contest to succeed him. The front-runner was Michael Portillo, backed by a clear majority of the Shadow Cabinet. The other contestants were Kenneth Clarke, Iain Duncan Smith, Michael Ancram and David Davis. MPs had to choose two to go forward to a ballot of the party membership. Ancram and Davis withdrew after they had finished bottom on a rerun first ballot and urged their supporters to vote for Duncan Smith. Portillo led on the first and second ballots but it was clear that he had peaked, adding only three more votes to his first ballot total, compared to Duncan Smith's 12 and Clarke's 20. Clarke finished top on the third and final ballot and Duncan Smith was one vote ahead of Portillo who was eliminated (Table 3.1). After the first ballot a disappointed Portillo had discussed with close aides how to withdraw even if he made it to the run-off, rather than wait to be eliminated. He began his gradual withdrawal from frontbench

Table 3.1 Conservative leadership ballot, 2001

	Round 1 (rerun)	Round 2	Change
Clarke	39	59	+20
Duncan Smith	42	54	+12
Portillo	50	53	+3
Davis	18	–	
Ancram	17	–	

politics, having shed support on the right partly because of his journey towards social liberalism and partly because of a reputation for disloyalty to William Hague.[3]

Clarke and Duncan Smith fought a bruising contest over ten weeks during the summer months of 2001. Clarke had Cabinet experience and greater voter appeal, but his pro-EU stance was a major handicap among the activists. The result of the 200,750 votes cast was fairly predictable: an elderly and Eurosceptical membership backed Duncan Smith by a margin of 3 to 2. Duncan Smith's support was clearly stronger in the constituencies than among MPs, and this did not bode well for his management of the Parliamentary Party. The election did nothing to unify the party and the electoral arrangements came under great criticism. There was general agreement that the campaign was too long and that the activists should probably have more say over who stood for election but less in the final choice of leader. Many activists would have found a choice between Clarke and Portillo (averted by only one vote among MPs) unappealing.

Duncan Smith's background was surprising for a Tory leader. It was not so much that he had never been to university nor been a member of a learned profession (neither had John Major or Winston Churchill) but that – uniquely for a Tory leader – he had never held a government post. Although the scale of his victory over Clarke in the constituencies confirmed his party's Euroscepticism, he understood that the party needed to talk less often and less shrilly about the issue and calculated that his impeccable Eurosceptic credentials equipped him to do this. And, although elected as a standard-bearer of the party's right wing, he also understood that the party needed to be taken seriously as a reformer of the public services.

Some would claim that Duncan Smith's leadership was doomed from the start. A number of party heavyweights, including Michael Portillo, Kenneth Clarke, Francis Maude and William Hague, refused to serve in his Shadow Cabinet. This was compensated somewhat by the return of Michael Howard as Shadow Chancellor and the emergence of Oliver Letwin as an effective spokesman on home affairs. But IDS's authority over many MPs was weakened by the expectation that Labour would easily win the next general election. Commentators (prompted by some Conservative MPs) speculated on when he would be forced to stand down.[4] He found it difficult to get a hearing from much of the media for his ideas because he was not thought to be a winner; his halting and generally unimpressive media performances contributed to this perception amongst Conservative MPs and the wider electorate. The leader's warning at the 2002 party conference to 'never underestimate the determination of the quiet man' was followed a year later with the claim that 'the quiet man is turning up the volume'. When he appealed to MPs for loyalty to his leadership and unity (in one speech he warned his MPs to 'unite or die'), critics (including former ministers and Whips from John Major's Cabinet) pointed to his own rebellious record over Maastricht. Maastricht had made his reputation, but it proved a handicap when it came to leading the party.

Greg Clark led a small Policy Unit in Central Office to work on new policies. Shadow ministers visited Europe to explore new ways of reforming the public services, based on the introduction of greater choice and competition. On health the party adopted the idea of a patient's passport to allow people to choose between hospitals for treatment and in education parents would be given passports to choose between schools, although fee-paying schools would not be allowed to ask parents to top up the dedicated sum. The party also announced plans to encourage charities and private companies to set up schools.

The Shadow Cabinet agreed to oppose the Government's introduction of top-up fees in higher education; it approved an increase in the state pension and a restoration of the link between pension up-rating and wage increases, as well as a scrapping of the congestion charge in London, and tougher action against asylum-seekers. There was a populist but not a free market touch to many of the policies.

At the party's Spring Forum in Harrogate in March 2002, Duncan Smith launched his project of making the Conservatives the party of social justice. The party's main task, he declared, was to help the vulnerable in society. In September, in a speech to mark the anniversary of his leadership, he spoke about the 'Five Giants', updating William Beveridge's 1942 analysis of the causes of poverty. The new problems he identified were failing schools, insecurity in old age, crime, poverty and substandard health care. Some colleagues did not understand the agenda and some simply lacked sympathy for it.

There were tensions between Michael Howard and Iain Duncan Smith over taxation. Opinion polls showed that tax cuts were not a priority for voters, who were usually more concerned about public services and were sceptical about any party cutting taxes. Howard was particularly cautious because he was convinced of the need to reassure voters that a Conservative government would place spending on public services ahead of tax cuts. But Duncan Smith pressed for action and was backed by the *Daily Mail*, the *Daily Telegraph* and many activists. The issue had not been resolved by the time Michael Howard assumed the leadership.

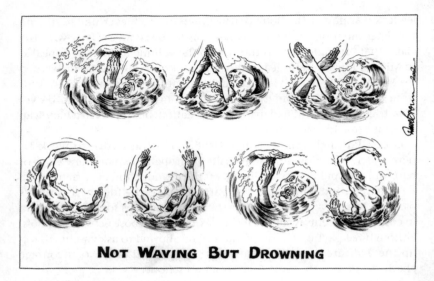

NOT WAVING BUT DROWNING

IDS's tax dilemma.

(Dave Brown, *Independent*, 23 December 2002)

Iain Duncan Smith, who had close links with neo-conservative circles in Washington DC, had no doubt of the case for supporting the US war on Iraq. But in the Commons vote in March 2003, 15 Conservative MPs voted against the war, and all the former Conservative Foreign Secretaries who spoke on the war – Lords Howe and Hurd and Malcolm Rifkind – were against it. Some Conservatives also voted against the Adoption and Children Bill in November 2002 which allowed, *inter alia*, adoption by unmarried couples, regardless of gender or sexual orientation.

Personnel problems at Central Office constantly made headlines. The leader's removal of his first Party Chairman, David Davis, when the latter was in the US, earned Davis's undying hostility. Davis was thought to have designs on the leadership and, according to Duncan Smith's friends, spent too much time in the tea-rooms in the Commons cultivating support. The new Chairman, Theresa May, also had an uneasy relationship with the leader. He did not approve of her claim in a party conference speech in 2002 that many people thought of the Conservatives as the 'nasty party', and he was lukewarm about her attempts to diversify the social background of candidates.

Duncan Smith suspected that some senior Central Office staff were open or closet Portillistas and were undermining him. On 14 February

2003, in what became know as the 'St Valentine's Day Massacre', he dismissed Mark MacGregor, a modernising chief executive in Central Office, without the approval of Theresa May, and then dismissed the Research Director, Rick Nye. He also sought but failed to remove the Campaigns Director, Stephen Gilbert, who had served the party for several years. Following a hostile reaction from MPs, activists and Board members, Gilbert stayed on. Other departures included his Chief of Staff, Jenny Ungless, and Director of Strategy, Dominic Cummings. Cummings had been recruited from heading the anti-euro 'No' campaign in February 2002, but had angered Duncan Smith by stating in public that 'The only thing less popular than the euro is the Conservative party.' The leader then appointed his fellow Maastricht rebel Barry Legg as chief executive, without consulting the Board (although it was constitutionally the final authority on such matters). Legg's appointment was a controversial step because of his association with Westminster Council's 'homes for votes' scandal of the 1980s. The Board formally objected to the appointment and Legg resigned two months later. MPs were bewildered, Central Office was not a happy headquarters and the incident further sapped the leader's already diminished authority.

The party's poor third place in the Brent East by-election on 18 September 2003 provided a depressing backcloth to the annual party conference. In what proved to be his final conference speech, Duncan Smith promised to extend consumers' choice in the public services and, in a passage that foreshadowed Michael Howard's 2005 general election campaign rhetoric, declared:

I believe in hard work, in rewarding people who play by the rules, in small government. I believe in punishing criminals, in trusting nurses, teachers, police officers. I believe in a low tax economy. I believe we all have a special duty of care for the most vulnerable people in our country – children, pensioners and the poor. And, most of all, I believe in the sovereign right of the British people to govern themselves.

The conference had been dominated by talk of an imminent leadership challenge, and when MPs returned to Westminster on 28 October it was announced that the necessary minimum of 25 Conservative MPs had written to the Chairman of the 1922 Committee, Sir Michael Spicer, to force a confidence vote in the leader. This would be the first time the new machinery had been used for this purpose. By now a growing number of MPs, Whips and even Shadow ministers openly favoured a change. Friends advised Duncan Smith to resign but he fought on, claiming that his resignation would only advertise the continued disunity within the party and its lack of loyalty to any leader. He lost the confidence vote by 90 to 75. Although he had retained the support of virtually all those MPs who had backed him when he was elected leader 25 months earlier, he had lost the crucial backing of the Whips.

'Unite or we die!'

(Patrick Blower, *Evening Standard*, 6 November 2002)

Faced with the prospect of another divisive leadership contest, many MPs decided that the party's interests would be best served if they could unite around one candidate. Michael Howard emerged as the favoured one; David Davis and Michael Ancram agreed, reluctantly, not to contest the leadership – partly in response to appeals to unite behind Howard and partly in acknowledgement of their own lack of support. Local associations were remarkably quiescent when presented with the fait accompli. It was something of a return to the old days when, in effect, senior figures in the party chose the leader.

Michael Howard had finished last of the five candidates in the leadership contest to succeed John Major in 1997 and seemed to have been overtaken by a younger generation. But he had served Duncan Smith loyally and had support across the party. He had authority and experience (having served in the Cabinets of Margaret Thatcher and John Major) and he was a formidable debater. But he was also a reminder of the Conservative past and critics recalled the wounding remark of his former Home Office colleague Ann Widdecombe that there was 'something of the night' about him.

Howard declared his candidacy at the Saatchi Gallery on 30 October. He had done little forward thinking about the leadership and, at short notice, Francis Maude, a senior figure on the modernising wing of the party, agreed to draft his speech (Howard abandoned an initial plan to make Maude Party Chairman out of deference to Duncan Smith, who complained that Maude had helped to destabilise his leadership). Howard's only substantive amendment to the draft was to insert a passage about his humble background and his parents being immigrants. In the speech, widely welcomed for its conciliatory tone, Howard promised to acknowledge Government achievements, not oppose for opposition's sake, and to lead the party from the centre. Maude also helped with Howard's 'British Dream' speech in February 2004. The new leader, keen to avoid the kind of public disunity that had so damaged the Conservative party's reputation, also discussed his Berlin speech about the EU beforehand with the leading pro-Europeans Lord Heseltine and Kenneth Clarke.

Howard was keen to emphasise a 'new broom' approach and to impose his authority. A key symbol of this was his decision to appoint a small Shadow Cabinet (12, compared to the outgoing 26) which met four mornings each week. He appointed David Davis as Spokesman on Home Affairs, Michael Ancram as Shadow Foreign Secretary, and Oliver Letwin as Shadow Chancellor. Tim Yeo took overall charge of 'public services', with the younger Tim Collins and Andrew Lansley respectively handling Education and Health but outside the Shadow Cabinet: a surprising decision, given the electoral importance of these issues. In July 2004, both were promoted to the Shadow Cabinet and Tim Yeo was moved to Environment.

Liam Fox and Lord Saatchi (whose advertising agency had handled the party's advertising at all general elections between 1979 and 1997) were appointed as Party Co-Chairmen. Saatchi was in charge of strategy and Fox took charge of campaigning, the constituencies and communicating with the media. Saatchi was a link with the party's election successes under Mrs Thatcher and a reminder of how the party had used tax to run effective negative campaigns against Labour. But some of Howard's advisers were convinced that the public mood had changed and wondered if he was adaptable enough to respond. As part of a reorganised Central Office (reduced from 11 to 3 departments),

Greg Clark headed the Research Department (with David Willetts, the Work and Pensions Shadow minister, appointed Chairman of a re-created Research Department, and given overall responsibility for policy). Will Harris, who had relaunched the BT Cellnet mobile telephone service as O2, became Director of Marketing, in charge of polling, advertising and membership. This appointment proved unsuccessful, and when Harris left in June 2004 no replacement was made.

Howard's small political office probably had more influence than his Shadow Cabinet. Rachel Whetstone, his political secretary, had served as his special adviser when he was Home Secretary; she knew Howard's thinking, helped write his speeches, voiced strong opinions on policies and personnel, and advised on key appointments. Stephen Sherbourne, a former political secretary to Mrs Thatcher, was made Chief of Staff; Guy Black, Director of the Press Complaints Commission, became Press Secretary; and David Cameron subsequently took over the policy development role from Willetts. Ed Vaizey, the party's candidate for Wantage, helped Howard with speech-writing and as the election approached was assisted by Michael Gove, another new candidate and an assistant editor of *The Times*. Steve Hilton, who ran a corporate social responsibility consultancy, helped with strategy, conducted focus groups and made strategy presentations to Howard and to the Shadow Cabinet until autumn 2004. Many of these had worked together in the party's Research Department under Andrew Lansley on the 1992 election campaign.

Six weeks after his election as leader, on 22 December 2003, Howard convened a strategy conference on the theme of 'Winning the Next Election'. Present were his political staff, the two Party Co-Chairmen and Oliver Letwin. Steve Hilton reported that voters, although content with the general state of the economy, were dissatisfied about asylum, crime, the public services and tax. Unfortunately for the Conservatives, they did not blame any particular party and, worse still, as he noted: 'There is zero belief that *we* would do better.' Furthermore, voters did not want tax cuts but greater value for money in public services. A member of the group recalled: 'The rants and moans were not going to be the basis for how people voted or for a change of government. People thought all parties break promises and are pretty well like one another. The electorate's cynicism and pessimism was better for the government than us because it made it difficult for us to break through – for that you need hope and enthusiasm.'

As a means of establishing that enthusiasm, Hilton floated the idea of a 'Timetable for Action'. Ronald Reagan, when running for the US presidency in 1980, was thought to have made an impact with his promises to take specific actions within hours and days of entering the White House. Howard, a great admirer of Reagan, was persuaded that a credible time-schedule for action would strengthen the Conservative message. This might be done by the party publishing a mock Conservative Queen's Speech for October 2004 – promising legislation to enforce accountability, control of taxation, reduction of regulations, fixed-term Parliaments and independence for the Office of National Statistics. Howard and Saatchi were uncomfortable with some of the proposals, particularly suggestions that the party be less adversarial and base its campaigning on a more positive vision, rather than the traditional anti-Labour message, and nothing came of the idea.

It did not take long for modernisers to express disappointment in Howard, just as they had done with his two predecessors. The party seemed, as under William Hague, to be reverting to issues that appealed to its core vote. But what mattered was attracting non-Conservatives and to do this the party had to change radically from the kind of policies which appealed to supporters (see Table 3.2). Modernisers argued that the party should focus on the voters it needed to win and not preach to the converted, and that the party should say what it stood for rather than what was wrong with Labour.

Table 3.2 What would attract voters back to the Tories?

	Tories (%)	Non-Tories (%)
Be more aggressive opposition	54	10
Commit to cut taxes	57	16
Higher priority to keep the £	67	22
Increase private sector role in NHS	61	29

Source: Populus, for *The Times*.

Many critics and even friends complained that Howard was not a strategist but a tactician, one who seized opportunities as they came day by day. As an established Parliamentarian, it was predictable that he would revel in adversarial frontbench politics and point scoring; his formative years in the Commons in the 1980s had been spent as a frontbencher at a time when his party was dominant. He was very much 'Michael Howard QC' in the parliamentary debate over the Hutton Report into the events leading to the death of Dr David Kelly. Howard had convinced himself that the report would be damaging to Blair. He was taken aback when it was not and performed poorly in the debate.

As the claims and counter-claims raged over Blair misleading the public about the case for going to war with Iraq, Howard came under party pressure to attack the Prime Minister over the issue, despite the party's initial support for the war. One member of his staff was urging him to use the Butler Report to abandon his support for the war and argued that the next election would be a referendum on Iraq. In an interview with the *Sunday Times* on 18 July 2004, Howard seemed to equivocate. He said he supported the war but would have joined the Labour rebels if he had known about the questionable intelligence about weapons. The interview was headlined 'I would not have voted for Iraq war says Howard' and provided ammunition for Labour (and some Conservative) critics of his 'opportunism'. Members of the White House Staff took note and the traditional close ties between the party and the Republicans became strained. By contrast, when Iain Duncan Smith had voted to support the war, Vice President Cheney had phoned him on the night of the vote to express appreciation. The war in Iraq and its consequences were damaging to Blair and the Government but did nothing to contribute to Conservative fortunes.

The party's lack of a clear vision became a source of frustration to Howard's team. At a meeting convened at Howard's home in April 2004, to discuss the failure to make progress in the polls, every member of the leader's inner circle, including Maurice Saatchi, argued for a clearly defined vision or 'big idea'. An outsider, George Bridges, quoted Viscount Slim's injunction that a leader had to offer his troops 'a noble object' to inspire them. Howard firmly rejected the demands, insisting that the role of a political leader was to solve people's problems, not indulge in conceptual theorising; 'Talking about small concrete measures to improve people's lives is what I am about, not having a big idea or a vision.' The decision set the tone for all the party's subsequent campaigning under Howard. One who was present recalled: 'The dye was cast then. We were not going to have a strategy.' A frustrated member of the group said: 'We were f****d. We never had a strategy.' Another said: 'In a way it was admirable but it is not the way to win elections today.'

Elections gave mixed results. There was progress in local government elections on 10 June 2004, but the European elections on the same day were a disappointment. The party fought a negative campaign, with its slogan of 'Let Down by Labour', trying to make it into a referendum on the Labour Government's performance. Blair's late decision to agree to a referendum on the forthcoming EU Constitution deprived the Conservatives of a key campaign message. UKIP, with its uncompromising call for Britain to leave the EU, managed to attract significant Conservative and Eurosceptic support. An appeal by Howard's office for Baroness Thatcher to warn Conservative supporters against the dangers of voting UKIP was embarrassingly rebuffed. 'She agrees with UKIP', said one of her staff. When the party finished fourth in the Hartlepool by-election on 30 September 2004 (having been second in 2001), the *Daily Telegraph*'s verdict was brutal: 'the worst by-election performance by an official Opposition in modern history'. Liam Fox made a ritual claim that private polls showed the party doing much better in the marginals. It was not.

The Saatchi–Fox dual chairmanship was not a success. The dividing lines of responsibility did not prove clear in practice and there was, perhaps inevitably, a struggle for supremacy. Lord Saatchi played a key role in handling the move from Central Office in Smith Square to new offices in Victoria Street (later renamed by Lynton Crosby 'Conservative Campaign Headquarters') – although several months later the building remained empty and without a tenant. Howard, however, was becoming impatient at the failure to implement a consistent political strategy and Saatchi's advocacy of a large tax-cutting programme had been rejected. 'Maurice Saatchi marginalised Liam Fox and then Howard marginalised Saatchi', said one insider.

Liam Fox managed to procure from President George W. Bush's campaign manager, Karl Rove, the 'Voter Vault' system, a computer programme for use in identifying key swing-voters in marginal seats. The party already possessed the programme but Fox managed to raise the money to commission Experian, an information services company, to operate it. The project was to target 838,000 voters in the 163 seats the Conservatives needed to win. Drawing upon demographic, opinion polling and 2001 census data, as well as canvass returns and MOSAIC, a commercial programme which divided households into broad social types, it identified 63 different types of voters. Target voters were those who had a high propensity to vote and had an affinity with (or not an aversion to) the party, but had not voted Conservative in 2001. Such voters were inundated with direct mail, visits from party workers and telephone calls. Party workers could use the data and postcodes to compare likely Conservative supporters with past records of voting pledges and local membership lists. The party learnt that from the model there was a 70 per cent chance of correctly identifying Conservative supporters; that its typical voter was aged 59, white, and had a household income of £43,000; and that the best predictor of voting Conservative was length of tenure of home ownership.

The party also benefited from a special seats exercise funded by Lord Ashcroft, a former party Treasurer. Ashcroft had been angered at the dispersal of party funds to some 180 seats in 2001 and favoured a more concentrated approach. He made available a sum up to £2 million through his Bearwood Corporate Services company. Forty-one local associations received money once Stephen Gilbert, the former party Director of Campaigning, had approved their business plan. Additional funds for other seats came from Lord Steinberg, chairman of Stanley Leisure, and the Midlands Industrial Council, a group of business leaders in the region. In all, some 80 associations received funds from these groups.

A key recruit was Lynton Crosby who arrived at Central Office on 18 October, six months after he had been appointed. Having helped the Australian Liberal Party leader, John Howard, to victory four times in succession, he had gained an unrivalled reputation for winning elections. The appointment was controversial for his past use of immigration as an issue in his election successes. As Campaign Director he was decisive and insisted on clear lines of authority. He believed in basing a campaign on simple, well-researched themes and messages and concentrating efforts on marginal seats. Crosby was irritated at charges that the party was pursuing a core vote strategy. Campaigning by posters, direct mail, leader's appearances, regional press advertising, polling and focus groups were all concentrated in the 163 marginal seats the party needed to form a government. On most mornings Crosby and George Bridges, a former political secretary to John Major in Number 10 and now a communications consultant, met Howard and his team (Rachel Whetstone, Guy Black, Stephen Sherbourne and David Cameron).

At the same time as the Crosby appointment, Howard appointed the 38-year-old MP David Cameron to replace David Willetts as Policy Coordinator, and George Bridges to head the Research Department as well as the War Room. Effectively, the David Cameron–George Bridges duo replaced the David Willetts–Greg Clark team. The new men were close to Howard who increasingly felt the need for a sharper edge to the projection of the policies. In effect, Lord Saatchi and Liam Fox were henceforth marginalised in discussions of electoral strategy.

Some long-serving backbenchers, as well as some Shadow Cabinet members, resented what they saw as not only the influence of the leader's office but also what they regarded as Howard's fast-tracking of a young generation of MPs, particularly David Cameron and George Osborne. Cameron and Osborne were sometimes held up as the party's equivalent of Labour's Brown and Blair of two decades earlier. They and some other members of the Howard team were referred to, sometimes disparagingly, as 'the Notting Hill set'; for the most part they were affluent, educated at public schools and Oxbridge, and were regarded as modernisers.

The policies were largely inherited from, or had been set in train by, Iain Duncan Smith using the work done under Greg Clark. Howard and Letwin waited on a study by David James (instigated by Howard, when he was Shadow Chancellor) for proposals to cut 'wasteful' public spending. Oliver Letwin's medium-term expenditure review in February 2004 tried to meet voters' concerns by promising that a Conservative government would match Labour's planned increases in spending on health and education. The party continued with its choice agenda for schools and hospital treatment and plans to elect local sheriffs, although the party's research showed that choice did not resonate at all with target voters. Voters thought that the health passport meant that patients could go abroad for treatment, and discipline in schools was a greater concern than choice. In March, Tim Yeo and the health spokesman Andrew Lansley, both influenced by Nick Sparrow's research, had argued strongly against the passport policy. Tim Collins, the education spokesman, was similarly unenthusiastic about the emphasis on choice on schools. Howard, supported by the Co-Chairmen, overruled them.

More difficult was the party's decision on the Government's proposal to introduce identity cards. Some Conservatives objected on civil libertarian grounds, some for cost reasons, but Howard had proposed a voluntary cards scheme when he had been Home Secretary. Friends of David Davis let it be known that he would rather resign than support the cards, and Howard let it be known that he would resign if the Shadow Cabinet did not back him. A crisis was in the making until the leader's aides interviewed each member of the Shadow Cabinet individually and won them over. The party voted for the bill on the second reading, abstained on the third, and vigorously opposed it in the House of Lords. In effect, the leader had had to overrule the Shadow Cabinet.

Tax had been a troublesome issue for the party since the 1992 general election when the party promised to cut taxes but then increased them. Although the party was sympathetic to the case for tax cuts ('it's in Conservative DNA', was often said) and backbenchers pressed hard for significant cuts, the party's research suggested a great deal of public disbelief in any party promising them. On a number of important issues there was not much difference between swing voters and loyal Conservative voters but on tax there was a marked difference: swing voters, in contrast to loyal Conservatives, were not in favour of tax cuts. Like Duncan Smith, Howard managed to keep Europe off the agenda. The party was now largely Eurosceptic; the issue was rarely brought up on the doorstep or in focus groups, and cross-party agreement about the need to hold a referendum on the EU Constitution stilled internal party controversy.

Immediate Sales, a self-contained operation within M&C Saatchi, was appointed to take over party communications in August 2004, although it had been working for the party since the start of the year. It was in charge of advertisements, posters, direct mail and on-line messages. It presented the campaign team with the slogan 'Are You Thinking What We're Thinking?' Following research, the slogan was launched on posters in February in the target seats. The agency argued that the party should exploit Labour's unpopularity by ensuring that the party's communications avoided gloss, were understated and worked with the grain of the public mood. Advertisements should be in a modest black-and-white format and messages should be handwritten to convey the impression that the ads reflected voters' views. The team pored over hundreds of verbatim quotations from the focus groups in search of ideas and slogans: one such was 'It's Not Racist to Impose Limits on Immigration'.

In the campaign headquarters, Gavin Barwell, the Director of Operations, led a team that monitored progress in the target seats. The party also established a call centre in the Midlands to maintain contact with Conservative voters and employed a staff of 50 at headquarters to contact the swing voters (see Chapter 11).

There was much change in the party's polling arrangements during the Parliament. YouGov polled for the party while Duncan Smith was leader. Under Michael Howard, negotiations with Nick Sparrow of ICM, the party's pollster in the 1997 and 2001 general elections, reached an advanced state. After the 2001 general election Sparrow had complained in a hard-hitting report to the party that

> the concentration on tax cuts and the euro were failing to ignite swing voter's interests in voting Conservative. But for months and years previously the research had advised against both these campaign themes. We can only conclude that a decision was taken to ignore the research. Indeed, from ICM the campaign looked to be only slightly influenced by the research, very largely it depended on political dogma.[5]

During early 2004, party leaders still resisted Sparrow's findings about the public's dislike of many party policies and its aversion to or disbelief in the promise of tax cuts. In public and in private he argued that the party would profit from a public disillusion with Labour only if the voters perceived that the Conservatives had genuinely changed and if they had positive reasons for voting for the party. In April 2004, Sparrow terminated his relationship with the party. He found that he appeared to be working to a wide range of people, including Howard, the two Co-Chairmen and the Marketing Director, among others, and objected to what he thought were attempts to add self-fulfilling questions to his surveys.

The party then turned to a newcomer in party polling, Johnny Heald, Research Director of Opinion Research Business (ORB). Heald was inexperienced as an in-house political pollster, although his father, Gordon, had long experience of polling for the party in the 1980s and 1990s. ORB was appointed in June 2004 to conduct surveys and focus groups with target voters. At these sessions Steven Hilton and George Bridges usually accompanied Heald. Overnight they would write a memo for Lynton Crosby and Michael Howard and the reports fed directly into election strategy, speeches and statements by the leader, and other communications. As discussed in Chapter 7, Lord Saatchi's claim at the party conference in 2004 that private polling showed the party to be winning in 103 of 130 Lab–Con marginals caused great embarrassment for ORB. It was inaccurate, out of line with national polls, and prompted a disbelieving Lord Ashcroft to commission a large programme of research in the marginals which produced a very different picture.

Sir Stanley Kalms, the former Chairman of Dixons, was party Treasurer under Duncan Smith. He was unhappy at the frequent changes in Central Office personnel (and the associated redundancy costs) and George Margan replaced him in 2003. Poor poll ratings proved a handicap in raising funds. Michael Howard appointed Jonathon Marland as Chief Executive of the Treasurer's department and Lord Hesketh was Chairman of the Foundation, a body which raised funds for the party's longer-term development. Wealthy benefactors made loans which were to be repaid with interest below the market rate; being repaid at below commercial rates meant that the identity of the donors could remain undisclosed.

Howard took much pride in unveiling a simple Conservative election message in ten words at the 2004 party conference, under the 'Timetable for Action' banner. Conservatives would promise: lower taxes, cleaner hospitals, more police, controlled immigration, school discipline. To these Howard added one other word: 'accountability', intended to break through the voters' mistrust of all politicians. The decision to highlight these five specific policy areas, along with the accountability theme and the 'Timetable for Action' concept, had been developed in intensive focus group research over the summer months. But the launch was something of an accident. The ten words had been included at the last minute in Howard's conference speech because of a concern to give party activists a simple way to communicate the party's policies, of which many voters were unaware. Not all advisers were pleased. The words 'lower taxes' and 'more police' were not supported by the research which had found that voters were more concerned about getting value for the taxes they paid and about the need for more respect in society (anticipating Tony Blair), and the need for tougher sentences.

Soon after the conference, Frank Luntz, an American campaign consultant, persuaded Howard that the 11 words should be re-presented as five commitments. Words were not actions. Howard was keen to focus on five specific commitments rather than a 'big idea' or vision (as some of his Shadow Cabinet and his campaign team had urged) because, according to a member of his staff, he was not an ideologue but a practical politician.

The party did not end the year in good spirits. The uplift in the polls that followed Michael Howard's election as leader had faded. The Conservative Party was not making ground with its new policies on public services and it and its leader seemed unable to take advantage of an unpopular Prime Minister and Labour Party.

Notes

1. See M. Garnett and P. Lynch, *Conservatives in Crisis?* (Manchester University Press, 2003), S. Ball and A. Seldon (eds), *Recovering Power: The Conservatives in Opposition since 1867* (Palgrave Macmillan, 2005).
2. See M. Gove, E. Vaizey and N. Bowis (eds), *A Blue Tomorrow* (Politico's, 2001).
3. S. Walters, *Tory Wars: Conservatives in Crisis* (Politico's, 2001).
4. A. Marr, *My Trade* (Macmillan, 2004).
5. Nick Sparrow, *A Review of ICM Research on Behalf of the Conservative Party* (ICM Research, 2001).

4
The Liberal Democrats and Others

In the first decade of the twenty-first century two parties still dominated British politics. However, in many areas of the country the Liberal Democrats had become the alternative to either Conservative or Labour, while in some places there were genuinely three-party contests. In Scotland and Wales four parties fought every seat (or, including the Scottish Socialist Party, five). Nationwide there were a few cases where minor parties earned some serious attention. Although the focus of the campaign was on the three main parties the 'also rans' must be remembered. At the end of the 2001 Parliament, the 659 MPs shared 11 different labels. In the European election of 2004, MEPS from eight parties were in the 79-member UK delegation. But in England in 2005, apart from the Independent, Dr Taylor, and Respect's George Galloway, only three parties had MPs. The Liberal Democrats had become a real force, pushing Labour into third place in some parts of the South West and coming ahead of the Conservatives in many urban areas.

The Liberal Democrats

In general elections from 1992 to 2001, the Liberal Democrat vote had remained around 18 per cent, but, largely thanks to successful targeting and tactical voting, the party's representation jumped from 22 MPs to 46 and then to 52.

The party did not increase its total number of councillors but it made striking advances in a number of cities where it replaced the Conservatives as the principal alternative to Labour; the party controlled Liverpool and, for a time, Sheffield, as well as winning Newcastle and Stockport and becoming the largest anti-Labour group in Bournemouth, Bristol, Cardiff, Leicester, Norwich, Portsmouth and Southampton. There were two spectacular by-election successes, jumping from third to first in Brent East in September 2003 and again in Leicester South in July 2004. The party also gained from sharing power with Labour in the Scottish Parliament and, for a time, in the Welsh Assembly.

Charles Kennedy, who had taken over from Paddy Ashdown in 1999 was seen as being to the left of his predecessor and much less close to Tony Blair. Although his health and his dedication were at times called into question, there was no challenge to his leadership and the party showed remarkable unity in its opposition to the war in Iraq.

The party prepared for the 2005 election with much the same leadership, organisation and strategy as in 2001. Lord Rennard, promoted to Chief Executive in 2003 from his position as Campaigns Director, worked closely with Lord Razzall as Campaign Chair and liaised with Charles Kennedy and his Chief of Staff, Lord Newby, as well as Sir Menzies Campbell. Alison Suttie was in charge of field operations and Sandy Walkington was recruited from BT to handle publicity.

The Liberal Democrats had much less money than their major rivals, but the data available through the Electoral Commission shows an annual income in 2003 of £3.5 billion and, as the election approached, more money came in from rich donors so that, for the first time since 1983, the party could sponsor some nationwide press advertising. During the campaign, Michael Brown, through his company, provided a record £2.4 million.

Once again there was an intense focus on target seats. It was assumed that the sitting MPs would, on the whole look after themselves as assiduous constituency members. The main effort was on the places in which the party was within 20 per cent of victory, although seats were not selected on a purely statistical basis; success in local elections and in membership recruitment were taken into account. There was a conscious switch of focus from Conservative to Labour seats, even though, among those with a less than 20 per cent deficit, 42 were Conservative and only 12 Labour. It was the continuing Liberal Democrat displacement of the Conservatives as the alternative to Labour in most of the big cities that gave the party hope. They drew publicity for their decapitation strategy, aimed ambitiously at toppling five Conservative frontbenchers whom they had run close in 2001 – Michael Howard, Oliver Letwin, David Davis, Theresa May and Tim Collins.

Paddy Ashdown had abandoned the established policy of equidistance between the big parties in his Chard speech of 9 May 1992 and argued for providing 'a non-socialist alternative to the Conservatives'. By 1997 there had developed a large measure of understanding with Labour.

But that was dissipated first by the overwhelming majority won single-handed by Labour in 1997 and then by the departure of Paddy Ashdown in 1999.

As Tony Blair captured the middle ground of politics there were those who wanted the Liberal Democrats to take over as the left-wing party. But to the body of experienced Liberal Democrat councillors that had limited appeal. On the whole, the party was fighting the Conservatives and they had no interest in frightening away potential Conservative deserters. Moreover, the Conservatives were in some disarray and the Liberal Democrats were keen to present themselves as the serious party of opposition. Realists knew that with a bridgehead of only 52 seats they could not hope to overtake the Conservatives but, with their clear-cut policy on Iraq, they could on occasion present themselves as the most significant critics of the Government.

The party followed moderate economic policies, but in September 2004 in the much-publicised *Orange Book*, David Laws, Ed Davey and other thrusting young MPs advocated, to the public dismay of many candidates, a wide diversity of ideas, many of them market-oriented. The chapter on the NHS by David Laws led to a misleading characterisation of the whole enterprise as a switch to the free market right.

Vincent Cable, who took over as an impressive Treasury spokesman in 2003, defended the most radical proposals – a top tax rate of 50 per cent for those with incomes over £100,000 and the replacement of council tax with a local income tax. The spending plans were extensive but the party assured a sceptical media that all its policies had been scrupulously costed. The Liberal Democrats profited from the fact that neither of its main rivals spent much effort on analysing or attacking its proposals.

Matthew Taylor, after consultation with fellow MPs, drafted the party manifesto. It headlined a ten-point programme 'Reasons to Vote Liberal Democrat': putting patients, not targets, first in the health service; scrapping student fees; diverting money from ID cards to pay for 10,000 more police officers; free personal care for the elderly; cleaner transport and cleaner energy; spending £1.5 billion on reduced class sizes; £100 a month extra for pensioners aged over 75; only one tax increase (on incomes over £100,000); a local income tax to replace the council tax, and a 'never again' promise on Iraq. Compared to the two other main parties, the policies appeared to target particular groups and offered little change in the delivery of public services.

Charles Kennedy was a more emollient leader than Paddy Ashdown. Some criticised him as 'too laid back' but he managed to keep his diverse followers together and, incredibly, to persuade them unitedly to oppose the decision to go to war over Iraq. After the hostilities and their bloody sequel the Liberal Democrats profited from this stance. Disillusioned supporters of Old Labour as well as Muslim voters were recruited. For the first time the Liberal Democrats had the clear support of a national newspaper, the *Independent*. The Liberal Democrats went into the election in good heart, adequately funded and hoping for at least 70 seats.

The United Kingdom Independence Party

UKIP was founded in 1993 with the clear goal of repudiating the Treaty of Rome. In the general election in 1997, it had been pushed aside by Sir James Goldsmith's lavishly funded Referendum Party, but UKIP came into prominence in 1999 when, thanks to proportional representation, it won three seats in the European Parliament. The party did not fare well in the 2001 general election when their 428 candidates secured, on average, 2.1 per cent of the vote, and all but six lost their deposits. But they built up a solid network of supporters, particularly among the elderly and in the southern coastal regions. In June 2004 the party seemed to take off, electing 12 MEPs and, with 16 per cent of the vote, driving the Liberal Democrats into fourth place. With the simple slogan 'No', insisted upon by their American adviser, Dick Morris, they recruited 10,000 members – even before their campaign received its spectacular boost from Robert Kilroy-Silk, the dismissed BBC chatshow host, who, at the last moment, emerged as their candidate in the East Midlands. But, as with the Greens in the 1989 European elections, their triumph was short-lived. One of their MEPs was immediately suspended because of a fraud charge and Robert Kilroy-Silk quickly became disillusioned with the party which would not elect him as their leader. The party also lost the support of its largest donor, the Yorkshire millionaire, Paul Sykes, who transferred his beneficence back to the Conservatives.

UKIP, from its new headquarters in Birmingham, continued to be very active. Its key figures were three MEPs: Roger Knapman (the Chairman), Nigel Farage and Graham Booth. The party managed to field 498 candidates on 5 May 2005.

Veritas

Robert Kilroy-Silk's acrimonious desertion from UKIP led him to found a new party, Veritas, launched on 2 February 2005. It had a right-wing Eurosceptic, politician-sceptic position. It recruited 33 candidates but failed to win any heavyweight endorsements. It was portrayed in the media as an ego-trip for its founder with jibes such as 'For Veritas read Vanitas'. He resigned from his own party two months after the election.

The Green Party

The Greens greatly valued having two MEPs from 1999 onwards. Caroline Lucas and Jean Lambert managed to attract some publicity for Green views; so did Darren Johnson in the London Assembly. They were delighted when the Scottish Parliament election of 2003 moved the party from one to seven MSPs. They also added steadily to their small company of local councillors with, most notably, seven in Oxford and six in Brighton (where they were to present their most serious parliamentary challenge). But in 2001 they had fielded a mere 145 candidates, and these on average only secured 2.8 per cent of the vote, with just ten saving their 5 per cent deposits. In 2005 they managed to place challengers in 183 seats.

The Greens tried to present themselves as a national party with more than ecological interests. They took a firm stand against intervention in Iraq and expressed strong views on transport. They remained an increasingly serious party, a good receptacle for protest votes, but they failed to find any single theme that attracted distinctive attention.

Respect

George Galloway, MP for Glasgow Central, was expelled from the Labour Party for his stance over Iraq, and on 25 January 2004 he announced the founding of Respect. The name was an acronym for 'Respect, Equality, Socialism, Peace, Environment, Community and Trade Unionism'. The main focus was on opposition to British involvement in Iraq, but the party sought be a wide-based coalition of left-wingers disillusioned with the policies of New Labour. It was comprised of three main elements: the Trotskyite Socialist Workers Party, Muslims, and Old Labour. Galloway was the dominant figure, and in the European election of 2004 its candidates stood under the label 'Respect the Unity Coalition, George Galloway' because their leader had the only nationally known name. The party made some headway in the East End of London and in July 2004 won a council by-election in Bethnal Green. George Galloway decided to stand for Westminster from there. The party had somewhat distant links with the Scottish Socialist Party and, to avoid splitting the left vote, in both 2004 and 2005 it decided to put up no candidates north of the border.

The British National Party

The British National Party, the successor to the National Front, attained increased prominence in the twenty-first century. In 2001 this openly racist group had put up 33 candidates who averaged 3.9 per cent of the vote and saved five deposits. But in Northern England and in the East End of London its candidates had made significant inroads in local government. Well-reported victories in Burnley, Oldham and Bradford, mainly at the expense of Labour, aroused cross-party anxiety. There were also serious race riots in Oldham and Bradford in the summer of 2001. Nick Griffin, the BNP leader since 1999, had a meeting with Jean-Marie Le Pen, the Front National leader, in Manchester in April 2004 at the outset of the European Parliament election. In that election the party won 4.9 per cent nationally and between 6.5 per cent and 8.9 per cent of the vote in four regions of the North and Midlands, coming quite near to electing an MEP. The BNP was encouraged to field 119 candidates in 2005 and, despite a dramatic exposé of its racism and violence in a BBC documentary on 15 July 2004, the party was ready to fight an aggressive campaign in its heartlands.

Plaid Cymru: The Party of Wales

In the first elections to the Welsh Assembly in 1999 Plaid Cymru broke out of its Welsh-speaking heartlands to win significant support in most parts of Wales, especially the Valleys. But the tide quickly receded. The party won only 14.3 per cent of the Welsh vote in the 2001 general election; in Assembly contests its vote fell from 30.6 per cent in 1999 to 20.5 per cent in 2003. In 2001 its Westminster representation went down from five to four; in the Assembly it declined from 17 MWAs (Members of the Welsh Assembly) in 1999 to 12 in 2003, and it was reduced from two MEPs to one in 2004. Plaid Cymru fell back especially in the South Wales Valleys where, in 1999, it had made its heaviest inroads outside the overwhelmingly Welsh-speaking area.

In 2003 Dafydd Iwan resigned as party President amid some controversy and in a subsequent election a triumvirate was elected to run the party: Dafydd Iwan as President, Elwyn Llwyd as the Westminster leader and Ieuwan Wyn Jones as the Assembly leader. There was some feeling that the party lost out through not having a single clear leader. Dafydd Trystan continued as General Secretary.

There were no major ideological struggles in the party. It clearly positioned itself to the left of Labour. It was firm in opposing military intervention in Iraq. But there was an impression that, in Wales at least, the Liberal Democrats were scooping up most of those who opposed Labour's role in Iraq. Moreover, on many points in the Plaid Cymru manifesto there was a heavy overlap with that of the Liberal Democrats.

The Scottish National Party

The SNP described itself as a 'democratic, left-wing party committed to Scottish Independence' aiming 'to create a just, caring and enterprising society by releasing Scotland's full potential as an independent nation in the mainstream of modern Europe'. In terms of votes it had been the second party in Scotland since 1997 and, in the first election to the Scottish Parliament in 1999, it ran Labour close. But in 2001 it fell from six to five Westminster MPs; in 2003 from 35 to 27 MSPs, and in 2004 from two to one MEP. But it had 178 councillors around Scotland. Its position as the largest opposition party in the Holyrood Parliament gave it a Scottish platform; however, disillusion with the new dispensation in Scotland rubbed off on it as much as on the governing Labour–Liberal Democrat coalition.

It had internal troubles and, after an unhappy European campaign in 2004, John Swinney, the SNP leader, felt obliged to resign: Alex Salmond, still a Westminster MP, returned to the job. The cut of 13 in the number of Scottish seats and the consequent redrawing of boundaries produced problems for the SNP, as it did for Labour, but these were smoothed over. The party was committed to fighting every seat but it had only a limited number of targets and in some areas it was being pressed hard by the Liberal Democrats.

The Scottish Socialist Party

The Trotskyite Scottish Socialist Party, headed by the well-known poll tax rebel Tommy Sheridan, built upon the one seat gained in the 1999 Scottish Parliament to secure six MSPs in 2003. But although they fought every Scottish seat in the 2001 general election, they secured only 3 per cent of the vote, even though ten candidates, mainly in Glasgow, saved their deposits. They did not seriously trouble the Labour hegemony in Scotland, although in 2005, Respect, not a close friend, chose to leave the left-wing challenge to them.

Northern Ireland

Since the 1960s the politics of Northern Ireland have become ever further removed from those of Great Britain and any residual overlap in party systems has disappeared. The attempts to establish a sustained multiparty regime, as envisaged by the Stormont Agreement of Easter 1998, stuttered. The obduracy of the IRA over weapons decommissioning was matched by the obduracy of Ian Paisley over having anything to do with Sinn Fein. Cooperation seemed impossible. The hardliners on each side won in votes. The extreme Sinn Fein and the extreme Democratic Unionist Party flourished at the expense of the moderate Social Democratic and Labour Party and the moderate Ulster Unionist Party. All sides prepared for the 2005 election on the assumption that the trend would continue.

Socialist Labour

This breakaway left-wing Labour group, inspired by the former miners' leader Arthur Scargill, put up 114 candidates in 2001, winning on average 1.4 per cent of the vote. The party was again present in 2005 as the smallest of the would-be national parties but it put up only 50 candidates.

Independents

Some candidates represented way-out movements, some sought to publicise local grievances. There were a few from ethnic minority groups and a few with very individual protests against the Iraq war. The most substantial candidates were Dr Richard Taylor who had won so spectacularly in Wyre Forest in 2001 in protest at the closure of an Accident and Emergency Unit, and Peter Law, a Welsh Assembly member who had resigned from the Labour Party because of the all-women candidate selection process in Blaenau Gwent.

5
The Coming of the Election

The idea of the near-term campaign, borrowed from the United States, is now firmly established in British elections. The Conservatives used it successfully before the opening of the 1992 general election. Before the campaign proper, a party launches new policies, rebuts opposition claims and mounts advertising and public relations initiatives, hoping to set the news agenda. The parties rehearse arguments and operations, test strong and weak points, striving to impress commentators and supporters and to put the political opposition on the back foot. A downside is that the prolonged and undeclared campaign actually extends electioneering by some two or three months and risks boring voters and the media. A political party may end up having little new to say for the election campaign.

During the first three months of 2005 the parties made a number of promises. Labour announced plans to help first-time house buyers and to increase paid maternity leave to nine months. The Liberal Democrats promised to increase maternity pay and to increase pensions for the over-75s. The Conservatives gradually released chapters of their manifesto, including pledges to abolish NHS waiting lists and to attack MRSA in hospitals, to cut council tax for the over-65s, to take new powers to deal with the problems of 'travellers', to clamp down on immigration and to tackle school discipline.

As the party in government, Labour had more opportunities, not least the unveiling of a budget. But planning for the campaign was handicapped by the continuing tensions between Gordon Brown and Tony Blair. The rivalry between the two central figures became a major news story on 6 January when broadcasters simultaneously covered Blair's monthly press conference in London and a much-trailed speech on international development delivered by Brown in Edinburgh. It was a battle of egos more than a great battle of principle. A meeting of the Parliamentary

Labour Party in early January castigated the two men and their camps for parading disunity at the top.[1] Labour made a short-term gain from the decision of the disillusioned Conservative MP Robert Jackson to join the party, on the grounds that Labour under Tony Blair best represented the values of One Nation Conservatives like himself.

Relations between Blair and Brown worsened again with the newspaper serialisation in January 2005 of the book *Brown's Britain* by the *Financial Times* journalist Robert Peston.[2] This account of relations between the two men and Blair's 'betrayal' over the leadership relied heavily on the Brown camp and contained the remarkable claim that Brown, on learning of Blair's decision to stay on as Prime Minister, said: 'There is nothing that you could ever say to me that I could believe.' Indeed a feature of the Government was the war of the books, as at least a dozen journalists wrote about Blair or Brown or both of them, usually from the viewpoint of one or the other camp. Peston's book was probably an embarrassment for Brown's supporters. A Cabinet minister commented: 'It laid bare Brown's ambitions and plotting. He realised that he had to row back.' Blairites encouraged press speculation that, after an election victory, Tony Blair would finally assert himself and move Gordon Brown from the Treasury to the Foreign Office, or retain him in a slimmed-down Treasury.

Although the two men met at weekly bilateral meetings, it was never clear that the Chancellor was fully part of Labour's election plans. It was known that he was unhappy over the structure and the strategy and wanted to have a bigger say in both. A leading figure complained: 'Gordon and his people are working to rule.' Meanwhile posters about the economy were being prepared and approved, but not by Brown, who was not a member of the campaign team, or by Milburn, who felt it was not part of his remit. Spencer Livermore, a Brown aide, was important in manoeuvring to get them approved. But the economy was certain to be an election issue, the budget on 16 March would be a defining moment and Brown had to be a central figure. A draft of the party's War Book stated: 'The economy must be made the foundation of the campaign; it is our biggest strength and the biggest Conservative threat.'

The advertising agency TBWA had tested Labour's five key pledges and a sixth was hurriedly added, apparently in response to Conservative plans to curb immigration. On 11 February Blair unveiled the six election pledges during a helicopter tour of six marginal constituencies on his way to address the spring party conference at Gateshead. The pledges were:

1. Your family better off
2. Your child achieving more

3. Your children with the best start
4. Your family treated better and faster
5. Your community safer
6. Your country's borders protected.

Labour also unveiled its ungrammatical election slogan: 'Britain Forward Not Back'.

In December, as part of the reshuffle after David Blunkett's resignation, David Miliband had been moved from his post as Minister for Schools to the Cabinet Office, with a remit to work on the manifesto and to make it a clear statement of New Labour philosophy. The manifesto drew largely on Labour's five-year plans; but additions included proposals to expand capacity in primary care and community hospitals, and effectively ending the school leaving age and allowing new providers of schools. Alan Milburn made a series of speeches promoting a third-term agenda for increasing choice for consumers and diversity of providers, all to promote social mobility.

Meanwhile, the local thrust to the campaign was organised by the Labour Contact project, a relationship management tool. Working on similar lines to the Conservatives' Voter Vault (see p. 39), party organisers added to the electoral register of voters, household data and information about the political views of target voters gathered by party canvassers and the party's call centre in Gosforth. On a database the party had a record of all contacts made with each target voter; the intention was to make seven contacts with each voter by polling day (see Chapter 11).

Private and public opinion polling was fairly reassuring for the party. In January an ICM poll showed Labour 3 per cent ahead of the Conservatives and with clear leads on the key issues. But the context was not as favourable for Labour as in January 2001, a similar stage in the previous Parliament. Then Labour's vote was 9 per cent higher (44 per cent against 35 per cent), and it enjoyed larger leads on the issues (see Table 5.1). The party, however, trailed on immigration, and there were concerns over the higher than usual Liberal Democrat support (up 3 per cent on 2001) and the disengagement that might erode the Labour vote. Feedback about Blair was also discouraging. Iraq had raised doubts among voters about his judgement and trustworthiness, but it was not the only cause of dissatisfaction with the Government: voters also blamed ministers for not tackling crime and asylum, for not achieving value for money in public services and for rewarding undeserving rather than hard-working citizens. Labour's campaign team acknowledged they had needed more forceful policies on immigration and asylum (where

Blunkett's resignation in December 2004 had delayed party plans). Some Conservative attacks were having an effect.

Table 5.1   Labour's lead over the Conservatives on issues, 2001 and 2005

	Jan 2001 (%)	Jan 2005 (%)
Tax	10	3
Schools	19	9
NHS	22	12
Economy	22	12
Crime	5	−3

Source: ICM.

'On today's election agenda is crime, and I know all there is to know about that!' (Blair (left) and Clarke (right).)

(Peter Brookes, *The Times*, 22 April 2005)

As Iraq had faded in late 2004, so Blair's ratings increased – modestly – and Michael Howard's dipped. 'Howard is a problem for the Conservatives, his ratings are in free-fall', said one closely involved in the Labour polling operation. Their research showed that the Conservatives still had major image problems: they were seen as divided and old-fashioned, and trailed Labour on economic competence.

Both leaders had problems. Many voters knew little about Howard – his modest background, his immigrant parents, and his family, and he was reluctant to play what he dismissed as 'personality politics'. Late in the day he conceded some ground and started to appear on public platforms with members of his family, and his wife, Sandra, accompanied him regularly. But how could Blair appease the voters' mood of cynicism and anger? Campbell and Gould suggested what became known as the 'masochism' strategy. Blair should appear personally on television programmes and take hostile questions from interviewers and members of the public; he had to show that he was engaged. Blair accepted that he had to be seen to be listening and working for the public's support.

Labour's message was focused on its record of economic success and stability, the investment made in public services and the Conservative threats of economic instability and cuts. Essentially the message was to warn, as the party's War Book stated, that 'Hardworking families will go back to having cuts and high interest rates if they vote Tory.'

In mid-March Philip Gould conducted his first focus group in four years. He claimed that, in addition to a Blair problem, asylum and immigration were a worry; there was a mix of racism, concern at the arrivals from the new EU member states and resentment that such people were getting 'something for nothing'. Linking his findings with those from public and private polls, he concluded that people wanted a fresh start, which the Conservatives promised, but also continuity. People appeared to want a reduced Labour majority as the way to force the Government to pay more attention to their interests. The War Book warned: 'TB must connect with the electorate, particularly the hard-working majority, and make it clear that he has not abandoned them', by showing greater candour, humility, willingness to listen, and dealing more with domestic and not overseas issues.

As the longest-serving members of the campaign team, Alastair Campbell (who had joined the campaign full time in February) and Philip Gould decided to try and repair relations between Brown and Blair, at least for the general election. Brown, they agreed, was indispensable if their key assets – the economy and the extra spending on public services – were to be at the centre of the campaign. They were convinced that for Blair to campaign without Brown at his side would cost the party many votes, but that Blair and Brown together would guarantee a decisive victory. Voters believed that Blair had lost his domestic focus and his old drive and energy. Campbell and Gould appealed to Brown and his aides to become fully involved in the campaign planning. 'I think Philip and Alastair were both kept awake at night by the thought that if Gordon did not come back, Tony could be humiliated', said one who was close to the discussions.

These negotiations took place over several weeks and agreement was not reached until the beginning of the campaign. Blair had discussions with many of his aides and with Milburn over what to do. Most said that Gordon Brown had to play a major role in the campaign, that Blair should decide for himself, but that he should think through the consequences for the third term of recalling Brown. Blair rejected Campbell's suggestion that he should consider standing down but, after some persuasion, he agreed to work more closely with his Chancellor. He accepted Brown's views about strategy and agreed to give him main billing alongside himself. Campbell and Gould also persuaded the two to appear together in a party election broadcast. It was also agreed that Brown would bring to the campaign headquarters 'his people', including Douglas Alexander, Ed Miliband, Ed Balls and the American campaign strategist Bob Shrum. An unspoken part of the 'deal' was that Brown would remain as Chancellor in a third term.

Inevitably, the new arrangement involved a diminution in the authority of Alan Milburn, although Blair rejected suggestions that Milburn should lose the title of Campaign Coordinator. It also involved some backtracking on Blair's part from his initial thoughts about the campaign strategy, although not about the manifesto (see above, p. 74). Some supporters of the Prime Minister thought that he had been mistaken to concede so much ground; the Chancellor would have to play a prominent role in the campaign, but Labour was always going to win decisively. A central figure, however, dismissed the reasoning: 'There was a danger of Tony and Gordon running two separate campaigns. The voters would have punished them, as they always punish divided parties.' And would Blair have won? 'Possibly but not by much.'

Brown then delivered a budget on 16 March offering a sweetener to pensioners (a one-off council tax rebate of £200), an increase in child tax credit and a rise in the stamp duty threshold to £120,000. Above all, it gave Brown the opportunity to celebrate his record of economic success, a boast that was endorsed by much of the media. A post-budget ICM poll reported that Labour's lead over the Conservatives on the economy had increased to 8 per cent. 'Vote now, pay later', warned Howard, and on 1 April, the Institute for Fiscal Studies (IFS) revealed that over the last-but-one full year average household incomes had fallen for the first time in ten years, largely as a consequence of Brown's tax and benefit changes. The main beneficiaries of Brown's policies had been children and pensioners.

David Cameron, assisted by George Bridges, began writing the Conservative manifesto in January. Having resisted suggestions to publish a mini-manifesto, he was determined to have a short and thematic document and not write at length just to interest the political reporters. From the turn of the year the party gradually launched details of the policies. Helped in part by events, they managed to set much of the pre-election news agenda. Already they had forced Blair into conceding a referendum on the EU Constitution. On education, the issues of parental choice, discipline and the expansion of popular schools were all long-established Conservative policies which Labour also now favoured. On 24 January, the Conservatives (emboldened by widespread focus group awareness of and support for the 'Australian system' of immigration decisions), proposed a points system, with annual quotas for immigration and for asylum-seekers and a 24-hour surveillance of ports and airports; Labour in turn also promised to introduce a points system for immigration. Michael Howard then complained about 'travellers' using the Human Rights Act to evade planning laws. The Roman Catholic Archbishop of Westminster, Cardinal Cormac Murphy O'Connor, backed the stricter line on permitting abortion expressed by Michael Howard (reducing the time limit on women having an abortion from 24 weeks to 22 or 20 weeks) in an interview with *Cosmopolitan* magazine. Blair told the same magazine that he 'personally dislikes the idea of abortion', but that he had no plans to reduce the current 24-week limit.

The Conservatives made their proposals for cutting 'government waste and bureaucracy' on the basis of the report from the company doctor, David James. The report claimed it was possible to cut a 'wasteful' £35 billion from public expenditure by freezing civil service recruitment and abolishing scores of quangos and Government bodies. The Conservatives' proposals went some way beyond Labour's planned efficiency savings, identified by Sir Peter Gershon a year previously, of £21.5 billion. They planned to make additional savings of their own of £13.5 billion. The party promised to spend £23 billion of the proceeds on extra investment in frontline services, and the rest on a reduction of the national debt, and a modest (£4 billion) cut in tax. The credibility of the James proposals was important if the Conservatives were to persuade voters that they would curb the growth of total spending and cut taxes without cutting spending on frontline services. Tax-and-spend for a time became a major theme; the Conservatives warned of further tax increases under Labour, and ministers warned of the cuts to public services that the Conservatives were planning, claiming they were equivalent to sacking every teacher, nurse and GP in the country. In truth, the last charge was misleading; the Conservatives planned to increase spending but at a lower rate than Labour over the next Parliament. The absence of Brown from Labour's campaign team hampered the effectiveness of Labour's response to James.

The Government (more specifically, Alastair Campbell) was blamed for the so-called 'Shylock' pictures on the party's website in early January for party members. The posters were designed to attack the Conservative economic plans ('pigs might fly') but critics complained that they were anti-Semitic in their depiction of Michael Howard and Oliver Letwin. 'Labour is riding high but fighting low', said Peter Riddell in *The Times* on 10 February 2005. The pictures were withdrawn after a few days.

The Conservatives found themselves embroiled in unwelcome controversy over spending and tax. On 25 March Michael Howard dismissed a party Vice-Chairman, Howard Flight, when *The Times* (of the same date) reported that he had stated at a private dinner that the party had plans to go beyond the already-proposed saving of £35 billion over the course of the Parliament in slowing the growth of spending. Howard also insisted on the deselection of Flight as the party candidate in Arundel and South Downs, a step widely considered as excessive. This followed Howard's pressure on two other prospective party candidates, Danny Kruger in Sedgefield and Adrian Hilton in Slough, to stand down because they had expressed allegedly off-message views. Howard's defenders claimed that he was demonstrating firm leadership and that the action was necessary to restore trust in politics. Flight was being dismissed, Howard claimed, because he was saying the party would say one thing in opposition and do something else in government. But he was also impatient at such irresponsibility; it smacked of the indiscipline of the Major period. Some senior figures, including Shadow ministers and Lynton Crosby, thought the dismissal could backfire. What is undeniable is that it was a gift to Labour, which had made little progress with its allegations that the Conservatives had a 'secret' agenda of spending cuts, and it increased its lead in the polls.

Until the eve of the election, Michael Howard tried to seize the initiative on tax. He knew that the tax cuts on offer fell far short of what many Conservative MPs, the *Daily Telegraph* and Lord Saatchi wanted. In early April he tried another tack and held secret discussions with Oliver Letwin, George Osborne and George Bridges about the possibility of pledging not to raise taxation over the next Parliament. This had echoes of what

William Hague had tried, to no avail, in 2001. In the end they decided that it was too late to make such a pledge.

The Conservatives also used personal cases to highlight populist concerns. On 2 March the party brought up the case of Margaret Dixon, a 69-year-old grandmother from Warrington, who had had her shoulder operation cancelled seven times. The tabloids called it the 'War of Mrs Dixon's shoulder' and 'Operation Dixon'. The next day her husband and daughter had tea with the Howard household in Pimlico. On 16 February Maria Hutchings, the mother of an autistic son, and a life-long Labour supporter, burst from a television audience to confront Tony Blair over the closing of her son's Special Educational Needs (SEN) school – although it was a Conservative-controlled local authority that wanted the boy to attend a mainstream school, in line with established thinking across all political parties. Michael Howard then gave her a platform at Conservative press conference on 7 March, to launch the Conservative SEN policy. The party made headlines and addressed voters' concerns, but 'the politics of grievances' was failing, according to the opinion polls, to win votes or add up to a clear strategy. At the end of the near-term campaign, the overall state of public opinion had hardly moved: Labour still had a slight lead among intending voters, and that would translate into a substantial lead in seats.

Not all Conservatives were happy at the narrow range of policies the party was promoting and its concentration on grievances which undoubtedly made headlines but were not winning votes. It reminded critics of William Hague's core vote appeals in 2001. But some in the leader's circle pointed to their own research showing that a result was that more voters knew what the party was saying and had a clearer impression of Howard.

Conservative strategists assumed and hoped for a low turnout – since this would maximise the effectiveness of the greater determination of the party's supporters to vote on polling day; they wanted to neutralise Labour's strengths on the economy, health and education; they also sought to maximise dissatisfaction with the government and its perceived failures to deliver improved public services. Although party strategists denied it, the campaign seemed designed to please the core vote, when the party needed to attract votes – and many of them – from non-Conservatives. The party would offer a change of direction based on traditional Conservative themes of value for money, cutting government waste and bureaucracy, and choice. Immigration had also emerged as a great source of disaffection in the focus groups of all parties, and people thought that parties should address it. Party strategists seized on a focus group member's claim that 'It's not racist to impose limits on immigration.'

There was ample survey and anecdotal evidence of voter disillusion with the Government, but also of unwillingness to believe that the Conservatives would do a better job. An elderly disillusioned Labour voter in Birmingham told a Conservative focus group: 'It's getting harder to vote Labour, but it's not getting easier to vote Tory.' In early March, Francis Maude commented: 'Labour is on the point of losing it. It remains to be seen if we are electable.'

Labour's campaign team was determined to make voters aware of a choice – Labour or Conservative, Blair or Howard. Voters were dissatisfied with the Government and Blair, but when faced with a choice of which party should be in government or which leader should be Prime Minister, Labour and Blair won decisively. 'We don't want it to be just a referendum on our record. We want to pose the choice and bring out the parts and dangers of their programme that they are hiding', Alan Milburn observed.

The Liberal Democrats entered the campaign on a higher base of polling support than ever before (18 per cent). In the previous two general elections the party had advanced during the course of campaign, thanks in part to the greater media attention it gained.

Labour campaigners expected to win and to win clearly, even if they would lose votes and seats. There was media speculation about how the size of majority might affect the relative standings of Blair and Brown during a third term; many commentators thought that a large majority would strengthen Blair and a slim one would undermine him. For Michael Howard the minimum acceptable result would be a hung Parliament, with a good increase in the Conservative share of the vote. It would be Blair's last general election and, in all probability, Howard's last, too. The Liberal Democrats were confident that their targeting would bring between 10 and 20 gains.

The parties concentrated on their differences and exaggerated the impact they would have. But were the differences so marked? The European Union was an unspoken issue, as was its influence over more than half of the legislation passing through Parliament. All parties accepted that the Scottish Parliament controlled its own legislation; they agreed that interest rates would continue to be decided by the Monetary Policy Committee of the Bank of England and that referendums would decide British entry to the euro and acceptance of the EU Constitution. On the key public services of health, education and pensions, the Conservatives pledged to match Labour spending, and all parties promised greater consumer choice. The Conservatives would have gone to war with Iraq, though not on the basis of the intelligence about weapons, and the Liberal Democrats would not have gone to war with Iraq at all. And all parties wanted the attention and votes of 'hard-working families'. Given the level of dissatisfaction with the major parties, it was appropriate for Philip Cowley to write in the *Guardian* on 16 April that the election would be a choice between 'The lesser of two evils. It is hardly the broad sunlit uplands, let alone the New Jerusalem. But it is where we're at.'

Chronology of the near-term campaign

January

1 Jan	As tsunami death toll nears 150,000, Blair remains on holiday despite spiralling criticism
	Freedom of Information Act (FOI) 2000 comes into force
3 Jan	Access under new FOI Act to Lord Goldsmith's advice on legality of Iraq war denied
4 Jan	Continuing violence in Iraq: Governor of Baghdad shot dead with six of his bodyguards
5 Jan	G. Brown begins week-long national campaign tour
	Writing in the *Guardian*, G. Brown outlines his own view of the direction Lab should be taking
6 Jan	Cons pledge to match Govt funding on international aid
	T. Blair assures G. Brown he will have 'central role' in election campaign
	T. Blair rules out TV leaders' debate
	M. Howard makes clear tax cuts will play central role in Cons campaign
9 Jan	Palestinian Authority presidential elections held
	R. Peston book published: claims Blair promised Brown he'd stand down before 2005 general election
11 Jan	*Independent* poll: Lab vote would increase by one-third if G. Brown leader
12 Jan	US Govt agrees to release four remaining British Guantanamo Bay prisoners
13 Jan	Lib Dems pledge to scrap Govt's child trust fund and use money to cut class sizes to 20
	Prince Harry wears Nazi uniform to fancy dress party
15 Jan	Con MP R. Jackson defects to Lab
16 Jan	M. Howard on BBC's *Breakfast with Frost* announces Cons' spending plans

17 Jan	James Report published: public spending cuts of £35 billion, £4 billion tax cuts
	Lib Dems and Lab say Cons' sums 'don't add up'
19 Jan	Blanket press coverage of new pictures of British soldiers abusing Iraqi prisoners
20 Jan	G.W. Bush sworn-in for second term
	Homelessness charities speak out over Lab right-to-buy plans
	Former chatshow host R. Kilroy-Silk quits UKIP, branding it 'A joke'
23 Jan	Cons on immigration: propose quota system on Australian model
24 Jan	Lib Dems pledge to increase maternity pay
	J. Prescott announces new plans aimed at helping first-time home buyers
25 Jan	EU and UN oppose Cons' immigration plans
29 Jan	*Telegraph*/YouGov poll: majority would reject EU Constitution in referendum
30 Jan	Elections held in Iraq
	Mail on Sunday prints Lab 'Shylock' posters next to image of Fagin: Lab accused of anti-Semitism
31 Jan	Controversial posters withdrawn from Lab website
	Cons plan voluntary and private orgs to find jobs for incapacity benefit claimants

February

1 Feb	Lab announces incapacity benefit cuts
	Ruth Kelly pledges 'zero tolerance' approach to 'low-level disruption' in classrooms
	Cons propose CCTV, random drug testing and metal detectors in schools
2 Feb	R. Kilroy-Silk launches new party Veritas
4 Feb	C. Blair calls chatshow *Richard and Judy* to complain T. Blair never buys her flowers
6 Feb	T. Blair becomes longest-serving Lab Prime Minister
	C. Clarke on *Breakfast with Frost*: Migrants mustn't become 'burden on society'
7 Feb	C. Clarke unveils immigration plans – points system to ensure migrants have 'right skills'
8 Feb	*Times*/Populus poll: Lab hits post-Iraq high
	Lib Dems launch five-point plan on civil liberties
	Daily Mail/YouGov poll: 78% think Lab not tough enough on immigration

10 Feb	Number of Scottish MPs cut from 72 to 59
	T. Blair on chatshow *Richard and Judy*
11 Feb	T. Blair unveils six election pledges with helicopter tour of six marginal constituencies
12 Feb	Press continues to be dominated by news that Charles and Camilla are to wed
	BBC claims violence in Iraq is returning to pre-election levels
	M. Howard reveals his grandfather may have entered UK as illegal immigrant, to pre-empt forthcoming biography
13 Feb	T. Blair closing Lab spring conference, promises he has abandoned the 'I know best' approach
14 Feb	Shi'a parties victorious in Iraq poll
	C. Kennedy begins week-long national tour
	Cons advocate health tests for asylum-seekers including screening for HIV and TB
16 Feb	M. Howard promises to abolish NHS waiting lists and eradicate MRSA 'superbug'
	Lib Dems target ethnic minority vote
17 Feb	Lab withdraws legal support from six councilors facing allegations of electoral fraud
18 Feb	T. Blair in *Jewish Chronicle* promises to 'never, ever, ever' attack Howard over Jewish beliefs
21 Feb	Cons pledge council tax cut for over-65s
	C. Kennedy announces birth of his baby will take priority over campaign
	BNP leader N. Griffin labels Cons' immigration plans 'a definite move onto our turf'
22 Feb	Govt criticised for trying to rush through Prevention of Terrorism Bill
23 Feb	Accusations that Lord Goldsmith changed mind over legality of Iraq war
24 Feb	Two British soldiers found guilty of abusing Iraqi prisoners; 18 more face trial
27 Feb	Lab announces paid maternity leave to increase to nine months by 2007
28 Feb	Lib Dems pledge 50% tax for those earning over £100,000

March

| 1 Mar | C. Clarke backs off over Prevention of Terrorism Bill house arrest clause |
| | Ongoing violence in Iraq: 115 killed in suicide bomb attack |

Cons unveil work permit plans aimed at avoiding upgrade to permanent residency

2 Mar   M. Howard uses specific case of Margaret Dixon to highlight broader NHS failures

4 Mar   T. Blair accuses Cons of 'ruthless exploitation' of M. Dixon
Greens launch campaign platform: the 'Radical Alternative' to Westminster politics

5 Mar   Lib Dems launch campaign slogan 'Real Alternative'

7 Mar   Cons: national curriculum to be reviewed 'head to toe' and political correctness 'rooted out'

9 Mar   *Sun* launches 'War on gipsy free-for-all'; *Daily Mail* gives similar emphasis

10 Mar   Lord Sainsbury donates £2 million to Lab
C. Clarke launches five-point 'tough action' plan on crime
C. Kennedy promises extra £100 monthly to over-75s

11 Mar   Concessions made to pass Terrorism Bill

13 Mar   M. Howard interview in *Cosmopolitan*: UK system 'tantamount to abortion on demand'
T. Blair on ITV all-female debate show

15 Mar   T. Blair warns against abortion becoming election issue

16 Mar   G. Brown delivers budget, satisfying speculation of pre-election giveaway. Pensioners, first-time home buyers and working families targeted

18 Mar   M. Howard confronted over views on gun control

20 Mar   Archbishop of Canterbury calls for urgent review of abortion laws

21 Mar   Lib Dems unveil manifesto for business
Govt accused of 'jumping on the Jamie Oliver bandwagon' in new plans for school dinners
Cons pledge new powers to prosecute 'travellers'

22 Mar   Judge in vote-rigging trial condemns postal vote system as 'open invitation to fraud'
Lib Dems launch ten pledges

24 Mar   Foreign Office lawyer E. Wilmshurt's resignation letter published: claims Lord Goldsmith changed legal advice twice in run-up to war
J. Straw rejects opposition calls for legal advice to be published

25 Mar   H. Flight, Con Vice-Chairman, sacked after claiming at private dinner that a Con Govt once in power would go further than James's £35 billion spending cuts

H. Flight refuses to stand down as parliamentary candidate and seeks legal advice

26 Mar *Guardian* and *Times* lead with Cons' 'turmoil' and 'disarray' as J. Reid, T. Blair and C. Kennedy all go on the offensive over Cons' spending plans

Lord Callaghan dies aged 92

27 Mar M. Howard defends H. Flight sacking

28 Mar Cons pledge increases in family tax credits

29 Mar Electoral Commission condemns postal vote system

31 Mar IFS study claims average income has fallen for first time in ten years: G. Brown taxes blamed

Notes

1. A. Rawnsley, 'Oh, Please Grow Up', *Observer*, 9 October 2005.
2. R. Peston, *Brown's Britain* (Start Books, 2005).

6
The National Campaign

The campaign, so long anticipated, had no sharp beginning. Parliament took its Easter recess from 24 March to 4 April, the day when Tony Blair was expected to announce the dissolution. However, out of respect for the Pope's death, the Prime Minister delayed his visit to the Queen for 24 hours. He finally went to Buckingham Palace at 11.05 a.m. on Tuesday 5 April. An hour later, standing outside 10 Downing Street, he said:

> It is a big choice, a fundamental choice … The challenge is to build on the progress made, to accelerate the changes, to widen still further the opportunities available to the British people and above all else to take that hard won economic stability, the investment in our public services and entrench it.

Michael Howard reacted by dismissing 'the smirking politics of Mr Blair, and the woolly thinking of the Liberal Democrats' and, taking an underdog stance, he suggested that the Prime Minister was already 'secretly grinning about the prospect of his third victory'. Tony Blair replied by telling his MPs to expect 'a rather nasty right-wing campaign'. The three main party leaders then made a rush to spend the afternoon electioneering: Tony Blair in the super-marginal South Dorset, Michael Howard in Birmingham and Manchester, and Charles Kennedy in other northern cities.

At the final Prime Minister's Questions the next day, there was some ritual sparring. Michael Howard tried to score on Labour's broken promises on National Insurance increases, on immigration, on top-up fees and on crime. His most palpable hit came when he asked how many Labour MPs were featuring Tony Blair in their election addresses. A misguided half-dozen raised their hands. Tony Blair, however, made a traditional riposte, pointing to what had happened under the last Conservative administration and particularly in the areas where Michael Howard had been responsible.

There was some hasty negotiation as the Government sought to push through pending legislation in the final 48 hours. Fourteen acts received the Royal Assent, but the bills authorising identification cards and casinos had to be abandoned.

When Parliament was prorogued on 10 April, only four weeks were left for the formal campaign. Some early time was lost because the party leaders decided to attend the funeral of Pope John Paul II in Rome on 8 April as well as the royal wedding reception at Windsor Castle on 9 April. Charles Kennedy lost a further day with the birth of his son on 12 April.

But for the rest of the campaign, there were no major distractions, although suicide bombings continued in Iraq and the receivership arrangements and rescue attempts for the collapsed MG-Rover firm in Birmingham continued to draw headlines. Tony Blair and Gordon Brown rushed there together on 8 April immediately after the Pope's funeral but there was little that they could do. The MG-Rover affair, however, did not prove to be the blow for Labour that many had expected; the car workers had been anticipating the collapse for some time and the reaction was surprisingly muted.

The Conservative and Labour parties both said they would abandon the usual early morning press conferences; their leaders would meet the media and make their announcements as they travelled round regional centres. The Liberal Democrats were content to follow routine with a 7.30 a.m. press conference. They felt vindicated when the other parties soon reverted to type, meeting the media almost every day at their adjacent headquarters in Victoria Street at varying times between 8.00 a.m. and 9.30 a.m.

The press conferences were all covered live on BBC News 24 and on Sky and repeated during the day on the BBC Parliament channel. They followed their familiar form, heavily geared to television with the first questions invariably rotating among the political editors from each of the main channels.

Often they were followed with a poster launch where the leader would unveil a monster hoarding on a trailer. Sometimes the poster was a one-off effort displayed nowhere else, but the christening ceremony guaranteed that the desired message got into most bulletins.

The polls are discussed at length in the next chapter, but it should be recorded that they did nothing to lend excitement to the campaign. Almost all showed a Labour lead of between 2 per cent and 6 per cent and it was widely pointed out that, because of the bias in the electoral system, any such advantage in votes would guarantee Labour a comfortable majority in seats. From the start the bookmakers offered odds of 16 to 1 on a Labour victory. Yet it should be recalled that YouGov found that, behind this apparent stability, there was much churning; some 25 per cent of voters changed their intentions during the campaign.

The party leaders made themselves available for exclusives with most of the newspapers; they also had their individual interviews with the main TV channels as well as appearing seriatim in the same edition of David Dimbleby's BBC *Question Time* on 28 April.

Chronology of the campaign, April to 5 May

Sat 2 Apr	Pope John Paul II dies
Mon 4 Apr	Verdict in Birmingham vote fraud case
Tue 5 Apr	Blair announces election date
Wed 6 Apr	Final Prime Minister's Questions
Thu 7 Apr	Parliament prorogued
	MG-Rover receivership
Fri 8 Apr	Pope's funeral
	Blair and Brown fly to Longbridge
Sat 9 Apr	Wedding of Prince of Wales and Camila Parker-Bowles
Sun 10 Apr	UN attacks Howard's false claims over immigration
Mon 11 Apr	Dissolution of Parliament
	Con launch
Tue 12 Apr	Green launch
	Kennedy baby
Wed 13 Apr	Lab launch
	Veritas launch
Thu 14 Apr	Kennedy stumbles at Lib Dem launch
	SNP launch
	UKIP launch
Mon 18 Apr	PC launch
	SSP launch
	Respect launch
Tue 19 Apr	Nominations close
	Pope Benedict XVI elected
Wed 20 Apr	UUP launch
	SDLP launch
Thu 21 Apr	DUP launch
	Sun backs Labour

Fri 22 Apr	IFS costings of party programmes published
Sat 23 Apr	BNP launch
Sun 24 Apr	Howard says Blair 'lied' on *Breakfast with Frost*
	Blair immigration speech
	Iraq stories resurface
Mon 25 Apr	New Con and Lab slogans
Tue 26 Apr	Postal vote applications end
	Sedgemore defects to Lib Dems
Thu 28 Apr	BBC *Question Time*
	Goldsmith's advice published
Fri 29 Apr	Sinn Fein launch
Mon 2 May	Bank Holiday
Tue 3 May	Soldier killed in Iraq, family blames Blair
Thu 5 May	Polling day

The parties made more than usual of their slogans, though they changed them mid-campaign. Labour moved from 'Forward Not Back' to 'If You Value It, Vote For It', and the Conservatives from the much-mocked but much-quoted 'Are You Thinking What We're Thinking?' to 'Taking a Stand on the Issues that Matter' (they felt that they could not go through to the end just asking a question). The Liberal Democrats stayed with their established theme 'The Real Alternative'. All parties engaged in national press advertising. The Conservatives started with a manuscript list of six points signed by Michael Howard.

The media once again tended to portray the election as a great bore and to lament the lack of colour and excitement. Less than usual was seen of the leaders moving around the country in battle buses with a large press entourage. For the most part they stayed based in London, making daily out-and-back helicopter trips to provincial centres and marginal seats. Once there, most of their time was taken up by local press and broadcast interviews together with staged photo opportunities, highlighting the theme of the day.

The need for security from terrorists, but equally the need for security from organised hecklers and show-stealers, meant that the leaders' movements were not advertised in advance and there were few walkabouts. A Channel 4 *Dispatches* programme broadcast later (23 May) suggested that the audiences in some of the televised events were packed with Labour Party faithful, though, in at least one case, the BBC was accused of adding hecklers to spice up a Howard gathering. Embarrassing encounters were not completely avoided. One of the most notable was on BBC *Question Time* on 28 April when Tony Blair was flummoxed

Michael Howard's election campaign.

(Steve Bell, *Guardian*, 7 April 2005)

by a lady with a cogent question about the absurd consequences of targeting for GP appointments. In Leeds on 20 April Tony Blair was confronted by a student who said: 'It is heartbreaking when you work so long to get a Labour Government in power and then they turn into a Conservative one.' Mr Blair acknowledged that he had heard many similar complaints, but argued: 'If you measure any government against perfection, you would vote for someone else. But you must measure us against the alternative, which is the Conservatives.' At a forum on 19 April Mr Howard was accused by a black police officer of pandering to fears over immigration and by another black officer for his attacks on political correctness. Critical feedback from their own side encouraged the party to move away from the immigration issue. All parties were sensitive about awkward questions from their own followers.

There were few major public meetings. Organised rallies for Michael Howard at Canary Wharf on 20 April and for Tony Blair in Huddersfield on 3 May were reported, but Charles Kennedy's open meeting in

It's not racist to impose limits on immigration.

ARE YOU THINKING WHAT WE'RE THINKING?   **CONSERVATIVE**

Cambridge with 600 in the audience and a 600 overflow was cited as altogether exceptional.

Nonetheless, there was some genuine engagement between the parties. On taxation, hospital management, immigration, council tax and Iraq, journalists made the leaders face up to challenges from the other side. But the campaign was diversified because, in pursuit of fresh headlines, each party raised new themes every day. Arguments over taxing and spending were prominent in the first days, as is shown in Chapters 8 and 9; Iraq was to the fore in the final week to the regret of both Conservative and Labour. Only the Liberal Democrats could benefit from the ventilation of this theme.

The parties had similar headquarters routines. An early morning meeting with some of the strategists would digest the media summaries and local reports prepared overnight by more junior staff.[1] The leader would then arrive for a senior meeting to discuss strategy and prepare for the press conference. Since the Liberal Democrats met the media at 7.30 a.m. Charles Kennedy had to be there at 7.00 a.m. In the late afternoon there would be a further meeting for the London-based staff to prepare for the next day.

The leaders' wives were unusually in evidence. Sarah Kennedy did not accompany her husband, but pictures of them both with their first child, Donald, born on 12 April, were prominent. Cherie Blair often travelled with her husband, while Sandra Howard did so almost all the time, promoting his image as a family man. She also contributed a web diary.

Manifesto launches provided the staple events of the campaign. The media could hardly ignore them, even when the parties were minor players. The major parties supplemented their main launch with special occasions to unveil business or rural manifestos as well as statements for Scotland and Wales.

The Conservative launch on 11 April saw Michael Howard use conventional soundbites, envisaging a 'battle for Britain' and asking the electorate to 'see how we've changed', adding: 'you don't have to settle for second-best'.

The party manifesto was brief and non-specific. The media noted that it was half the length of the 2001 document and only a third that of the 1997 one. It emphasised the party's pledges on tax, crime and immigration, along with value for money and accountability. It contained no surprises and, as critics noted, it was hardly a programme for government.

The Labour Party took the Mermaid Theatre in the City for a spectacular affair on 13 April to hear Tony Blair give his last manifesto launch. The Cabinet was assembled at the back of the stage behind the Prime Minister and his presumed successor, Gordon Brown. Ruth Kelly, Patricia Hewitt, Alistair Darling, John Reid and John Prescott were arrayed with them behind ceremonial plinths. The press noted, suspiciously, that Jack Straw was not in the front line-up. The manifesto was packed with policies for the third term. It was clearly New Labour and commentators noted that Gordon Brown accepted the mantras of 'choice' and 'diversity'. The manifesto promised to 'personalise public services', to 'help hard-working families' and to maintain economic stability. The manifesto also said that the Government would campaign 'wholeheartedly' for a 'Yes' vote in a referendum on the proposed European Constitution, although the subject was hardly raised again during the campaign. Blairites claimed that the manifesto for a third term could 'entrench' a progressive consensus along the lines of 1945.

The Liberal Democrat launch on 14 April was made memorable by the confusion of the exhausted new father, Charles Kennedy, when challenged to explain the party's scheme for a local income tax. But the party stood by its proposals for a 50 per cent tax on incomes over £100,000 and for restoring the link between pensions and average earnings.

The minor parties' campaigns got little coverage in the media but each launch earned a paragraph or two, at least in the broadsheets. Robert Kilroy-Silk's Veritas and the BNP were noted for their attacks on multiculturalism, and the Greens for their doom-laden warnings on pollution. George Galloway's Respect and UKIP each tried to suggest that they were more than single-issue parties. The SNP and Plaid Cymru each emphasised an anti-war and left-wing nationalist stance.

A key element in Labour's campaign lay in the prominence given to Gordon Brown and his relationship with Tony Blair. After prolonged negotiations they had agreed at the last moment to work together and the media were denied the opportunity to write again and again about the feud. The strategy meetings now included Brownites: Ed Balls, Donald Alexander, David Miliband, Spencer Livermore and Bob Shrum. On 6 April the Prime Minister made plain that the Chancellor would keep his job: 'He is the most successful Chancellor in 100 years. We would be crazy to put that at risk.'

Blair and Brown were repeatedly shown campaigning harmoniously together. At a joint news conference on 23 April, Gordon Brown appealed to disaffected Labour voters to stick with the party: 'only a Labour Government can bring the sort of society traditionalist Labour voters believe in'. This was part of a concerted effort to present Labour as a team, in contrast to the Conservatives who so often seemed to present Michael Howard alone. The partnership certainly heartened Labour's campaign team. The election was plainly a last hurrah for both Blair and Howard. But, unlike Howard, Blair had an obvious successor.

The economy was put at the forefront of the party's case for re-election and Gordon Brown fared reasonably well in the early arguments over finance. The Howard Flight affair had made the Conservatives cautious about tax-cutting promises. Of the £12 billion they hoped to save by cost-cutting, £4 billion would go to reducing government borrowing, £4 billion to new expenditure on police and other services, and £4 billion to tax cuts (£1.7 billion specifically for pensioners' income tax and £1.3 billion for pensioners' council tax).

The Conservatives were embarrassed by their earlier talk of £35 billion of cuts. Commentators pointed out that the final argument was over £12 billion, less than 2 per cent of GDP. The Conservative proposals were described as 'an incoherent mess' in a Labour Party dossier, and Gordon Brown argued that 'Mr Letwin has a black hole of £18.9 billion in year one, £18.5 billion in year two, and £14.4 billion in year three.' Oliver Letwin firmly refuted him: 'On our plans we can reduce borrowing and avoid the tax rises that are implied by Labour's post-election spending plans.' Michael Howard said repeatedly: 'If Labour gets in again, taxes will go up again.' Gordon Brown, of course, reiterated the promise not to raise income tax and came near to an assurance that he would not raise National Insurance, 'although no sensible Chancellor would make pledges on every single tax'.

On 26 April the much respected Institute for Fiscal Studies (IFS) offered a verdict, arguing that Labour's spending plans for the next economic cycle could still leave an £11 billion funding gap and that Gordon Brown had 'consistently over-estimated tax revenue'. But the IFS also expressed scepticism about the Conservatives' prospects of achieving cost-cutting savings of £12 billion; the IFS went on to say that the Liberal Democrat proposals, since they were based on the same Treasury figures as Labour's, would be equally at risk.

However, Robert Chote, Director of the IFS, pointed to the remarkable convergence of the parties' plans all centring on spending about 40 per cent of GDP, all accepting the Chancellor's Golden Rule, and all approving the Bank of England's control over interest rates.

Specific financial issues came up. On 21 April Michael Howard promised to raise the threshold for Stamp Duty on house purchases to £250,000 and on 20 April he promised to abort the pending council tax revaluation for homes in England, pointing to the expense and unfairness of the recent revaluation in Wales. He defended the council tax but complained that Labour had used it as a form of 'stealth tax'. The Liberal Democrats soldiered on with their substitution of a local income tax for the 'fundamentally unfair' council tax, and were mocked by the other parties for the technical complications and unfairness of the proposal.

Despite opposition complaints the Conservatives fought an animated campaign. They denied making the theme of immigration and asylum the centrepiece of their campaign; it provided the main theme of only one press conference. But they had a big poster: 'It's Not Racist to Impose Limits on Immigration'.

There certainly were Conservative candidates who annoyed moderates in the party by giving heavy prominence to the subject. Michael Howard said it was an issue that must not be 'swept under the carpet'; immigration was out of control and Tony Blair was 'pussyfooting about the subject'. Peter Hain protested at the Conservatives' 'scurrilous, right-wing, ugly tactics'.

To neutralise asylum and immigration Tony Blair gave his best speech of the campaign. He said on 24 April at Dover: 'I think that most people recognise the huge contribution that immigrants have made to this country', and then dealt, point by point, with the arguments over the desirability and scale of current immigration and the administrative problems of monitoring it. He called the Conservative policies 'incoherent babble ... an attempt deliberately to exploit people's fears, to suggest that, for reasons of political correctness, those in power don't care to deal with the issue'. The Prime Minister referred specifically to the Conservative proposals to withdraw from the International Convention on Refugees and to process asylum-seekers on some offshore 'fantasy island'. Mr Howard, who was frank about his own refugee roots, argued: 'we have to limit the circumstances that people apply for asylum in this country'.

UKIP and BNP pointed to the influx from the new members of the EU and demanded a total stop to all immigration.

As the Conservatives failed to make any progress in the polls, stories of internal unhappiness emerged. Some suggested that with their meagre manifesto the party seemed to run out of steam and there were complaints of a lack of vision and inspiration. Others criticised the extent to which it was presented as a one-man campaign. In contrast to the Prime Minister, flanked on three occasions by his whole Cabinet, and continuously seen travelling with Gordon Brown, stories about the Conservatives showed Michael Howard alone. There was comment on the limited prominence given to Oliver Letwin, Michael Ancram and David Davis compared to the lesser-known and more junior David Cameron, George Osborne and Andrew Lansley.

On 19 April Michael Howard felt forced to deny that senior figures had urged him to get away from his emphasis on immigration. He said that it was only one of his five priorities. Norman Tebbit pressed him to be even tougher; on the BBC *Today* programme on 28 April he called for a stronger campaign on immigration and for making more of tax cuts. On the same day, on BBC2, Kenneth Clarke wanted to move on from immigration and said that he was not sure that he would have sanctioned the 'liar' poster (see p. 79). 'I have not used that word myself; I am an old parliamentarian.' David Mellor in the *Evening Standard* on 19 April had cried: 'Wake up, Michael, it's the economy, stupid. Unless you get a grip on that you're toast.' A leaked letter to candidates from Lynton Crosby in mid-April suggested a hard slog ahead, and Michael Howard confirmed his underdog status when on 25 April he likened his position to being two goals down at half time (referring to his team, Liverpool, which the day before had recovered from a two-goal deficit to win the European Cup). Liam Fox later took up the analogy, suggesting that the election would be 'very close' and would 'go to penalties'. But as the polls continued to offer a bleak message, the Conservatives seemed to have little more to say. As one Howard adviser noted, 'Four weeks is a long time. You have got to have a lot of policy in reserve.'

The campaign had its trivia. The Conservative candidate in the marginal South Dorset seat was exposed for faking a photograph. John Prescott was caught gratuitously abusing a local journalist in South Wales. There were riotous scenes in the Mile End Road during the George Galloway assault on Oona King's Bethnal Green seat; it seems to have been the roughest of all constituency campaigns – on 19 April a gang on Muslim zealots, objecting to any participation in voting ('anyone who votes is an unbeliever'), attacked a mosque and then a Galloway meeting. Oona King was later pelted with eggs by Bengali youths wearing Respect badges.

The possibility of postal vote fraud was repeatedly brought up. On 5 April six Labour councillors in Birmingham were unseated by an election court for systematic fraud in the 2004 elections, and the judge referred to procedures 'worthy of a banana republic'. On 7 April a former Blackburn councillor was sent to prison for three and a half years for improper gathering of postal votes. On 4 May the police arrested two men in Bradford, one of them a Conservative councillor, for postal ballot fraud. Statistics appeared showing the threefold increase in postal vote applications, and a poll suggested a handsome Labour lead among those applying. All parties were criticised for collecting the voting envelopes rather than leaving them to be sent by post. After an emergency meeting on 21 April, called by the Department for Constitutional Affairs, the Electoral Commission launched press advertisements clarifying voters' rights.

Labour boasted of its spending on health but Michael Howard made a major point of NHS inefficiency. He referred particularly to the hospital virus, MRSA, which had killed his mother-in-law, and he advocated the return of hospital matrons with full authority over ward cleanliness. He also reverted frequently to the problems of law and order and in particular of 'yobs'; he cited the mugging of his wife. He accused Tony Blair of being complacent about crime, trying 'to keep it off the front pages with a blizzard of misleading denials'. On 21 April Home Office figures showed that recorded crime had fallen by 5 per cent but violent crime had risen by 9 per cent. David Davis, as Shadow spokesman, announced a six-point plan to 'make life a misery for criminals', saying that violence and lawlessness were spreading in Britain's inner cities: 'Let me tell Mr Blair straight: life in Britain is very different outside your security bubble.' But all parties were promising an increase in police numbers: the Conservatives by 5,000 a year, the Liberal Democrats by 10,000 over five years and the Labour Party by 25,000 community support officers. All parties said they would reduce police paperwork.

Education was brought into the campaign with promises to expand nursery education and with recurrent references to top-up fees for students which every party except Labour had promised to abolish. There were occasional comments on the issues that seemed missing from the national campaign. Little was heard of housing or transport or nuclear energy or, surprisingly, of fox hunting. More importantly, despite the efforts of the minor parties, very little was said about Europe, although on 18 April Tony Blair did admit that the coming Parliament would not see a referendum on joining the euro.

The campaign saw a few headlined changes of allegiance. Pa
a Labour MP who had defected to the Liberal Democra
returned to his old party on election eve, though he was 1
again. Stephen Wilkinson, the Labour candidate for Ribble Valley (a saℓ
Conservative seat) suddenly joined the Liberal Democrats on 6 April.
Brian Sedgemore, a veteran left-wing Labour MP, not standing again,
joined the Liberal Democrats on 25 April. Derek Cattall, a leading figure
in Tony Blair's Sedgefield constituency party, decided to support Reg
Keys, the grieving father of an Iraq casualty, who was standing against
the Prime Minister. Greg Dyke, the former Director-General of the BBC
and a generous Labour Party donor, announced two days before the
poll he would support the Liberal Democrats because 'another Blair
Government would be a danger to democracy'. On the day after her
election defeat in Peterborough, former Labour MP Helen Clark switched
to the Conservative Party.

On 23 April, Channel 4 News, followed by the *Mail on Sunday,* revealed
the contents of the Attorney-General's March 2003 advice to the Cabinet
on the legality of going to war without a further UN resolution. Lord
Goldsmith firmly denied that he had been leant on to give a legal green
light for military action. On 27 April the Government released the full
text, 'since so much was already in the public domain'. Tony Blair claimed
that 'the smoking gun has turned into a damp squib'. The Conservatives
made much of it with a poster:

> If He's Prepared to Lie
> to Take Us to War
> He's Prepared to Lie
> to Win an Election.

Indeed, during the 24 April *Breakfast with Frost*, Michael Howard accused
Mr Blair of repeatedly lying to the public: 'He's told lies to win elections.
On the one thing where he's taken a stand in the eight years he's been
Prime Minister, which was taking us to war, he didn't even tell the truth
about that.'

Charles Kennedy observed that Conservative criticisms were 'clap-trap';
they were 'the principal cheer-leaders for George Bush and Tony Blair in
this war in the first place'. Gordon Brown firmly endorsed Tony Blair's
decision in March 2003, but agreed that Parliament should almost always
be consulted about going to war. Plaid Cymru and the Greens continued
to demand the impeachment of Tony Blair.

The Liberal Democrats, who had been planning to develop the Iraq theme in the final week of the campaign, were delighted to exploit the Attorney-General story and they ran with the Iraq issue for the remaining days. They quoted their new recruit, Brian Sedgemore, speaking of Blair's 'stomach-turning lies'. Charles Kennedy pointed out that his was the only major party to oppose intervention and claimed that the election could be 'a referendum on the war'. The party placed advertisements in the *Daily Mail* and *Daily Mirror* on 25 April emphasising its opposition to Iraq policies. The death of Anthony Wakefield, a British soldier in Iraq, and the bitter comments of his widow on 4 May kept Iraq in the public eye to the end.

The trust issue rumbled on throughout the campaign. The Conservatives ran a film in 80 cinemas with the theme song 'Take that look off your face' over an image of Tony Blair. All candidates reported adverse doorstep comments on Tony Blair. 'You can't believe a word he says', was a Conservative mantra. Some Labour MPs revealed their eagerness for a change of leader, and there seems to have been a considerable response to Polly Toynbee's repeated advice in the *Guardian* to vote Labour 'holding your nose'.

On 21 April the *Sun* ended speculation by giving a critical endorsement to Labour by releasing red smoke over their Wapping headquarters. Rupert Murdoch's other flagship, *The Times*, followed suit and so did the *Financial Times*. Except for the *Express,* which switched to the Conservatives in 2004, every paper confirmed its 2001 preference, but many plainly did so reluctantly, choosing the lesser evil.

But in the end Labour got firmer press support than the Conservatives. On 4 May, the *Sun* robustly argued: 'Tony Blair is the same decent family man he was on that first day [in 1997]. The *Sun* believes he is worthy of your vote', while the *Mirror* told its readers: 'It has to be Labour. Today there is a chance to make sure that the Conservatives never again get the opportunity to ruin the country. This means voting Labour. Voting to destroy the Tories.' This contrasted with the *Daily Mail* which, under the headline 'GIVE BLAIR A BLOODY NOSE', wrote: 'Our support for a Conservative victory – which we concede is unlikely – is superseded by an even greater imperative: to destroy the power of an overwhelmingly arrogant Mr Blair.' The *Daily Telegraph* observed: 'Other newspapers have urged their readers to vote tactically, so as to return Labour with a reduced majority. That sounds like stupid advice.'

In the last days, Michael Howard, inspired by Lynton Crosby, unveiled a 'timetable for action' listing eight things that a Conservative government would do in the first days after taking office:

The people have had enough of spin and smirk – they just want someone who'll make things work. It's no use being a man of destiny if you can't be bothered with details. People don't want a date with destiny. Most just want a date with the dentist.

The two big parties focused their national offensives on each other, even though, as Chapter 11 shows, much of the battleground was between one or other of them and the Liberal Democrats. Charles Kennedy indicated firmly that in a hung Parliament there would be no prospect of a deal with Labour. It was only in the last days that Labour turned any fire on the Liberal Democrats. Tony Blair energetically warned voters against 'letting the Conservatives in by the back door' by voting Liberal Democrat. Labour expressed worries about the lavish Tory concentration on target voters in target marginals and about tactical voting by people who did not want a Conservative government but wanted to give Labour a bloody nose.

In the final days, Labour speakers warned about complacency, namely that 'if one in ten don't vote' the Conservatives could come back. They stressed achievements in health and education, bolstered by their new slogan 'If You Value It Vote For It'. There was an effort to counteract the deliberate leak of an Alastair Campbell memo which the *Sunday Times* misleadingly headlined on its front page as 'CAMPBELL: WE'RE HOME AND DRY' (24 April).

The weather on 5 May was cloudy but mostly dry – though bouts of heavy rain were reported from Aberdeen and Manchester. The BBC and ITN jointly sponsored an exit poll to be revealed the moment the booths closed at 10.00 p.m. It showed, accurately, a 3 per cent lead for Labour which the broadcasters translated, accurately, into a clear Labour majority of 66 seats. The first result, Sunderland South, came in at 10.46 p.m., but the next was 40 minutes later, and only five had reported by midnight. By 4.25 a.m., as Labour was winning the 324th seat that guaranteed its majority, Michael Howard formally conceded. By breakfast time, 619 counts were completed. Most of the remaining seats were from Northern Ireland where Sinn Fein and DUP victories increased the polarisation of the province's politics.

Tony Blair was disappointed not to have got the three-figure endorsement he had hoped for, and the television coverage of the results was made memorable by a passionate speech directed at Tony Blair by Reg Keys, the anti-Iraq war candidate in Sedgefield, as well as by the larger-than-life George Galloway shouting 'This is for Iraq' as his victory in Bethnal Green was announced. The campaign had been literally painful for Blair, suffering from a slipped disc and a heavy cold.

VOTE LABOUR
ON THURSDAY OR WAKE UP
WITH MICHAEL HOWARD.
If one in 10 Labour voters don't vote, the Tories win.   Labour
www.labour.org.uk

The overall result was clear enough. Labour had won a comfortable majority, but it was on only 35.2 per cent of the vote: the lowest support ever for a single-party government. The Conservatives made a net gain of 32 seats over 2001 and Liberal Democrats a net gain of 11, most of them at Labour's expense. Three junior ministers were defeated but no famous heads fell; Tim Collins, the Conservatives' Education spokesman, was the only victim of the Liberal Democrat decapitation strategy.

The turnout at 61 per cent was slightly up on the abysmal low of 2001 but, as Appendix 1 shows, the outcome was more varied. At noon Tony Blair went to the Palace to report to the Queen, and by early evening his Cabinet changes had been announced.

"IF YOU VOTE FOR *HIM* YOU GET *HIM* !"

(Nicholas Garland, *Daily Telegraph*, 4 May 2005)

Note

1. Personnel changed from day to day but the key figures at the main meetings seem to have been: Liberal Democrats – Charles Kennedy, Lord Rennard, Lord Razzall, Lord Newby, Sir Menzies Campbell, Matthew Taylor and Shirley Williams, who all attended quite often; Conservatives: Michael Howard, Lynton Crosby, Liam Fox, Lord Saatchi, George Bridges, David Cameron, and from Howard's office Stephen Sherbourne and Rachel Whetstone; Labour: Tony Blair, Gordon Brown, Alan Milburn, Douglas Alexander, Alastair Campbell, Matt Carter and Lord Gould.

7
Public Polls and Private Polls

It is now inconceivable for a political party to campaign without the benefit of polling. Although some 80 per cent of what the polls find comes into the public domain as a result of polls commissioned by the press and broadcasters, the private polls have the advantages of providing virtually instant reactions to campaign events, helping in the planning and monitoring of strategies, and enabling the pre-testing of specific concepts, phraseology and communication materials.

The election saw more campaign polls than 2001 but even less movement in their findings. Certainly polls, public and private, had an effect on the campaign – on the morale of the participants and on the expectations of the public. But the media paid less attention to them than in past elections (see Chapters 8 and 9).

There were substantial changes in the political polling industry during the 2001 Parliament, both in the main players and in their methodology. After a pause and an open competition *The Times* in 2002 chose to move from MORI to Populus which Andrew Cooper had recently founded. The *Daily Telegraph* in 2002 abandoned its long association with Gallup and switched to YouGov, the online pollsters headed by Peter Kellner and Stephan Shakespeare, but with Anthony King continuing to write up the findings. The third paper publishing regular monthly polls, the *Guardian,* stuck with ICM under Nick Sparrow. Both YouGov and ICM did occasional work for other papers and broadcasters. Harris and Gallup abandoned political polling for newspapers but NOP under Nick Moon published *ad hoc* surveys for several media outlets and worked for the *Independent* during the election. MORI contributed polls for the *Financial Times*, the *Observer* and the *Evening Standard* and others and, working with NOP conducted the 5 May exit poll sponsored jointly by the BBC and ITV. A new operation, Communicate Research under Andrew Hawkins, polled for the *Independent on Sunday*. The British Election Survey at Essex published four polls in the *Mail on Sunday*, with their data collected by YouGov (notably Anthony Wells's pollingreport.co.uk).

Early in 2005, the pollsters united to form the British Polling Council which established agreed standards for its members, including making available the breakdowns of their findings. Each pollster maintained an informative internet site. Only MORI continued to use face-to-face interviews with respondents selected on a quota basis (though they did some telephone polling on a quota basis and used telephone polls for their final forecast). Apart from YouGov with its on-line panel, all the other companies depended on telephone interviews with a random sample and all had their own formulae for weighting their results for likelihood of voting and for the representativeness of their sample in terms of age, class, gender, car ownership, newspaper reading and other variables.

The 2001 drop in turnout to 59 per cent had been disproportionately great in working-class constituencies and was a source of great anxiety to pollsters; in past times, when turnout averaged 75 per cent, they had not found it so necessary to modify their raw figures. The most difficult and controversial aspect of weighting was allowance for past voting. How far could respondents be trusted to remember whether and how they cast their ballots three or four years earlier? All the telephone pollsters did make their own allowances for reports of past voting and argued that if they had not done so they would have been recording Labour leads of 10–15 per cent, not 2–7 per cent. MORI (which in early April reported a unique rogue poll that put the Conservatives ahead) concentrated on a ten-point scale about likelihood of voting and quoted the figures for those who said they were ten-out-of-ten 'certain to vote'. Others used a ten-point scale adjusted in different ways. Pollsters expressed anxiety about the greatly increased number of postal voters (tripled from the 5 per cent in 2001) but they obeyed the Electoral Commission guidance against reporting how they were dividing before the count began.

The 53 nationwide polls published during the campaign compare with 29 in 2001 and 49 in 1997. Their detailed breakdowns were promptly posted on their webstites.

The findings on voting intention showed a remarkable stability (see Table 7.1). On a rolling average of all the polls, Labour's lead always lay between 7 per cent and 4 per cent. YouGov seems to have had the most stable series of findings. The Liberal Democrats were disappointed that the polls failed to show the substantial upsurge in the campaign they had expected. Their gain during the campaign was less than 2 per cent. The Conservatives became dismayed as the faint hope offered by some of the early polls dissipated. Labour feared that polls were too flattering, but took comfort in their continuing lead and in the cushion offered to them by the bias in the electoral system.

Table 7.1 Voting intention during the campaign

Opinion polls 2005	Date published	Sample size	Field. dates	Con (%)	Lab (%)	Lib Dem (%)	Lab lead over Con
2001 result (GB)				33	42	19	9
ICM/*Guardian*	5.4	1507	1/3.4	34	37	21	3
MORI/*FT*	5.4	1001	1/3.4	39	34	21	−5
NOP/*Independent*	5.4	956	1/3.4	33	36	21	3
Populus/*Times*	5.4	1513	1/3.4	35	37	19	2
YouGov*/Sky	6.4	1735	5.4	36	36	21	0
YouGov*/*Telegraph*	8.4	5108	5/6.4	35	36	21	1
ICM/*S. Telegraph*	10.4	1012	7/8.4	34	38	20	4
YouGov*/*S. Times*	10.4	1552	7/9.4	35	37	21	2
MORI/*Observer*	10.4	1004	7/9.4	33	40	19	7
ICM/GMTV-*Mirror*	11.4	1009	9.4	33	38	22	5
YouGov*/*Telegraph*	11.4	1514	8/10.4	36	36	20	0
NOP/*Independent*	12.4	956	8/10.4	32	38	21	6
MORI/*E. Standard*	13.4	1973	7/11.4	35	39	21	4
ICM/*Guardian*	14.4	1524	10/12.4	33	39	21	6
YouGov*/*Telegraph*	15.4	2240	12/14.4	33	38	22	5
Communicate/*IOS*	17.4	1000	11/15.4	34	40	20	6
ICM/*S. Telegraph*	17.4	1521	13/15.4	30	40	22	10
YouGov*/*S. Times*	17.4	1482	14/16.4	35	36	23	1
ICM/ GMTV-*Mirror*	18.4	1005	16.4	33	41	20	8
Populus/*Times*	19.4	1000	14/17.4	31	40	21	9
YouGov*/*Telegraph*	18.4	2011	15/17.4	33	36	23	3
NOP/*Independent*	19.4	958	15/17.4	32	37	21	5
MORI/*FT*	19.4	1005	15/18.4	32	40	21	8
Populus/*Times*-ITV	20.4	1424	15/18.4	33	39	21	6
ICM/*Guardian*	21.4	1513	17/19.4	33	39	22	6
MORI/*Sun*	21.4	1001	18/19.4	32	39	22	7
YouGov*/*Telegraph*	22.4	1474	19/21.4	34	37	22	3
Populus/*Times*-ITV	23.4	1400	19/22.4	33	41	20	8
Communicate/*IOS*	24.4	1003	19/22.4	35	40	18	5
ICM/*S. Telegraph*	24.4	1524	20/22.4	33	39	21	6
YouGov*/*S. Times*	24.4	1490	21/23.4	33	37	23	4
ICM/ GMTV-*Mirror*	25.5	1015	23.4	33	39	20	6
YouGov*/*Telegraph*	25.5	1831	22/24.4	33	37	24	4
NOP/*Independent*	26.4	959	22/24.4	30	40	21	10
MORI/*FT*	27.4	2256	21/25.4	34	36	23	2
Populus/*Times*-ITV	28.4	1430	23/26.4	31	40	21	9
ICM/*Guardian*	28.4	1547	24/26.4	33	40	20	7
YouGov*/*Telegraph*	29.4	2070	26/28.4	32	36	24	4

Communicate/*IOS*	1.5	1091	23/28.4	31	39	23	8
ICM/*S. Telegraph*	1.5	1532	27/29.4	31	39	22	8
MORI/*Observer*	1.5	1007	28/29.4	33	36	22	3
Populus/*Times*-ITV	2.5	1427	27/30.4	29	42	21	13
YouGov*/*S. Times*	1.5	1400	28/30.4	33	36	23	3
YouGov*/*Telegraph*	2.5	1309	29.4/1.5	33	36	24	3
MORI/*FT*	3.5	1009	29.4/1.5	29	39	22	10
YouGov*/Sky News	4.5	2368	2/3.5	32	36	25	4
ICM/*Guardian*	5.5	1532	1/3.5	32	38	22	6
NOP/*Independent*	5.5	1000	1/3.5	33	36	23	3
Populus/*Times*	5.5	2042	2/3.5	32	38	21	6
YouGov*/*Telegraph*	5.5	3962	2/3.5	32	37	24	5
MORI/*E. Standard*	5.5	1632	3/4.5	33	38	23	5
2005 result (GB)				33	36	23	3

* Sampled from a panel of internet users.
The Populus polls include every four days those based on a daily tracking poll of 350 respondents.
There were also three 'normal' polls by Populus on 5 April and 19 and 5 May.
On election eve Harrisinteractive under Humphrey Taylor returned to British polling with an on-line survey showing a 38/33/22 per cent division of the vote.

Source: David Cowling.

Labour actually won by 3 per cent. NOP legitimately boasted of being exactly right, but every other final poll (except Communicate which had to interview before 1 May) put Labour ahead by between 3 per cent and 6 per cent, comfortably within the accepted margin of error. The pollsters were relieved. The industry still had uncomfortable memories of 1992 when they were all about 8 per cent out in their estimates of the gap between the parties.

There were few constituency polls but there were two rolling polls. Populus interviewed 350 people a day, cumulating the last four days' findings to provide a trend line on voting intention and two days' findings for issue questions. The British Election Survey at Essex University also published its own rolling poll daily on the web, conducted by YouGov, cumulating the last six days' findings. It was alone in putting the Conservatives ahead in the first week of the campaign.

Some of the most interesting polls were on issues and on leaders. The campaign certainly did not help the Conservatives. The Essex University British Election Survey asked daily which party was performing best and which worst in the campaign. At the end of the battle the Liberal Democrats triumphed (best minus worst, +17%); the judgement on Labour's efforts was only just positive (+4%); the Conservative campaign got the worst marks (–18%) (see Figure 7.1). YouGov comparing its findings in early April and early May discovered that on every major issue Labour improved its position relative to the Conservatives, even on issues where it was at a disadvantage.

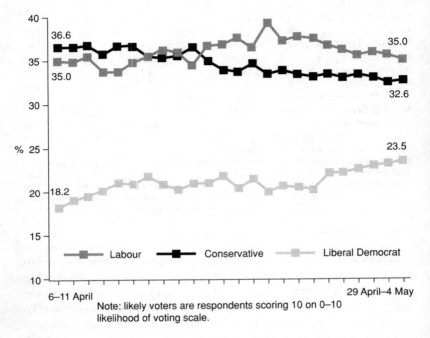

Figure 7.1   Voting intention among likely voters (decideds plus leaners)

Source: British Election Study 2005 Rolling Campaign Panel Survey <www.essex.ac.uk/bes/2005/Rolling%20campaign.htm> accessed 3 June 2005.

Table 7.2   Changes in party ratings

'Here is a list of problems facing the country. Could you say, for each of them, which political party you personally think would handle them best?' (Figures show Lab lead over Con.)

	5–6 April	3–4 May	Change
The economy overall	14	22	+8
The NHS	8	13	+5
Education & schools	5	7	+2
Taxation	−5	0	+5
Law and order	−14	−11	+3
Asylum & immigration	−26	−23	+3

YouGov data also showed that, apart from Iraq, it was Labour's issues that increased in importance to the voter as the campaign advanced and that Tony Blair, despite all the doorstep evidence of his unpopularity, had an increasing advantage over Michael Howard.

The scale of Labour's private polling programme dwarfed that of the Conservatives and Liberal Democrats. As noted on p. 24, Labour revised its polling arrangements in September 2004. Stan Greenberg was redeployed to work on polling in marginal seats and Mark Penn took over the strategic polling. Penn had less political polling experience than Greenberg, although he had polled for Clinton in 1996. Blair seems to have appreciated his reports more than Greenberg's detailed analyses and rigorously tested sets of tables. The two pollsters also differed in their identification of target voters: Penn suggested women with children; Greenberg emphasised pensioners. Philip Gould gave regular presentations to 'political' sessions of the Cabinet, drawing on Greenberg's work and other polling.

Before the election was called Penn polled monthly and then conducted six tracking polls with a sample of over 2,100 voters during the four weeks of the campaign. The findings were reported to a small group: Tony Blair, Gordon Brown, Alastair Campbell, Philip Gould, Alan Milburn and Matt Carter. The trends were generally reassuring for the party, and the pollster regularly emphasised the importance of the economy as Labour's main electoral draw. On 17 April he wrote to Blair that he should 'drive the election to the point where it came down to one central question: "Who do you trust with the future of the economy?"' His reports also advised how Labour could combat its weaknesses. On immigration it should remind voters of its actions (for example, ID cards and border controls) but also attack the underlying Conservatives' underlying racism, although 'This message should be carried by others than the Prime Minister.' Penn also noted the ignorance of Liberal Democrat policies on crime and drugs among that party's supporters – and their rejection of these policies when they were informed. He urged the party to exploit this Lib Dem weakness and in his final report advised: 'The drug issue is a complete surprise (to Lib Dem voters). So this means: here is a lot of power in a credible attack on this because it is new information.'

Between November 2004 and mid-March 2005, when his budget ran out, Greenberg surveyed 130 marginals, segmented according to census and MOSAIC data. In an interview, he reported Labour's weakness in a segment of seats he called the 'south-east middle class' (in fact, they were mainly working class). He emphasised the party's vulnerability on immigration and voters' belief that the Government was not tackling it, but reported a slight overall Labour lead in the marginals. (In nine weekly polls between January and March, ORB for the Conservatives found the two main parties running virtually level.) During the election campaign he added questions to Populus surveys and the raw data was analysed to test the relative strengths of the economy and immigration as influences on the vote.

Labour also mounted an ambitious focus group operation among target voters. TBWA did one each night, usually in the London area. The party's head of political strategy, Greg Cook, conducted groups in marginal seats in the second half of 2004. Gould did three or four a week, and his associate, Alice Cartner-Morley, did four a week. Certain themes recurred in the groups. Labour's strong points were the economy, Blair and Brown coming together and hostility to Howard. Weak points were Iraq (which was helping the Liberal Democrats and, for voters and the media, submerged the party's economic agenda) and voter cynicism because of immigration, asylum and Iraq.

A private Gould memo to Blair on 26 April struck a triumphant note, suggesting that Labour had 'won the election, the only question left is how large the majority is'. The endorsement might be a reluctant one, but 'The election is effectively won, the task now is to blast through to a three figure majority which is within our grasp.' After his group with lapsed Labour voters in Streatham on the eve of polling day he predicted that voters would give 'a conditional endorsement for a third term'; that Labour's vote would be between 36 per cent and 38 per cent, the Conservatives' between 32 per cent and 33 per cent, and the Liberal Democrats' between 22 per cent and 24 per cent; and Labour would have a majority of 90 seats.

In addition, Labour commissioned a weekly tracking poll from YouGov for six months before the election as well a monthly internet poll of 300 by Penn. Labour did not lack for data about voters nor for a variety of sources.

ORB was the third company to poll for the Conservatives in the Parliament. Following Nick Sparrow's decision to sever his relationship with the party (see p. 42), ORB was selected from a shortlist (for which one of the criteria, at Howard's insistence, was that any agency should not also poll for the media). Under Johnny Heald, ORB conducted tracking polls in the target seats (130 Labour-held and 33 Liberal Democrat-held), again among the target voters. These were voters who had backed Labour in 2001 but had become disillusioned and did not rule out voting Conservative. According to a Conservative who attended some of the groups: 'They are pissed off with Labour but have not moved over to us.'

During the election campaign ORB polled 500 potential voters every night, combining these to give a 1,500 sample every third evening. The details were initially sent to five people in campaign headquarters; Crosby, Gavin Barwell, Mark Textor (a business partner of Lynton Crosby), George Bridges and Ian Corby, and then more widely discussed at morning strategy meetings. The polls showed the Conservatives running level with Labour on many party attributes, enjoying leads on standards in hospitals, immigration and cracking down on crime. It trailed badly on helping families, having strong leadership and keeping mortgage interest rates low. Above all, the party made no inroads on Labour's big lead on the crucial questions of economic management.

ORB also conducted more than 90 focus groups, again of target voters in target seats, between June 2004 and the election. Heald moderated the groups, which were also attended by George Bridges (Director of the party's Research Department) and Steve Hilton. Overnight they wrote a report for Crosby and Howard. The findings convinced Howard and Crosby that they were dealing with the issues that bothered voters. They also shaped much of the party's strategy, slogans and posters, and informed to a considerable degree the language that Howard used in his public statements. They determined the five issues that formed the centrepiece of the campaign (see p. 43), were crucial in stiffening resistance to right-wing demands for the party to offer bigger tax cuts, and helped to formulate direct mail attacks on Liberal Democrats. On the other hand, research showing that voters did not fully understand or rate highly the idea of choice in health and schools, echoing earlier ICM research, did not dissuade the leader from continuing with the policies.

As in the Labour polls and groups, immigration and asylum were major concerns. 'People were reluctant to bring immigration up, but when somebody mentioned it, it took off. Everybody seemed bothered about it, largely for the pressures it seemed to be putting on the public services', said one Conservative. During the pre-campaign period the focus groups reported an improvement in Howard's standing every time he made a high-profile and controversial statement, for example on 'travellers' or immigration. This led to 'taking a stand' as a tactic – and, eventually, a slogan – by the Conservatives. But the groups also reported a worry over Howard's apparent lack of passion. The most disheartening finding was that the narrower Labour's lead appeared to be, the more it encouraged Labour doubters to return.

The Conservatives were embroiled in controversy when an ORB survey was reported in the *Financial Times* on 6 October 2004 alleging that the Conservatives had 39 per cent of the vote compared to Labour's 32 per cent in Labour-held marginals. The survey conclusions (but not the data) were presented by Lord Saatchi as evidence that the party was on track for victory, which the survey did not show or claim. The claims caused surprise because they were out of line with all other polls at the time. In fact, the survey had been conducted between 5 and 11 August 2004 with a sample of just over 1,000, hardly a sufficient basis on which to make such a bold claim about 163 seats. The apparent discrepancy led one pollster to complain to the Market Research Society that the full survey be published, in accordance with the MRS's code of conduct.[1] ORB strenuously defended its position on the grounds that it had no prior knowledge of Lord Saatchi's analysis or his intention to make it public. On his arrival Lynton Crosby immediately restricted the circulation of the polls and there were no more leaks.

From January 2005 until after the general election Lord Ashcroft commissioned an ambitious programme of polls and focus groups by Populus and YouGov in Lab–Con and Lib Dem–Con marginal seats. His research confounded Lord Saatchi's claims that the Conservatives had clear leads in the all-important marginals and Liam Fox's boasts that the party was doing better in them than in the national polls. Lord Ashcroft's findings were not comforting for the party and after the election he published a strong attack on what he regarded as the party's failure to get the best value from polls and on the large number of seats the party targeted (see pp. 171–2).

The Liberal Democrat programme, named PTV (Project Target Voter), followed the same model as in 2001 and 1997. Julian Ingram and Derek Martin, formerly Chairman of Martin Hamblin GfK, did a tracking study of target voters in 40 marginal seats. The findings were reported each night to Lord Rennard and Lord Razzall and a fuller presentation was made each Sunday to the whole campaign team. The broad findings of the research confirmed many of the findings of other private as well as public polls: Howard's standing with target voters was poor; Kennedy outscored other party leaders on a number of leader attributes; and Blair, although seen as a strong leader, had lost the trust of many. Iraq, according to the research, had already detached people from Labour and there was little indication that Iraq would further damage the party. Among the targets, about twice as many target voters supported Liberal Democrat proposals for a local income tax as opposed it.

The parties could have shared much of their polling data as the surveys concurred on so many of their strengths and weaknesses. A Conservative reported that the overwhelming sentiment coming from the target voters was, depressingly, 'Better the devil you know.' And a Labour pollster, with some relief, summarised the collective reaction of the focus groups as 'Let's stick with what we've got.'

There were a number of differences between Labour and Conservative approaches to the use of research. Labour appears to have circulated more widely most of the polling and focus group material during the campaign – between 12 and 20 people saw the findings. The Conservative use was more restricted and a number of Shadow ministers, with an expertise in the area, felt excluded from the exercise in the months preceding the election. Labour's research was greater in scale and employed a variety of agencies; the Lord Ashcroft exercise operated outside the control of the Conservative and was not made available during the campaign. There was greater continuity of key personnel on the Labour side. Campbell, Gould and Greenberg, as well as Blair and Brown, had all been involved with the polling for two previous general elections. On the Conservative side, Crosby was experienced but not in a British election, and the other key figures had not been centrally involved in the polling at previous general elections. Selective findings of Labour's focus groups in marginal seats, showing weaknesses in Labour support, were leaked to the *Guardian* on 27 April. At the time, party leaders were worried that expectations of an easy Labour victory were encouraging some Labour supporters not to bother to vote. Even if the British Polling Council had wished to take action over the breach of its guidelines, it could not, because Labour's US pollsters were not members. A little-noted feature was that for the first time in a British general election, a company, YouGov, had polled for both the Labour and Conservative parties.

Note

1. Rule B14 of the code states: 'Researchers must not knowingly allow the dissemination of conclusions from a marketing research project which are not adequately supported by the data. They must always be prepared to make available the technical information necessary to assess the validity of any published findings.'

8
On Air[1]

Martin Harrison

Rarely have the years between elections brought such uncertainty for broadcasters. As the election approached the BBC was still raw from one of its gravest clashes with government, which had cost it a Chairman and Director-General and led to important changes in the management of its news operations. Charter renewal was in its early stages, always a delicate period, and severe job cuts were threatening. ITV was digesting the merger of Granada and Carlton into a single company covering England and Wales and attempting to stem the erosion of ITV1 viewing figures. Independent Television News had lost the contract to supply news to Channel Five and its future seemed in doubt. A majority of homes now had access to a wider choice of radio and television channels by cable, satellite or digital terrestrial transmissions. Audiences were more fragmented than ever and the competition for market share more intense.[2] Almost all the new channels were election-free, making it easier than ever to avoid the campaign. Many voters did just that. However, the happy few who revel in elections now had five 24-hour news channels to choose from: the 'veteran' Sky News, BBC News 24, the ITV News Channel, Radio Five Live and Parliament TV.

For all this backdrop of technological, commercial and political vicissitudes, the main challenge to broadcasters, as in 2001, was how to engage the voters, many of whom were thought to be indifferent, antipathetic or simply convinced the outcome was a foregone conclusion. In 2001, the broadcasters had given the problem their best shot – and turnout fell. Much wringing of hands ensued among both politicians and broadcasters. The politicians then continued as before. The BBC, true to type, commissioned a report. Several initiatives emerged, primarily aimed at young voters. Most sunk without trace, though the youth-oriented *7 O 'Clock News* survived on BBC3, as did *The Daily Politics*, a relatively light-hearted current affairs magazine, running three mornings a week on BBC2. There had been excellent single programmes on current issues, news agendas had been fine-tuned in a more 'popular' direction and several younger newsreaders had been brought to the fore. Yet the BBC still carried no regular political programming in primetime and its flagship show, *Panorama*, stayed firmly in its Sunday evening graveyard slot. A report commissioned by the BBC governors found that the Corporation was outgunned by ITV at peak times – which was not saying all that much.[3] The governors' new chairman, Michael Grade, warned that the rise of rival news networks meant that 'serious news values [were] under increasing strain'.[4]

In all, the broadcasters had made little progress towards reconnecting the disconnected. Yet huge numbers of people had taken to the streets in protest over countryside issues and the war in Iraq. The potential was there – but could it be enlisted for traditional electoral politics? Reflecting that the broadcasters had simply bored the viewers in 2001, Nick Pollard of Sky News promised that 2005 would bring a more imaginative approach. But that would depend on whether the politicians would play their part.[5]

For at least two years political reporting on all channels had been looking to May 2005 as the likely election date. In October 2004, Michael Howard had made the traditional call for a televised leaders' debate and was no less traditionally rebuffed. February 2005 brought the surest signs that polling day was approaching: senior politicians began popping up in programmes to which they would normally give a wide berth. All three party leaders appeared on *Woman's Hour* (Radio 4) and chat shows like *Richard and Judy* (teatime on Channel 4) and *The Steve Wright Show* (mornings on Channel Five). Michael Howard took part in Channel 4's youth programme, *T4*, donned a flak jacket to join police on a drug raid and visited the cast of *Coronation Street*. These outings were seen mainly as a vehicle for showing the leaders in a more human light, as well as a good way of reaching the daytime audience with its many retired and unemployed people, and parents of small children. For Labour, the aim was to 'rebuild the Prime Minister's relationship with the British people', no less.[6]

The talk shows and their like were an element in Labour's 'masochism strategy'. They were not, however, without risk. *Richard and Judy* gave Blair the softest possible ride – but he had to admit he never sent Cherie flowers (so much for the 'women's vote'). On Channel 5, the mother of an autistic child told him he was 'talking rubbish' about special needs education. Another time, a hospital worker asked him whether he would be 'prepared to wipe somebody's backside for five pounds an hour'. The most disconcerting TV encounter was with a women who had pulled out several teeth with pliers because she was unable to find an NHS dentist, showing her gums in evidence.[7] He also encountered 'Little Ant and Little Dec', two ten-year-old *enfants terribles* with a regular slot on *Ant and Dec's Saturday Night Takeaway* (ITV1). According to David Hill, a senior Labour spin doctor, its audience of 7–8 million made this the perfect forum in which to show Blair as 'accessible, clear, nice'. The interview moved from the cheeky ('My dad says you're mad. Are you mad?') to the crass ('If you make an ugly smell, do people pretend not to notice because you is the Prime Minister?'). As the pair presented Blair with a pair of panties for Cherie he reportedly looked towards his aides and said, 'I don't believe this.' Margaret Thatcher, who once famously set a benchmark in political marketing by cuddling a new-born calf, could never have imagined it would come to this.[8] There had to be better ways than this of reconnecting politicians and people; better ways also than *Vote for Me*, a reality show on ITV1, where political novices competed to be a candidate for a mythical political party. The winner was an ex-convict who advocated castrating paedophiles, a massive prison building programme, deporting immigrants, repealing the Human Rights Act and legalising most drugs.[9]

During February the Conservatives won substantial coverage for policy statements on immigration and asylum, pensions, crime and hospital cleaning. They also scored over the 'battle of Margaret Dixon's shoulder' – a sad tale of repeated postponements of a much-needed operation, illustrating the state of the NHS. Again they won substantial coverage on all channels, despite editors' wariness about 'shroud waving'. However, any ground they may have won was compromised by the Howard Flight affair, discussed on p. 60. This was reported at some length and buried their proposals on the family. (Radio 4's *PM* declared the episode had 'dominated' a campaign that had not yet officially begun.) Earlier, Blair had travelled by helicopter to Labour's spring conference at Gateshead by a circuitous route successfully designed to attract maximum regional news coverage. During this warm-up phase, *Panorama* (BBC1) tackled the highly sensitive topic of the manipulation of intelligence over Iraq. With all these preliminaries it was perhaps not surprising that, on 4 March, Radio 4's *Feedback* aired the first complaint of 'too much election news' – a month before the formal start.[10] But what provoked the biggest political stir during this period was not a political programme at all: a denunciation of the quality of school dinners by Jamie Oliver, a TV chef, triggered widespread public discussion and had politicians scurrying to be seen to be 'doing something'.

Finally, Radio 4's 8 a.m. news declared on 5 April, 'The phoney war is over.' Blair's formal announcement came live on the lunchtime news. Where the much-derided launch of the 2001 campaign had come in a glow of religiosity from a school hall of hymn-singing non-voters, the Prime Minister now spoke in front of Number 10 with all the associations with state, power and continuity that the scene carried. Here was New Labour as party-of-government in word and symbol. A shirt-sleeved Michael Howard, already campaigning, and projecting energy, purpose, commitment and enthusiasm, although lacking comparable authority, promptly took up the challenge.

In tackling the election, radio and television offered an essentially familiar mix: news, with the greatest reach, offered highly compressed hard news packages, usually focused on the three main leaders and peppered with soundbites, complemented with analysis, commentary and softer features. Beyond that lay the customary panoply of current affairs magazines, programmes examining specific issues or campaign strategies and extended interviews with the political leaders. Changes remained modest, with the exception of a *Question Time* featuring the three main party leaders. However valid and professional this all was, it held little promise of engaging the indifferent and the disenchanted.[11]

One thing that changed little was the volume of news output.[12] Programmes were not extended, apart from ITV's lunchtime news, which was moving to a revised schedule, and Radio 4's *World at One* which ran for a full hour on days when there was no *Election Call* phone-in. The 15 news programmes monitored for this study devoted 49 per cent of their time to the election. Channel 4 News gave it 70 per cent of airtime at lunchtime and 62 per cent at 7 p.m. The main BBC1 and ITV1 bulletins and the 7 p.m. edition of Five News gave the campaign between 50 per cent and 60 per cent of their time. Radio 4's full-scale bulletins at 6 p.m. and midnight carried 42 per cent and 33 per cent respectively. The 8 a.m., 1 p.m. and 10 p.m programmes, which headed 'magazine' sections that concentrated heavily on the election, carried less. The late morning Five News, with 22 per cent on the election, was by far the least involved.

The election produced none of those 'breaking news' moments that are meat and drink to the rolling news services. More prosaically, they carried the party news conferences around breakfast time. Later, BBC News 24, ITV News and Radio Five Live drew heavily on a common stock of material with their parent organisations – though their more modest budgets meant they frequently provided simpler presentation. Sky News offered a stand-alone mix of news, interviews and features. Audiences had increased since 2001, but the main political significance of these channels still lay in enabling everyone involved in the campaign to keep a running check on the other actors and launch instant rebuttals. Parliament TV was a case apart. It carried not only the morning news conferences in full but also many speeches in full, whether live or recorded. This was a service for a tiny few. But where else could one come across not only Tony Blair at the top of his form but also Margaret Beckett addressing a somnolent crowd in Erewash? Or be exposed to the sneers, jibes and invective of a warm-up speaker at a Michael Howard rally as well as to Howard himself at his most expansive? Here, at least, anyone who wished to do so could hear senior politicians without the salami-slicing routines of bulletin editors. Sometimes one learned; sometimes limitations were cruelly exposed.

In 2001, some editors kept with the election because there were no big stories they could turn away to. This election was peppered with them: the demise of MG-Rover, the illness, death and funeral of John Paul II and the election of his successor, a royal wedding, the conviction of a failed asylum-seeker for killing a policeman and a particularly horrific attack on a young mother. All were reported at considerable length, sometimes pushing the campaign down the agenda or even eclipsing it. On the day of the Pope's funeral, when the three main party leaders were in Rome, total election coverage on the sampled programmes amounted to under three minutes.[13]

That story and the royal wedding were, conventionally speaking, not political. The others did not initially arise in an electoral frame, but all in different ways, had a strong electoral resonance. The MG-Rover collapse was covered predominantly as an industrial and human story but obviously called for a response from the politicians. In the event, although there was much speculation about the likely electoral fallout, the partisan exchanges that ensued were more muted than might have been expected – partly, no doubt, because opposition parties had no alternatives to offer. Even so, the Conservatives might have been expected to make more of this blot on the rosy picture that Gordon Brown was painting of the state of the economy. Reporting of the terrorist trial avoided direct reference to the election but the Conservatives promptly seized on the episode to attack the Government for incompetence over immigration and asylum. The murderous assault on a young mother was never fully absorbed into the campaign exchanges but came just as the Conservatives were making much of an increase in violent crime. Finally, coverage of the current situation in Iraq was kept carefully separate from the controversy over the decision to go to war – until a British soldier was killed two days before polling. No party sought to make political capital out of this, but one network carried a report in which his widow was asked, 'Do you blame Tony Blair?' 'Yes', came the response.

These very different instances not only show how unexpected events can affect the volume and shape of coverage and take a campaign in unexpected and even unwanted directions. They also show how blurred the distinction was between what is held to relate to the election and what is not. This discussion will concentrate on explicit election material, but this does not imply that it alone may have influenced the outcome – especially given the prominence of sensitive issues like immigration, crime and Iraq. It was the apparent good fortune of the Conservatives that two of the big stories of the period gave them ammunition. Only 'apparent' because it could well be that the time they were seen pursuing themes eventually hampered their hopes of shedding their image as 'the nasty party'.

Despite the competition from other stories, the election was usually top on every channel, though it was less dominant than in 2001. In the 28 days before polling the BBC led at lunchtime on 19 days to ITV's 12, in the early evening on 14 days to ITV's 15 and later in the evening on 21 days compared with 20. The least likely to put the election top was Five News. That possibly apart, the similarities between the play the election received in the different programmes were more substantial than the differences. The same in a large measure held true for the stories receiving top billing in the election package, when appropriate allowance is made for the time of day. The election lead in the main BBC1 and ITV1 evening bulletins was as near as made no difference identical on at least 21 of the final 28 days of the campaign with a further couple doubtful. Among the handful where the lead was significantly different were 24 April with 'Leaders mark poverty day' on the BBC and 'Which of these three men do you trust?' on ITV. Or, on 29 April, the BBC had 'Blair warns: don't let the Conservatives in by the back door', when ITV ran with 'Growing anger over GP appointments'. More usually, differences were essentially stylistic, with 'Conservatives under pressure on tax and spend' (BBC1, 12 April) echoed by ITV's 'Less tax: Conservative plans under fire'. And so on.

Over the campaign, the balance of headlines on both channels arguably ran slightly in the Conservatives' favour – scarcely surprising after Labour had been in power for eight years. The Liberal Democrats rarely see their preferred issues topping the news, and this time their launch lost top billing to the outcome of the terrorist trial. The on-line time they explicitly carried the lead was with an unilluminating reference to Lib Dem educational policy (BBC1, 7 April). Yet they probably had the greatest grounds for satisfaction. That opportune leak of the Attorney-General's advice on the legality of the Iraq war, which so profoundly influenced the final stages of the campaign, was assuredly one of 'their' issues.

Professionals would pick many differences in the handling of particular stories by different channels, and even different programmes from the same network. But lay viewers may well have felt they were much of a muchness. Just as the parties had converged on many points of policy, so there was convergence and consensus about the stories to report and how to interpret them. Contributors like Andrew Marr, Mark Mardell, Nick Robinson and Elinor Goodman, all increasingly deployed as analysts as well as reporters, brought a highly individual stamp to their work. Yet, even here, the differences between what they said as often as not lay more in nuances and emphases than in substance. Much of the output was good; very little was in any respect outstanding. Was there no place for the occasional whiff of heterodoxy, originality or humour? The one clear instance of a programme taking its own course was the evening when Channel 4 News led on a report about declining social mobility which none of the other channels covered. It was also Channel 4 News that had the nerve to break the Attorney-General's advice on the legal case for the Iraq war (the BBC had the story but hesitated a shade too long, to the chagrin of many of its journalists: this was the only point where the legacy of the Gilligan affair may have caused a loss of corporate nerve). The one programme that might have developed a new approach was the late morning edition of Five News. Less committed to hard news reporting, more willing to offer discussions and relatively fluffy items, it appeared to be looking for a formula that would match the interests of the groups more likely to be available at that time of day. However, the content was never coherent or consistent enough to constitute a viable alternative to the established models. Will one develop in time for 2009?

The flow of news went through several phases (see Figure 8.1). The initial emphasis was chiefly on taxation and public expenditure. Each party's plans were reported in turn and immediately dismissed by opponents because they did not add up. Aware that these avalanches of figures were likely to bemuse many voters, most networks subjected the competing versions to scrutiny, identifying uncertainties and scaling down hyperboles, often with the aid of the Institute for Fiscal Studies.

The BBC's Evan Davis did sterling work along these lines. He and others greatly irritated Gordon Brown by suggesting taxes would have to be raised. Andrew Dilnot (late of the IFS) contributed a particularly incisive critique, contending that the tax and spend debate was ludicrously

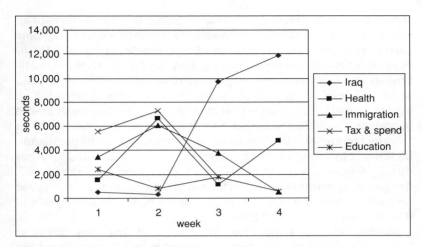

Figure 8.1 Time allotted to the major news themes

preoccupied with purported exact numbers in matters which probably lay within the margin of error. Numbers, he provocatively suggested, could be a substitute for having something to say. He noted the absence of any discussion of the costs of the 'choice' to which all parties now appeared to subscribe.[14] The impossibility of leaving the parties a free run in such matters was never better illustrated than when Labour launched a poster denouncing 'Tory cuts' of £35 billion. Labour refused to take questions, but a quick-witted Nick Robinson nevertheless made the point that a lesser increase was not a cut. Brown was again not pleased – but Robinson was doing what reporters are supposed to do. This 'marking' of the parties was not new, but it was conducted more systematically and across a wider range of policy in this election than previously, whether on air or by referring the audience to websites like Channel 4's 'FactCheck'. However, it had the unintended consequence of tying coverage closer than ever to the parties' agendas.[15]

By the middle of the campaign, tax and spend was played out, though it never completely disappeared. Other issues came into prominence, notably health, education, crime and asylum/immigration. Here again, the parties' proposals were summarised and assessed in the news and aired at greater length in a range of other programmes or documented on the channel's website. The more charged the issue, the more useful more measured documentation could be: for instance, in distinguishing between asylum-seekers, failed asylum-seekers and legal and illegal economic migrants – terms which were sometimes blurred by the politicians, not always accidentally. With the political argument so narrowly focused on who had the harshest line, the broadcasters offered a wider and more balanced range of views and scrutiny of the politicians' proposals. In *The Paxman Interviews*, Jeremy Paxman grilled the Prime Minister closely, though inconclusively, on the number of failed asylum-seekers, and Michael Howard on his plans to set immigration quotas and establish an extraterritorial holding camp. Constituency vox pops frequently voiced opposition to more immigration, including some from immigrants, but ITN also reported Scotland's need of immigration to counter population decline and East Anglia's need for immigrant agricultural workers and bus drivers. *Tonight* (ITV1) and Five News vividly documented the squalid, dangerous conditions under which would-be illegal immigrants lived at Sangatte. *Panorama* followed a number of East Europeans who came to Britain as legal economic migrants.

Neither big party wanted Iraq as an issue. At first, they had their way. It received fewer than three minutes of news coverage during the first fortnight of the campaign (though it was raised on *Newsnight* and *Jonathan Dimbleby*, among others). But with the partial disclosure of the Attorney-General's advice, leaked on 23 April, it became the top story. Taking 37 per cent of issue coverage, it dominated the remainder of the campaign. There is nothing journalists relish more than a leak, particularly of material a government is so determined not to disclose. (Did nobody in Whitehall foresee this?) Sometimes the herd instinct takes over and a sense of proportion is lost. With all channels leaping on the story, arguably that happened here. Since few journalists have a confident grasp of legal English, initial reporting was uneven. Each outlet now imported a professor of international law to unpack and assess Lord Goldsmith's paper and pronounce it a competent professional job. Interest then shifted to the highly arcane question of whether, by delivering his conclusions to Cabinet orally, the Attorney-General had met the statutory requirement to present it in printed form. One wonders how many voters' decision hung on the answer. Ultimately, all the activity brought no smoking gun to light; tough-minded editing might have moved the coverage on with greater dispatch.

The Iraq issue was very closely associated with 'trust'. 'Trust' is a factor in any election, present in every promise and every challenge to opponents' figures. But never before had it been so explicitly and prominently an issue in itself, starting with Michael Howard's assertion, 'This election is about trust.'[16] However, it was not until 23 April that ITV's late News led bluntly on Howard's allegation: 'Blair lied' (over Iraq). BBC1 preferred 'Blair rallies Labour to vote', following up in fairly muted terms. At midnight Radio 4 gave it a mere eight seconds. The next evening, ITV again played the story strongly but BBC1 aired a world poverty day item before Howard's onslaught. Both channels reported Labour's rebuttal but comment concentrated on the escalation of language more than on Howard's charge either then or when he widened the indictment beyond Iraq. Howard ensured further coverage by reiterating his allegations. However, he also ensured that interviewers would subsequently want to know whether he himself ever lied. Perhaps he forgot the reporting of his assertion that Iraq was the only issue on which Blair had stood firm as well as his comment to Jeremy Paxman that 'Mr Blair doesn't believe that there should be any limit on immigration into this country.'[17]

The issues receiving most attention in the news, shown in Table 8.1, corresponded reasonably with rankings in an ICM poll at the start of the campaign. Iraq was the major exception. Not initially in the ICM list, it shot up to third position by the end of the campaign.[18] Iraq was given an estimated 368 minutes in news coverage (and much more elsewhere) – a third more than the next issue, tax and spend. Housing, which just squeezed into the list, received a mere 40 minutes. In short, coverage focused heavily on a very restricted range of questions (and sometimes on only a few aspects of those questions). One matter not in the table, because it was not an issue in the normal sense, was postal voting. Following several court cases and further alleged irregularities, related questions surfaced several times during the campaign, incidentally deepening anxieties about trust. It would have ranked sixth.

Table 8.1 Relative importance of issues in radio and television news

	BBC1	ITV1	C4	C5	R4	All	2001
Iraq	1	2=	1	1	3	1	–
Tax & spend	2	2=	2	2	1	2	5
Health	4	4	3	5=	2	3	3
Immigration/asylum	3	1	4	3	4	4	8
Law and order	6	6	5	4	5	5	7
Education	5	10	8	5=	6	6	6
Economy general	8	5	6	–	7	7	–
Trust	9	7=	10=	7	8	8	–
Pensions	7	7=	–	–	10	9	–
Housing	12	9	7	8	–	10	9

The narrow range of issues in no small measure reflected the reluctance of Labour and the Conservatives to join battle on Europe, the environment and global warming, local government funding, urban regeneration, energy policy, the way ahead in Iraq (Lib Dems apart), the 'war on terrorism', the Trident missile programme or homelessness – let alone such wider questions as the size of the state. Conservative plans for pensions were reported in some detail and discussed for a day or so, but Labour's refusal to address the issue in advance of a report by Adair Turner – after polling day – prevented it from receiving the attention it deserved. The minor parties seized on some neglected issues: Europe by UKIP and Veritas, Trident by the SNP and SSP, environmental questions by the Greens, and so on. But no issue gained substantial attention unless both Labour and the Conservatives accepted it. The broadcasters ran very many pieces on 'forgotten' concerns; Channel 4 carried an hour-long programme, *Election Unspun: What They'll Never Tell You*, explaining why politicians were so unwilling to engage on issues like the environment, pensions or nuclear power. But in the absence of response from the parties these remained isolated initiatives.

BBC1 ran a *My Britain* series, paralleled on Five by *If I were Prime Minister*. These brief pieces used outsiders – some well-known, others not – to speak on topics like constitutional reform, secondary education, reading standards in school, moral issues in the campaign and the preoccupations of pensioners. Although uneven, they offered a refreshing variety of faces and voices and a glimpse of some of the other questions the election might well have been 'about'. While such initiatives were now unremarkable, what a contrast they provided with the days when the notion that anyone not sponsored by a party might have access to the airwaves on a matter of public policy during an election campaign would have met an appalled veto.

In this new world, who was covered seemed scarcely less important than what issues were reported. Campaigns had been heavily 'presidential' for over a generation. Table 8.2 confirms that this election was no exception. Although Blair's picture was absent from many election addresses and the party manifesto, he continued to dominate broadcast coverage, accounting for 55 per cent of quotations from Labour politicians. However, the figure was down on 2001. With Blair now an uncertain asset, Brown, the successful Chancellor, became a key player. He was cited less frequently than in 2001 (when he was campaign coordinator), but the number of times he was quoted was less important than what he said and when – notably in supporting Blair at the launch and in his emphatic 'Yes', when asked whether he would have made the same decisions as Blair on Iraq. He was shown at Blair's side, even relaxed and accepting a Bank Holiday ice cream. Body-language experts suggested such shots revealed underlying tensions, but to less sophisticated eyes they simply signalled sound partnership. Blair was also seen with other colleagues. To some, the manifesto launch looked like a quiz show set, to others a revivalist meeting; the sight of ministers brandishing the manifesto stirred uneasy

Table 8.2   Politicians quoted in television and radio news (number of times)

	BBC1	ITV1	C4	C5	R4	Total
Labour						
Blair	85	68	46	33	85	317
Brown	25	12	10	6	16	69
Reid	9	8	3	2	6	28
Clarke	5	4	5	1	6	21
Milburn	3	4	4	3	5	19
Darling	2	2	1	–	6	11
Prescott	1	4	2	–	2	9
Straw	2	2	1	–	2	7
Beckett	–	3	–	–	3	6
Hutton	1	–	3	–	2	6
Jowell	2	–	–	2	2	6
37 Others	18	13	24	6	15	76
Lib-Dems						
Kennedy	73	66	34	24	77	274
Campbell	16	6	8	2	8	40
M. Taylor	5	2	2	1	7	17
Cable	3	3	2	–	4	12
Sedgemore	2	3	1	1	4	11
Burstow	2	1	4	–	1	8
Oaten	2	2	–	1	2	7
Hughes	2	2	1	1	1	7
36 Others	22	11	14	3	10	60
Conservatives						
Howard	94	96	54	32	109	385
Fox	9	3	7	1	9	29
Letwin	6	4	1	2	8	21
Davis	2	4	3	3	–	12
Spelman	3	–	3	1	4	11
Widdecombe	2	2	1	1	1	7
Herbert	1	2	1	2	1	7
Osborne	–	–	4	–	2	6
34 Others	19	12	18	7	14	70
Other parties						
Salmond (SNP)	10	7	2	3	7	29
Knapmann (UKIP)	6	4	2	1	4	15
Galloway (Respect)	3	3	3	2	3	14
Kilroy-Silk (Veritas)	4	3	3	–	4	14
Llwyd (Plaid)	6	3	3	–	2	14
Taylor (Green)	4	2	–	1	6	13
Paisley (DUP)	4	1	–	–	3	8
Griffin (BNP)	2	1	2	–	2	7
Sturgeon (SNP)	2	4	–	–	1	7
Trimble	3	1	1	–	2	7
Adams (SF)	1	1	1	–	3	6
29 Others	19	6	9	3	6	43

memories of an earlier 'little red book'. But what it visually conveyed was that here was an experienced governmental team – something the Conservatives could never match. (But why was the Foreign Secretary relegated to the gloom of the back row?)

Howard tallied 70 per cent of quotations from Conservative politicians, compared with Hague's 56 per cent, while the number of colleagues reported six or more times dropped from ten to seven, three of them featured from force of circumstance rather than deliberate choice. As a new leader, Howard needed both to make himself better known and to scotch the old tag that there was 'something of the night' about him. Yet he also needed to show strength in depth. While Shadow ministers made many appearances outside the news, scarcely any established themselves in the news itself even in non-speaking roles. The result came perilously close to presenting the party as a one-man band rather than a team prepared to take over the reins of government.

Most of the 'others' in Table 8.2 spoke for ten seconds or so in constituency reports and were heard no more. The 37 people cited six or more times included only five women and none from an ethnic minority. In this, news coverage mainly reflected the character of Britain's senior politicians – though when women were called to speak at party news conferences little reached the bulletins. Women featured much more prominently outside the news programmes, particularly in constituency reports; there were even occasional all-women panels. Members of ethnic minorities appeared fairly frequently as vox pops from areas like Blackburn, Bradford, Leicester and Birmingham but were less likely to feature in other items.

'Real people' were very much the fashion. But many that one saw were mere window-dressing, marshalled at every televised event from every available age, gender and ethnic group to frame the leader with supportive faces. Some were even shifted around from event to event as mobile Potemkin villagers – a dodge that reporters soon exposed. Blair had said that his party needed to 'get right to the grass roots and talk to people'.[19] But once the campaign was under way he was seen only twice meeting anyone outside the fan club. In one, as he gladhanded towards a rally, a woman cried, 'I don't shake hands with murderers'; in the other he encountered a student from a Labour family in a Leeds Starbucks, failing to convince her he was not a Tory in sheep's clothing. Otherwise, apart from occasional dissident noises-off, he moved in a strictly controlled invitation-only world. The Conservatives seemed very slightly more relaxed, but Michael Howard was little more likely to meet an ordinary person than Tony Blair. The Conservatives certainly did not appreciate

The Hecklers, a rather light-hearted programme tucked away on BBC3, which few would have noticed had the Conservatives not complained. It gave several young people a rudimentary training in heckling at one of Howard's meetings. They were not very good, were speedily ejected and had minimal impact. What was striking about it, however, were the clips of classic heckles from the past, showing that election meetings have not always been as contrived, controlled, sanitised and bloodless. There was a time when real people could gain admission to meetings and voice their dissent – and when party leaders could handle them.

Unlike the parties, the broadcasting organisations made a genuine attempt to involve members of the public. The BBC fitted out a double-decker bus as a mobile studio, visiting 26 towns and generating many items reflecting local concerns. Sky News 'embedded' Kay Burley in Rossendale and Darwen for a fortnight to convey the flavour of the campaign in a single constituency. There were constituency reports on most of the other channels, many drawing on local residents rather than candidates. Andrew Marr lamented what he called the 'fashion for the ignorant and uninterested'.[20] Some 'real people' indeed displayed ignorance, indifference and antipathy about politics and politicians. Yet meaningful engagement

Howard, Blair and Kennedy.

(Peter Brookes, *The Times*, 7 April 2005)

could not but encounter the darker side of democratic politics. Roger Mosey, head of BBC television news, later commented that 'the most common response our teams found around the country was disaffection with the process and little sense that it mattered'.[21]

ITV1's daily *Ballot Box Jury* had 'jurors' from around the country questioning a politician from their own homes and commenting on the outcome. Hailed as a 'unique interactive experiment', it proved an unwieldy format; yet here, as elsewhere, it could bring up off-the-agenda questions like same-sex marriage.[22] There was one blazing moment when George Galloway objected to a tendentious introduction and walked out, vowing never to speak to ITN again. *The Daily Politics*, which had a 'real people' correspondent on a motor scooter, had a nice line in seeking the views of slightly offbeat groups: prisoners and prison officers, a boxing gym, a caving group, a male voice choir, visitors to the Harrogate flower show, care home residents, 'travellers' and pigeon fanciers (a much misunderstood minority, it transpired). *The Politics Show* worked from a narrowboat, travelling by canal from Oldham to Birmingham, interviewing people on the towpath and picking up matters of local concern, such as the impact of the decline in manufacturing on a Potteries family. Five News dispatched a reporter in a red Mini to gather vox pops around the country. Her eclectic taste in transport included a 'ferry 'cross the Mersey', a cable car, an amphibious vehicle and a funfair ride on Blackpool pleasure beach, ending in a long screech as she plunged downwards. There was a marked distinction between features that introduced 'real people' but then allowed them no more than a fleeting few seconds, and others that were more committed to allowing them time to make their point. Among these was that old standby, *Election Call* on Radio 4. Among the earliest and most successful attempts to bring voters into direct contact with senior politicians, it had fallen on hard times. Shifted from after breakfast to early afternoon and shortened, its diminished status was humiliatingly evident when Blair declined to appear and passed his slot to Jack Straw. Sally Magnusson's *Politics Roadshow*, which went on tour, *Jonathan Dimbleby* and Radio 4's long-running *Any Questions* were also based on lay questioning of the politicians. What we did not see was politicians facing questions by experts in their field.[23]

The highlight, a coup for the BBC after protracted negotiations, was *Question Time Leaders Special*, which attracted over 4 million people to see each leader facing a half-hour of questions from an invited and, in principle, balanced audience. Kennedy was well received, and had an easy ride. Howard roused livelier reactions, positive and negative. (An

Asian man charged him with hating asylum-seekers.) The most striking moment, over Iraq, was his revelation that he would have been prepared to go to war on terms which the Attorney-General had said would be illegal. By the final session the audience was fully fired up. Blair faced a barrage of hostile questions, particularly about Iraq. At one point he was told he should resign. However, the point that featured prominently in next day's papers came when a woman complained that, to meet targets, her GP refused to give appointments more than 48 hours ahead. Blair appeared incredulous but the questioner stood her ground, supported by others in the audience. Finally, he conceded that some targets might have to be revisited. It is rare to see a senior politician confronted so sharply with the law of unintended consequences, and this was ammunition to those who argued that Blair was 'out of touch'. The session ended in hubbub. Commenting subsequently, foreign correspondents expressed surprise at calls for Blair to resign; this would be unimaginable in France and the United States. But to whose credit or discredit was that?

For all the value of 'citizen questioning', it does not supplant the professionals. The leaders made the round of the networks in time-honoured fashion. And there were, of course, many other interviews with ministers and their Shadows. While these were a necessary element in campaign ritual, only a few attracted much wider attention. One possible exception was *The Paxman Interviews* on BBC1 in which the leaders were subjected to the interviewer's *de haut en bas* interrogations. On another occasion John Humphrys harried Jack Straw for a full 15 minutes over the Attorney-General's advice.[24] Although Paxman's interviews attracted professional admiration, Jon Snow questioned the aggressive style of some interviewers and a sharp discussion ensued.[25] It was in many respects a false argument: aggression may be appropriate in some circumstances; a softer approach may work in others. Adam Boulton, interviewing Blair for his *Boulton Factor* programme, elicited confirmation that the euro had been kicked into the long grass for the foreseeable future. And Snow's urbane interview with Howard included this exchange, which encapsulated the Conservatives' strategic uncertainties:

Howard: To have a world-class health service and a world-class educational system we've got to spend money.
Snow: Does that mean you've become a party of big government?
Howard: No. We're committed to smaller government.[26]

The problem of so much of the interviewing was less one of style than of its tendency to look backward, to accommodate to the short-term pragmatism of so many of the politicians. Repeatedly pressed on facts and tactics, rarely were they really challenged intellectually or made to focus on the long term.

Roughly 62 per cent of election news coverage was devoted explicitly to 'issues', ranging from 73 per cent for Channel 4 News to 52 per cent for Five News. The remainder included reports of the leaders' travels with accompanying photo opportunities – as ITV's 'Outsider' observed, even the minor parties now staged photo opportunities: the Greens on their bikes spoke in perfect soundbites.[27] There were fewer walkabouts, partly for security reasons, but also because, despite the secrecy surrounding the leaders' movements, opposing parties proved remarkably skilful at sniffing them out and filling the screen with their placards.

Polls received under 3 per cent of the coverage, usually far down the running order. The BBC's Peter Snow was as enthusiastic and devoted to huge computer graphics as ever, tirelessly scrutinising every flicker in party support, including some within potential sampling error. His projections of the shape of the new House of Commons based on a two-party model roused understandable Liberal Democrat ire. The BBC had a three-party graphic up its sleeve for results night, but the party unsurprisingly thought that a trifle late in the day. ITV News regularly carried Populus polls, with a briefer, simpler and less flamboyant presentation. And major bulletins were usually rounded off with the political editors' take on how the campaign was developing.[28] The principal innovation was the scrutiny of body language. This was a regular feature of Five News. Channel 4 News carried several items on it and a full edition of *The Election Unspun*, with a professor of social psychology, best known for a similar role with the *Big Brother* 'reality' series. This substantial commitment of airtime produced very occasional insights and mild fun at the expense of politicians, but made a minuscule contribution to political understanding.

Broadcasters looked back on 2005 without the angst of 2001 but with little elation. While turnout increased slightly, a *Newsbeat* poll (Radio 1) found only 31 per cent of first-time voters planning to vote, compared with 38 per cent at the same stage in 2001.[29] Sky News ran an 'index of interest' ('interested' minus 'uninterested') which never rose higher than –26. Chris Shaw of Five reflected that, despite a huge expenditure of money and effort, the campaign 'didn't come alive'. The broadcasters had indeed made a vast and varied effort. Yet given the context and the narrow ground over which the election was fought, was there any way in which it could legitimately have been made more compelling? While a poll subsequently showed 3 per cent of people saying they would have liked to have had more coverage, the remainder divided about equally between those who thought coverage was about right and those who said there had been too much.

Broadcasters clearly felt that the parties could have done more to help them. John Etchingham of Sky described their control as 'absolutely stifling', ITN's Nick Robinson found them 'ruthless about access to the leaders' and Alastair Stewart, also of ITN, spoke of 'an iron grip over who would talk to us and on what subject'.[30] The effectiveness of that control may explain why journalists agreed that they experienced little pressure from the parties. Yet the politicians at times had reason to feel hard done by. A late evening 'satirical' programme on Radio 4 described all three leaders as 'arseholes', while the *Today* programme employed a resident 'poet' whose doggerel culminated with the immortal line, 'They're lying, they're lying, they're lying.' This was a far cry from the days when the BBC dropped a sketch by Michael Bentine with a junk sailing up the Thames and sinking the Palace of Westminster. Now, in an episode of *Dr Who*, a space ship crashed through Big Ben and into the Thames. Nobody raised an eyebrow.

The party broadcasts

Unloved and derided, party election broadcasts are the longest-established way in which radio, then television, have participated in elections. Now a shrunken shadow of their former selves (and Labour had asked the Electoral Commission to consider allowing 60-second spots), they remained the one occasion when the parties address voters with no external intervention.[31] So they merit a shade more attention than their reputation and tiny fraction of airtime might suggest.

Traditionally the broadcasts courted wavering voters, rallied core support or tried to do both. More recently a further function emerged: to extend the reach of the message by attracting the attention of other media. The only one to bid successfully for that wider resonance was Labour's first broadcast. It was widely trailed in the press, because the party brought in a star producer, Anthony Minghella, and because it addressed the problematic Blair–Brown relationship. Blair and Brown were the only two characters, depicted as old friends and equals, looking back on their common ideals and achievements and pondering the future. Viewers were never addressed directly; this was an oblique soft-sell about 'a partnership that's worked'. One critic likened it to an ageing couple surveying their marriage, with so many 'ups' and only fleetingly evoked 'downs'. Initially, it seemed persuasive, at least for those prepared to be persuaded. Revisiting it, one wondered. This appeared to be a single conversation, albeit with breaks. So why did both men switch from shirt-sleeves to collar and tie and back again? Why were they in Blair's room in the Commons at one moment, in a kitchen the next, and then as suddenly back where they were? Why did they appear to talk past each other so much, and why celebrate togetherness almost entirely in single shot? Minghella was too old a hand to leave apparent continuity breaks accidentally, so why were they there? Intriguing but quite irrelevant. The important point was that, despite some derisive criticism, the programme apparently worked.[32] Labour had deftly used this early occasion to demonstrate a united leadership *urbi et orbi*.

Labour's second programme attracted no such attention. It was a skilfully crafted assault on Howard. The soundtrack was Barbra Streisand's 'The Way We Were', a beautifully sung recollection of a broken relationship, running over a sequence of stills of Howard, with captions recalling his record as minister and in opposition – high interest rates, unemployment, cuts in police numbers, Black Wednesday, opposition to the minimum wage. The song ended wistfully wondering, 'if we had the chance to do it all again …'. In short, the Conservatives had not really changed. Negative campaigning at its most negative and personal, yet not one nasty word!

Labour's other broadcasts were more orthodox. The third, which had a voice-over by Prunella Scales, had members of the older generation comparing how it was before the NHS and how it is now. If the Tories returned, what would happen to people who could not afford to pay? The fourth appealed to the 'mums' vote, with sunlit scenes in playgrounds and at schools, tax credits, new schools, a free NHS – again contrasted with 'Tory charges'. The final broadcast warned it would take only one person in ten voting for a third party to let the Tories in by the back door, bringing charges for operations, high interest rates, unemployment, mortgages at risk and loss of tax credits. In all, this was a skilful series aimed at reminding the disenchanted of Labour achievements and playing the fear factor quite hard. It was also quite unscrupulous in reiterating allegations about £35 billion in Tory cuts and that charges would be imposed for NHS operations, and in repeating discredited contentions about letting the Conservatives in by the back door.[33]

The Conservatives needed both to introduce Howard and to persuade voters that he and the party had truly changed: the man who famously had 'something of the night' about him had now to be promoted as Mr Nice Guy. He was presented, amid a sequence of beautiful Britain shots, as a believer in Britain, coming from a humble background, who was not born into Conservatism but chose it. A succession of manifestly 'real' people speaking manifestly unreal dialogue, endorsed the party over frontline services, immigration, crime, the family and education. Howard promised to 'tell it how it is' and speak up for the 'forgotten majority'. 'The choice is yours.' The next programme argued that Britain needed a new government and the Conservatives had just the team: Oliver Letwin, Liam Fox, Caroline Spelman and David Willetts were glimpsed so fleetingly as to be unpersuasive. Howard emphasised that he had attended a state school and that crime fell while he was Home Secretary. The Conservatives stood for limits to immigration, more police, longer sentences, better discipline in schools and accountable government: 'I *will* do it.'

The broadcast on 26 April was remarkable for its underlying pessimism. This was the 'last chance' to 'send a message'. Reward Blair for eight years of broken promises – crime, council tax, discipline in schools, 5,000 deaths a year from MRSA. The Liberal Democrats would abolish life sentences for murder, allow unchecked immigration and give prisoners the vote. Howard, by contrast, had taken a stand on crime. Finally, voters were again urged to 'send that message'. This was not the language of a party expecting victory. The final programme again hit at Labour's broken promises, scornfully dismissed the Liberal Democrats and again offered near-subliminal glimpses of the Shadow Cabinet. It was 'now or never'. The problem with the series was that it was so heavily negative and said little of substance about the better world awaiting if the party won. Those who thought that the Conservatives were the 'nasty party' were given insufficient reasons to revise that view.

The Liberal Democrats set out to show that they were credible as the 'real alternative'. Kennedy, astride a huge floor map of the United Kingdom, stepped from 'England' to 'Scotland' to demonstrate that in power they did make a difference, particularly in health and care of the elderly, aided by testimonial vox pops from 'real people'. The next three programmes offered sketches followed by a message from Kennedy, brightly lit and to camera against a coal-black background. One presented used-car dealers of the Arthur Daley variety. Would you buy a used car from Labour with its broken promises on fees in higher education, dental services and Iraq?; could you trust the Conservatives on Iraq? Another opened with a man lying injured in the street. A man with a red rosette and a man with a blue rosette arrived and began bickering over him until a man in a yellow T-shirt came on the scene and immediately gave assistance.

Finally came the 'story of a journey' as Kennedy recounted the growing success of the Liberal Democrats under his leadership and how he had met the biggest test of his leadership over Iraq. He spoke of his marriage and the recent arrival of baby Donald. In short, viewers were encouraged to see him as an amiable, down-to-earth character, capable and tough if he had to be but avoiding the sterile confrontational manner of the other parties. And, as always, the party projected itself as the nice guy, who could exercise power productively yet was not contaminated by it – the classic stance of third parties for decades.

The Scottish National Party's approach combined economy and a recognition of the virtues of repetition. It ran the same broadcast three times. Introduced by Scotland's most famous (non-resident) son, Sean Connery, sounding like some ancient mariner, it offered beautiful landscapes and 'real people' clips expressing personal and patriotic pride. Alex Salmond explained why, even though there was now a Scottish Parliament, Westminster elections remained important; even during the campaign the other parties were ignoring Scotland. The SNP alone would defend Scotland over a wide range of issues. The SNP, claimed Connery, was the most trusted party of all.

Plaid Cymru's message was little different in essence. Adam Price read a speech rather badly to an inert public meeting, citing the sad plight of a Wales that was not a priority for the London parties. Wales was only a tiny blip on their radar. Plaid Cymru would never turn its back on Wales. In a rather more modern style, Dafydd Iwan complained to camera of economic decline and lamented the state of health care (a responsibility of the Welsh Assembly, not Westminster). Price complained that young people were unable to find a home, and promised that Plaid would campaign to see that the Prime Minister and ministers were accountable: 'Blair should pay for his crimes.' Labour's time had come and gone.

The remaining parties had little hope of immediate success at Westminster, but took the opportunity to give their policies a rare airing and to attempt to build for the future. The Scottish Socialist Party's broadcast was set in a vast school meals kitchen, with contributors dressed in the appropriate working entire. A criticism of junk food equated it with the junk policies of the four Scottish Tory parties. The speakers, a succession of its MSPs, claimed that the SSP was the Robin Hood of Scottish politics and launched a full-blooded attack on excess profits, unemployment, low pay and inadequate pensions, and on Blair with blood on his hands over Iraq, with a culminating call for an independent Socialist Scotland.

The Greens and Scottish Greens offered localised versions under their common banner of 'People, Planet, Peace'. Both versions sought to demonstrate the parties' electoral credibility by emphasising Green successes, in European or local elections or in the Scottish Parliament, and paraded current councillors or MSPs or, in the English version, their candidate in the seat where they thought they had the greatest chance of success. Both stressed distinctive green policies, domestically on issues like climate change and transport; externally on Iraq and Trident.

In a genre where hyperbole is the norm, UKIP excelled. Its apocalyptic opening warned that Britain was being watched by an alien world, depicting London being overwhelmed by a monstrous blue octopus – what else but the EU? UKIP would fight for an independent Britain. Roger Knapman's rallying cry was 'We want our country back.' This was the only party that was wholly committed to the task. So much, so expected. But UKIP needed to show it was not a single-issue party. Clips by candidates favoured cuts in immigration (a black woman), the ability of home owners to defend their homes, stopping student fees, higher pensions. The European Union was corrupt, while the other parties were characterised by lies and deceit.

Although there was predictable hostility to the BNP having a broadcast, it was rather less vociferous than for the National Front in 2001. Shot mainly in monochrome, it featured a soundtrack by Nick Griffin, accompanying himself on guitar in something akin to a country and western style. The film told the tale of a Falklands veteran, now homeless, sleeping rough, scavenging for food and searching trash piles along the Embankment. There were flats for Iraqis and Afghans, but not for him. To their shame, the Tories had let in many asylum-seekers. Griffin, now in colour outside Halifax police station, where he had been charged, delivered a final, defiant speech, with dark references to heroin and the 'grooming' of young girls.

The verdict

On the stroke of ten on 5 May the BBC and ITV1 switched instantly to a projection of the result: a Labour majority of 66 – the product of an exit poll organised jointly by the two networks. The final instants before those figures were flashed up were to be most tense moment of a long evening and night. Presented by David Dimbleby, at a circular desk, with Andrew Marr and Professor Anthony King, BBC1 coverage came from a vast two-storey studio, styled, according to one critic, like a 1990s wine bar, with numerous bays and alcoves to house discussants and commentators.[34] ITV used a version of its election 2005 set, backed by a honeycomb of dimly illuminated offices. Sky offered digital viewers 16 interactive screens. Both the senior networks hosted parties for 'personalities' and political guests; ITV won the party stakes hands down, with its boat on the Thames and Lady Thatcher as senior guest. ITV had Gerald Scarfe as resident cartoonist. Labour had a group of youngsters in the north painting in a huge floor map of the constituencies. ITV had Alastair Stewart with what looked like a giant snakes-and-ladders board. Both networks had ambitious computer graphics charting progress towards a majority – but only the BBC had the inimitable Peter Snow to interpret them.

The exit poll brought an instant dilemma. Could it be believed? Old hands were wary. Many had painful memories of earlier years when they had been pointed in the wrong direction. This time the poll came remarkably close – but nobody was prepared to bet their shirt on that until some real results came in, so all political invitees ventured that their party had done just a bit better than the poll suggested. Apart from such speculation and tours of the key counts where nothing of consequence could yet be said, attention moved to speculation whether Sunderland South, which was sure to declare first, would beat its own record for the fastest count. In the event it failed by seconds. Then the result, live on all networks, Chris Mullin's victory speech and rapid graphics displaying the votes, party shares and swing. All a far cry from the early days when these matters had to be worked out with slide rules.

That single result led to some cogitation about whether it chimed with the exit poll. Even with computers, it was some while before the slow trickle of results showed a clear pattern and commentators could relax in the knowledge that the voters had produced the right result for the pollsters. By midnight there was no room for doubt: Labour was home and dry, and the pattern of results in the marginals, about which political editors had shown such uncertainty during the final stages of the campaign, was now clearer. There was no longer any suspense, save for those personally engaged in seats where the outcome was still uncertain. Under two hours after the polls closed, discussion had already moved on to when the transition of Labour leadership might take place, the chances for a fourth Labour term and the future of the Conservative leadership.

For those who stayed on through the night, there were occasional deviations from the general pattern to exclaim over and explain, but few memorable moments.[35] One was the result at Sedgefield, where Reg Keys, whose soldier son had died in Iraq, made an impassioned attack on Blair who, looking rigidly ahead with a woman wearing a 'BLIAR' hat close by, had no alternative but to experience the father's raw emotion. The other, deep into the night, came when Jeremy Paxman, interviewing George Galloway, opened by asking whether he was proud to have defeated one of the few black women MPs. After the question had been put and rejected three times, Galloway, never the most even-tempered of interviewees, walked out. Despite such a moment of infelicity, to put it at its mildest, the delivery of the results was an impressive operation by both the television networks and radio – in some respects a Cinderella, yet as always delivering an uncluttered yet effective service.

And so the long march towards the 2009 campaign got under way. It will be fought with new leaders for the two largest parties, presumably with fresh issues and, perhaps, with a less predictable outcome. However that may be, the problems for parties and broadcasters with which the 2005 campaign opened remained unresolved at its end, and the challenge to both sides in discovering fresh approaches to more successfully engaging the voters was undiminished.

Notes

1. Thanks to Wendy Harrison, Alison Harrison and Bryan Shaw for assistance and support.
2. According to a City Broadcasting report audiences for terrestrial TV had fallen 6 per cent in five years and by 15 per cent among 16–34-year-olds (*Observer*, 18 July 2004).
3. *Guardian*, 16 February 2005.
4. *Daily Telegraph*, 25 January 2005.
5. *Guardian*, 24 February 2005.
6. *Guardian*, 18 February 2005.
7. *Observer*, 3 April 2005.
8. The editor of *The New Yorker*, David Remnick, gives a full account of the episode in the *Observer* (1 May 2005). Blair remarked to Remnick, 'It was a piece of fun ... [It's] always a battle, isn't it, between the modern world in which people expect their leaders to be a lot more accessible ... and the dignity of the office? And you've got to be careful that you don't compromise the one in the attempt to enter into the other.' Indeed.
9. *The Economist*, 22 January 2005.
10. On the same day the *Daily Telegraph* published a YouGov poll in which 40 per cent agreed the campaign so far was 'childish', 38 per cent that it was 'negative' and 35 per cent that it was 'boring'.
11. The BBC's policy was to go with trusted strands rather than invent new ones (*Guardian*, 9 May 2005).
12. Unless otherwise indicated, statistical data relate to 410 news bulletins on BBC1, ITV1, Channel 4, Channel 5 and Radio 4 between 7 April and 4 May, excluding headlines, commercial breaks, regional inserts and weather.
13. Similarly, Channel 4 News carried an immensely sad story about a terminal cancer patient without linking it to the election (midday, 19 April).
14. *More or Less*, Radio 4, 26 April.
15. Nick Robinson, *Guardian*, 9 May 2005.
16. Channel 4 News, 5 April 2005.
17. *The Paxman Interview* BBC1, 18 April 2005 (Kennedy), 20 April 2005 (Blair), 22 April 2005 (Howard). Transcripts at <http://news.bbc.co.uk>.

18. *Guardian*, 5 and 24 April 2005.
19. *Dispatches,* Channel 4, 23 May 2005.
20. 'Why Do We Waste Time on Those Who Don't Care?' *Daily Telegraph*, 13 April 2005.
21. *Observer*, 8 May 2005.
22. ITV News, 12.30 p.m., 18 April 2005.
23. Blair was reported to have pulled out of a commercial radio show, *UK Leaders Live*, at which representatives of the BMA, teaching unions and civil liberties groups would have questioned him (*Guardian*, 2 May 2005). Both leaders had some difficult passages during phone-ins. Howard encountered a black policeman who accused him of pandering to fascists (BBC1, 6 p.m., 19 April 2005), while another policeman flatly contradicted Blair on law and order.
24. *Today*, 25 April 2005. Transcript in *Independent*, 26 April 2005. In the same issue Steve Richards criticised Paxman for treating the three party leaders 'as naughty pupils who deserved a scolding'.
25. See Snow's interview with Vanessa Thorpe, 'Snow wants Paxman to Show Respect' , *Observer*, 17 April 2005. He was interviewed on *Today*, 18 April 2005. Also Kevin Marsh, 'Soft Sofas and No Hard Questions', *Observer*, 17 April 2005, and Humphrys' defence of his interviewing style, *Guardian*, 2 May 2005 and 30 June 2005.
26. *Guardian*, 9 May 2005. One of the very few other items to consider this fundamental question of the role and size of the state was a discussion between Jonathan Freedland and John O'Sullivan on *Talking Politics*, 30 April 2005.
27. ITV News, 12.30 p.m., 22 April 2005.
28. These commentaries were mostly high on pragmatism, low on critical evaluation. Peter Oborne made a scathing attack on the parties' 'anti-democratic' approach to the campaign, assailing the 'stupifying banality of the parties' pledges' in *Why Politicians Can't Tell the Truth,* Channel 4, 25 April 2005. Earlier, Channel 4 had run *How to Win Power*, a not uncritical account of the rise of political marketing (18 April 2005).
29. If so, this would have been a lower proportion of the age group than voted for contestants in the 'reality shows' *Big Brother* or *Pop Idol* (*Daily Telegraph*, 7 March 2005; also *Guardian*, 3 May 2005).
30. All quotations here from the *Guardian*, 9 May 2005.
31. *Guardian*, 26 June 2001.
32. Peter Bradshaw, 'A Nightmare on Downing Street 3', and Mark Lawson, 'The Hard Sell: Hosing Down the Leaders', both *Guardian*, 12 April 2005. Here, as for the most part elsewhere, the radio version was closely modelled on the television broadcast. Most TV broadcasts on the major networks went out early in the evening (Sky was an exception), while most radio versions were transmitted around 10.45 p.m. on Radio 4.
33. Channel 4 News ran a set of three 'spoof' party broadcasts. The 'Labour' spoof took the 'fear factor' that little bit further by featuring a young woman waking from a one-night stand and realising she had made a terrible mistake, but found she was unable to get rid of the man for another five years, 29 April 2005.
34. *Daily Telegraph*, 7 May 2005.
35. The audience was estimated at just under 7 million – 1 million down on 2001 and 4 million below 1997. BBC viewing peaked around the time of the first result at around 6 million to ITV's 1.7 million.

9
The Press: Still for Labour, Despite Blair

Margaret Scammell and Martin Harrop

The papers began the 2005 election without appetite, anticipating a reprise of 2001's Labour landslide. Yet as the campaign developed, so the press was able to develop considerable passion over the Iraq war and the Prime Minister's part in it. As election day approached, so the intense debate about the war gave way in its turn to broader judgements about the country's future direction. 'Vote Blair but get Labour' became the pragmatic theme of some pro-Labour papers while much of the anti-Labour press was keener to give Blair a bloody nose than to embrace Michael Howard's distinctly limited agenda.

Overall, Labour's support in the press declined from its high water mark of 2001. The *Daily Express*, the *Sunday Express* and the *Sunday Times* returned to the Conservative fold. The *Independent* and the *Independent on Sunday* planted themselves more firmly in the Liberal Democrat camp while the *Daily Star* declined to endorse Labour. As a result, only five of the ten national newspapers and four of the nine Sunday papers supported Labour. However, these pro-Labour papers still commanded more than half the total market by circulation and by historic standards the party's performance in the press remained strong. In the newspapers, as in the electorate, the Conservatives were unable to mount a decisive challenge to Labour's leading position.

The press since 2001

The market for national newspapers continued to shrink, while remaining fiercely competitive (Tables 9.1 and 9.2). This secular decline in both paid

119

circulation and readership must inevitably reduce the direct impact of the press on an electorate which increasingly chooses whether, how and when to consume campaign news and opinion (one additional option being, of course, the papers' own websites).

Table 9.1   Partisanship and circulation of national daily newspapers

Name of paper Ownership group (Chairman) Editor Preferred result	Circulation[1] (2001 in brackets) (000s)	Readership[2] (2001 in brackets) (000s)	% of readers in social grade[3] (2001 in brackets)	
			ABC1	C2DE
Mirror Trinity Mirror (Sir Victor Blank) Richard Wallace Labour victory	1,602 (2,056)	4,657 (5,733)	38 (34)	61 (67)
Express Northern and Shell (Richard Desmond) Peter Hill Conservative victory	884 (929)	2,132 (2,168)	60 (64)	40 (37)
Sun News International (Rupert Murdoch) Rebekah Wade Labour victory	3,098 (3,288)	8,825 (9,591)	37 (33)	63 (67)
Daily Mail Daily Mail and General Trust (Viscount Rothermere) Paul Dacre Not a Labour victory	2,278 (2,337)	5,740 (5,564)	66 (64)	34 (36)
Daily Star Northern and Shell (Richard Desmond) Dawn Neesom No preference declared	735 (585)	1,965 (1,460)	33 (27)	67 (72)
Daily Telegraph Telegraph Group (& The Business) (Barclay brothers) Martin Newland Conservative victory	868 (989)	2181 (2,235)	87 (86)	13 (14)
Guardian Scott Trust (Paul Myners) Alan Rusbridger Labour victory[4]	327 (362)	1,068 (1,024)	89 (88)	11 (12)

The Times	654	1,655	87	13
News International	(667)	(1,575)	(88)	(13)
(Rupert Murdoch)				
Robert Thomson				
Labour victory[5]				
Independent	226	643	87	13
Independent Newspapers	(197)	(571)	(89)	(12)
(Tony O'Reilly)				
Simon Kelner				
More Liberal Democrats				
Financial Times	132	453	92	8
Pearson	(176)	(598)	(92)	(7)
(Lord Stevenson)				
Andrew Gowers				
Labour victory				

Notes:
1. Average net total circulation in the United Kingdom. Source: Audit Bureau of Circulation (April 2005).
2. Source: National Readership Survey (January 2004–December 2004).
3. Calculated from National Readership Survey (January 2004–December 2004), which classifies the population 15 or over as follows: ABC1 (professional, administrative, managerial and other non-manual) – 54 per cent (2001: 50 per cent); C2DE (skilled manual, semi-skilled or unskilled, and residual) – 46 per cent (2001: 49 per cent).
4. Also increased number of Liberal Democrats.
5. Also a larger Conservative opposition.

Table 9.2 Partisanship and circulation of national Sunday newspapers

	Preferred 2005	Winner (2001)	Circulation[1] (000s)	Readership[2] (000s)
News of the World	Lab	(Lab)	3,417	9,490
Sunday Mirror	Lab	(Lab)	1,441	4,851
The People	Lab	(Lab)	870	2,217
Mail on Sunday	Not Lab	(Con)	2,336	6,329
Sunday Express	Con	(Lab)	866	2,214
Sunday Times	Con	(Lab)	1,197	3,272
Observer	Lab	(Lab)	405	1,163
Sunday Telegraph	Con	(Con)	660	2,045
Independent on Sunday	Lib Dem[3]	(Lab)	176	666

Notes:
1. Source: Audit Bureau of Circulation (April 2005).
2. Source: National Readership Survey (January–December 2004).
3. But 'where the realistic choice is between Labour and Conservative, we prefer Labour' (*Independent on Sunday*, 1 May 2005).

The *Mirror* continued to suffer heavily in the tabloid wars, with its readership now only half that of 1987. Its experiment of adopting a heavier diet of political news proved detrimental to sales. In 2004, the *Mirror*'s editor Piers Morgan paid the price for his vigorous anti-war coverage when he was dismissed after the paper's owners acknowledged that it had published fake pictures of British soldiers torturing Iraqi prisoners. Although the red tops generally suffered a larger fall in readership than did the quality papers, there were exceptions. With an increase in readership over 2001, Richard Desmond's *Daily Star* showed that celebrity, sex and sport was still a winning formula.

Conditions were less depressed, though still difficult, in the middle and at the top of the market. In 2003, the *Independent*, relaunched in compact format, gained an immediate increase in sales. *The Times* turned compact soon afterwards, and by the time of the election its circulation also remained close to 2001 levels. But despite the positive impact of the new format on sales, 'tabloidisation' led to a vigorous debate about quality. 'What are newspapers for?' asked the *Guardian*'s editor, Alan Rusbridger,[1] speculating fearfully about a future in which all former broadsheets would find themselves converging on the mid-market tabloid territory controlled by the *Daily Mail*.

Much media excitement was generated by activities at the *Daily Telegraph*. In 2003, Charles Moore stepped down after eight years as editor and then, later in the year, Lord Black of Crossharbour was forced to resign as chairman of Hollinger International amid accusations of financial impropriety. In June 2004, Hollinger sold the *Telegraph* and associated titles to the Barclay brothers.

Politically, the Iraq war was the key event of the inter-election period. Before the invasion the balance of press opinion had been broadly favourable. Only three dailies, the *Mirror*, the *Guardian* and the *Independent*, were clearly opposed to the war, while six titles offered support: *The Times*, the *Telegraph*, the *Mail*, the *Express*, the *Sun* and the *Star*. The position of some newspapers on the war clearly influenced their approach to the subsequent election; the anti-war *Mirror,* for instance, failed to register its old enthusiasm for a Labour victory. But for much of the press, Iraq was a war fought substantially in retrospect. With the Hutton and Butler Inquiries compounding suspicion that Britain had been spun into war, papers such as the *Mail* and the *Express* experienced no difficulty in reconciling their support for the war with vigorous opposition to the Prime Minister's accounts of it. So the election campaign opened with the press – as well as the opposition parties – ready to question the Prime Minister's credibility.

How individual papers covered the campaign

The press began its coverage in weary fashion. The election date had been extensively trailed, the Conservatives appeared to offer little genuine threat and the media in general were reluctant to give an apathetic public another overdose of election coverage. However, in the event the campaign did succeed in capturing significant press attention, generating a comparable number of front-page leads and editorials as 2001 (Table 9.3). Only two titles, the *Sun* and *The Times*, reduced attention in both their front pages and leader columns. With the exception of the *Sun* and the *Star,* all the papers found some reasons for excitement. The Conservative press was somewhat more comfortable with Michael Howard than with his predecessor, while the *Express,* returning to the Tory fold following its flirtation with Labour in 2001, helped to restore the sense of a partisan battle. Above all, Tony Blair's position at the core of the campaign allowed the press to present its coverage in a strikingly personal, and often highly critical, manner.

Table 9.3 Profile of press content

	Mean number of pages		Front-page lead stories on election		Editorials on election (% of all editorials)	
	2005	2001	2005	2001	2005	2001
Mirror	70	59	7	12	62	54
Express	76	76	11	2	50	45
Sun	58	56	7	9	57	70
Daily Mail	83	84	12	9	84	84
Daily Star	67	53	2	4	47	31
Daily Telegraph	50	53	16	15	42	66
Guardian	101	121	18	15	44	53
The Times	108	79	16	18	37	39
Independent	110	49	15	17	53	33
Financial Times	58	63	18	17	20	23

Note: Front-page leads and editorials analysis cover the 21 issues between 12 April and 5 May 2001. Page count is based on Monday to Friday issues only; the increased pagination for the *Independent* and *The Times* reflects their move to a tabloid format.

The *Daily Mail* led the way with a sustained barrage of criticism of the Prime Minister and his Government throughout the campaign. The paper began with stories of vote-rigging, accusing Labour of threatening democracy through its relaxation of the rules for postal voting. But it found an even more strident voice on asylum and immigration, launching a succession of stories buttressing Conservative claims that the asylum system was in chaos. 'MURDERED BECAUSE WE'VE LOST CONTROL OF OUR BORDERS' was its headline on 14 April over its report of the trial of an illegal immigrant who had killed a policeman. When the Attorney-General's advice on the legality of the Iraq war was revealed in the penultimate week, the *Mail* turned its considerable weaponry on Labour's leader. Blair's trustworthiness had become the key issue, it reported, and its editorial left no doubt as to where the *Mail* stood: 'we can no longer believe a word he says'. Subsequent publication of the full text of the legal advice on Iraq provided the *Mail* with what it treated as a smoking gun: 'BLAIR LIED AND LIED AGAIN', was the lead. Its editorial drove home the point: 'it is hard to recall any recent Prime Minister who has so demeaned his office ... He is unfit to be Prime Minister.'

Throughout the campaign, the *Mail* stayed close to the Conservative agenda of immigration, asylum, crime, tax and pensions. Nonetheless, its fire concentrated on denouncing Labour rather than promoting the Conservatives. Despite praising Michael Howard's achievement in restoring credibility to what had been a 'shambolic rabble', the *Mail* was not inspired by the Conservative offer. Rather, the thrust of its final advice was to 'give Mr Blair a bloody nose'. He was the 'fake-tanned' premier, who had run 'an utterly dishonest election', avoiding the key issues and lying not just about Conservative policies but also about Iraq. Labour's leader was 'up to his neck in sleaze'. Even the Government's claims of economic success had turned sour as Britain had dropped down the league table of competitiveness and Gordon Brown had become a spendthrift. The Conservatives offered sensible policies on the economy and Europe as well as 'hope of restoring integrity in public life'; for these reasons, the *Mail* supported them. But its preference was 'superseded by an even greater imperative: to diminish the power of overweeningly arrogant Mr Blair'.

The strategy of the *Daily Express* resembled that of the *Mail*. It echoed the *Mail*'s shrill coverage of immigration, crime, Government incompetence and Blair's 'lies'. With its traditional Conservative allegiance re-established, the *Express* was far more committed than in 2001. It significantly increased its front-page election coverage, seizing every opportunity to emphasise Labour's shortcomings. The strap line 'Blair's Britain' accompanied stories of crime, health service failure and, in a curiously old-fashioned touch, abuse of welfare benefits. Blair's Britain had become a 'truly terrible place' in which ordinary people were denied the right of self-defence while the unemployed were offered a 'spongers' bonanza'. Blair had debased the word 'integrity', said its eve-of-poll leader: 'we need to get Labour out and put the Conservatives in'.

By comparison with the *Mail* and the *Express*, the *Sun* had a relatively quiet and indecisive election. It was slow to engage with the campaign, declaring itself bored with the contest. The paper eventually declared for Labour, but pragmatically and despite its own largely conservative agenda. It announced its decision with a self-referential front page with an image of red smoke arising papal-style from its own headquarters. But the actual endorsement was grudging: 'ONE LAST CHANCE', declared the headline. Immigration was a 'disgrace', pensions a mess and welfare reform patchy; the Conservatives talked 'good sense' on crime and immigration. The paper offered two reasons for voting 'Blair and Brown': 'standing firm on Iraq and the lack of a real alternative'.

As the campaign progressed, the *Sun* began to warm to its work. It became Blair's best, and sometimes *only*, friend in the daily press. It kept bad news off the front page, preferring either its own routine 'rock the vote' campaign or more commonly no politics at all. It was also prepared to defend the Prime Minister over Iraq. Michael Howard, its editorial said on 28 April, had descended into the gutter; and by calling Blair a liar the Conservatives had exposed their own hypocrisy. In the *Sun*'s view, Labour's leader had shown extraordinary courage over Iraq. The paper published a letter from Jalal Talabani, President of Iraq, expressing his thanks to Blair for helping to depose Saddam Hussein. It posed the question that Blair himself repeatedly asked: would the world be a better place if there had been no war and Saddam had stayed in power? As the election moved into polling week, the *Sun* also championed Labour's line that a protest vote for the Liberal Democrats would let in the Conservatives.

On the eve of the poll, the *Sun* published a remarkable interview with Tony and Cherie Blair. Its front page trumpeted the coup with 'WHY SIZE MATTERS' and 'Cherie says Tony needs a big one … a big majority.' The story ran across three inside pages, revealing – among other private matters – that Blair was a 'five times a night man'. It was an astonishingly personal end to a highly personal press campaign; for Quentin Letts, in the next day's *Mail*, the interview was 'jaw-droppingly vulgar'.

The *Daily Mirror* is traditionally Labour's strongest supporter and during the darkest days of the 1980s, it was sometimes its only ally. However, relations with New Labour had often proved uncomfortable as the party increased its focus on the best-selling *Sun* and *Mail*. In addition, the *Mirror* had been an outspoken critic of the Iraq war. The dismissal of Piers Morgan as editor in 2004 might have been expected to help Labour, but the *Mirror*'s commitment at this election was less assured than usual. The 'simple truth', its leader declared, was that even though things had got better, people simply did not believe Labour any more. Blair had four weeks to restore trust.

In the event, the *Mirror* concealed its reservations by reducing its overall election coverage and by using traditional knocking copy. It variously described the Conservatives as 'right-wing, nasty, bigoted and ruthless'; desperate politicians exploiting fears with lies about immigration; conmen on the economy; and hypocrites on education. On Iraq, the *Mirror* held its tongue. Much like the *Sun*, it kept the story off the front page but its editorial support for Blair was less fulsome: 'Mr Howard says Mr Blair is a liar. Of course, others think that and it will decide how they vote ... But for the leader of the Opposition to base his campaign on screeching "liar, liar, liar" at the Prime Minister is pathetic.'

Whenever the *Mirror* was in doubt, it targeted the Conservative leader. On polling day, its front page showed an image of Howard the vampire, lying in a coffin with a wooden stake through his heart, under the headline 'VOTE LABOUR – THERE'S TOO MUCH AT STAKE'. Inside, a double-page spread on 'DRACULALAND' revisited the *Sun's* 1992 classic, 'Nightmare on Kinnock Street'. The *Mirror* offered a speculative account of 'what Britain could become if you don't vote Labour today': 'unemployment is three million and the elderly are dying of cold as pensioners plan to march on No 10'. However, the tone of its editorial made clear that the wounds of Iraq had failed to heal: 'we led the opposition and still think it was wrong to go to war'. The *Mirror* 'understands the doubters', it said, 'but it has to be Labour'. Rather than letting Michael Howard in through the 'DRACDOOR', the voters should send the Conservatives 'crashing towards oblivion'.

The *Daily Star* had supported Labour in 2001. Although it did not formally declare a preference this time, its tone was firmly conservative. It focused on attacking the Prime Minister. Tony Blair had made a shambles of immigration and crime, and on these issues his reputation was 'damaged beyond repair'; 'surely we deserve a better leader than this'. The paper urged the 'formidable' Michael Howard to 'put the boot' into the Prime Minister. The *Star's* news pages offered little coverage of the campaign but did feature disparaging stories of 'Muslim loonies' seeking to hijack the election through abuse of postal votes.

The quality papers included an abundance of issues, poll and battleground analyses, but avoided the special pull-out sections of recent elections, thus reducing the need to fill excessive space. Perhaps as a result, the editorials, not the celebrity commentators, were restored as the primary definers of each paper's political approach. The titles to watch most keenly were the *Daily Telegraph*, with its new owners and editor, and the *Independent*, whose tabloid turn had been accompanied by a bolder presentational style.

Charles Moore's *Telegraph* had robustly supported the Conservatives at the previous two elections but under its new editor, Martin Newland, the paper fought a curiously restrained campaign. The paper admired parts of the Tory programme, notably the proposed reforms of pensions, the police and council tax. However, it soon tired of the emphasis on immigration, repeatedly urging a switch of focus to tax cuts. 'It's about tax', complained its editorial on 12 April. The paper agreed with criticisms from party grandees about the Conservative election strategy: Michael Howard 'believed in lower taxes and smaller government; this must be his message for the rest of the campaign'.

The *Telegraph* had supported the invasion of Iraq and continued to do so. Because of this, and despite its often vociferous criticisms of Blair, it chose not to join the 'liar Blair' chorus of the Conservative tabloids. The Prime Minister had made the right decision even if he had employed the wrong arguments. While his failure to share the full text of the Attorney-General's legal advice with the Cabinet was 'reprehensible', and damaged what was already a 'tattered reputation', the controversy was more important to Labour activists than to the country at large. In the *Telegraph*'s view, 'his party seems certain never to forgive him for the Iraq war, even if the British people do'. Charles Moore, still retained as a columnist, captured the paper's position: 'for any reason you mention, Blair should go. Except Iraq.' The *Telegraph* ended its lukewarm election with a tepid endorsement of the Conservatives. It could not pretend it was happy with a Tory campaign that had majored on side issues rather than taxation. Even so, the overall equation remained clear: 'small government + freedom + low tax = vote Tory'.

The reinvigorated *Independent* offered the most distinctive treatment of the election by any newspaper. It was one of the few titles to increase its circulation during April and claimed a minor exclusive with the defection to the Liberal Democrats of outgoing Labour MP Brian Sedgemore. Uniquely in the national press, it regretted the end of the contest: 'against expectations this has been a far from boring four weeks'. It had been a 'frantic, intense, argumentative and often fascinating' campaign, in which ordinary people in the street and in the studio audiences had been the 'unsung heroes', asking the commonsense questions that cut through political double-speak.

The paper exploited its compact format to eye-catching effect, devoting its front pages to single stories, normally with large pictures or graphics and bold headlines but occasionally text only. This style of presentation reinforced the sense of a politically engaged newspaper. The *Independent* was willing to leave the pack in an attempt to drive forward its agenda of the environment and world poverty. While traditionalists might question whether newspapers of record should seek to set the agenda in this way, the paper's energetic treatment of such issues seemed a sufficient riposte.

In any case, the *Independent* made full play with Iraq, the issue that dominated the final 10 days before polling. 'Did Blair mislead us?' it asked on 29 April, with the legal arguments for and against splitting its front page. Its editorial equivocated over Blair's integrity but pronounced him guilty of a 'profound misjudgement with terrible results'. As polling day approached, the paper's liberal leanings – evident from its earlier commentary on the manifestos – became sharper. Its leader on 4 May declared it vital that 'the forces of liberalism prevail'. It liked the Liberal Democrats on Iraq, civil liberties, Europe and immigration; but since the party had no hope of overall victory, it could not offer a total endorsement. 'Instead, we seek an outcome in which there is a significantly larger force of Liberal Democrat MPs'; and it favoured the replacement of Tony Blair by Gordon Brown sooner rather than later.

By contrast, the tabloid *Times* was much like the old broadsheet *Times*; just more compact. Together with the *Financial Times*, it provided the most detached and neutral coverage of the election. In keeping with its custom, its editorials throughout the campaign highlighted the merits of a cross-party selection of individual candidates, including Education Secretary Ruth Kelly. On the national contest, *The Times* again endorsed Labour but in a highly qualified way. The Conservatives had 'an almost plausible leader' in Michael Howard but still desperately needed an influx of fresh talent. The Liberal Democrats were disappointing, still very much 'a work in progress', and their wooing of the left threatened long-term self-harm. The paper urged candidate-based voting where, for example, a Conservative moderate faced an unreconstructed old Labourite – or any candidate who 'claims to read the *Guardian*'. The best result would be a smaller but still viable Labour majority with a larger Conservative opposition.

The election became a game of two halves for the *Guardian*. For the first ten days its editorial tone and headline framing were clearly both pro-Labour and anti-Conservative. The paper acclaimed Labour's manifesto, which promised 'giant strides towards making this a society which marries economic efficiency and social justice in a modern and lasting manner'. By contrast, the paper was offended by the Conservative stance on immigration and alarmed by the party's negative and dangerous manifesto. Michael Howard's dream for Britain was 'more like a nightmare'.   *Guardian*

In the second half of the campaign the paper's temporarily submerged misgivings about Blair's style, the Iraq war and civil liberties resurfaced. Under the headline 'hidden agendas', the paper's editorial writers complained that Labour was hiding from the key issues of tax, National Insurance, pensions, Europe and Iraq. Labour was turning all difficult issues into no-go areas; 'this is immature, arrogant and old-fashioned politics'. In the penultimate week of the campaign, the paper suggested that government attempts to curb judicial power, not least by denying the right of appeal to failed asylum-seekers, amounted to an 'undemocratic and harmful attack on human rights and due process'. Its leader concluded that the 'retreat from the rule of law and civil rights remains the deepest flaw in the Blair administration'.

Eventually, the *Guardian* took the advice of star columnist Polly Toynbee who at the outset had urged readers to 'hold your nose and vote Labour'. Iraq especially made for a difficult choice, and there were powerful reasons to favour the Liberal Democrats. However, given the imperative of keeping the Tories at bay the paper urged readers to use their heads and hearts and re-elect Labour, with an increased presence for the Liberal Democrats.

The *Financial Times* backed Labour for the fourth election in succession. 'It is not yet time for a change', its editorial pronounced on 3 May. Labour had proved unconvincing on public spending and worrying on tax, but the Conservatives still did not have a programme for government, just a half-baked list of grievances. There was a strong case to be made for a smaller state and lower taxes, but 'Mr Howard has not made it'. Paradoxically, the paper found cause for celebration in a campaign comprising 'shallow slogans' and little serious debate: 'the vigour of the debate about things that do not matter emphasises the extent of cross-party consensus on the things that do'. It suggested that there was no longer a contest between pro- and anti-business parties and the paper did indeed limit its own coverage of the campaign, focusing its reduced resources on its core business coverage.

In the post-devolution era, the Scottish press expresses limited enthusiasm for British general elections. As *Scotland on Sunday* pointed out, voting Labour for more hip replacements in Surrey is not a concept likely to inspire its readers. Although no parties were exempt from the gloomy outlook of Scottish journalists, the Conservatives came in for the most consistent criticism. On election day, the *Daily Record*'s front page ran a series of images showing Michael Howard gradually morphing into Margaret Thatcher, under the heading, 'ARE YOU THINKING WHAT WE'RE THINKING?' The *Sunday Mail* was equally partisan: 'the Tories say they are 2–0 down. Let's make it 10–0 at the final whistle and keep them out of Downing Street.' In the main, the quality Scottish papers also rejected the Conservatives while offering only insipid support for Labour. The *Herald* judged that the best result would be for 'Labour to be returned to power with a much reduced majority that causes Mr Blair to stand down much earlier than planned'. This position was upheld in the *Sunday Herald*: 'The best outcome? A bloody nose for Mr Blair.' *Scotland on Sunday* also embraced 'tactical voting aimed at cutting UK and Scottish Labour down to size', while warning that 'the Tories are non-starters as a party of government'. The *Sunday Post* observed that 'the Lib Dems seem the only fresh thing in the election shop'. It too raised the awkward position of the role of Scotland in British elections, this time with reference to the Conservatives: 'even after three weeks of campaigning, they are known mainly for wanting to keep immigrants out ... which isn't too helpful in Scotland where we're actively trying to attract immigrants'.

The campaign in progress

As judged by lead stories and editorials, the press agenda at this election was strikingly different from 2001 and 1997 (Table 9.4). The major development was, of course, Iraq, but immigration and asylum preoccupied the papers to almost the same extent. Moreover, the European Union and the euro, which had dominated coverage of the previous two elections, were almost entirely absent this time.

The issue agenda of 2005 was firmly anti-Labour. Five of the seven main topics created difficulties for the party: Iraq, immigration/asylum, Tony Blair himself, the collapse of MG-Rover and the abuse of postal voting. The Conservatives could hardly have wished for more favourable terrain; their stance on immigration, in particular, was reinforced by all the popular tabloids bar the *Mirror*. By contrast, Labour's historic strengths in the public services, and its more recent advance in economic management, received limited highlighting on the front pages and from the leader writers. Overall, the press agenda came far closer to the Tory wish-list than to Labour's.

Although the issue agenda favoured the Conservatives, the Labour party received far more press coverage than did the Conservatives. Table 9.5 shows the extent of Labour's dominance. Of those front leads focusing

Table 9.4   Front-page lead stories and editorials about the election, by topic

| | Front-page lead stories | | | Editorials | | |
| | 2005 | | (2001) | 2005 | | (2001) |
	Number	%	(%)	Number	%	(%)
Party strategies/prospects	22	17	(14)	27	11	(7)
Iraq war/Iraq	15	12	(–)	22	9	(–)
Immigration/asylum	14	11	(4)	20	8	(8)
Blair	14	11	(–)	17	7	(–)
MG-Rover	9	7	(–)	4	2	(–)
Taxation/public spending	8	6	(6)	14	6	(5)
Postal voting/voter registration	7	6	(–)	6	2	(–)
Opinion polls	6	5	(9)	–	–	(1)
Exhortation to vote/advice on voting	4	3	(3)	16	7	(6)
Law and order	4	3	(–)	16	7	(–)
Health	4	3	(2)	12	5	(7)
Other leaders	3	2	(2)	16	7	(6)
Pensions	3	2	(–)	8	3	(–)
Terrorism	3	2	(–)	3	1	(–)
Education	2	2	(–)	10	4	(–)
Economy	2	2	(–)	9	4	(–)
Manifestos	–		(2)	21	8	(5)
Other	7	6	(58)	24	10	(55)
Total	*127*	*100*	*(100)*	*245*	*101*	*100*

on parties, three in four concerned Labour; similarly, most party-based editorials examined Labour. The governing party typically receives more coverage than the opposition and the press always focuses more on the leading party when its victory is assumed. In this campaign, too, news stories such as the MG-Rover closure naturally highlighted Government action. Even so, the extent to which Labour dominated press coverage was wholly exceptional.

Of course, coverage is one thing but content is another. Much of the coverage of Labour was critical as the Conservative tabloids judged there to be more mileage (and perhaps more sales) in attacking Tony Blair than in defending Michael Howard. To an extent unmatched in any recent campaign, press coverage of the 2005 election focused not just on a single party but also on a single individual. For many newspapers, the election was a referendum not so much on the Government as on the Prime Minister. Thus the word 'Blair' occurred 31 times in the headlines of front-page leads during the campaign. By contrast, 'Howard' appeared just five times, less often than 'Brown' and indeed the football star 'Rooney'

(Table 9.6). The 'issue' of Tony Blair commanded as many front pages and editorials as did that of immigration and asylum.

Table 9.5　Election coverage of political parties in front-page lead stories and editorials (daily newspapers)

	2005 Number	%	(2001) (%)
Front-page lead stories			
Conservative	12	19	(22)
Labour	47	73	(54)
Liberal Democrat	–	–	(–)
Other	–	–	(2)
More than one party	5	8	(22)
Total	*64*	*100*	*(100)*
Editorials			
Conservative	30	14	(17)
Labour	121	56	(52)
Liberal Democrat	14	6	(3)
Other	2	1	(2)
More than one party	50	23	(26)
Total	*217*	*100*	*(100)*

Labour's attempts to promote the Blair-Brown team failed to diffuse the spotlight on the Prime Minister. From the middle of the third week, Blair's conduct and integrity became the central focus as the newspapers debated whether he had misled Parliament, the country and indeed his Cabinet. Whatever a paper's position on the war itself, there was widespread agreement that Iraq had severely reduced the Prime Minister's political capital. With a Labour victory widely expected, most papers speculated that Blair's days in Downing Street were strictly numbered. The most likely scenario, suggested the *Telegraph* on 2 May, was that the country would go to bed with Blair on polling day and wake up with Brown.

The flow of news across the election is reflected in the front-page headlines, summarised in Table 9.6. In the first week, the main topics were immigration and asylum, MG-Rover and postal vote-rigging. These issues rather overshadowed the launch of the main parties' manifestos. Nonetheless, the manifestos still received significant coverage at a stage of the campaign when the battle lines were still being drawn up. In the main, the judgement was that the Conservatives failed to set out a distinct programme for government while Labour succeeded in demonstrating a continuing commitment to reform.

ny Blair, Labour rally, Enfield, 1 May.

an Milburn, Labour Campaign Coordinator.

3 Alastair Campbell, Labour Campaign Adviser

4 John Prescott, Ilkeston, Derbyshire.

5 Philip Gould and Matt Carter, Labour Party headquarters.

6 Labour battle bus.

7 Labour pre-election poster.

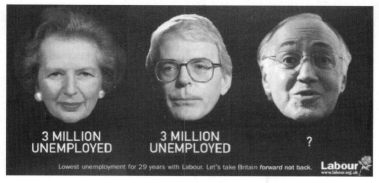

8 Labour election poster.

9 Gordon Brown and Tony Blair, Labour rally, Gillingham, Kent, 2 May.

10 Gordon Brown, opening a new building at
Tulloch Training Academy, Inverness, 21 April.

12 Lord Saatchi, Conservative Co-Chairm

1 Michael Howard, launching the Conservative
manifesto, London, 11 April.

13 Liam Fox, Conservative Co-Chairma
poster laun

4 Rachel Whetstone, George Bridges with Michael Howard.

15 Lynton Crosby, Conserva
Campaign Direc

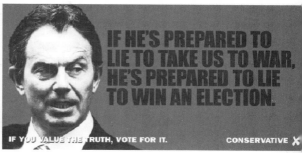

IF HE'S PREPARED TO LIE TO TAKE US TO WAR, HE'S PREPARED TO LIE TO WIN AN ELECTION.

IF YOU VALUE THE TRUTH, VOTE FOR IT. CONSERVATIVE ✗

Guy Black, Press Secretary
Michael Howard.

Imagine 5 more years of it.

Violent crime soars but Labour puts gloss on it

Daily Telegraph, 22 October 2004

ARE YOU THINKING WHAT WE'RE THINKING? VOTE CONSERVATIVE

17 and 18 Conservative election posters

19 Sandra and Michael Howard,
awaiting the Folkestone and Hythe constituency count, 5 May.

20 Charles Kennedy, Liberal Democrat 'Mini rally', Aberdeen, 29 April.

21 Charles Kenn⸱
Near Inverness, 23 A

22 Lord Rennard, Liberal Democrat
Chief Executive.

23 Alex Salmond, SNP leader.

Elwyn Llwyd, Plaid Cymru
liamentary leader.

25 George Galloway, Respect leader

27 Robert Kilroy-Silk, Veritas leader.

Darren Johnson, Green Party co-spokesman.

28 Roger Knapman, UKIP leader.

29 The count, Folkestone and Hythe.

30 Reg Keys' speech, Sedgefield count.

31 Sarah, Charles and Donald Kennedy, election ni

32 Sandra and Michael Howard.

Table 9.6 Front-page lead stories, 12 April–5 May 2005

Date	Mirror	Express	Sun	Daily Mail	Daily Star	Daily Telegraph	Guardian	The Times	Independent	Financial Times
April 12	(I knew I was innocent – freed mother)	(Camilla groomed to be Queen)	(Crazed Rooney thumps Coleen)	Illegal immigrants given 48 hours to vanish	(Dyer in new roast shock)	Labour 'lie' [about to Tory spending plans] goes up in flames	Labour plea to anti-war voters	Parties warned against inflaming race tension	Iraq: is the tide turning?	MG-Rover directors offer £49m
13	(Coleen flees after Rooney bust-up)	Migrant madness	(Rooney goes with hookers)	(The aspirin lifesaver)	(Rooney: I didn't hit Coleen)	A taxing day for Labour	New fears over postal votes	Doctors desert Labour	(Tesco's profits)	Blair risks fight over juries
14	The toxic terrorist	Shame: patient kicked out of NHS hospital	Terrorist: he wanted you dead	Murdered because we don't control our borders	(Celebrity wrestling)	Asylum crisis left al-Qaeda free to plot	17 years for poison plot	Al-Qaeda plot to poison Britain	The big choice [party policies]	Blair guarded on business tax
15	(Prince Harry flunks army tests)	MRSA is out of control	(Coleen: Wayne's the love of my life)	Labour: blame us for three more PC's murder years	(Big Bro: three more years)	Labour: we're sorry for murder of DC Oake	Rover's £400m accounting puzzle	Fraud fear as postal voting soars 500% in marginals	(Britons throw away food)	Blair went against advice on Rover loan
16	Rover's bitter end	Rover: it's all over	5,000 on the scrap heap at Rover	Hero PC 'to get George Cross'	(Rooney told to take piano lessons)	(Bird flu outbreak threat)	5,000 jobs go in Rover collapse	End of the road as Rover rescue collapses	Michael Howard meets his match	£150m aid for Rover workers

Table 9.6 continued

Date	Mirror	Express	Sun	Daily Mail	Daily Star	Daily Telegraph	Guardian	The Times	Independent	Financial Times
18	(Rio Ferdinand and Chelsea meet again)	(Queen to save nervy Camilla)	Britain needs your McDonald's vote	(Murder at Hell's Kitchen)	(Knives out in Hell's Kitchen)	Howard pledges £1.7bn pension boost	Blair retreats from EU vote	Tory tax boost for pensions	The green issue	(State set to outsource services)
19	(Psychopath knifeman freed to kill)	Labour threat to state pension	(Why was he out?)	(A million children have a mobile)	(Rotted brain of psychopath killer)	Blair won't rule out pensions means testing	Top Tories in pleas to Howard	Howard faces flak as Labour streches lead	(The woman who fought George Bush)	Setback for Howard on tax
20	(God's rottweiler: Pope Benedict XVI)	(The £750,000 speed trap)	(From Hitler Youth to Papa Ratzi)	Tory curb on council tax	(£1,000 fine to fly the flag)	('God's rottweiler' is new Pope)	(Vatican insider is new Pope)	(Pope is Benedict XVI)	(The boy who became Pope)	(German conservative is Pope)
21	Blair: I will reclaim the streets	Petition on hospital ward dumped in skip	The Sun says: one last chance	No Idea! Blair on illegal immigration number	Muslim loonies hijack election	How Prescott put £1bn on council tax	Tory letter exposes party fears	Secret loans bolster Tory campaign	I will not take election win as vindication of Iraq – Blair	CBI warns Labour on raising taxes
22	(Left for dead)	(Toddler sees mum knifed by maniac)	(Boy, 2, sees mum butchered)	(Horror in England's safest corner)	(Gazza: my life on coke)	(Victims of a violent Britain)	Row over £11bn tax black hole	(A mother, a victim, another statistic)	Tory candidates ignite race row	(Cadbury chief slams investor groups)

No.										
23	(First picture of Abigail and mummy)	(Stab mum: couple arrested)	(Dad Pitt)	(Boy who saw his mummy stabbed)	(Grapple girl's secrets)	Boarding schools for state pupils	Blair hits back over migrants	Tory's two-faced migrant campaign	Nuclear power? Yes please, says Blair	Brown faces blow on growth
25	(Posh and Becks: we will survive)	(Torment of knifed Abigail's husband)	(Black Cats: we're back)	(15,000 a month by phone scam)	(Becks deals Posh killer blow)	Poorest pay for state school failures	Opposition goes on Iraq offensive	(Taxman grabs charity cash)	A government at bay: fears over legality of Iraq war	Industry leaders back Labour
26	Crime victims to get lawyers and legal aid	President Blair: insult to Queen	Is this election boring or what?	Liar taunts haunt Blair	(High noon for Becks)	(Judges fear curbs on Thatcher's power)	Brown claims Thatcher's legacy	Fraud inquiry as millions vote by post	Labour MP defects to Lib Dems over Iraq	Brown is firm on Euro entry
27	(Rio in street brawl)	(Road camera fines soaring)	(I love you, mummy)	(My beautiful brave mummy)	(£100m macho the day)	(He held a knife to my baby's throat)	Private poll reveals Labour fears	Tories taunt 'liar' Blair	(Hollow victory: Syria leaves Lebanon)	Howard galvanises the Tory vote
28	Blair's air scare	The big lie	(24-hour guard on Abi)	Blair lied and lied again	(Muslim loonies bribe terror kids)	I never lie, says Blair, as doubt cast on war	Government's secret legal advice on Iraq war	Blair ditches the Euro	The legal advice we weren't allowed to see	Blow to Blair over Iraq war
29	(Britain's sickest paedophile)	Our sons died for Iraq lies	(Tom's new girl is a virgin)	Blair's betrayal of our soldiers	(Telly cooks like footie yobs)	Blair haunted by spectre of Iraq	Blair's dark day as Iraq row erupts	Blair anoints Brown as next premier	Did Blair mislead us?	Brown comes to Blair's rescue

Table 9.6 *continued*

Date	Mirror	Express	Sun	Daily Mail	Daily Star	Daily Telegraph	Guardian	The Times	Independent	Financial Times
30	(Jessie jilts lover)	Too many migrants, say Asians	(Abi suspect in court)	The doctor won't see you now	(Soap deal eases love split)	Brown would gives MPs last word on war	Hunt lobby bids to oust Labour MPs	Post vote hotline signals action on fraud	Lib Dem vote will not let in Tories	Labour fears for its majority
May 2	(Rooney: hero to zero)	(Why 70% of children are badly behaved)	(Huntley beaten by prison attacker)	Blair's insult to our dead troops	(Rooney too rude for kids)	Blair battles to shore up Labour vote in marginals	Battle for the middle classes	(Gang held in hunt for killers of British hostage)	Blair to upgrade Britain's nuclear weapons	Labour targets key marginals
3	My daddy is a hero	British soldier dies a hero	(Naz held on 'hit-run')	My daddy dies a hero	(Orlando set for Corrie part)	Kennedy pulls rug on pact with Labour	Poll reveals fragile Labour lead	(Cancer checks on all spices)	Iraq: the issue that won't go away	Labour extends its poll lead
4	(Mourinho's Mersey misery)	(Teacher raped in class by boy of 15)	Why size matters: Tony needs a big majority	(Why was rape boy at school?)	'Mythical' Muslims out to hijack the election	Teacher raped by boy with violent history	Blair banks on economy in final push	Fraud arrest as postal voting brings chaos	The final reckoning	Blair rejects NI rise for NHS
5	Vote Labour: there's too much at stake	(Teacher who tackled yobs freed)	Come on, you reds	(Vaccine could end cervical cancer)	(Brad 'n Angelina's love romps)	Blair heads for historic third term	Polls say Labour will win historic third term	Blair set for third term as Lib Dems advance	The campaign is over. Now Britain decides	Labour hopes high as fight ends

Both the *Telegraph* and the *Financial Times* were disappointed by the Conservative proposals. By promising to match Labour's spending on public services, the Tories had left themselves a 'footling' amount for tax cuts, the *Telegraph* complained. The party had missed the opportunity to make the case for the smaller state, said the *Financial Times*, and had chosen instead to target voters' baser instincts on Europe, crime and immigration. *The Times* and the *Independent* agreed that the Conservatives sounded positively 'Blairite' on public spending. The main distinguishing feature of the Tory manifesto, according to the *Independent*, was its strong 'British tone'. But this gave the proposals a distasteful edge: 'an illiberal campaign disguised as sweet reason'. For the *Guardian*, the Conservatives did not have a programme for government, 'just a list of grievances'. In *The Times*, Peter Riddell suggested that the Conservatives were following a deliberate 'dog-whistle' strategy; since victory was a fantasy, they had settled on a sensible programme to boost their status in opposition. The popular press divided in predictable fashion. The *Mail*, the *Express* and the *Star* were delighted by Howard's tough stand on immigration and crime, the *Sun* told Howard to concentrate on reducing tax, while the *Mirror* thought Howard 'looked like a dunce' in his efforts to square increased public spending with tax cuts.

By contrast, Labour's manifesto was certainly considered a programme for government, and for the *Financial Times* and the *Telegraph*, altogether too much government. The *FT*'s leader judged that Labour's campaign slogan should really be 'Britain Backwards, Not Forwards'. Certainly, Labour's manifesto was a 'coherent and ambitious' programme for extending the state, but as it drove spending back to 1980s levels, so it risked a return to the fiscal crises of that decade. The manifesto was 'composed by control freaks', said the *Telegraph*, and would extend the state's reach into the lives of ordinary people. *The Times* found the programme 'solid, sensible in many parts, painfully worthy in others'; it was strong on public service reform, crime and foreign policy but 'this overall is a workmanlike tome which appears fearful of passion'. According to the *Independent*, the pledge not to increase income tax was the most eye-catching promise in Labour's 'weighty production', but the paper was disappointed with the low priority given to green issues and to Europe.

The *Guardian*, the *Sun* and the *Mirror* were supportive to varying degrees, though each made the point that Labour must now deliver. 'Blair still has a big job to do', said the *Sun*, while the *Mirror* warned that if Labour failed again it would deserve to be thrown out. Predictably, the *Mail* found plenty to dismay Middle Britain, which it said would be hit by increases in National Insurance. The *Express* was even more dismissive. It relegated Labour's manifesto to the second item in its leader column: 'No one can believe Labour's election manifesto is worth wasting time on. After lying to us on everything from tax to tuition fees … Tony Blair and his party have lost all credibility.'

The Liberal Democrat proposals were awaited with unusual interest since much analysis of the battleground seats had noted the party's opportunity for further gains. As the *Guardian* leader put it, this is 'Charlie's chance'. However, in the event, normal service resumed as the Liberal Democrat manifesto received slight coverage, much of it focused on how Charlie's chance became Charlie's gaffe. Fatigued from attending the birth of his son, Kennedy appeared confused over his party's proposals for a local income tax, providing the press with some easy sport. 'Mr Kennedy … produced the most gloriously amateur performance in British public life since Eddie the Eagle Edwards', wrote Quentin Letts in the *Mail*. The 'knackered dad' had lost the plot, according to the red tops. The *Sun* suggested that Kennedy should hand over to someone who might make more sense: 'How about his son Donald?'

The *Guardian*, the *Financial Times* and *The Times* agreed that the Liberal Democrat manifesto positioned the party to the left of Labour. The *FT* took fright; the manifesto was an 'unreal alternative' and there would be a danger of excessive public spending and taxation if, as in Scotland, the Liberal Democrats held the balance of power. The party had abandoned 'the market-oriented, less intrusive government that is liberalism's proud heritage'. With its large share of Liberal Democrat readers (Table 9.7), the *Independent* was more sympathetic. It welcomed a 'genuine alternative' and viewed the manifesto as a 'refreshing' programme which, in its treatment of tax, immigration, the environment and foreign policy, offered something different from the 'crowd-pleasing' policies of the other parties.

In the second week of the campaign, the broadsheets reported internal disquiet in the Conservative campaign as Labour stretched its lead in the opinion polls. But it was the Iraq issue which really brought the campaign to life. On 24 April the controversy began with a leak to the *Mail on Sunday* and Channel 4 News, summarising Lord Goldsmith's legal advice about the Iraq invasion, and continued with Michel Howard accusing Blair of lying. The *Independent* was delighted that the war was 'where it ought to be' – at the centre of the election. It added a little more fuel to the fire with the story of Brian Sedgemore's defection to the Liberal Democrats. Sedgemore urged everyone 'to give Blair a bloody nose', accusing the Prime Minister of contempt for Parliament, the Cabinet and the rule of law. The *Mail* and the *Express* needed no encouragement and the words 'Blair' and 'liar' were scarcely separated in their pages thereafter. 'Now for a real fight', said the *Star* (26 April). The *Financial Times* reported its own MORI poll proclaiming that Michael Howard was succeeding in galvanising the Tory vote, while the Conservative leader himself explained in an interview with *The Times* 'why I have come to despise Tony Blair'. It was an extraordinarily bitter week for Blair, but only the *Sun* still claimed to be bored: 'Is this the dullest election ever ... YES OR GNOME?' declared its front page, as it enlisted garden gnomes to its rock-the-vote campaign.

Table 9.7   Party supported by daily newspaper readers, 2004

Newspaper		Party supported by readers		.
		Con (%)	Lab (%)	Lib Dem (%)
Daily Telegraph	2004	61	15	17
	2001	65	16	14
Daily Mail	2004	53	21	17
	2001	55	24	17
Financial Times	2004	45	23	24
	2001	48	30	21
Express	2004	41	29	19
	2001	43	33	19
The Times	2004	40	26	29
	2001	40	28	26
Sun	2004	31	41	13
	2001	29	52	11
Daily Star	2004	17	53	16
	2001	21	56	17
Independent	2004	12	36	39
	2001	12	38	44
Mirror	2004	15	60	18
	2001	11	71	13
Guardian	2004	5	44	37
	2001	6	52	34

Note: Whole sample: Con 31 per cent, Lab 35 per cent, Lib Dem 23 per cent, Other 11 per cent. Source for 2004: MORI Voting Intention Aggregate ('certainty of voting, 10/10'). Base: 21,727 adults interviewed July–December 2004, of whom 16,337 gave a voting intention.

The death of Anthony Wakefield, a British soldier killed in action in Iraq on 2 May, kept the war on the front pages into the final week. 'MY DADDY IS A HERO', was the headline in the *Mirror*; 'BRITISH SOLDIER DIES A HERO', said the *Express*; 'MY DADDY DIES A HERO', wrote the

Mail. Both the *Mail* and the *Express* went on to quote the soldier's widow, who blamed the Prime Minister for the death. However, as polling day approached, the papers turned their attention to speculation about the result, reporting headline polls that continued to favour Labour. As polling day dawned, the papers were united in their prediction: the Labour Party was heading for a historic third term.

The Sundays and weeklies

In the Sunday papers, much as in the dailies, support for Labour weakened but without collapsing. The *Sunday Express* and the *Sunday Times* returned to their Conservative home, while the *Independent on Sunday* embraced the Liberal Democrats. The other pro-Labour papers maintained their loyalty, but at a lower level of intensity than in 1997 or even 2001 (Table 9.2).

The traditional Labour tabloids – the *People*, the *Sunday Mirror* and the *News of the World* – remained faithful but in large measure their case for the government now rested on Conservative inadequacy. The *Sunday Mirror*'s theme was typical: 'VOTE LABOUR, THERE REALLY IS NO ALTERNATIVE'. The paper agreed that Labour had become a Government in decline: 'the prime minister, so long the mainstay of his party, has been more a liability than an asset. Iraq has damaged his credibility and there is also the inevitable contempt that comes with familiarity.' Yet although things should have been better under Labour, 'under the Conservatives they will only get worse'.

The *People* pursued a similar line, suggesting that even though 'there will be those who wish to give Mr Blair a bloody nose', tactical voting should be resisted: 'protest votes, or not voting at all, are votes for the Tories. And that could produce the unthinkable. Tony Blair leaving Number 10 by the front door. As Michael Howard slithers in through the back.' The *News of the World*, too, was 'not without apprehension' in supporting a Government that 'has sneakily hiked National Insurance and refused to rule out further rises'. However, the Conservatives 'have failed to come up with a convincing long-term plan to slash the tax burden and to cut the size of the state … Labour aren't Champions League material. But they DO play in the Premiership. The Tories are just a Coca-Cola Championship team.'

In the mid-market, the *Mail on Sunday* offered an even sharper critique of Mr Blair. Again, however, it could summon only limited endorsement of the Conservatives. The Prime Minister had constructed 'an administration based on a personality cult': 'it is Mr Blair who has corrupted the institutions of this country and taken us into a war of aggression, in a secret agreement with a foreign power'. The paper concluded that 'nobody who believes in honesty, in the rule of law, in justice, democracy or in Britain as a fair and well-governed nation can possibly cast a ballot for Tony Blair'. But, like the *Daily Mail*, the *Mail on Sunday* was guarded in its support for the opposition. True, Michael Howard 'has a much better grasp of what is truly valuable about this country', while Charles Kennedy had 'stood against the tide of opinion and fashion' in opposing the war in Iraq. Further than that, though, the *Mail on Sunday* was not prepared to go. Its final editorial offered no comment whatever on the policies of either the Conservatives or the Liberal Democrats.

By contrast, the *Sunday Express* did provide strong support for the Conservatives. Like its daily counterpart, the paper revelled in its return to the Tory fold, luxuriating in a clash of political philosophies invisible to the rest of the press. 'In its heart,' wrote the leader writers, 'Labour believes that the Government is better at spending your money than you are, while the Conservatives believe that how we spend our hard-earned cash should be left up to us.' Under the headline, 'VOTE HOWARD, SACK BLAIR', the *Sunday Express* charted the failure of Labour's meddling: soldiers left without body armour; judges transformed into lapdogs; small businesses into form-fillers; classrooms into war zones and the elderly into means-tested serfs of the Chancellor. Meanwhile, 'the work-shy continue to sit at home on incapacity benefit'. Unlike the Prime Minister, Michael Howard was 'a leader of real weight, intellect and authority' who would 'lead and manage this country, rather than just preach to it'. Uniquely among the Sundays, the *Express*'s vigorous advocacy echoed the adversarial style of press campaigns from 20 years ago.

Among the broadsheets, the most significant move came from the *Sunday Times*. The paper found little in the campaign to inspire 'those preparing to trudge to the polls'. On the one hand, Labour's record was no better than mixed. Brown had been lucky on the economy, Tony Blair had failed to make the 'honest case' for war and the Government had virtually vanquished the idea of a neutral civil service. Above all, a huge increase in public spending had produced only limited results while higher taxes had damaged incentives and growth. On the other hand, the Tories were not much better, offering only 'Labour-lite: no significant tax cuts and plenty of extra public spending'. In the end, the paper decided to return to the Conservative Party for its instincts rather than its policies: 'Labour's arrogance needs to be curbed and the Tories need to be given a better platform in opposition on which to start building a genuine alternative. A vote for the Conservatives is the only way to achieve both of these aims.'

The *Sunday Telegraph* again endorsed the Conservatives though also in a rather measured way. Its critique of Labour focused, unusually, on economic management: the Government's claim to economic competence reflected the groundwork laid by the Major Government and would in any case soon be tested by the effects of uncontrolled public spending. But under the headline 'SOMETHING OF THE RIGHT', the paper did seek to build a positive case for the Conservatives. Mr Howard offered 'all the right instincts on law and order' while also seeking to bring private sector discipline to the public services. He also offered a better strategy for redefining Britain's membership of the European Union. The paper concluded that after eight years of 'New' Labour, 'what Mr Howard has to offer would be, in the true sense of the word, completely and refreshingly new'.

The *Observer* and the *Independent on Sunday* continued to speak with similar anti-Conservative voices. Both papers gave considerable credit to the Government. The *Observer* argued that Labour remained 'the only party committed to ending poverty and building social justice', while the *Independent on Sunday* also noted Labour's 'valuable if unfinished achievement in promoting social justice'. Both papers also expressed disquiet over the Conservative approach; the *Observer* suggested that 'the Tories have fought a shabby, racist campaign', while the *Independent on Sunday* condemned Mr Howard's 'distasteful campaign'.

Yet although the analyses were similar, the papers drew different conclusions. Under the headline, 'LABOUR IS THE RIGHT CHOICE', the *Observer* suggested that 'the way to get a Labour government in most constituencies is to turn out and vote for one'. However, 'voters with sitting Liberal Democrat MPs should return them and voters choosing in marginal contests between a Tory and a Lib Dem should back Charles Kennedy'. The *Independent on Sunday* offered a fuller endorsement of the Liberal Democrats, the party which had 'provided the real opposition to the war'. It suggested that 'where the realistic choice is between Labour and Conservatives, we prefer Labour, but the values for which this newspaper stands are best promoted by voting – where they can win – for the Liberal Democrats'. This conclusion represented a shift away from the paper's support for Labour at the two preceding elections.

The weekly political journals maintained their allegiances from last time. The *New Statesman* (circulation 24,000) and *The Economist* (153,000) again supported Labour while the *Spectator* (66,000) warmly embraced the Conservatives. Like the liberal Sundays, the *New Statesman* respected the Government's goal of social justice: 'Labour's commitment to beating poverty and improving public services deserves support.' True, Mr Blair had prosecuted 'a murderous, illegal war', but even so, 'we owe it to millions of poor people here and abroad to ensure Labour – not Mr Blair, not even Mr Brown, but its MPs, its activists, its union supporters – remains the party in power. Then, at least, the voices of the deprived will be heard, however faintly, where it matters.'

The Economist also retained its support for Labour, albeit from a more right-wing perspective. The magazine judged that the Prime Minister remained the best conservative on offer: 'Mr Blair has continued to hog the centre-right ground in British politics, as he as done ever since becoming Labour's leader in 1994.' The magazine's pre-election cover showed a cheery Mr Blair under the headline 'THERE IS NO ALTERNATIVE (ALAS)'. Specifically, the Tories lacked a distinctive position on both public spending and the health service while the Liberal Democrats were sound on immigration but 'opposed to two things that commend Mr Blair strongly to this newspaper: his top-up fees for universities; and, of course the Iraq War'. The conclusion was that 'Tony Blair, for all his flaws, remains the best centre-right option there is.'

The Spectator instructed its readers that 'this is no time for dwelling on any deficiencies in Tory personnel or programmes'. Rather, 'it is time to vote Conservative in a spirit of optimism and confidence, not least because the Tories are the only party remotely interested in the democratic freedoms of this country'. Mr Blair's Government was 'clapped-out, deceitful, nannying and discredited', leading to the conclusion that 'we can't just drift on with a Labour administration that has plainly run out of money, hope and ideas. Vote Conservative for freedom, democracy and taxpayer value.'

Advertising

Despite limits on national campaign spending, the major parties found room in their budgets for more press advertising than in 2001, though total volume remained well down on the high-rolling 1980s (Table 9.8). Labour was once again the most extravagant party, offering a series of full-page insertions drawing attention initially to the Government's achievements and then, towards the end of the campaign, to the dangers posed by a Conservative victory. Probably reflecting increased volume, electors' ability to recall advertising also grew. In a post-election poll (5–10 May), MORI found that 48 per cent of respondents recalled seeing political advertisements in newspapers during the campaign, compared to 37 per cent in 2001. Recall of Conservative and Labour advertisements was neck and neck.

However, the most distinctive feature of press advertising in this campaign was the Government's attempt to improve turnout. This theme accounted for half the total material. The Electoral Commission ran a single, and much repeated, full-page item advising electors not to sit on the fence (complete with unimaginative drawing of said fence). In addition, a number of Government departments and agencies joined together in a rather more informative effort to explain the procedure for voting by post.

Table 9.8   Election advertising in national daily and Sunday newspapers

	Number of insertions	*Number of pages*
Political parties		
Conservative	4	4.0
Labour	22	22.0
Liberal Democrat	13	8.9
Pressure groups		
GMB	3	3.0
Other trade unions	3	3.0
Christian Aid	4	3.5
Other	10	3.9
Public agencies		
Electoral Commission	28	28.0
Eight agencies[1]	28	16.1
Total	*115*	*92.4*

Note:
1. Information campaign on postal voting procedures by eight agencies and departments, including the Scotland Office, the Home Office and the Department for Constitutional Affairs.

Conclusion

At the outset, few observers would have expected the press to make a vigorous contribution to this campaign. In the newspapers, as in the electorate, dealignment is the long-term trend. Traditional displays of press partisanship seem out of place in an era in which many electors (including newspaper readers) no longer even take the trouble to vote. Furthermore, newspapers are preoccupied by the problems of their own declining but competitive market. They have little choice but to become more commercial in outlook, a goal difficult to reconcile with the pursuit of traditional party politics.

And indeed the election did play in a low key for parts of the press. At the bottom end, the *Daily Star* largely succeeded in keeping the election off its front pages. The *Mirror* was constrained in its enthusiasm for Labour by its opposition to the Iraq war, while the *Sun* found difficulty in expressing an authentic commitment to Labour's cause. Even at the top end, the *Financial Times* judged that an election with a predictable outcome and few differences between the fiscal approaches of the major parties did not merit undue attention.

Elsewhere, however, the campaign did stimulate the political instincts that still form part of the press's genetic code. Both the *Daily Express* and the *Sunday Express* ran traditional Conservative campaigns redolent of the 1980s. The disappearance of the European issue might have been expected to hinder the *Mail*, but it found immigration and asylum perfectly serviceable alternatives with which to pursue its xenophobic agenda. Above all, the papers did much to initiate and sustain the sharpest moments of the campaign with the controversy over the Prime Minister's role in the Iraq.

The final outcome in the press resembled that in the wider electorate, not necessarily because either influences the other but because each observes the same campaign. Labour's support among newspapers declined while remaining at a historically high level. For most papers, as for most voters, criticism of the Prime Minister did not translate into an embrace of the Conservative alternative. Indeed, many newspapers experienced difficulty in identifying what the Conservative alternative was, a point best illustrated by the *Guardian*'s scathing dismissal of the Tory manifesto as nothing more than 'a list of grievances'. So the press, again like the electorate, found itself basing its judgement on the overall performance and detailed prospectus provided by the governing party.

Note

1. Alan Rusbridger, 'Hugo Young Lecture: What are Newspapers For?' Sheffield University, 9 March 2005.

10
MPs and Candidates

Byron Criddle

The election was contested by 3,555 candidates of whom 2,834 (80 per cent) were men and 721 (20 per cent) women. The average number of candidates per constituency was 5.5 compared to 5.0 in 2001. A slight increase in voter turnout was thus paralleled by a small increase in candidate participation. The Labour and Conservative parties fought 627 mainland constituencies, avoiding the Speaker's seat of Glasgow NE; the Liberal Democrats fielded 626 candidates, avoiding the Speaker's seat and the Wyre Forest constituency of the Independent MP, Dr Richard Taylor; the SNP fought all 59 Scottish seats including that of the Speaker, and Plaid Cymru contested all 40 Welsh seats. Three minor parties fielded more than 100 candidates: UKIP (496), the Green Party (183) and the BNP (119).[1]

The new intake of MPs totalled 123 (19 per cent), slightly up on 2001 when the figure was 99 (15 per cent). The new MPs comprised 40 Labour (11 per cent of the PLP), 54 Conservative (28 per cent of the party's MPs) and 20 Liberal Democrats (32 per cent of the party's MPs); the minor parties' intake made up the rest – two SNP, three DUP, two SDLP, one Sinn Fein and one independent. Of the 123, only four were former MPs returning after earlier defeats: Sir Malcolm Rifkind, Christopher Fraser and David Evennett (all Conservative), and Revd William McCrea (DUP). This was a small number of 'retreads', virtually all of the Conservatives swept aside in the Labour landslides of 1997 and 2001 having finally given up hope. Three others stood and were beaten: David Martin, Stephen Day and Roger Knapman (now as leader of UKIP), and the former Labour MP Keith Darvill sought to recover his seat lost in 2001. Four other former MPs also stood and lost: the former Conservative MP David Mudd stood in his Falmouth and Camborne seat as an Independent, the ex-Labour MP Dave Nellist contested his former Coventry NE seat for the Socialist Alternative Party, the former Liberal Democrat MP Mike Carr fought Rossendale & Darwen and the former SNP MP Douglas Henderson, who had been ousted from Aberdeenshire East as long ago as 1979, returned to the fray in Dumfries and Galloway at the age of 69.[2]

The turnover of MPs in 2005 was, with 61 seats changing hands,[3] less dependent than in 2001 on a large number of retirements, because although these in 2005 totalled 86, not all of them were replaced, due to the reduced number of Scottish seats from 72 to 59. Labour's 58 departing MPs comprised the usual mix of the old, the disaffected, the dislodged and those ambitious for other careers. Leading the exodus of the elderly was the 73-year-old Father of the House, Tam Dalyell, who had served for 43 years since winning the West Lothian byelection in June 1962. A Scottish laird who replaced a coal miner in 1962, he managed throughout his long career to eschew use of his seventeenth-century baronetcy, and in retiring halved the number of Old Etonian Labour MPs from two to one. Originally a Labour moderate and Europhile, he had latterly taken to rebellion, notably over military campaigns, dubbing Tony Blair a 'war criminal' for the Iraq war. He would otherwise be recalled for his dogged pursuit of Margaret Thatcher over the sinking of the *Belgrano* in the Falklands War and for posing the anti-Scottish devolution West Lothian Question. Others of his age retiring included Kevin McNamara (b. 1934), whose Hull North by-election victory of January 1966 had prompted Harold Wilson's successful dash to the country and a Labour majority of 97; Tom Cox (b. 1930), leaving Tooting reluctantly after 35 years; and – oldest of all – Bill O'Brien (b. 1929) leaving Normanton after 22 years. The long-serving, though younger, former minister in the Wilson and Callaghan Governments, Denzil Davies (b. 1938) retired from Llanelli after 35 years. One current and four former Cabinet ministers were retiring, two to take up diplomatic posts: Paul Boateng, at the age of 53, was leaving to become High Commissioner in South Africa, and Helen Liddell (aged 54) to a similar post in Australia. Of similar age, and therefore unusual to be leaving, were Estelle Morris (b. 1952) who had resigned from a stressful tenure as Education Secretary, and the former Culture Secretary Chris Smith (b. 1951), the first MP to announce his homosexuality, and latterly to his being HIV-positive. More explicable in terms of age was the exit of the former Cabinet minister Dr Jack Cunningham (b. 1939) after 35 years, his retirement leaving Margaret Beckett and Michael Meacher as the only remaining MPs to have served in the last (Callaghan) Labour Government before Tony Blair's. Two former

Chief Whips were also leaving: Ann Taylor (b. 1947) and Derek Foster (b. 1937), the latter – like all of the last five-mentioned – receiving a peerage, notwithstanding his disaffection at having failed to be offered a Cabinet job in 1997, and later having described the Blair Government as 'not fit to lick the boots' of the post-war Attlee administration.

A further group of retiring Labour MPs were those dislodged by the Scottish Boundary Commissioners. Thirteen Scottish Labour MPs retired, some less willingly than others. One, Malcolm Savidge, was beaten in a contest for his redrawn Aberdeen North seat by the MP for the abolished Aberdeen Central, Frank Doran. Bill Tynan objected to boundary changes in the Hamilton area, but retired, as did Jimmy Wray in Glasgow. These casualties apart, peerages eased the situation in other cases, such as Lewis Moonie, who quit to make room for Gordon Brown in the redrawn Kirkcaldy seat; George Foulkes, whose Ayrshire seat was redrawn to incorporate the Ayr constituency, and the relatively young Lynda Clark (b. 1949), who fell on her sword to provide a seat for Alistair Darling among the reduced number of Edinburgh constituencies. Both Helen Liddell's departure for Canberra and Irene Adams's for the Lords also eased the pressure caused by the Boundary Commissioners in Lanarkshire and Renfrewshire.

There was a small group of underaged retiring Labour MPs from the 1997 intake, all still in their forties. Two of these, Iain Coleman and Debra Shipley, retired on health grounds; the others were the junior minister Ivor Caplin (b. 1958) and Julia Drown (b. 1962), who was off to spend more time with her young family, having in the previous Parliament received fairly short shrift from Speaker Boothroyd when calling for breast-feeding to be permitted at Westminster. Another of Labour's 1997 intake, Jane Griffiths (b. 1954), who had criticised sexism at Westminster, had no choice about her departure, having been deselected at Reading East. The older Helen Jackson (b. 1939) also quit, citing her disenchantment with the Commons vote to return partially to allegedly un-family-friendly late-night sittings. Disenchantment also appeared to feature in the departure at the age of 61 and after 22 years of the former Sports Minister Tony Banks, who revealed his dislike at having to deal with constituents' problems and of being 'abused by journalists', before disappearing with a peerage and a change of name, to Baron Stratford.

A final group of the departing brought colour to the Whips' cheeks: the serially rebellious Harry Barnes (b. 1936), Alice Mahon (b. 1937), Brian Sedgemore (b. 1937) and Llew Smith (b. 1944) left the Commons, the last two not entirely quietly: Brian Sedgemore made an orchestrated defection to the Liberal Democrats in the middle of the election campaign, and

Llew Smith gave tacit support to the successful rebel candidacy against the woman selected as his replacement in Blaenau Gwent.

Leading the Conservative exodus, in terms of longevity, was Sir Teddy Taylor (b. 1937), who had served a total of 40 years since his election for Glasgow Cathcart (1964–79) and, after an 11-month gap, for Southend East (1980–2005). A junior minister in the Heath Government until resigning over Europe, his career was noted for both his Euroscepticism and his opposition to Scottish devolution; he had been one of a group of rebels against the Maastricht Treaty who lost the Whip under the Major Government. From his generation too was Sir Sydney Chapman (b. 1935), who was first elected in 1974, and Marion Roe (b. 1936). They were accompanied by four former Cabinet ministers: Virginia Bottomley (b. 1948), who had sat since 1984; Sir Brian Mawhinney (b. 1940), first elected in 1979; Gillian Shephard (b. 1940), elected in 1983, and – most exceptionally given his age – Michael Portillo (b. 1953), who had contested the leadership as recently as 2001 after a political career taken up almost on leaving university, but having, as he put it, lost his appetite for 'the cut and thrust of the Chamber' and taken to dispassionate television and press commentary, was leaving for a career in the media.

Four other Conservative retirees were leaving either unwillingly or after unflattering publicity. Michael Trend (b. 1952), who had sat for Windsor since 1987, retired after criticism over his Commons allowances claims. Jonathan Sayeed (b. 1948) – noted mainly for the defeat in 1983 at Bristol East of Tony Benn, which served to exclude the latter from an impending Labour leadership ballot – left right on the eve of the election following criticisms from the Parliamentary Standards Committee concerning his links to a company charging for tours of the Palace of Westminster. Nick Hawkins (b. 1957) was leaving because he was deselected at Surrey Heath, and Howard Flight was forced out close to the election by a decision of the party leader. Two other retiring Conservatives were evidently disaffected: James Cran (b. 1944) had sat since 1987 but had received press attention for his non-participation in the Commons for some time; Archie Norman (b. 1954), who had entered from the world of commerce as MP for Tunbridge Wells as recently as 1997, was leaving disillusioned with the ways of politics. Promoted into the party organisation by William Hague to encourage McKinsey-style management, unhierarchical teamwork and clear desks, he left frustrated at the world of Westminster which he saw as hidebound by tradition and out of step with the country it was meant to run. He saw himself as 'not a politician's politician', preferring the world of business 'where people are really interested in outcomes'.

He said: 'I was the first FTSE100 chairman to be elected to the House of Commons – I'll probably be the last.'

Efforts were made in mid-2004, allegedly by the Opposition Whips' Office, to augment the rather small numbers of retiring Conservative MPs by producing a list of supposed 'bed-blocking' members who were said not to be pulling their weight and were to be urged to make way for younger more enthusiastic candidates. The list included some august names, notably Sir Peter Tapsell, Michael Mates, Sir John Butterfill, and even the former Cabinet ministers Kenneth Clarke and Stephen Dorrell. The notion was dismissed by one of the named – Derek Conway – who retaliated by blaming the 'Notting Hill set' of ambitious young metropolitans, and threatened to sue over any criticism of his Commons attendance record, and an apology had to be issued by the *Daily Telegraph* (which had mounted the story) to Sir John Butterfill, whose quadruple heart bypass had kept him away from the House.

Most of the departing Liberal Democrats were at or near retiring age: Paul Tyler (b. 1941), Jenny Tonge (b. 1941), David Chidgey (b. 1942), John Burnett (b. 1945) and Sir Archie Kirkwood (b. 1946). Sir Archie, who had sat for 22 years, by retiring was making available a secure seat for his colleague Michael Moore in the Scottish Borders where the Boundary Commissioners had rolled two Liberal Democrat seats into one. Nigel Jones (b. 1948), who had represented Cheltenham since 1992 and had earlier suffered a sword attack by a deranged constituent in which an aide was killed, left on grounds of ill-health. Less conventional was the departure of Richard Allan who had captured Sheffield Hallam in 1997, at the age of 39; he had made his mark as a leader in the computer revolution at Westminster.

Three Northern Ireland MPs left the scene: the Ulster Unionist Revd Martin Smyth (b. 1931), the SDLP MP Seamus Mallon (b. 1936) and the former SDLP leader and Nobel Peace Prize winner John Hume (b. 1937), who had relinquished all his political offices, exhausted after a career which had culminated in his party being marginalised by the electoral advance of Sinn Fein. He had represented Foyle since 1983. Finally, three floor-crossers left Westminster, two of them former Conservatives. Robert Jackson, MP for Wantage since 1983, a Clarke-voting Europhile who had voted with Labour on the EU Nice Treaty and higher student fees, had taken the Labour Whip in January 2005, though his intention to retire had been announced as early as November 2001. Andrew Hunter, MP for Basingstoke since 1983, who had a long history of support for Ulster Unionism, had sat as an Independent Conservative from the time he announced his intention to retire in 2002 and formally joined Revd Ian Paisley's DUP in 2004. More eccentric was Paul Marsden, a surprising Labour victor at Shrewsbury in 1997, who had crossed the floor to the Liberal Democrats in 2001 after rebelling against the bombing of Afghanistan and claiming intimidation by the Whips, had subsequently announced his intention to retire, and then, in the course of an election campaign he was not fighting, declared his intention to rejoin the Labour Party.

For significant innovation in candidate selection procedures after 2001 it was necessary, as ever, to look to the Labour Party. Soon after the 2001 election the Government introduced legislation to restore selection by way of all-women shortlists, a practice that had been discontinued in 1996 after an industrial tribunal had declared it discriminatory and so unlawful. In consequence, it was alleged, the number of women elected in 2001 dropped for the first time since 1983. The Sex Discrimination (Election Candidates) Act 2002 amended section 13 of the Sex Discrimination Act 1975 to permit parties to adopt measures to reduce inequality in the number of men and women elected, without forcing parties to adopt them. Although Conservative MPs spoke against all-women shortlists in debates on this Bill, its passage inevitably put the matter of women candidates on the agenda, encouraged both by lobbyists and by academic advocates of greater numbers of women MPs.[4]

Following the legalising of all women shortlists, Labour's National Executive Committee (NEC) decided in January 2002 that the party's 'long-term objective is to achieve 50:50 gender representation; [that] we need to target regions currently with less than 25 per cent women representation, [and that] these regions should ultimately achieve not less than 35 per cent ... [and that] the NEC is to be given the authority to intervene in selections and late selections to ensure progress is made'. The targeted regions – with under 25 per cent women MPs – were Wales (with only 12 per cent, or four, women MPs), North (13 per cent, four), South East (18 per cent, four), East Midlands (21 per cent, six), Yorkshire and Humber (23 per cent, eleven) and West Midlands (24 per cent, ten). In order to attain the minimum 35 per cent target it was calculated that retiring male MPs would need to be replaced by the following number of women candidates: eight in Wales, seven in the North, four in the South East, four in the East Midlands, six in Yorkshire-Humber, and five in the East Midlands. In the North West (where 27 per cent, or 17 MPs were already women), and London (where 27 per cent, or 15 already were) smaller increases in female MPs were required – five in the North West and four in London. Two other regions, Eastern and South West, were deemed already to have achieved 35 per cent gender representation by female MPs and were merely 'expected to continue work towards

50%, but at least maintain the 35% threshold'. Scotland, meanwhile, was exempt from all of this because of the problem caused by fitting existing MPs – many of whom were Cabinet ministers – into the reduced number of parliamentary seats. To assist this process of feminisation, late-retiring MPs – defined as those announcing their retirement after December 2002 – were to be automatically replaced through all-women shortlists, though with discretion remaining with the NEC 'to authorise exemptions in special circumstances'.

From the above list of 'unfeminised' regions it can be seen that pressure was on certain areas; notably Wales, where eight new women candidates were deemed necessary. In the event only six Welsh MPs retired – and one of those was a woman – but all were replaced by women, five of them by way of all-women shortlists. However, two of the new Welsh women candidates were defeated at the election, and one of them – Maggie Jones at Blaenau Gwent – by a rebel Labour man, Peter Law, who ran against her because of her imposition on the constituency by means of an all-women shortlist. Mr Law was the sitting Welsh Assembly member for the constituency, and was seen as the 'favourite son' expecting to follow the retiring Llew Smith into the Westminster seat. It was a common theme of Labour's advocates of all-women shortlists that they were the only way of blocking otherwise unstoppable local heirs-apparent – all normally men. But with Mr Law the issue was not just one of gender; he had the tacit backing of the left-winger Llew Smith, according to whom 'they are parachuting in Blairites who have traditionally voted with the right wing and the Party is very much against it'. Llew Smith was also irked that the Blaenau Gwent all-women shortlist was imposed even though he had announced his retirement before the date after which such shortlists were to be mandatory. Peter Law's much-publicised resistance saw his sensational capture of the seat as an Independent with a 9,000 majority, despite undergoing an operation for a brain tumour at the start of the campaign.

Other resistance to the imposition of all-women shortlists came from the advocates of more black and Asian MPs, who claimed that non-white women were never selected from such lists, and that the only way of ensuring more ethnic minority MPs was to have open shortlists (meaning, in Labour's case, lists that were 50:50 male–female) in seats where black and Asian populations were large. Thus, eventually, the seats of Ealing Acton & Shepherd's Bush, Dewsbury, Tooting, Brent East and Brent South were all designated for open shortlists, and non-white candidates were duly selected in all except Ealing Acton & Shepherd's Bush, where the white 'favourite son' local council leader, Andrew Slaughter, was chosen.

At Brent East, a seat which had been lost to the Liberal Democrats in a 2003 by-election, the selection was tortuous, leading at first to the selection of the white male candidate, Robert Evans, who had lost the by-election but who, following appeals by two aspiring Muslims, Shahid Malik and Yasmin Quereshi, was replaced by Ms Quereshi – who would have become the first female Muslim MP had she not failed to recapture the formerly safe Labour seat at the general election. Open shortlists in such seats were not conceded easily by the NEC, and it was due to the persistence of the ambitious Shahid Malik who had been excluded from contention at Burnley by an all-women shortlist and who also happened to be an NEC member, that an open shortlist was permitted at Dewsbury and which saw his selection. In West Ham, a seat with a majority non-white population being vacated by the white Tony Banks, the NEC, despite much pressure from black activists, imposed an all-women shortlist which saw the victory of the white woman – Lyn Brown – over five black women, one of whom was the locally based and strongly tipped Dawn Butler. It was the view of Simon Woodley, coordinator of the lobbying organisation Operation Black Vote, that 'Labour's equality agenda shoves blacks and Asians to the back of the queue; all women shortlists will be all white women shortlists'. Shahid Malik, for his part, said he was 'fully signed-up to all women shortlists', and, despite Labour Party Chairman Ian McCartney suggesting all-black shortlists were 'not ruled out in the future', he opposed that currently unlawful option. It so happened that in March 2005, on the eve of the election following the late retirement of Paul Boateng at Brent South, an unofficial all-black shortlist was constructed by way of an open shortlist consisting of two non-white men and two non-white women, and it was thus that the black GMB union officer Dawn Butler, who had recently been thwarted at West Ham, was selected. In this case – as in Brent East – the claims of race and gender were simultaneously met, if with a different outcome: Dawn Butler was elected for Brent South on 5 May.

Labour's 40-strong new intake of MPs bore the heavy imprint of the all-women shortlist policy: 26, or two-thirds, of the new MPs were women, 23 of whom had come from all-women shortlists.[5] In fact, in the 48 seats where retiring Labour MPs had been replaced by new candidates, 33 of them had been women (30 from all-women shortlists), but seven of these seats were lost at the election. The rest of the new intake (14) were men, some being the supposed 'favourite sons' backed by the party or unions. With many retiring MPs not announcing their exit until close to the election, it was open to the NEC under its late retirement procedure to vary shortlisting arrangements in order to ease the way for, mostly, male government special advisers and party staffers. Although the most prominent of these, Ed Balls, the Chief Economic Adviser at the Treasury, had been selected at Normanton in July 2004, a clutch of other Whitehall political aides came in at the last minute: Ed Miliband (Doncaster North), Pat McFadden (Wolverhampton SE) and Ian Austin (Dudley North). But despite the 'favourite son' charge against such people, it was clear that a number of the women selected could be seen as 'favourite daughters', for they too had come from the ranks of ministerial aides, such as Kitty Ussher (Burnley) and Alison Seabeck (Plymouth Devonport), or had been senior party staffers, such as Jessica Morden (Newport East) and Natascha Engel (Derbyshire NE). Equally, from union employment came the GMB official Dawn Butler (Brent South). Labour's new intake thus represented not merely the intended further feminisation of the Parliamentary Labour Party (PLP), but the march of the apparatchiks – male and female. Labour, as the new 'natural party of government', was seeking to use a centralised system of candidate selection to transfer reliable favoured policy advisers and party staffers from state or party bureaucracies to parliamentary and ministerial careers.

Reflecting Labour's top-down approach to candidate selection and in response to big rebellions over the Iraq war and foundation hospitals toward the end of the 2001 Parliament, the Chief Whip, Hilary Armstrong, was rumoured to be intending to carpet the hardcore rebels. The party's reselection rules for MPs already gave the Whips the opportunity to report critically on the member's parliamentary behaviour, but of the few Labour MPs who had problems securing reselection, only one – George Galloway – was actually dispatched by the leadership. Already menaced by the boundary revisions in Glasgow, Mr Galloway was at first suspended and then in October 2003 expelled from the party for his remarks on an Arab TV station that President Bush and Tony Blair were attacking Iraq 'like wolves' and in other interviews that the Iraq war was 'illegal' and that 'the best thing British troops can do is to refuse illegal orders'. He was also facing press-driven allegations at having profited financially from the Saddam Hussein regime, allegations over which he secured damages from the *Daily Telegraph*. His creation of his own party, Respect, and relocation to London to contest and win from Labour the Bethnal Green & Bow seat held by the black Jewish MP Oona King (who had herself to fend off a deselection attempt in a heavily Muslim seat for her defence of the Iraq war), was a remarkable achievement for an expelled rebel.

The only Labour MP formally deselected was Jane Griffiths at Reading East; she was replaced by local councillor Tony Page, who had two past convictions for indecency, by a vote of 145 to 96 in February 2004. Her demise was due more to personal than political factors. A somewhat eccentric Blair loyalist elected in 1997, she had established a reputation as a critic of the macho ways of Westminster and had complained of sexist incidents and of MPs having affairs and drinking to excess. She also had poor relations with the large ruling Labour group on Reading Council and with her parliamentary neighbour and former Deputy Leader of the Council, Martin Salter. The seat was lost to the Conservatives at the election. Another of Labour's 1997 female intake, Helen Clark (formerly Brinton) faced a deselection vote at Peterborough in January 2004 but survived by 11 votes. A loyalist latterly taken to parliamentary rebellion, she had attracted a fair amount of critical press attention over the years, much of it concerning her private life, and whilst she avoided deselection, she lost the seat at the election. After the election she joined the Conservative Party. The veteran Tom Cox, MP for Tooting since 1970, who had been resisting attempts to retire him for many years, finally succumbed, after failing to win an automatic reselection vote, by withdrawing. In the subsequent selection the nomination went to the civil rights lawyer Sadiq Khan. As ever, the murky waters of Birmingham politics delayed the reselection of Roger Godsiff (Sparkbrook & Small Heath) and Khalid Mahmood (Perry Barr); in both seats local ward branches had been suspended, but both men were, on the eve of the election, reselected with over 50 per cent of the votes cast by wards and affiliated organisations – the necessary procedure in order to avoid a full-scale contested reselection. It was understood that Mr Godsiff, noted as an accomplished union fixer, had only secured the threshold because of the votes of his former employers, the GMB. His retention of the ethnically diverse constituency had been fraught ever since his acquisition of it in 1992, but his uncertain future was to be resolved by the Boundary Commission's recommended removal of the seat from the Birmingham map after the election.

Given the Conservative Party's repeated rejection of such structural reforms as all-women shortlists – specifically criticised by Iain Duncan Smith during his leadership – it was unlikely the party would match Labour's innovation in candidate selection after 2001. Nor, arguably, did instability at the top of the party – two changes of leadership, three changes of the party chairmanship – provide a secure setting for significant innovation. Responsibility for the candidates office passed in 2001 to Trish (later Baroness) Morris, as Vice Chairman for Candidates. Unlike previous holders of the post she was not or had not been an MP, and whilst favourable to greater professionalism in the candidate screening process, she was opposed to all-women shortlists. She had additional support from Gillian Shephard MP, and in September 2004 Andrew Mackay MP was drafted it with responsibility for 'target seats'; in effect his role was to deal with crises concerning candidate selections in the run-up to the campaign, with application of a 'truncated selection procedure', involving centrally imposed shortlists, as at Arundel and South Downs and Bedfordshire Mid, where MPs were replaced in a hurry.

The prime concern at Central Office was to improve the process of assessing and training would-be candidates, and not to change the actual process of candidate selection. An occupational psychologist, Professor Jo Sylvester, was brought in to produce a revised procedure for candidate screening designed to test more effectively ability and potential. The Parliamentary Selection Board at which aspiring candidates were screened was renamed the Parliamentary Assessment Board and was intended to become a more rigorous means of determining the capacity of and assessing the training needs of applicants. The list of approved candidates was expanded from some 600 to about 1,000 so as to offer greater choice to constituencies, and the proportion of women on the list rose to 25 per cent. The only change in candidate selection processes was the use in seven Labour-held target seats of primary elections to select candidates. In these seats – none of which were very high on the list of winnable seats, and only one of which was actually captured on 5 May – anyone on the electoral register who was marked as a Conservative 'pledge' could attend a hustings meeting and vote on the shortlisted candidates. Thus the 'selectorate' was expanded towards the Conservative electorate and away from the assumed prejudices of the narrower membership. That said, the characteristics of the candidates selected by this means in these seven seats were similar to those chosen by more conventional means: although three of the seven were women, a higher than average proportion, five had attended public schools (one of which Eton), and the occupations covered – law, medicine, banking, the armed forces and business – were entirely traditional.

Characteristic of Conservative caution in the matter of selection processes was the pamphlet produced in 2002 by Andrew Lansley MP, former head of the Conservative Research Department, and a Vice Chairman under William Hague's leadership.[6] Its recommendations were slight; that there should be an 'A' list of about 100 of the most highly approved candidates, comprising equal numbers of men and women and 'several drawn from ethnic minorities', which should be brought to the notice of key-seat Conservative Associations in order to encourage the selection of higher quality and female candidates, and secondly that there should be postal balloting in candidate selection to enable 'a higher proportion of younger members to participate'. Mr Lansley was keen to point out that neither of these proposals implied 'women only shortlists', but he urged at least one third of selections in safe and winnable seats to be of women and of 'a number of candidates from ethnic minorities'. These proposals, neither of which were adopted, represented more the politics of exhortation than of Labour's social engineering, as did Central Office officials' visits to top target seats to encourage local selectors, in the words of one official, to 'look beyond the characteristics of the Association to the wider constituency when developing a profile of the best candidate for that constituency'. Whilst Central Office set great store by these changes, even if the revamped means of screening and training candidates improved candidate quality in the long run, it was not clear how they addressed – as did Labour's very direct measures – the matter of demographic representativeness. Nor would changes in candidate screening bear fruit in May 2005, because three-quarters (33) of the new Conservative intake of 54 MPs were candidates recycled from earlier elections; some were into their third electoral contest and ten were being elected in seats they had fought in 2001. Central Office saw virtue in this, assuming the equivalence of an incumbency effect for locally known candidates. But these were people who had been on the candidates' list for upwards of ten years. And the number of women in the new intake – six – did not represent anything like the 25 per cent of the expanded candidates' list who were women. What could be taken to represent innovation in the new intake was the election of two ethnic minority MPs, Adam Afriye (Windsor) and Shailesh Vara (Cambridgeshire NW), though there was no great novelty in this: the party had previously elected an Asian candidate, Nirj Deva, at Brentford and Isleworth (1992–97).

A number of disputes involving Conservative candidates reflected the concerns of gender, race and sexual preference. A clutch of women candidates were replaced – at Colne Valley, Calder Valley and Cleethorpes – invariably with allegations of sexism from the departing candidates. A handful of candidates in target seats were open about their homosexuality, but at Falmouth and Camborne, such a candidate, Ashley Crossley, was continuously challenged by homophobic elements in the local association right up to the eve of the campaign, and a disgruntled former aide of the sitting Labour MP Candy Atherton alleged at an industrial tribunal (which rejected his allegations) that even Ms Atherton had sought to exploit Mr Crossley's lifestyle; the seat fell to the previously third-placed Liberal Democrats at the election. A dispute fuelled by racism flared at Bradford West following the selection of a 34-year-old British Airways executive Haroon Rashid, with claims by officers of the association that the constituency had been 'promised a white candidate'. Haroon Rashid was suspended as candidate whilst claims of ballot-rigging at his selection were investigated, but he was reinstated in January 2005. Racial factors also lay behind a reported move to deselect the MP Ann Winterton at Congleton, following two incidents involving her telling racist jokes.

Only two Conservative MPs were formally deselected: Nicholas Hawkins and Howard Flight. A third, Jonathan Sayeed, abruptly announced his retirement in March 2005 after being having been suspended from the Commons following a critical report on him by the Standards and Privileges Committee. The deselection of Nick Hawkins at Surrey Heath appeared more personal than political. His relations with local officials had deteriorated after the breakdown of his marriage in 1999 and, amid allegations of poor communications, arrogance and scruffiness, he lost a reselection ballot in February 2004. He in turn blamed Freemasonry and 'a large group of ethnic minority people' whom he claimed had voted in his deselection ballot. A postal ballot of the full membership confirmed his defeat, and he was replaced in one of the safest of Conservative seats by *The Times* journalist Michael Gove. Much more politically salient was the ousting – by the Party leader – of Howard Flight from Arundel and South Downs in the eve of the campaign in March 2005 A bluff, congenial, pin-striped banker from the right of the party, Mr Flight had held Shadow Treasury posts, but, in a bugged speech to a Thatcherite audience, he implied that tax cuts well in excess of those publicly stated would be introduced by a Conservative government. To kill the damaging electoral impact of this statement Michael Howard immediately sacked him from his party post and withdrew the Whip, declaring: 'We will not say one thing in private and another thing in public; everyone in the party has to sign up to that; if not, they're out; Howard Flight will not be a Conservative candidate at the next election.' Mr Flight considered legal action, but the election was imminent and Andrew Mackay saw Flight's sacking as 'playing well' with the public. Central Office offered the constituency a ten-strong shortlist from which they selected Nick Herbert from the Conservative think tank Reform, a man whose right-wing views on the economy fairly well matched those of Howard Flight.

No innovation attended Liberal Democrat candidate selections after 2001. An attempt to ape Labour was thwarted at the 2001 party conference, when delegates rejected a proposal for all-women shortlists – an event rather over-dramatically described by Shirley Williams as 'the second longest suicide vote in history'. Instead of grasping that nettle, the party opted for a target of 40 per cent of female candidates in winnable seats, without any obvious means of its achievement – its only relevant rule being that shortlists should be one-third female. The reality that the party had so few obviously winnable seats made it unlikely that ambitious male candidates would easily stand aside to allow women a clear run. With its realistic strategy of targeting campaigning on winnable seats, competition for such seats was inevitably intense.

The number of women candidates fielded by the three parties was 433, comprising 166 Labour, 122 Conservative and 145 Liberal Democrat. The total number of women MPs rose to 128, the highest figure ever, though an increase of only ten on 2001. (See Tables 10.1 and 10.2.) The total was comprised of 98 Labour (28 per cent of the PLP), 17 Conservative (9 per cent of Conservative MPs), ten Liberal Democrat (16 per cent of Liberal Democrat MPs), and three representing Northern Ireland parties.

Table 10.1   Women candidates, 2001–05

	Labour	Conservative	Liberal Democrat
2005	166 (26%)	122 (19%)	145 (23%)
2001	148 (23%)	93 (15%)	140 (22%)

Table 10.2   Women MPs, 2001–05

	2001	By-elections 2001–05	Retiring 2005	Defeated 2005	New MPs 2005	Total
Labour	95	–	–14	–9	+26	98
Con	14	–	–3	–	+6	17
Lib Dem	5	+1	–1	–1	+6	10
SNP	1	–	–	–1	–	0
UUP	1	–	–	–	–	1
DUP	1	–	–	–	–	1
Sinn Fein	1	–	–	–	–	1
Total	118	+1	–18	–11	+38	128

The 38 new women MPs comprised 31 per cent of the new intake, and the new total of 128 women MPs, 20 per cent of the House of Commons. In weight of numbers, Labour's contribution was paramount, though almost as many women Labour MPs retired or were beaten (23) as were newly elected (26). Three Conservative women had retired, and in the 18 Conservative-held seats where MPs had been replaced, three new women had been selected at Chipping Barnet, Basingstoke and Mid Bedfordshire. In addition to holding these seats, only three other women were elected in seats captured by the Conservatives, at Putney and St Albans (from Labour) and at Guildford (from the Liberal Democrats) because in its top 50 target seats the party had selected women in only six. Proportionately the greatest contribution to the enhanced number of women MPs came from the Liberal Democrats who doubled their complement from five to ten, even though women had been fielded in only six of their 20 top target seats.

The number of candidates from ethnic minorities contesting the election for the main parties doubled to 117: 34 Labour, 41 Conservative and 42 Liberal Democrat, but the number of non-white MPs rose by only three, from 12 (all Labour) in 2001 to 15 (13 Labour and two Conservative) in 2005.[7] The Liberal Democrats had won the Leicester South by-election with an Asian candidate – Parmjit Singh Gill – in 2004, but he was defeated at the general election. Labour lost Paul Boateng (Brent South) through retirement and Oona King (Bethnal Green & Bow) through defeat, but gained Shahid Malik (Dewsbury), Sadiq Khan (Tooting) and Dawn Butler (Brent South). The House now had four Muslim MPs, all Labour, though a Muslim woman, Yasmin Quereshi, had failed to recapture the former Labour seat of Brent East. There were only two female non-white MPs, Dawn Butler and the re-elected Diane Abbott – both of Afro-Caribbean parentage. The Conservatives elected their first black candidate (of Anglo-Ghanaian parentage), the IT businessman Adam Afriye at Windsor, and the Ugandan Asian lawyer Shailesh Vara at Cambridgeshire NW. But given the political reality that electable non-white candidates were most likely to be those fielded in predominantly non-white constituencies, Labour's monopoly (after 1997) of all such seats made it unlikely that the other parties would make any significant contribution to increasing the number of ethnic minority MPs.

The number of Jewish MPs returned at the election was 26: 11 Labour, 12 Conservative and three Liberal Democrat. In one case – at Hornsey & Wood Green – one member of the Jewish community, Labour's Barbara Roche, was ousted by another, the Liberal Democrat Lynne Featherstone. At Richmond Park, Susan Kramer was replacing her retiring Liberal Democrat colleague, Jenny Tonge, who had earlier been dropped as a Liberal Democrat spokesman for sympathising with Palestinian suicide bombers. Four of the new Conservative intake, Brooks Newmark (Braintree), Grant Shapps (Welwyn Hatfield), Lee Scott (Ilford N) and the returning Sir Malcolm Rifkind (Kensington & Chelsea), were from the Jewish community.

The oldest MP in 2005 was Labour's Piara Khabra who was born in either November 1922 or 1924, but was certainly an octogenarian. There remained only one other member born in the 1920s – Revd Ian Paisley, born in April 1926, and so, in 2005, in his eightieth year. Taking 1 January 2005 as the calculation point, 11 other MPs were in their seventies: the Labour MPs Sir Gerald Kaufman (b. June 1930), Robert Wareing (b. August 1930), Alan Williams (b. October 1930), Gwyneth Dunwoody (b. December 1930), Dennis Skinner (b. February 1932), David Winnick (b. June 1933), Joe Benton (b. September 1933) and Austin Mitchell (b. September 1934); the Conservatives Sir Peter Tapsell (b. February 1930) and Michael Mates (b. June 1934); and the Independent MP Dr Richard Taylor (b. July 1934). At the other end of the age range were three MPs in their twenties, all of whom were newly elected Liberal Democrats: Jo Swinson, the youngest, was the only MP born in the 1980s (b. February 1980), Julia Goldsworthy (b. September 1978) and Dan Rogerson (b. July 1975). The next youngest MPs were also Liberal Democrats: Jenny Willott (b. May 1974) and Sarah Teather (b. June 1974). The youngest Labour MP was Andrew Gwynne (b. June 1974) and the youngest Conservative Jeremy Wright (b. October 1972). Liberal Democrat MPs had the youngest age profile, with 61 per cent being under 50, compared to 56 per cent of the Conservatives and only 37 per cent of the PLP. The Labour benches were distinctly ageing, with 44 per cent in their fifties and with the highest median age of 53. (See Table 10.3.)

Table 10.3 Age of candidates

Age (at 1 Jan 2005)	Labour Elected	Labour Unelected	Conservative Elected	Conservative Unelected	Lib Dem Elected	Lib Dem Unelected
20–29	–	50	–	57	3	51
30–39	39	78	36	179	17	144
40–49	91	82	75	134	18	171
50–59	158	45	56	46	18	152
60–69	58	14	29	11	6	41
70–79	8	1	2	–	–	3
80–89	1	–	–	–	–	–
Unknown	–	2	–	2	–	2
Median age						
2005	53	40	48	38	46	45
2001	50	40	48	38	47	45

As in 2001, the MP with the longest service was Sir Peter Tapsell who had sat for 44 years since first winning Nottingham West from Labour in 1959. Whilst he was the last survivor from the 1950s, his absence from the House between 1964 and 1966 meant he was not the member with the longest unbroken service: that distinction went to the Labour MP and former junior minister Alan Williams who won Swansea West from the Conservatives in 1964 and retained the seat continuously thereafter. He therefore became Father of the House in 2005. Apart from him, only two other MPs, both Labour, remained from the 1960s: Gwyneth Dunwoody and David Winnick, who had both been elected in 1966 but had subsequently interrupted service. Mrs Dunwoody, with a total service of 35 years, was the most senior woman MP. After these four veterans, the Commons' senior ranks comprised 37 MPs elected in the four elections – or at by-elections – during the 1970s. The longest-surviving, all from the 1970 election, were Labour's Sir Gerald Kaufman, Michael Meacher, John Prescott, Dennis Skinner and Gavin Strang; the Conservatives' Kenneth Clarke, Sir Patrick Cormack, John Gummer, Sir Alan Haselhurst and John Horam (elected in 1970 as a Labour MP); and the Revd Ian Paisley. The Conservative MP Sir Nicholas Winterton and the Liberal Democrat Alan Beith entered the House at by-elections in 1971 and 1973 respectively. Following them came 11 survivors of the two elections of 1974: the Labour MPs Margaret Beckett, Robin Cook and Bruce George, and the Conservatives Michael Ancram, Michael Mates, Sir Malcolm Rifkind, Sir Michael Spicer, Sir John Stanley, Anthony Steen, Peter Viggers and Sir George Young. Finally, from the 1979 election or by-elections preceding it, were seven Labour MPs – Frank Dobson, Frank Field, David Marshall, Austin Mitchell, Jack Straw, Barry Sheerman and Geoffrey Robinson; five Conservatives – Peter Bottomley, Stephen Dorrell, Douglas Hogg, Andrew Mackay and Richard Shepherd; and the Speaker, Michael Martin, then a Labour MP. These 41 survivors of the 1950s, 1960s and 1970s comprised only 6 per cent of the House elected in 2005, though three of their number were in the Labour Cabinet – Margaret Beckett, John Prescott and Jack Straw.

From the two elections of the 1980s, or by-elections preceding them, there remained 52 Labour, 46 Conservative and six Liberal Democrat MPs, comprising 16 per cent of the House, and including the Prime Minister, the Chancellor of the Exchequer and the Leader of the Opposition. But by May 2005 the parliamentary experience of the overwhelming majority of MPs extended no further back than the 1990s, a decade of Conservative decline and Labour growth. (See Table 10.4.) MPs of this era were conditioned to a culture in which Labour was the 'natural party of government' and the Conservatives were seen as unelectable. However, since 1945 the average span of an MP's incumbency has been 15 years and one month – equivalent to the duration of three or four Parliaments.

Thus the big Labour intake of 1945 was largely eroded by 1959, and the Conservative one of 1983, by 1997. Given Labour's wafer-thin majorities in many seats held in 2005, and the potential for destabilisation by the boundary revision, the expected life-span of Labour's large 1997 intake was probably running true to form. Already by 2005 retirements and defeats had removed one-third of that intake, reducing it from 180 to 126.

Table 10.4 Parliamentary experience of MPs

First elected	Labour	Conservative	Lib Dem
1950–59	–	1	–
1960–69	3	–	–
1970–79	15	19	1
1980–87	52	46	6
1988–92	59	28	2
1993–97	138	27	19
1997(July)–2001	44	26	13
2001(Nov)–05	44	51	21
Total	*355*	*198*	*62*

Family connections of MPs were slightly changed from 2001. Five husband and wife pairs were returned: Ann and Alan Keen (Labour), Ed Balls and Yvette Cooper (Labour), Ann and Sir Nicholas Winterton (Conservative), Andrew Mackay and Julie Kirkbride (Conservative), and Peter and Iris Robinson (DUP). Oddly, the Keens, the Wintertons, the Robinsons and the Balls–Cooper duo all sat for adjacent constituencies. The House now had a pair of brothers – David and Ed Miliband (Labour) to add to the sisters Angela and Maria Eagle (Labour) and Ann Keen and Sylvia Heal (Labour). Eighteen MPs were the children of former members: Hilary Armstrong, Charlotte Atkins, Hilary Benn, Mark Fisher, Lindsay Hoyle, Ian McCartney, Alison Seabeck, Dari Taylor – all Labour (though Mark Fisher's father had been a Conservative MP); and James Arbuthnot, Dominic Grieve, Douglas Hogg, Bernard Jenkin, Francis Maude, Andrew Mitchell, Nicholas Soames, Bill Wiggin, and the newcomers Nick Hurd and Richard Benyon – all Conservatives. Ten MPs were the grandchildren of former members: Hilary Benn, Fiona Mactaggart and Mark Todd – all Labour (although the grandfathers of the latter two had been Conservative MPs); the Conservatives Geoffrey Clifton-Brown, Philip Dunne, Douglas Hogg, Nick Hurd and Nicholas Soames, and the Liberal Democrats John Thurso and Sir Robert Smith (though the latter's grandfather was a Conservative). The Conservative newcomer Charles Walker was (from the age of seven) the stepson of the former Conservative MP Sir Christopher Chataway; and the new Labour MP for Burnley, Kitty Ussher, the niece of the retiring Conservative MP Virginia Bottomley. Nick Hurd, entering the House in 2005 as MP for Ruislip-Northwood, was joining the very small band of MPs whose families had served in four successive generations: his great-grandfather, Sir Percy Hurd, sat for Frome from 1918 and then Devizes until 1945; his grandfather, Sir Anthony Hurd, was MP for Newbury 1945–64; and his father, Douglas Hurd, represented Mid Oxon/Witney 1974–92.

The educational background of Labour and Conservative candidates revealed in Table 10.5 remained much as it had been over four previous elections. Graduates provided four-fifths of Conservative MPs, two-thirds of Labour MPs and two-thirds of both parties' unelected candidates. A more important social indicator was the proportion of candidates who had attended public schools[8] – again unchanged over 20 years, with three out of five Conservative and one in six Labour MPs drawn from such schools, but whereas the new Labour intake in 2005 reflected this pattern (with seven out of 40 MPs from fee-paying schools), the new Conservative intake was less elitist with fewer than half from private schools and fewer with the elitist pedigree of 'public school and Oxbridge' – only 22 per cent

Table 10.5   Education of candidates

	Labour		Conservative		Lib Dem	
	Elected	*Unelected*	*Elected*	*Unelected*	*Elected*	*Unelected*
Secondary	38	20	7	48	4	64
Secondary + poly/coll	86	71	16	83	6	159
Secondary + univ	168	135	57	146	28	220
Public school	1	2	4	13	–	6
Public sch + poly/coll	4	5	11	23	3	15
Public sch + univ	58	35	103	116	21	97
Unknown	–	4	–	–	–	3
Total	355	272	198	429	62	564
Oxford	40	19	49	35	11	39
Cambridge	18	14	37	23	8	27
Other univs	168	137	74	204	30	251
All Univs	226	170	160	262	49	317
	(64%)	(63%)	(81%)	(61%)	(79%)	(56%)
Eton	1	–	15	5	1	2
Harrow	–	–	–	6	–	–
Winchester	–	–	1	1	–	–
Other public schools	62	42	102	140	23	116
All Public Schools	63	42	118	152	24	118
	(18%)	(15%)	(60%)	(35%)	(39%)	(21%)

Table 10.6   Occupation of candidates

	Labour		Conservative		Lib Dem	
	Elected	Unelected	Elected	Unelected	Elected	Unelected
Professions						
Barrister	10	10	22	22	2	9
Solicitor	18	13	18	24	2	21
Doctor/dentist/optician	1	–	3	9	2	10
Architect/surveyor	1	2	4	6	2	5
Civil/chartered engineer	4	5	1	13	–	24
Accountant	3	4	5	25	2	25
Civil service/local government	22	24	3	3	3	32
Armed services	1	2	13	13	–	8
Teachers: university	16	7	–	–	3	21
poly/college	25	10	–	3	–	9
school	32	19	6	17	9	62
Other consultancies	1	14	1	12	–	18
Scientific/research	7	2	–	–	–	12
Total	*141*	*112*	*76*	*147*	*25*	*256*
	(40%)	*(41%)*	*(38%)*	*(34%)*	*(40%)*	*(45%)*
Business						
Company director	4	15	23	34	6	13
Company executive	6	18	41	70	7	51
Commerce/insurance	1	6	7	30	3	46
Managerial/clerical	11	4	1	12	2	18
General business	3	6	3	14	–	17
Total	*25*	*49*	*75*	*160*	*18*	*145*
	(7%)	*(18%)*	*(38%)*	*(37%)*	*(29%)*	*(26%)*
Miscellaneous						
Misc. white collar	70	52	4	33	4	51
Politician/political organiser	60	27	20	40	7	39
Publisher/journalist	24	13	14	24	5	14
Farmer	–	–	6	14	2	4
Housewife	–	–	1	3	–	14
Student	–	5	–	3	–	7
Total	*154*	*97*	*45*	*117*	*18*	*129*
	(43%)	*(36%)*	*(23%)*	*(27%)*	*(29%)*	*(23%)*
Manual						
Miner	10	–	1	–	–	1
Skilled worker	20	7	–	3	1	26
Semi-skilled	5	4	1	2	–	3
Total	*35*	*11*	*2*	*5*	*1*	*30*
	(10%)	*(4%)*	*(1%)*	*(1%)*	*(2%)*	*(5%)*
Unknown	–	3	–	–	–	4
Grand total	*355*	*272*	*198*	*429*	*62*	*564*

of newcomers compared to 35 per cent in the entire Parliamentary Party. Meanwhile the Liberal Democrats increased their reliance on the privately educated with half of their 20-strong new intake from fee-paying schools, including 30 per cent from public school and Oxbridge.

The Commons' Etonian component fell from 18 to 17, of whom there were 15 Conservatives, one Labour and one Liberal Democrat.[9] Amongst the five unelected Old Etonian Conservative candidates were two young merchant bankers who offered hope from so unexpected a quarter to the party's modernisers: Kim Humphreys (Anglo-Chinese) and Kwasi Kwarteng (of Ghanaian parentage).

Finally, occupation (Table 10.6). Conservative MPs continued to be drawn equally from business and the professions – predominantly law. This was as true of the 54-strong new intake as of all Conservative MPs. But Labour MPs were increasingly drawn from the ranks of professional politicians, who dominated the new intake and who had come to rival the weight of the teaching profession. Ever fewer Labour MPs were drawn from business, or from manual work (only two in the new intake), leaving the Liberal Democrats uniquely drawing their candidates from all social categories – from Old Etonian academic to Tyneside roadsweeper.

With the main theme in candidate selection after 2001 having been greater demographic representativeness, much hinged on Labour's electoral prospects, for if its electoral tide continued to ebb at the next election, many of the expanded number of women MPs it had provided through social engineering would be lost, and the other parties' resistance to structural change in selection procedures would be placed under more pressure.

Notes

1. Source: House of Commons Library Research Paper 05/33.
2. Other former Conservative MPs such as Phillip Oppenheim and Lady Olga Maitland unsuccessfully sought selection, as did the disgraced ex-Cabinet minister Jonathan Aitken, whose attempt to stand again in his former Thanet South seat was greeted by Michael Howard's dismissal that 'his days as a Conservative MP are over'.
3. This total includes Brent East, won initially by the Liberal Democrats at a 2003 by-election, and held in 2005; Lagan Valley where the UUP MP Jeffrey Donaldson switched to the DUP in 2004 and retained the seat for his new party in 2005; and three redrawn Scottish seats which were notionally taken to be Labour-held seats but were lost in 2005.
4. See Laura Shepherd-Robinson and Joni Lovenduski, *Women and Candidate Selection in British Political Parties* (Fawcett Society, 2002); and Sarah Childs, *New Labour's Women MPs* (Routledge, 2004).

5. Of Labour's 26 new women MPs, the 23 selected from all-women shortlists were: Helen Goodman (Bishop Auckland), Kerry McCartney (Bristol East), Kitty Ussher (Burnley), Natascha Engel (Derbyshire NE), Roberta Blackman-Woods (City of Durham), Meg Hillier (Hackney South and Shoreditch), Sharon Hodgson (Gateshead East and Washington West), Linda Riordan (Halifax), Celia Barlow (Hove), Diana Johnson (Hull North), Emily Thornberry (Islington South & Finsbury), Rosie Cooper (Lancashire West), Nia Griffith (Llanelli), Jessica Morden (Newport East), Alison Seabeck (Plymouth Devonport), Sarah McCarthy-Fry (Portsmouth North), Angela Smith (Sheffield Hillsborough), Lynda Waltho (Stourbridge), Sian James (Swansea East), Anne Snelgrove (Swindon South), Mary Creagh (Wakefield), Lyn Brown (West Ham) and Barbara Keeley (Worsley). Labour's three new women MPs selected from open shortlists were: Katy Clark (Ayrshire North & Arran), Dawn Butler (Brent South) and Meg Moon (Bridgend).
6. Andrew Lansley, *Do the Right Thing* (C-Change, 2002).
7. There is no uniformity in the counting of ethnic minority candidates. The pressure group Operation Black Vote produced a list headed 'Black Candidates' which included candidates of Anglo-Chinese and Anglo-Lebanese origin. Its totals for each party were Labour 29, Conservative 41 and Liberal Democrat 40. Other lists included candidates of Greek origin. The figures cited in this chapter are for all ethnic minority candidates, including those of Chinese, Greek, Turkish, Cypriot, as well as of African, Afro-Caribbean and South Asian origin.
8. Traditionally this table distinguishes between state secondary and public (that is, private) schools. Formerly, the term 'public school' referred to fee-paying schools listed as belonging to the Headmasters' Conference or the Girls' School Association, but for the purposes of this analysis it is now applied to all independent schools.
9. One Conservative Old Etonian, John Wilkinson, retired; two others were newly elected – Nick Hurd and Philip Dunne. One Labour Old Etonian, Tam Dalyell, retired; and one Liberal Democrat, David Rendel, was defeated.

11
Constituency Campaigning

The 2005 election was mainly a national struggle carried on by the parties through the national media, but it also contained 646 separate constituency fights that took different forms in different regions, as well as in safe and marginal seats. The Duke of Wellington's adage 'You can no more describe a battlefield than you can describe a ballroom' applies to political warfare. All candidates are constrained by the same legal rules on timing and expenses and behaviour. But some are inventive and energetic while others are despairing and idle. Local conditions vary greatly. The press tries to tell the story but journalists discover that election reporting can be extraordinarily frustrating. They know that something may be going on 'out there' but they find it very difficult to fathom. So do the candidates. Yet they are close to the ground and intensely involved. Therefore, in our efforts to portray what went on across the country, we once again rely heavily on the responses to a questionnaire sent out to a limited number of candidates of all main parties and in all regions.

The broad picture of how much of the campaign touched ordinary voters is offered by MORI's post-election poll, comparing the impact of various attempts to reach the voters in 2001 and 2005 (Table 11.1).

Despite the leaders' prominence in every news bulletin, less than half the electorate had seen them on the air and only a fifth remembered doorstep contact with any party. NOP's post-election poll (Table 11.2) offers further light on the limited penetration of the campaign.

But these tables may give a misleading picture of what happened in the campaign. The strategists at the centre were not concerned with the mass of the electorate. Their increasingly professionalised efforts were focused much more narrowly. Parties have always concentrated on the seats they hope either to win or to save from losing. But in recent years the emphasis on targeting has become much more emphatic. The British parties drew heavily on US and Australian campaigning experience, working 'under the radar' on the voters who could make the difference. Reference was often made to the overwhelming concentration of the Republican and Democratic parties on swing voters in Ohio during the 2004 US election. The last election results always show which seats are statistically most marginal and obviously there is a focus on the 100 or so which have the greatest potential for changing hands.

Table 11.1 Campaign experiences of the electorate

'*During the past few weeks, have you ...?*', (If 'Yes') '*Which party was that?*' (2001 in brackets)

	All %	Con %	Lab %	Lib Dem %
Received leaflets	89(69)	71(43)	71(40)	65(23)
Saw TV PEBs*	70(58)	58(39)	61(43)	63(28)
Saw posters	62(50)	47(31)	40(35)	26 (7)
Saw leaders on TV	46(43)	41(47)	43(32)	37(23)
Saw press advertisements	48(37)	23(48)	35(25)	37(23)
Heard radio PEBs*	20(16)	13(10)	15(10)	27(11)
Was called on by a party	21(14)	10 (6)	8 (7)	12 (7)
Received personal letter	21(12)	14 (6)	12 (6)	6 (2)
Was telephoned	7 (5)	3 (2)	3 (3)	1 (0)
Helped party	3 (3)	1 (1)	1 (1)	1 (1)
Visited party website	4 (2)	2 (1)	2 (1)	1 (0)
Used internet	7 (2)	4 (1)	5 (2)	4 (0)
Attended meeting	2 (1)	1 (0)	1 (1)	1 (1)
Received party video	3 (1)	1 (0)	2 (1)	1 (0)
Received party email	3 (1)	1 (1)	1 (1)	1 (0)

*PEBs = party election broadcasts.
Source: MORI, 5–10 May 2005.

Table 11.2 Sources of Information about the election

'*How much of your news and information about the election did you get from ...?*'

	A lot (%)	Some (%)	A little (%)	None (%)	Don't Know (%)
TV	48.0	24.1	16.1	11.4	0.4
Newspapers	22.8	25.3	20.9	30.5	0.4
Party literature	17.2	24.1	28.5	29.9	0.3
Radio	10.6	16.8	22.4	49.1	1.0
Friends, family	5.7	13.1	22.6	58.4	0.3
Internet	3.3	4.5	7.7	83.1	1.4
Magazines	1.5	5.3	9.8	82.5	0.9

Source: NOP (n=1,937).

But targeting has become ever more sophisticated. The parties are interested in identifying the particular electors who might switch sides or at least be converted from non-voting to voting. Labour and Conservative campaign organisers visited the US in the summer of 2004 to study new developments for fighting the 'ground war' and the latest 'hi-tech field ops'. Drawing heavily on the American experience, marketing experts have developed increasingly precise techniques for identifying sub-groups of potentially volatile voters. MOSAIC and other databases have been constructed which show the social characteristics of each postcode area, dividing the public into 11 social groups and 61 categories. Information about professional organisations makes it possible to identify doctors or schoolmasters or small-business men. The Conservatives imported Voter Vault and Labour developed Labour Contact.

Moreover, where constituency parties were moderately efficient, some evidence about past voting records was available (although the Data Protection Act presents an inhibition which is not always easy to evade). During the election there were complaints that, while there were 45 million citizens with votes to cast, the parties were only interested in a few seats and a few hundred thousand voters who could affect the outcome. This explains in part why many candidates said they felt neglected by their party headquarters and why commentators sometimes qualified their analysis of the national campaign by referring to the 'ground war', about which they knew little. One Conservative observed with telling precision: 'There are 7.4 million voters in the target seats but it will be 838,000 who decide the election.'

Labour targeting was naturally defensive. They had a majority of nearly 170 seats and, apart from planning the recovery of two by-election losses, there was little expectation of gaining seats. They put resources into the 107 most obviously vulnerable seats, making seven contacts with each voter and, theoretically, each contact was recorded on their database.

The Liberal Democrats were aggressive. They assumed that incumbent MPs could look after themselves (although in a few cases, notably Newbury, special help was given). In essence, they worked on their 20 or 30 best hopes. There was a special emphasis on Labour-held seats which were remotely within range: including, for example, Cambridge, where they had been 20 per cent behind in 2001. They did not choose seats on a narrow statistical basis but allowed for places where local government advances or a large student or Muslim population gave them hope.

The Conservatives faced more of a challenge. They required 85 gains to end Labour's clear majority and 158 gains for an absolute victory. Some in Central Office, including Maurice Saatchi, argued that, to be credible, they must fight on the broadest front, seeking an outright win. Others, more sceptical, wanted to focus on the seats where a real advance could be made. Several rich donors made this point. Under Duncan Smith the party selected 95 target seats, a figure Lord Saatchi increased to over 160, the number required to win the election. This was a political decision that senior organisers readily acknowledged was far too large. 'But we were stuck with it', said a senior executive at party headquarters.

A notable sceptic about the exercise was Lord Ashcroft, a former party treasurer and a millionaire donor. In 2004, aided by Stephen Gilbert (who had recently been Conservative Head of Campaigning), he set about offering funds to Conservative Constituency Associations in winnable seats if they could produce a plausible business plan on how to spend the money. Arguing that, to be effective, targeting must be planned well in advance, Lord Ashcroft liked to quote Lord Chesterfield: 'You can't fatten a pig on market day.'

Fewer than 50 constituencies took up Ashcroft's offer, and during the year before the election he spent some £2 million, giving the money unconditionally to candidates and their teams to help in their efforts to promote themselves and to contact target voters. He sponsored polls and focus groups in his chosen constituencies as well as nationally. At first Central Office was uneasy about this independent enterprise but, in due course, they became reconciled as Lord Ashcroft made his data available to them. But his emphasis on the 40 or 50 realistically winnable seats was at odds with Maurice Saatchi's approach, and in the aftermath Lord Ashcroft produced a factual, but intrinsically polemical, attack on the 2005 strategy, *Smell the Coffee: A Wake-up Call for the Conservative Party*. He wrote:

> Far from being a plucky but ultimately unsuccessful attempt to confound expectations, the Conservative targeting strategy was a disaster waiting to happen. The purpose of selecting targets is to maximise the number of seats gained with the level of resources available. The Tories scatter-gun approach produced precisely the opposite result.[1]

Lord Ashcroft claimed that in his targets the swing was greater than in other marginals – but by less than 1 per cent, and even that may give a false impression because those seats where the Associations and candidates were successful must already have shown a 'get up and go' spirit to win the funding. The Ashcroft research provided evidence that in November 2004 the Conservative candidates were being out-campaigned by the MPs they were challenging. Incumbency is a great advantage; it offers the candidate parliamentary resources and easy access to local publicity; after the dissolution that benefit dies away and the parties became almost equal in level of activity.

Lord Ashcroft's poll in 130 marginals found that the national campaign had made voters decidedly less favourable to both the main parties but more favourable to the Liberal Democrats; the impact of the local campaign was also negative for both Conservative and Labour – but less so than that of the national campaign.

The choice of targets and the allocation of money or staff was essentially a London decision. Headquarters could support professional agents. They could supply centralised low-cost printing and provide elegant copy for locally delivered leaflets or direct mail. They could also allocate time on their centralised phone banks for those who could be reached through publicly available telephone numbers. Politicians, like pollsters, face difficulties over telephone approaches because 30 per cent of people are ex-directory and many others only use mobiles. Labour had 120 callers making 2 million calls from their communications centre at Gosforth, near Newcastle-upon-Tyne. Besides systematised telephoning, much work was done there on producing and sending out by post or email well-designed literature with local adaptations. Both sides in Victoria Street claimed to have sent more and better-directed mail in the seats that mattered than in 2001.

The Conservative Party, in addition to a 40-phone facility in Victoria Street, set up a smaller-scale call centre at Coleshill Manor, near Coventry, and further outfits in Kent, the south-west and Yorkshire. One Conservative in a safe seat said: 'We did no phone canvassing but I sat by a well-advertised number for four hours a day, taking on average 20 calls each shift.' A Liberal Democrat in a tight race complained that while his party 'respected the rules against cold calling TPS [Telephone Preference Service[2]]-registered voters, the Tories did not'. But the TPS rules are ambiguous and, while all parties claimed to follow them, all complained of what others were doing. The same Liberal Democrat acknowledged the efficiency of his opponent's efforts in general, mentioning the role of Lord Ashcroft's subvention to the constituency.

The Conservatives had 120 full-time agents, mostly in safe seats. They had 26 regional organisers, paid centrally. Many marginals employed full-time workers on a short-term contract. Some of the best were recent graduates with political enthusiasm but no long-term intention of staying in a political organisation. The Labour Party had a similar number of centrally paid organisers in the field. The Liberal Democrats were employing about 100 full-timers when the campaign began.

All parties stressed the need for decentralisation and for campaigning to be done on a regional or local basis. Labour emphasised the importance of MPs being presented as specifically local champions. From the beginning of 2005 they had been sending a letter, designed and printed at the call centre, to every elector; DVDs were distributed in 60 marginals, showing the candidate speaking with local people and mentioning improvements – in particular local hospitals or schools – and with the Prime Minister seen talking about the constituency. There were serious efforts to copy the traditional Liberal Democrat style of emphasis on parish pump issues. However, there were those in Victoria Street HQ who commented wryly that in the end it was the most centralised and coordinated campaign ever. But that is the way that local campaigning is conducted on a professional basis today.

All major parties used the free post to distribute one central constituency message. Most of the election addresses were centrally printed for reasons of cost. This led to some standardisation, but there was plenty of scope for localised material expounding the candidate's views and qualification and dealing with local issues. In target seats the voter would be bombarded by up to seven pieces of hand-delivered material from each of the parties, and the numbers of contacts were monitored at the call centres.

The ever-developing internet played its part in the campaign. But it was certainly not 'an internet election'. As Table 11.2 shows, only 8 per cent of the public claimed to have paid 'a lot' or 'some' attention to politics on-line. The BBC provided much the most frequently visited website; it was seen as providing solid information and neutral comment. Channel 4's FactCheck website offered admirable verification of over 100 election claims. The parties all maintained their own sites and a few thousand regularly logged on. There was a lot of entertaining blogging as enthusiasts either set up sites to put forth their own commentaries and propaganda or posted comments on sites provided by the broadcasters and others. Over 50 candidates maintained a personal blog throughout the campaign, as did Sandra Howard. Although the internet may not have reached – let alone influenced – many voters, the parties' private intranets were enormously important in enabling daily or twice daily instant messages to every candidate with opportunities, perhaps underused, for feedback. As one Labour insider said: 'We don't reach the mass public through the internet but it does allow us to promote the three Ms: to spread our Message to our own people, to Mobilise them and to get Money out of them.'[3]

The election was probably more invisible than ever. A national poster campaign has to be spread evenly across all seats; if the posters are concentrated in marginals they have to be charged against constituency expenses. Labour had fewer posters than in 1997 or 2001. The Liberal Democrats spent about £1.5 million on advertising nationally and locally, mainly on hoardings.

Over most of the country it was hard to spot window bills or front-gate placards, let alone advertisements for public meetings. Most candidates subscribed to the view that 'public meetings are now something of the past'. One said: 'I had one – a launch meeting at the Town Hall. But only the faithful turned up.'

Such meetings as occurred were mostly poorly attended cross-party gatherings organised by churches or other local bodies. Senior frontbenchers travelled the country but, apart from media interviews, they could be used only for canvassing and enthusing the faithful. Labour strategists talked of getting direct to the people by sending ministers to shopping centres, not to elite lunches. Alan Milburn proclaimed: 'We want direct communication every day', and wherever Tony Blair travelled there was an attempt to show him talking to 'ordinary people'. But a television programme cast doubt on how 'ordinary' they were, showing how party members were systematically used to create the impression of 'real people' strongly supporting Labour.[4] There was scepticism about the efficacy of such activities on all sides. A Conservative commented:

One seriously doubted the surge of so-called VIPs who come out of the woodwork at election time – descend on constituencies they know nothing about – waste the time of the candidate and are generally unknown to the average voter, leaving after an hour or two having made no impact at all. Every party suffers from these people who think the public know them. A futile exercise.

Postal voting had some impact. The number of postal votes granted rose from 4 per cent in 2001 to 12 per cent in 2005. But the postal turnout was higher: 15 per cent of valid votes were cast by post, compared with 5 per cent in 2001. There were great variations; in eight English seats over 20,000 postal votes were issued. The highest percentages were Stevenage (45 per cent), Newcastle-upon-Tyne (45 per cent) and Rushcliffe (39 per cent); at the other extreme were 13 of the 18 seats in Northern Ireland, where more stringent conditions apply (Antrim South (1.1 per cent) came bottom). Glasgow East (3.1 per cent) was lowest in Scotland, Hull East (4.1 per cent) in England, and Ceredigion (5.5 per cent) in Wales.

Polling evidence suggests that, in contrast to a generation earlier, when the Conservatives outscored the other parties, postal votes were divided relatively proportionately between the parties. An accumulation of MORI's campaign polls suggested that intending postal voters divided 34 per cent Conservative to 38 per cent Labour and 22 per cent Liberal Democrat. However an ICM poll for the *Guardian* found that 17 per cent of their respondents claimed to have applied for a postal vote and that, of these, 45 per cent intended to vote Labour, 27 per cent Conservative and 25 per cent Liberal Democrat. The Ashcroft study, confined to 130 marginals, found that a little over 20 per cent of voters in those seats had applied to vote by post, with Liberal Democrats being slightly the most energetic in doing so.

The criticisms of the all-postal voting imposed in four regions in the 2004 European elections encouraged concern. There were repeated references to the Birmingham judge's suggestion on 5 April that current postal voting procedures were 'worthy of a banana republic'. Protests about the activities of all parties in collecting postal ballots and handing them in to the town hall were heard, and the Electoral Commission publicly deplored the practice. Local government officials and the police were alerted and were much more involved than in previous contests. But actually, it does not seem that fraud was at all widespread outside a few inner-city wards. There were no election petitions and remarkably few prosecutions. However, the fact that many people had already posted their votes before the end of April did affect the tempo of the campaign.

Attitudes to party headquarters varied widely. One Labour MP complained that the headquarters' emails contained 'No useful campaigning ideas – no suggestions of how to tie in local with national themes – just a lot of petty debating points.' But one Conservative reported that the campaign was 'more focused and efficient, protective and supportive than any I have known. We had our money's worth from Central Office.' Another said that Conservative messages from headquarters made no impact. 'We ignored them wrong in tone and wrong in emphasis.' But candidates in marginal seats paid much warmer tributes to headquarters' back-up activities, and this reflected the concentration of HQ activities.

Although there was a greater policy divide between Labour and the Liberal Democrats than in 2001, there were still plenty of informal efforts to exchange votes where it could make a difference. There were websites such as <www.tacticalvoter.net> designed to help the troubled citizen to assess the local situation and to facilitate contacts with the like-minded. There also were constituencies in which a party with no hope of winning ran a token campaign. The most extreme example seems to have been in New Forest East, where the Labour candidate explicitly recommended support for the Liberal Democrat who was seeking to oust the Conservative, Julian Lewis. It appears that this effort backfired in a similar way to the Liberal Democrats' decapitation strategy aimed at Conservative frontbenchers: local voters were alienated.

With 70,000 voters in the average constituency, a lot of activists are needed if there is to be comprehensive personal contact. Although one candidate boasted of 1,000 helpers, very few candidates had support on that level: '80–50 less than last time'; 'about 20'; 'six real activists but 100 gave a few hours'. The average reported was 150–200, with only a slight falling off from 2001.

For many, the methods tended to be the tried and tested: 'Very traditional. No phone, all done knocking on doors. With 3,400 square miles it is difficult – but it works!' A few candidates stressed the increase in the use of telephone banks and direct mail. Some candidates seemed unaware of the extent of centralised campaigning with headquarters preparing material and making direct contact with voters by email, by post and by telephone. At least in constituencies running serious campaigns, computers were used to mark up the electoral register and print sticky labels, as well as to monitor campaign activities. With party workers in short supply, envelope-stuffing machines were sometimes in evidence. It was noted that volunteer workers were much better adapted to the new technologies than in 2001, and accepted the disciplines of segmenting the campaign to identified groupings. A veteran Labour candidate spoke for many when he wrote:

> Canvassing gets less every election as the limbs of an ageing party (and candidate) stiffen and our numbers shrink. But you must distinguish between canvassing which is to put the case and is used to get ID information about the voters and canvassing which is leafleting where the candidate and a small band race down the street, speaking friendlily to anyone who passes, putting leaflets in every letter box and dashing believing that word will spread that the candidate has been there. The first kind of canvassing needs a lot of manpower and only makes sense if you are organised to put on a full polling day operation, knocking up non-voters – and we were only organised to do that in one ward.

Reporting their canvassing encounters, candidates stressed the prominence of immigration as an issue and noted how little was said about Europe. Worries about the local school or the local hospital came up much more than the headline national issues. Some mentioned Iraq; but others in the Midlands noted its absence, at least until Lord Goldsmith's advice was published in the last week. Candidates of all parties commented on the hostility to Blair. Phrases such as 'loathing' and 'damaged goods' recurred. 'We are getting hammered on the streets', commented one Labour strategist. Yet two-thirds of Conservative respondents to our questionnaires also commented critically on their own leader, 'All Howard and no team; a basic error.' There was unhappiness about Michael Howard calling Blair a 'liar': 'a mistake – made us look nasty'. Conservatives could make play with the absence of references to the Prime Minister in Labour leaflets, but Michael Howard was almost equally missing from Conservative posters and local literature. A senior Liberal Democrat put it pithily: 'Blair discredited; Howard disliked; Kennedy not "Prime Ministerial".'

Direct mail has become increasingly targeted and personalised. The greater central resources at the disposal of the Labour and Conservative parties enabled them to add a local flavour to their messages – to a greater extent than the Liberal Democrats. Conservative mail concentrated on their five themes, and used the local press for messages with a local angle. The most successful (in terms of eliciting replies from voters) was the pledge to cut council tax for pensioners, and candidates regarded the attack on Liberal Democrat proposals for a local income tax as effective. Research into local leaflets by Justin Fisher for the Joseph Rowntree Reform Trust provides some support for Michael Howard's contention that it was the media not the party which was obsessed with immigration. As a topic it featured in party leaflets fewer times than education, pensions, health and crime. Labour claimed to have sent out 10 million items of direct mail from its call centre in Gosforth. Its themes of 'Britain Forward Not Back' and 'If You Value It Vote For It' were used in direct mail to target voters about schools, pensions, hospitals, and so on. The two main parties also used direct mail to attack Liberal Democrat policies on crime and drugs.

Constituency campaigning is changing rapidly, decaying in most places yet becoming more sophisticated and targeted in marginal seats. One senior figure at the centre claimed that 2005 was 'a radically different campaign' with a new-style professionalism, micromanaged from the centre to reach, unobtrusively, a minority of voters in a minority of seats. The national campaign may have shaped voters' perceptions of the parties, but targeting was about getting supporters to vote on polling day. To judge by the evidence set out in Appendix 2, and indeed by Lord Ashcroft, its effectiveness may have been limited. Turnout stayed low and the variations in swing were mostly small. Perhaps, since on the whole parties were targeting the same seats, their efforts were mutually cancelling. The Conservative Party certainly concentrated on too broad a front of seats; mass targeting was a contradiction in terms.

Notes

1. Michael Ashcroft, *Smell the Coffee: A Wake-up Call for the Conservative Party* (London: Michael Ashcroft, 2005), p. 100.
2. Companies involved in direct selling are not permitted to call people who have registered with the TPS.
3. For a full commentary, see S. Coleman and S. Ward (eds), *Spinning the Web: Online Campaigning in the 2005 General Election* (Hansard Society, July 2005).
4. See Gaby Hinsliff, 'How Labour Used its Election Troops to Fake Popular Support', *Observer*, 3 May 2005, and above, pp. 106–7.

12
The Campaign Reassessed

Recent general election campaigns have gained a bad press and 2005 was no exception. The tabloids complained that it was dreary and the broadsheets that it was either trivial or nasty or both. The published polls showed little movement in the parties' support, apart from a late rise by the Liberal Democrats. YouGov found that over the four weeks of the campaign as many as a quarter of the electorate changed its voting intention but no party made a net gain. A Labour victory was never in doubt, although the size of the majority was. As we showed in Chapters 8 and 9, the tabloids reduced their coverage – partly out of editorial choice and partly because of the absence of what they regarded as memorable events; the Pope's death and funeral, and the royal wedding were rivals for coverage.

A theme running through the feedback from target voters across the three main parties was the mood of 'better the devil you know' and 'stick with what we've got', a compound of disillusion with Labour and Blair and an unwillingness to change to the Conservatives and Howard. Many voters seemed to be assessing the balance between the risk of the Conservatives returning and a desire to punish Labour. Reports on voters spoke of cynicism and distrust of all politicians, anger over immigration and asylum and disappointment with Labour's failure to deliver on public services and crime. The campaign did not reverse such well-established signs of apathy as low turnout, voter disengagement and the turning away from the main political parties. In a post-election briefing note about the public mood, Philip Gould wrote:

> They felt cut out, bored, detached and disempowered. They did not believe what politicians said and did not trust their motivations. The election just washed over them, leaving them more cynical than ever.

If there was one thing I would draw from this election it is this: people are switching off from politics.[1]

But after the 2001 general election the politicians had promised something different next time. Voter apathy became a staple of media comment and a research project for academics and the newly established Electoral Commission. Politicians across all parties spoke of their intention to listen to voters more, to be more interactive, to abandon top-down politics and to be more localist (using the local media and stressing local issues through personalised messages, the internet and local candidates). They would also cut back on the use of the battle bus and the early morning London press conferences; mechanisms that, they claimed, allowed the Metropolitan journalists to 'hijack' the election with their agendas. Instead, politicians would have more contact with 'real' voters and the regional and local media. This happened to a limited extent. But the one innovation that might have stimulated interest – a party leaders' debate – was vetoed by Tony Blair, as previous front-runners in elections have always done.

A nightmare election. (Blair (left) and Prescott (right).)

(Steve Bell, *Guardian*, 6 May 2005)

There was certainly less spontaneous contact between the leaders and the voters than in previous elections. Rallies and visits were staged before invited audiences and, more than ever, were geared to generating favourable pictures for press and television. A veteran Labour MP reported in response to our questionnaire: 'I've never known a campaign where the disconnect between national and local was so total. I wondered at times whether the rest of the country was having an election. Or was it just us?' Reporters took to writing about the almost secretive unveiling of a poster and the leader's one-minute speech, all for the cameras; they pointed out that Labour officials shielded Blair from journalists' questions and that the 'ordinary voters' he was supposed to address or mingle with were often vetted party workers or supporters who provided an enthusiastic 'backfill' for the cameras. In *The Times*, Ben Macintyre wrote; 'I doubt that Tony Blair met a single unvetted voter.'[2] If so, it was not a total success: Blair met and was abused by voters in the street and in the television studios. A Labour MP commented: 'I think a sensible party should have sent Blair to commune with the voters of my constituency and left the national job to me. I'd have done it so much better and given us a good programme to govern while he'd have learnt something.' Candidates also regretted the lack of personal contact. Some part of this reaction stemmed from resentment, particularly in non-marginal seats, of feeling bypassed by party headquarters and by the national media, and of being largely ignored by voters.

Of course growing concern over security, particularly since 9/11, has imposed limits on voters' access to their political leaders. But party managers, with memories of John Prescott's punch and Blair's embarrassing encounter outside a Birmingham hospital with Sharron Storer in 2001 – who complained in front of the nation's media about the delays in the treatment of her husband's cancer – also feared that contact with the public might be unpredictable or even troublesome. A memorable incident in the 2005 campaign was a television audience's questioning of Tony Blair about problems in booking appointments with GPs; the Prime Minister appeared unaware of a side-effect of one of his health service targets (see p. 109). Conservatives and Labour people complained about the other side's personalised campaigning, Liberal Democrats about both Labour and the Conservatives, and both Labour and Liberal Democrats about Conservative negativism on immigration and asylum and introducing tactics of 'dog-whistling' and 'grievance politics'.

The parties may have had exciting plans for reshaping the political agenda, but it was hard to discern a great clash of ideas. Blair's manifesto was New Labour in its policies but the themes of choice and diversity were muted in the campaign. The Conservative advocacy of a smaller state was lost as the party's pledges involved an increasing role for central government and a promise of a significant increase in state spending, although not as large as Labour's. Over the following five years the Conservatives were planning to increase state spending by 4 per cent per annum, Labour by 5 per cent. In many areas (see pp. 62–3), there was convergence between Conservative and Labour. The two main parties stuck to their battlegrounds, the economy and spending on services for Labour and public safety and security issues for the Conservatives – immigration, asylum, crime, school discipline. And complex issues affecting the EU, transport, local government finance, pensions (except for David Willetts on the Conservative side) and energy were virtually off-limit.

The Conservatives

The Conservatives took pride in running a disciplined campaign and maintaining their morale to the end, and gave credit for both to Lynton Crosby. 'He took over a bad hand but played it well', wrote a disaffected frontbencher. The result could be and was seen either as a stage on the road to recovery or, for the pessimists, another bad defeat. Seats were gained but vote share hardly improved. Targeting helped the party to capture seats from Liberal Democrats, in spite of a fall in vote share; indeed, in 25 of the 33 seats gained, the party's percentage actually fell. But overall, it was hardly successful. Lord Ashcroft said that the party's resources were spread too thinly across 164 seats, which he dismissed as 'a scatter-gun approach'. The party certainly motivated its core support. Questioned by YouGov about the importance of the election to the future of the UK, 66 per cent of Conservatives rated it 'very' or 'extremely important', compared to only 51 per cent of Labour voters and 47 per cent of Liberal Democrats.

Pessimists noted that Conservative gains were largely in the South East of England, the share of vote hardly changed, and the party was down a million votes on its catastrophic defeat in 1997. The party continued to trail Labour badly on the key issues of the economy, health and education and failed to broaden its position from its long-standing strengths on crime and immigration – or to break out of its traditional southern English heartland. Over succeeding days the sense of disappointment among modernising Conservative Shadow ministers increased. Typical remarks were 'terrible', 'a wasted eight years', 'a disgraceful result considering that Labour was there for the taking', and 'Labour was seen to have failed but we did not persuade people to make the change'. Another said:

'We got their attention but what they saw they did not like.' But even senior figures on the right muttered about the lack of vision or genuine alternative to Labour; they had wanted more on tax cuts and hostility to Europe.

Michael Howard was Michael Howard, for good and ill. Labour regarded him as a bonus and they had targeted him in the 2004 European election campaign. In 2005 they again attacked him in their posters and advertisements. He carried his party's message to a greater extent than Blair carried Labour's and more than virtually any other party leader had done in any recent election. Blair and Kennedy did not overshadow their colleagues to the same degree that they had in 2001, but Howard dominated his party's coverage to a greater extent than William Hague had in 2001. Across the terrestrial television channels and Radio 4, Blair was quoted in a ratio of 4.5 to 1 over Gordon Brown, Kennedy in a ratio of 7 to 1 to his next prominent colleague Menzies Campbell, but Howard in a ratio of 13 to 1 over his nearest colleague Liam Fox (see p. 105). But in the press Blair dominated – the papers not so much carrying his messages as discussing him, and often his problems – and against Labour's wishes.

Other secondary Shadow ministers like David Davis and Oliver Letwin played a modest role, albeit they were defending marginal seats; but John Redwood, Michael Ancram and Tim Yeo – let alone previous party leaders like John Major, William Hague and Iain Duncan Smith – hardly registered at all. Opinion polls during the Parliament had shown that most of the Shadow Cabinet were unknown to the public and the campaign was a missed opportunity to change that, although Andrew Lansley, George Osborne (in lieu of Letwin who had come across poorly in focus groups) and David Cameron took the opportunity to shine.

Many party candidates admitted that Michael Howard was a weakness for the party and a number expressed unhappiness over his calling Blair a liar. Typical of the responses were:

- 'Calling Blair a liar was mistake'
- 'I indicated I did not think it was right to call Blair a liar'
- 'Towards the end of the campaign I picked up some hostility to MH's decision to call Blair a liar. Whether it was statistically significant is another matter'
- 'Made us look nasty. Caused me a real problem. BUT campaign was very professional, no leaks, good literature'
- 'It created controversy and was therefore a loser for us'.

YouGov found that while Blair and Kennedy improved their ratings by 3 per cent over the campaign on the question of who would make 'the best Prime Minister', Howard's rating fell by 1 per cent. When voters were asked to choose between a government led by Blair and one led by Howard, Blair's initial lead of 12 per cent increased to 19 per cent by the end of the campaign. A Harris poll found that only 49 per cent of Conservatives would vote for their leader if the election were about choosing a Prime Minister, while 64 per cent of Labour and 59 per cent of Liberal Democrats would vote for their respective party leaders. Howard's admirers hoped that his competence and experience would more than compensate for his perceived lack of charisma and warmth. Among voters it did not.

A dilemma for the Conservatives was that the more successfully they campaigned and the more likely a hung Parliament became, so it might stimulate floating Labour voters to turn out. A post-election survey by Populus for Lord Ashcroft commented: 'the closer to polling day people made their decision, the less likely they were to vote Tory'.[3] And the more Conservative attacks on Labour struck home, so disillusioned Labour supporters might switch to the Liberal Democrats. A party pollster spoke of the swing voters' dislike of Blair, but added: 'Once they get a sniff of the Conservatives coming back, they say, "I'm going to vote".' Some commentators detected a counter to this in Howard's mid-campaign appeals to voters to 'Send Mr Blair a message' and to 'wipe the smile off his face', seemed designed primarily to stop Labour winning a substantial majority. Labour publicists warned journalists of Lynton Crosby's so-called 'Queensland gambit', referring to a 1995 state election in Queensland, when the conservative coalition – responding to private polling data that voters did not want to dismiss the state Labour administration but just teach it a lesson – concentrated its message on the theme 'Put Labour under pressure': a strategy which led to a surprise victory for the coalition.

Howard and Crosby were dismissive of complaints that a tax and immigration campaign (a characterisation they disputed) was a core vote strategy, like William Hague's tax and euro appeal in 2001. Crosby's remit was to win the election. In an interview, he said:

The reason we went for 163 target seats is because we wanted to win. The issues we fought on were chosen from numerous interviews with target voters in the target seats to enable us to win the election.

Some party strategists were dismissive of Lord Ashcroft's plan to concentrate resources on 50 winnable seats. 'That is a strategy for losing. How can we inspire our troops with that?' said one. The most important issues for Conservative voters, according to YouGov, were immigration and asylum (mentioned by 63 per cent), crime (42 per cent) and tax (38 per cent). Labour's battleground was health (60 per cent), the economy (54 per cent) and education (37 per cent). The battlegrounds for the two main parties had not changed much over three successive general elections. But whereas Labour's three issues rose in salience (between 3 per cent and 8 per cent) over the campaign, the Conservative issues declined (between 3 per cent and 6 per cent). It was only the rise in salience of Iraq in the latter stages that, according to YouGov, qualified Labour's success in the battle of the agenda.

Lynton Crosby and Michael Howard found no appetite among voters for bigger tax cuts, as demanded by the party's right wing. As the leader stated in his post-election Centre for Policy Studies lecture, voters did not believe promises of tax cuts, while they feared that cuts would mean reduced spending on public services.[4] He and Oliver Letwin believed that their targeted and modest cuts were more credible than a general reduction in income tax rates. But the modest scale of the proposed tax reductions and a programme that would increase spending, although by less than Labour's plans, meant that for the second successive election the Conservatives had effectively ceded the tax and spending debate to Labour. MORI (*Financial Times*, 19 April) reported that by 41 per cent to 30 per cent, Labour was more trusted to spend money wisely on public services. Moreover, if 80 per cent expected a future Labour government to increase taxes, 67 per cent expected the same of a future Conservative government.

Immigration was the one issue on which the Conservative Party had a commanding lead, but it was never intended to be as dominant in the campaign as it became. Although the party held only one press conference on immigration and more were held on pensions, education and health, and the same balance applied to the direct mail themes in the constituencies (see p. 177), the media chose to discuss it at length. A former party leader commented that 'concentration on immigration did not swing voters', and a Shadow minister spoke of it not attracting liberal-minded Conservatives. But Labour's research in marginal seats from late 2003 frequently registered concern on immigration and complaints that the Government had been negligent.

Several target voters from all parties regarded immigration as a symbol of many failings – social decay, the running down of the NHS, the abuse of the benefits system, the lack of social control and the country going in the wrong direction. The Labour pollster Stan Greenberg thought that the Tory slogan 'Are You Thinking What We're Thinking?' was effective because many people resented feeling that they were not being allowed to talk about the issue. In an interview, he said:

> The strategy was working and the Conservatives should've presented themselves as defending people who played by the rules. Instead Howard moved onto a mean-spirited attack on targets like gypsies. They should've made a bigger statement on the basis of immigration about how government could help ordinary people. Their slogan should've been 'A government for playing by the rules'.

The Conservatives may have set the media agenda with the issue (see Chapters 8 and 9), but may already have gained what votes they could from it. In the penultimate week Michael Howard announced that his campaign was changing tack, perhaps in response to pressure from David Cameron who argued that the issue was taking attention away from other Conservative policies. The party aborted a plan to raise the issue of how reunions of families from the Indian subcontinent were being exploited to abuse the immigration system. After polling day both Howard and Crosby privately expressed regret that they had not stuck to the original plan.

No doubt the journalists contributed to making immigration a high-profile theme – the most covered issue in the national press – by raising it so often at press conferences and broadcast interviews. But following William Hague's experience of how the media reported his 2001 campaign, this should have been anticipated. A Shadow minister who agreed that the party had to raise the immigration issue, added, in an interview with the authors: 'But we should have seen the risks. You can't blame the media. You have to realise how they will play it and what noise the racist and anti-racist lobbies will make. They lit the blue touch-paper.' Certainly some Conservative candidates were unhappy at the effect of the combination of the media focus on immigration and Howard's high profile. But Howard was defiant: 'If we had not discussed this important issue people would have demanded to know why and I would have been failing in my duty', he said.

Immigration could not beat the economy. When Populus studied voters who thought that Labour were best for managing the economy and that the Conservatives were best on immigration, the voting intentions split Labour 48 per cent, Conservatives 16 per cent and Liberal Democrats 26 per cent. Conceding the economy to Labour was a major failing. A key figure in the campaign headquarters said:

We let Gordon Brown off too lightly. He got away with too much in the first term. We could not undermine Labour in just four months. We should've been hammering away at stealth taxes, debt and lack of competitiveness, the downside of Brown.

One closely associated with the Conservative polling said: 'We had the right issues, the ones that bothered voters. But the economy trumped everything. Gordon Brown has got away with the perception that it is well run, even though individuals do not feel better off.'

Although Howard had used the term 'liar' some months before, its impact was magnified during the election campaign. The strategist in campaign headquarters quoted above was unrepentant: 'Character is important and we had to deal with it, and the focus groups said nothing about the liar charge. As ever, it was when it was picked up by the media that it became a problem.' The poster accusing Blair of being a liar had been designed to head off expected Labour attacks on Conservative spending 'cuts' on public services (see p. 79). The recommendation by Howard's advisers to run it on 26 April was taken when Iraq was dominating the agenda. Although it attracted great media interest, there was no increase in Conservative support. Private polling had earlier warned against raising the 'liar' charge and Howard, while accepting responsibility for the statement, was not made aware of the research.

Perhaps Howard could have used different language, as in Parliament, or allowed another frontbench spokesman to make the charge. According to George Osborne, in his review of the 2004 Bush campaign: 'character attacks on his [Bush's] opponent almost never came from the President's own lips. They came out anonymously in TV ads or by e-mail from the campaign's HQ. Mr Bush has gone out of his way praise John Kerry's record in Vietnam, even as his campaign tears it apart.'[5] For all Blair's poor ratings on trust he still led the Conservative leader on most leader attributes, according to the polls. A party pollster said: 'People thought Blair was a liar, but they think this of most politicians and Howard's trust rating was no higher than Blair's anyway.'

Conservative modernisers believed that the party's progress had to be measured more in improved perceptions of the party than in gains in seats and votes, welcome though these would be. For them the party, doomed to certain defeat in 2005, had to position itself for a longer-term recovery, demonstrate that it could reach out beyond its core vote and improve its image. This did not happen. Many negative attributes were still associated with the party. It trailed Labour on favourable attributes but led it on unfavourable ones, often by decisive margins (see Table

Table 12.1   Party images

'Irrespective of how you intend to vote (or have already voted by post), which of the following statements do you think apply more to the Conservative Party and which apply more to the Labour Party?'

	Applies more to …			Don't know	Lab minus Con (%)
	Con (%)	Lab (%)	Both/neither		
It seems to have succeeded in moving on and left its past behind it	17	42	24	17	25
Its leaders are prepared to take tough and unpopular decisions	19	42	28	11	23
Even if I don't always agree with it, at least its heart is in the right place	22	40	22	17	18
It is led by people of real ability	19	36	34	12	17
The kind of society it wants is broadly the kind of society I want	33	40	19	8	7
It seems to chop and change all the time: you can never be quite sure what it stands for	35	26	26	12	−9
It is too extreme	29	16	33	22	−13
It seems to want to divide people instead of bringing them together	41	20	25	14	−21
It seems rather old and tired	44	18	27	10	−26
It seems to appeal to one section of society rather than to the whole country	48	20	22	10	−28
It seems stuck in the past	45	11	27	17	−34
It has very little chance of winning this election	63	6	16	15	−57

Source: Populus. Fieldwork 29 April–1 May.

12.1). It was seen as stuck in the past, sectional, divisive, extreme, not having its heart in the right place and being old and tired. Post-election surveys by Populus found that potential Conservative voters were put off by what they regarded as the negativism and aggressiveness of the party's campaign.

A problem dawning on some Conservatives was that in spite of changing leaders, policies and slogans – all of which the party had done to death over the previous decade – support obstinately remained in the 31–34 per cent range. The party's image was such a handicap that it was difficult to see any strategy that could have delivered an election victory. A Populus poll found that once a relatively popular policy was identified as a Conservative one, support for it immediately fell away. Labour polling picked up a mood for change but this never translated into support for the Conservatives. The swing of the electoral pendulum or more professional campaigns would not be enough in the absence of a clear and agreed sense of direction.

Labour

Some Labour campaigners had mixed feelings about the party's campaign, perhaps mirroring the mixed nature of the result. Compared to 2001, the party lost in seats and in share of vote; it had shed 4 million votes from 1997. Its share of the total vote was 6 per cent down on 2001, the lowest for any party winning a majority of seats and only 0.2 per cent more than Neil Kinnock had gained in defeat in 1992. It was a grudging mandate.

But Labour won the election, and for an unprecedented third successive time, and its margin of victory over all parties was a comfortable 66 seats. Tony Blair, on the point of resigning in 2004 and damaged by taking the country into an unpopular war, deserves credit for his political comeback. He had become the greatest election winner in the party's history.

The outcome seemed to reflect the overwhelming message of private and public surveys. Voters wanted Labour back but with a substantially reduced majority: 'They felt that the records of Labour and Blair did not warrant another landslide and that the Conservatives were not yet ready for government', said Philip Gould in one of his notes to Blair. A narrowly defeated female Labour MP reflected that the remarks of a lapsed Labour supporter spoke for many: 'We wanted Labour back but with a smaller majority and your loss is part of the price.' 'And I voted against the war and wanted Gordon to take over from Tony', the former MP added.

Much of Labour's campaign had been decided late in the day, a consequence of the last-minute agreement of Blair and Brown to share the limelight. The two men in effect decided the line for the day at a 7 o'clock meeting each morning. If the manifesto was Blair's, the campaign message was Brown's. Contrary to Blair's intentions during the previous autumn, Labour's main dividing line was over the economy – the Government's record on inflation, interest rates, economic growth and investment in public services. Health, education and plans for increasing choice and diversity – the Blair agenda – were supportive but less robust themes. A central figure in headquarters thought that the campaign had been 'like flying by the seat of our pants', and that no one person appeared to be in charge. 'It was difficult to see who was coordinating and people just got on with their jobs.'

Though never as single-issue-oriented as the Conservatives had been over income tax in 1992, Labour hammered its own record on the economy. 'Do not risk going back' to the boom and bust and high levels of inflation and interest rates when the Conservatives were last in office, was the party's message. The economy featured relentlessly on posters and advertisements. Brown's high profile reinforced the economic message as well as reminding hesitant Labour voters that they were voting not for Blair alone. Of Labour's press conferences, four were on health, five on education and eleven on the economy, including business, globalisation and world poverty. Party polling showed that the main reason Labour identifiers remained loyal was the economy – 38 per cent mentioned that as the reason for staying with Labour.

Nationally, the party showed much less 'message discipline' than in the two previous general elections and probably less than the Conservatives. In a memo (17 April), Mark Penn complained of 'Sound-bite confusion: currently there seem to be several stories and several sound-bites every day.' A good illustration of the lack of coordination was seen in the events following Tony Blair's speech on Saturday 23 April when he warned lukewarm Labour supporters not to take victory for granted. The same day Alastair Campbell leaked his memo to the *Sunday Times* which misleadingly reported it on 24 April as triumphant (headlined on the front page, 'WE'RE HOME AND DRY'), and two days later Alan Milburn, in part to counter the report of the Campbell memo, released to the *Guardian* internal Labour Party reports warning that a number of Labour marginal seats were at risk: 'Private poll reveals Labour fears. Neck and neck in key marginals', was the front-page headline on 27 April. There was widespread disdain for the party's six pledges, for being too wordy and too bland, and, although revised during the campaign to make them more specific, they were not much used.

Voters, helped by the media, confounded Labour hopes that Iraq was water under the bridge and that any damage had already been incurred. In the last ten days of the campaign the revival of the question of the legality of the case for the war reinforced doubts about Blair's trustworthiness. 'We have lost the best part of five campaigning days because of Iraq', said one strategist. Labour's release of the full version of the Attorney-General's leaked memorandum was a forlorn attempt to close down the issue. 'We

have to get people off Iraq and onto the economy; we have two ⌣ ..
do this. This requires us to be tough with the Conservatives' (Report from
a focus group held on 30 April). There was a clear disjunction between
the voters' and the media's interest in Iraq. On the day the election was
announced, YouGov found that voters ranked Iraq 11th out of 12 issues,
and even by the end of the campaign, only joint 8th out of 12. But Iraq
was the second most covered topic on the press front pages and editorials
and the first for the broadcasters. Labour pollsters reckoned they lost
between 2 per cent and 3 per cent of their vote in the last week, largely
to the Liberal Democrats because of Iraq. An election-day poll for Sky
News found that one in four Liberal Democrat voters said they would
have voted Labour 'but did not do so because of Iraq'. YouGov found
that 15 per cent of identifiers with Labour voted Lib Dem, often because
of Iraq. Perhaps the concentration in the last week on 'Don't let the
Conservatives in by the back door' resulted in the party overlooking the
Liberal Democrats. Although Labour had attacked the Liberal Democrats
on crime and drugs with direct mail locally, the first national attack by
Blair came only two days before polling day.

But Iraq and distrust of Blair did not help the Conservatives, as it might
have done in the predominantly two-party system of a generation ago;
the party had supported the war. Populus found that of those who lost
trust in Blair over Iraq, 30 per cent would still vote Labour, 28 per cent
Liberal Democrat and only 25 per cent Conservative.

Tony Blair remained his party's chief standard-bearer, but he quickly
realised that he was no longer the asset he had once been. Reporters
observing the interaction between Blair and Brown on the campaign
trail claimed to notice, as did some senior staff in party headquarters,
Blair's deference to the Chancellor and the latter's solicitude for the
Prime Minister. An insider said that he was aware of a metaphorical
transfer of power from Blair to Brown during the campaign. But the
combination of the two men was effective, with Brown appealing more
to party supporters and Blair to Middle England. In spite of the control
party officials exercised over Blair's tour, he found the campaign tiring,
partly because of the highly personalised and hostile questions from
voters in the television studios, but more so because of a slipped disc.

Some Labour candidates kept their distance from Blair, although for
the most part these were the predictable critics. But even supporters of
the Prime Minister openly admitted that Gordon Brown would have
produced a more substantial Labour victory. 'Iraq and Blair (and they
were inseparable) were a millstone around our necks', said one Labour
candidate in a marginal seat. But high-profile Labour critics of both the

war and of Blair – like Clare Short and Frank Dobson – also suffered heavy swings against them. Although there are some campaign appearances a party leader cannot delegate, and Blair appeared at all of the televised press conferences and set-piece television interviews, he was less prominent on television and radio compared to 1997 and 2001, and shared the spotlight more with colleagues than either Howard or Kennedy (see Chapter 8).

Yet for all the external and internal criticism, Labour led on the measures of campaigning strength. YouGov found that Labour was ahead of the Conservatives on 14 of 18 issues and increased its lead on many of them during the campaign. By the end of the campaign Labour led on the key issues of the economy by 22 per cent, the NHS by 13 per cent and education and schools by 7 per cent. Labour also reduced its deficits to the Conservatives on tax, immigration and law and order. Labour's seven large private polls during the campaign found a slight weakening in its rating on a number of issues and attributes, but an increase in its lead over the Conservatives, because of the decline in that party's standing. These figures give rise to a paradox. Labour may have lost the media agenda because of the prominence (see Chapters 8 and 9) of Iraq, Blair and immigration/asylum. As Maggie Scammell and Martin Harrop claim in Chapter 9, 'Overall, the press agenda came far closer to the Tory wish-list than to Labour's.' But, in spite of this unfavourable terrain, it appears to have comprehensively won the campaign agenda, measured by surveys of the major concerns of voters. The Conservatives, on the other hand, appear to have won the media agenda but lost the campaign.

The Liberal Democrats

The Liberal Democrats emerged with an increase of ten seats and 3.7 per cent in votes. No doubt the party attracted its usual share of protest voters and those who wanted to express a plague on both Tory and Labour houses. But there were now positive reasons for voting for it because of its distinctive positions, favouring increasing income tax, ending tuition fees and opposing the Iraq war. It gained from the last two, though they are hardly likely to be key factors at the next general election. The party also invested more heavily than before in press and poster advertising and opinion polling, doubling its total spend compared to 2001.

A consequence is that the party has established its identity to the left of the Labour party. It gained voters disillusioned with Labour and its policies were clearly designed to appeal to public service professionals, students, the elderly and war protesters. Perhaps because of its new positioning it lost a net three seats to Conservatives. A YouGov survey asking voters to place themselves on a left–right scale confirmed the nature of the party's support. Among Liberal Democrats, 43 per cent placed themselves left of centre; among Labour supporters, 44 per cent did; but among Conservatives, only 7 per cent did. YouGov also found that Lib Dem supporters ranked health (40 per cent), education (33 per cent) and Iraq (33 per cent) as the main issues affecting their vote. Except for the last, the profile matched that of Labour voters. The question remained: when the Liberal Democrats claim they are the real alternative, is it to the Conservatives, or Labour, or both?

Should the Liberal Democrats have done even better, given the problems of the other two parties and the media interest in Iraq? In response to our survey, candidates said they had not been helped by policies on local income tax, giving prisoners the right to vote or allowing 16-year-olds to drink alcohol legally. Some strategists wondered if they needed to broaden from the focus on targeting. In the South East their vote increased by 4 per cent but they gained only one seat, whereas the Conservatives gained ten seats for an extra 0.5 per cent of the vote (see pp. 197 et seq.).

Conclusion

For most people decisions about voting were decided by factors which long predated the four weeks of the campaign or even the four years of the Parliament. One therefore has to retain a sense of caution in assessing what impact on the outcome different party decisions during the campaign might have had. What if Blair had not been so ready to support President Bush over Iraq? What if he had made way for Brown during 2004? Either step would surely have increased Labour's lead. What if Howard had been more radical over tax cuts, as the right wished, or had more fully embraced the modernisers' agenda?

The YouGov surveys of the parties' images (Table 12.1) and the voters' ratings of party leaders and party policies show that approval of Labour's values and identification with the party (46 per cent) comfortably exceeded its 36 per cent share of the vote on 5 May; that approval of the Conservative Party's values was below its 33 per cent share of the vote and its share of identifiers (34 per cent), and that the Liberal Democrats' vote exceeded their share of identifiers (14 per cent). Labour could argue therefore that it won the election without getting its maximum vote out on polling day and that the Conservative Party effectively sweated its base, to use marketing terms. For much of the post-war period, Labour led the Conservatives on questions about voters' party identification but failed to get enough of its (largely working class) supporters to vote.

The Conservatives managed to overcome their handicap by getting their supporters to the polling stations. Now, however, the Conservative Party is so far behind Labour that effective organisation alone will not overcome the handicap. In a nutshell, to win next time Labour needs only to mobilise the full potential support suggested by the ratings, whereas the bigger challenge for the Conservatives is to reach out considerably beyond existing supporters, after its failure yet again to do so.

Vernon Bogdanor observed in the *Financial Times* that oppositions as well as governments can lose elections. Four of the previous six elections – 1983, 1987, 1992 and 2001 – saw the return of the Government against an unelectable opposition: elections appear to have become as much a referendum on the opposition as the government of the day, so reversing the conventional wisdom.

The low turnout and the expectations of a certain Labour victory appear to have affected the parties' fortunes differently. A post-election ICM survey found that 41 per cent of non-voters would have voted Labour and only 27 per cent Conservative, had they voted, and that nearly half of non-voters said that they did not vote because Labour was bound to win. Labour's appeal in the last few days to its unenthusiastic supporters was therefore successful enough to win the election, although many remained unmoved. There was, however, no hidden Conservative majority waiting to be mobilised.[6]

The 2005 election represented another step towards a new style or Americanisation of British campaigns. The near-term campaign (see Chapter 5) is now firmly established. Parties make greater use of new technology, particularly computers, email and the internet. They self-consciously adopt campaign strategies; recruit professionals from the polling, public relations and media industries; and focus on message development, discipline and rebuttal. Targeting has become more rigorous: this is data-driven campaigning, relying on sophisticated computer software to collect and analyse data about individual voters. If old-style campaigns were about local party activists mobilising their party's loyal supporters on polling day, targeting is about cultivating those who will vote but are yet to decide which party to vote for. Not all voters or seats are equal when it comes to the allocation of party resources.

Many commentators admitted that 2005 was a difficult election to interpret. They could follow the national campaign but knew little of the 'ground war' fought by the parties in their target seats. Party managers claimed that national opinion polls were not an accurate guide to what was going on in these 100–150 seats where the election would be decided. Party managers, aware of the decline in the number of party activists in the constituencies, increasingly used professional staff at various centres to direct 'local' operations.

The Labour and Conservative parties certainly drew to a greater extent than ever before on campaign methods from other countries and were willing to import campaign expertise. Campaign specialists from the US Democratic party were a notable presence in the Labour campaign, and the Conservatives had an Australian as their key strategist and imported from down under 'dog-whistle' tactics and a 'Queensland gambit'.

Finally, because of a greater fragmentation of political choice, it has become more difficult to talk about a 'national' election result. Party strategies have to take account of different local political circumstances; national political messages are less useful. Within the Labour and Conservative camps there was some concern, although Liberal Democrat satisfaction, about the shift from a two-dimensional to the three-dimensional political environment. After the election, Labour and Conservative acknowledged their limited success in coping with tactical voting.

Notes

1. Philip Gould, private memo.
2. See *Dispatches: The Dirty Tricks Election*, Channel 4, 23 May, and Patrick Barkham et al., 'Stage-Managed Rings of Confidence', *Guardian*, 5 May 2005.
3. Michael Ashcroft, *Smell the Coffee: A Wake-up Call for the Conservative Party* (London: Michael Ashcroft, 2005), p. 89.
4. See Michael Howard's post-election analysis, 'Reflections on the Election: Tax', CPS lecture, 27 June 2005.
5. 'Bush's Lesson for the Tories', *The Times*, 31 August 2004.
6. See P. Kellner, 'Clearing the Fog. What Really happened in the 2005 Election Campaign', *Political Quarterly*, October 2005.

13
Conclusion

On 6 May 2005, Tony Blair stood outside Number 10 and said: 'I have listened and I have learnt. And I think I have a very clear idea of what the British people now expect from this government for a third term.' The ideas he mentioned bore an uncanny resemblance to the points that the Conservative Party had emphasised during the election. He was a more subdued Prime Minister compared to the one who had stood outside Number 10 following the 1997 and 2001 elections. The front page of *The Times* was headlined 'BLAIR LIMPS BACK' and the *Guardian* declared: 'TIME IS RUNNING OUT'. The front cover of *The Economist* depicted Blair with the headline 'OUCH!' Its verdict was that voters appeared to want a result that punished Tony Blair in a way that would not produce a Conservative return to power, and they got it.

In the early hours of 6 May Michael Howard announced his resignation as party leader, the third successive Conservative leader to resign on the morrow of a general election defeat. He added that his resignation would take effect once the party's rules for electing his successor had been revised. The Conservative leader also claimed that his campaign and the result had 'Sent Mr Blair a message'.

All three parties had some reasons to be pleased. Tony Blair had led his party to a third historic victory. He had made a remarkable political comeback from his troubles in 2004 and achieved a clear working majority. Iraq had damaged him but without helping the Conservatives. Michael Howard could point to the net gain of 33 seats and claim that the party was on the road to recovery. The Liberal Democrats achieved the largest number of seats for a third party in over 80 years and their best vote since they were formed in 1988.

But the three party leaders also had reason to be disappointed. Tony Blair had received a substantial rebuff – the Labour Party had lost 6 per cent of their vote since 2001 and they were forming a government with the lowest vote share ever; there were many reports of the voters' disillusion with the Government's record and distrust of the Prime Minister. It was no wonder that the party had not wanted to make the election into a referendum on its record and its leader.

The Conservatives were chastened that the gain of seats was achieved with a negligible increase (0.5 per cent) in vote share and little progress in recovering from long-standing weaknesses in the North and in the major cities. The party's image had not improved. It remained marooned around the 33 per cent share of the electorate it had had for the last ten years.

For the Liberal Democrats, satisfaction soon gave way to a suspicion that they could and should have done better faced with two unpopular parties. Their net gain of ten seats was what a uniform swing would have produced. Senior figures wondered if the party needed a more persuasive national campaign to complement the well-established targeting with its focus on local campaigning. This had gained 26 seats in 1997, but only six in the 2001 and ten in 2005, and there was disappointment in the number of targets won.[1]

In Scotland Labour fell from 56 to 41 seats, a loss due largely to a reduction in the number of seats from 72 to 59. The SNP increased its seats from five to six, but its vote of 17.7 per cent was its lowest since 1987. In Scotland and Wales, the nationalists again fared worse in Westminster than in devolution elections.

Politics in Northern Ireland, as ever, took a different direction: the main interest lay in which party would win the battles within each of the two communities. Most notable was the decline of the once-dominant Unionist Party; the defeat of David Trimble, the former First Minister of the power-sharing Executive; and the rise of Ian Paisley's DUP (with a gain of four seats) as the major voice for the Protestant population.

Table 13.1 shows that the social class divide is perhaps weaker than ever when it comes to voting. The Conservative share of the A/B (or professional middle class) vote continued to decline; its lead of 32 per cent over Labour in 1992 among A/B voters fell to 9 per cent in 2005, according to MORI. There is perhaps no more striking measure of how New Labour, even when its vote share fell, has managed to capture a large part of what had been the Conservative core vote. The Conservatives continued to lead among the over-65s, but were seriously behind Labour among the young and the middle-aged.

Table 13.1 Voting and demography, 2005

		Vote 2005					Change since 2001				Turnout	
		Con	Lab	Lib Dem	Oth	Lab Lead	Con	Lab	Lib Dem	Swing	2005	Change
		(%)	(%)	(%)	(%)	(%)					(%)	
All		33	36	23	8	3	0	–6	4	3	61	2
Gender	Men	34	34	22	10	*	2	–8	4	5	62	1
	Women	32	38	23	7	6	–1	–4	4	1.5	61	3
Age	18–24	28	38	26	8	10	1	–3	2	2	37	–2
	25–34	25	38	27	10	13	1	–13	8	7	49	3
	35–44	27	41	23	9	14	–1	–4	4	1.5	61	2
	45–54	31	35	25	9	4	–1	–6	5	2.5	65	0
	55–64	39	31	22	8	–8	0	–6	5	3	71	2
	65+	41	35	18	6	–6	1	–4	1	2.5	75	5
Social	AB	37	28	29	6	–9	–2	–2	4	0	71	3
Class	C1	37	32	23	8	–5	1	–6	3	3.5	62	2
	C2	33	40	19	8	7	4	–9	4	6.5	58	2
	DE	25	48	18	9	23	1	–7	5	4	54	1
Housing	Owned	44	29	20	7	–15	1	–3	1	2	71	3
tenure	Mortgaged	31	36	25	8	5	0	–6	5	3	60	1
	Social renter	16	55	19	10	39	–2	–5	5	1.5	51	–1
	Private renter	27	36	28	9	9	–1	–4	3	1.5	51	5
2001 Vote	Con	90	2	6	2	–88	–10	2	6	–6	80	–20
(reported)[1]	Lab	8	72	15	5	64	8	–28	15	18	71	–29
	Lib Dem	12	6	78	4	–6	12	6	–22	3	75	–25
Region	East Midlands	37	39	18	6	2	0	–6	3	3	63	2
	Eastern	43	30	22	5	–13	1	–7	5	4	64	2
	Greater Lon.	32	39	22	7	7	2	–8	5	5	58	3
	North East	20	53	23	4	33	–1	–6	6	2.5	57	1
	North West	29	45	21	5	16	0	–6	4	3	57	1
	Scotland	16	40	23	21	24	0	–4	7	2	61	3
	South East	45	24	25	6	–21	2	–5	1	3.5	64	2
	South West	39	23	33	5	–16	0	–3	2	1.5	67	2
	Wales	21	43	18	18	22	0	–6	4	3	62	0
	West Midlands	35	39	19	7	4	0	–6	4	3	61	3
	Yorks/Humb.	29	44	21	6	15	–1	–5	4	2	59	2
Men	18–24	33	34	25	8	1	4	–4	–1	4	39	–4
by age	25–34	29	33	27	11	4	5	–19	8	12	49	2
	35–54	31	36	22	11	5	2	–7	3	4.5	64	0
	55+	40	33	20	7	–7	1	–6	4	3.5	74	1
Women	18–24	22	43	26	9	21	–2	–2	3	0	35	–1
by age	25–34	21	43	28	8	22	–4	–6	9	1	48	2
	35–54	27	40	25	8	13	–4	–3	5	–0.5	61	1
	55+	41	34	20	5	–7	1	–4	2	2.5	73	6

* Denotes a figure of less than 1 per cent but not zero.

Note:

1. Change figures asume report of 2001 vote is accurate.

Base: 'Absolutely certain to vote' (n=10,986)

Total n=17,959

Source: MORI surveys for the *Observer*, the *Financial Times*, the *Sun*, the *Evening Standard* and the *Sunday Mirror*.

John Curtice, Steve Fisher and Michael Steed analyse in some detail the main features of the election results in Appendix 2. Their key points include the following:

1. Labour's share of the GB vote (36.2 per cent) was the lowest ever for a single-party majority government, and the fall in vote (5.8 per cent) was the greatest any incumbent Labour Government had ever suffered. But the Conservatives' advance was negligible (0.5 per cent); the party won a smaller vote than in any election between 1857 and 1997. As a result, the combined Conservative and Labour vote (69.4 per cent) was the lowest since 1923.

2. The Liberal Democrats won their third highest share of the vote since 1929 and the most seats since 1923. The period since 1997 is the first ever period of Labour rule during which Britain's main third party has increased its vote. There were also more 'other' votes (7.9 per cent) than at any time since 1918.

3. The electorate's judgement was no less of a 'national' one than it has been at other recent general elections. Party performance varied from one constituency to another by around as much as has been the norm in the recent past.

4. Labour lost ground most heavily in seats it was defending. This was particularly true of constituencies with large Muslim and student populations, seats where the Liberal Democrats made their strongest advances. This suggests that the Liberal Democrats' success rested at least in part on their opposition to the Iraq war and university tuition 'top-up' fees. How Labour MPs had voted on the Iraq war, foundation hospitals or the anti-terror laws made little difference to their performance, although there was a slight boost for Labour MPs who voted against top-up fees.

5. The Conservatives made little advance outside the South East, where the party may perhaps have been helped by the regional trends in house prices and unemployment.

6. Tactical voting continued to be important. Liberal Democrat voters living in seats that Labour was defending against a challenger were still inclined to vote tactically for Labour, although Labour voters may have been somewhat less willing to reciprocate in those seats where the Liberal Democrats were contesting a seat with the Conservatives. Meanwhile, third-place Conservatives seemed more willing than before to switch tactically to the Liberal Democrats.

7. The most successful minor parties were the British National Party (BNP), the Greens, Respect and the United Kingdom Independence

Party (UKIP). The BNP recorded the best performance ever by a far-right party in a general election and the Greens did better than in any previous general election. While UKIP did not match the performance of the Referendum Party in 1997, it still advanced on 2001. Respect's anti-war platform proved relatively popular in constituencies with large numbers of Muslims.

8. Turnout (61.2 per cent) was only a little above the record low in 2001. It was highest in marginal seats and lowest in safe Labour seats, suggesting that voters may have stayed at home not just because they believed that the result was a foregone conclusion but also because of disillusion with Labour. The increased use of postal voting does not appear to have helped to increase turnout.

9. Even though Labour lost 14 more seats than it would have done if swing had been uniform, the advantage it continued to derive from the electoral system was decisive in delivering it an overall majority. If the Conservatives had enjoyed a three-point lead in votes, the party would still have had fewer seats than Labour, let alone secured an overall majority. The introduction of new constituency boundaries will help to reduce but will far from eliminate this 'bias'.

10. One in seven MPs is now not attached either to the Conservatives or to Labour, enough to produce a hung Parliament in most post-war elections. If this pattern continues, there is a significant chance that future British elections will produce hung Parliaments.

The Conservatives disagreed about the success of their targeting. Although they gained 33 seats (5 per cent of all seats) for an increase of 0.5 per cent in share of the vote, Lord Ashcroft, in his *Smell the Coffee*, was highly critical of the exercise. He pointed out that the party gained only 30 of the 139 Con/Lab target seats in England and Wales. With a national swing in England and Wales from Labour to Conservative of 3.5 per cent the party should have gained more seats, on a uniform swing, than it did. And some of its gains were a consequence of Labour voters switching to the Liberal Democrats. It was significant that in the top 80 target seats, the swing from Labour to Conservative averaged 3.4 per cent, hardly different from the average in England and Wales as a whole.

The 2005 general election confirmed once more that the Conservative Party was no longer Britain's natural party of government and that it had also surrendered to Labour its reputation as the party of economic competence. The electoral successes of right-wing parties in the United States, using moral majority issues, and in Australia, using cultural grievances, hardly seemed applicable in twenty-first-century Britain.

Conservative modernisers expressed concern over the influence of a socially unrepresentative party membership and over the extent to which the values and issue preferences of its voters were untypical of most of the electorate; they also worried over the strong pro-Labour bias of the electoral system. More than ever, perhaps, the party would have to rely on some outside event – like the 'winter of discontent' or an economic crisis – for its recovery. In 1951 and 1979 it had recovered power following the implosion of a weak Labour Government and an economic crisis. The war with Iraq was clearly a major event, but on this the party agreed with the Government. And now the Liberal Democrats were a possible repository for dissatisfied Labour voters. How would the party be able to gain the 40 per cent of the vote it needed to become the largest party at the next general election, let alone even more to win an overall majority? In view of the party's poor standing with voters, the experience of 2005 suggests that improvements in campaigning or targeting are likely to play only a small part in attracting substantially more votes.

Post-election surveys reported that more than a quarter of those who supported Liberal Democrat candidates had voted tactically, often to thwart Labour. There was a swing to the Liberal Democrats from both Labour and the Conservatives, but of the 187 seats in which the Liberal Democrats finished second, Labour held 104. The party faced a strategic dilemma, and an opportunity, for the next Parliament.

At Labour's election manifesto launch, Tony Blair had raised the possibility that a third term would provide New Labour with an opportunity to entrench a progressive consensus, just as Clement Attlee had done after 1945. In her different way Mrs Thatcher after 1979 also set the agenda for a generation. Critics might note, however, that Attlee had done his work in one term and Thatcher hers largely in two terms. Although the scale of Labour's success in seats owed much to the electoral system, the party's potential for doing even better next time (without Iraq again being a major issue) remained intact (see pp. 193–4). Blair could console himself with the emergence of a progressive centre-left majority in the election: Labour and the Liberal Democrats together gained 52 per cent of the vote. A potential worry for Labour, however, was that if the main concerns of voters moved from the economy and public services, on which it held a clear advantage, to crime and security issues (for example, immigration and terrorism), the agenda would be more favourable to the Conservatives.

Among voters, Britain has moved towards a three-party system to a greater extent than at any general election since 1945. It was scant consolation that the Conservative and Labour parties together combined

70 per cent of the vote was an improvement on the European elections a year earlier, when their combined share fell below 50 per cent. The fragmentation of political choice, emerging from the decline of aggregate support for the two main parties, the growth of minor parties, and the different line-ups of parties in various parts of the UK, means that British general elections now give less of a national verdict. With 91 MPs not connected to the Labour or Conservative parties, the chances of a hung Parliament would be greatly increased if the electoral system were not so favourable to Labour.

In the eight weeks following polling day in 2005, political debate in Britain was dominated by various issues, the Government's scheme for ID cards, the uncertain future of the European Constitution and the Government's decision not to proceed with a referendum on it, and terrorism – none of which had received more than perfunctory mention in the campaign.

Note

1. R. Grayson, 'The Liberal Democrats Face a Long Journey', *Independent*, 14 May 2005, p. 31.

Appendix 1: The Voting Statistics

Table A1.1 Votes and seats, 1945–2005

	Electorate	Votes	Con	Lab	Lib Dem	Nat	Comm	Other
1945	73.3%	100%–640	39.8%–213	48.3%–393	9.1%–12	0.2%	0.4%–2	2.1%–20
	32,836,419	24,082,612	9,577,667	11,632,191	2,197,191	46,612	102,760	525,491
1950	84.0%	100%–625	43.5%–299	46.1%–315	9.1%–9	0.1%	0.3%	0.9%–2
	34,269,770	28,772,671	12,502,567	13,266,592	2,621,548	27,288	91,746	262,930
1951	82.5%	100%–625	48.%–321	48.8%–295	2.5%–6	0.1%	0.1%	0.5%–3
	34,645,573	28,595,668	13,717,538	13,948,605	730,556	18,219	21,640	159,110
1955	76.8%	100%–630	49.7%–345	46.4%–277	2.7%–6	0.2%	0.1%	0.8%–2
	34,858,263	26,760,493	13,311,936	12,404,970	722,405	57,231	33,144	230,807
1959	78.7%	100%–630	49.4%–365	43.8%–258	5.9%–6	0.4%	0.1%	0.5%–1
	35,397,080	27,859,241	13,749,830	12,215,538	1,638,571	99,309	30,897	145,090
1964	77.1%	100%–630	43.4%–304	44.1%–317	11.2%–9	0.5%	0.2%	0.6%
	35,892,572	27,655,374	12,001,396	12,205,814	3,092,878	133,551	45,932	169,431
1966	75.8%	100%–630	41.9%–253	47.9%–363	8.5%–12	0.7%	0.2%	0.7%–2
	35,964,684	27,263,606	11,418,433	13,064,951	2,327,533	189,545	62,112	201,032
1970	72.0%	100%–630	46.4%–330	43.%–288	7.5%–6	1.3%–1	0.1%	1.7%–5
	39,342,013	28,344,798	13,145,123	12,178,295	2,117,033	381,819	37,970	486,557
Feb. '74	78.1%	100%–635	37.8%–297	37.1%–301	19.3%–14	2.6%–9	0.1%	3.1%–14
	39,770,724	31,340,162	11,872,180	11,646,391	6,058,744	804,554	32,743	958,293
Oct. '74	72.8%	100%–635	35.8%–277	39.2%–319	18.3%–13	3.5%–14	0.1%	3.1%–12
	40,072,971	29,189,178	10,464,817	11,457,079	5,346,754	1,005,938	17,426	897,164
1979	76.0%	100%–635	43.9%–339	37.%–269	13.8%–11	2.%–4	0.1%	3.2%–12
	41,093,264	31,221,361	13,697,923	11,532,218	4,313,804	636,890	38,116	1,001,447

	Electorate	Votes	Con	Lab	Lib Dem	Nat	Comm	Other
1983	72.7%	100%–650	42.4%–397	27.6%–209	25.4%–23	1.5%–4	0.2%	2.9%–17
	42,197,344	30,671,136	13,012,315	8,456,934	7,780,949	457,676	53,848	90,875
1987	75.3%	100%–650	42.3%–376	30.8%–229	22.6%–22	1.7%–6	0.3%	2.3%–17
	43,181,321	32,536,137	13,763,066	10,029,778	7,341,290	543,559	89,753	762,615
1992	77.7%	100%–651	41.9%–336	34.4%–271	17.8%–20	2.3%–7	0.5%	3.%–17
	43,249,721	33,612,693	14,092,891	11,559,735	5,999,384	783,991	171,927	1,004,765
1997	71.5%	100%–659	30.7%–165	43.2%–418	16.8%–46	2.5%–10	0.2%	6.6%–20
	43,757,478	31,286,597	9,602,857	13,516,632	5,242,894	782,570	63,991	2,077,653
2001	59.4%	100%–659	31.7%–166	40.7%–412	18.3%–52	2.5%–9	0.6%	6.2%–20
	44,403,238	26,368,798	8,357,622	10,724,895	4,812,833	660,197	166,487	1,646,764
2005	61.2%	100%–646	32.4%–198	35.2%–356	22.0%–62	2.2%–9	–	8.2%–22
	44,261,545	27,123,652	8,772,473	9,547,944	5,981,874	567,105	–	2,234,267

Source for 2005: *The Times Guide to the House of Commons, 2005.*

Minor party votes (GB 2005)

Party	Votes	% Share	Av. vote %	Candidates	Lost deposits
UKIP	605,173	3.2	2.8	496	458
BNP	192,706	0.7	4.3	119	85
Greens	283,477	1.0	3.4	202	178
Respect	68,094	0.3	6.8	26	9
SSP	43,514	0.2	2.0	62	56
Socialist Labour	20,192	0.1	0.8	50	49
Veritas	40,481	0.1	1.3	33	32

Table A1.2 National and regional results

United Kingdom

| | Seats won in 2005 (change since 2001) | | | | | Share of votes cast 2005 (% change since 2001) | | | | |
	Con	Lab	Lib Dem	Nat & Other		Turnout	Con	Lab	Lib Dem	Nat	Other
England	194 (+29)	286 (−37)	47 (+7)	2 (+1)		61.1 (+2.0)	35.7 (+0.5)	35.5 (−6)	22.9 (+3.5)	0 (0)	5.9 (+2.0)
South	126 (+20)	45 (−13)	25 (0)	0 (0)		62.8 (+2.40)	40.0 (+1.5)	28.7 (−5.8)	25.4 (+2.6)	0 (0)	5.9 (+1.7)
Midlands	49 (+7)	69 (−9)	6 (+2)	1 (0)		61.9 (+1.7)	37.0 (−0.1)	36.9 (−6.2)	19.7 (+3.9)	0 (0)	6.4 (+2.4)
North	19 (+2)	133 (−6)	10 (+4)	0 (0)		57.8 (+1.5)	27.2 (−1.7)	49.6 (−6.1)	23.3 (+6.2)	0 (0)	5.4 (+1.9)
Wales	3 (+3)	29 (−5)	4 (+2)	4 (0)		62.4 (+1.1)	21.4 (+0.4)	42.7 (−5.9)	18.4 (+4.6)	12.6 (−1.7)	5.0 (+2.7)
Scotland	1 (+1)	41 (−5)	11 (+2)	6 (+2)		60.6 (+2.6)	15.8 (+0.3)	39.5 (−4.4)	22.6 (+6.3)	17.7 (−2.4)	4.4 (+0.2)
Great Britain	198 (+32)	356 (−47)	62 (+10)	12 (+3)		61.1 (+2.0)	33.2 (+0.5)	36.2 (−5.8)	22.6 (+3.8)	2.2 (−0.4)	5.7 (+1.8)
Northern Ireland	0 (0)	0 (0)	0 (0)	18 (0)		62.9 (−5.1)	0 (0)	0 (0)	0 (0)	2.2 (−0.3)	100.0 (0)
United Kingdom	198 (+32)	356 (−47)	62 (+10)	30 (+3)		61.2 (+1.8)	32.4 (+0.7)	35.2 (−5.5)	22 (+3.8)	2.2 (−0.3)	8.2 (+1.4)

Regions

| | Seats won in 2005 (change since 2001) | | | | | Share of votes cast 2005 (% change since 2001) | | | | |
	Con	Lab	Lib Dem	Nat & Other		Turnout	Con	Lab	Lib Dem	Nat	Other
South East	104 (+18)	71 (−19)	15 (0)	1 (+1)		64.4 (+2.8)	45.0 (+2.3)	24.4. (−5.0)	25.4 (+1.7)	0 (0)	5.5 (+3.2)
Greater London	21 (+8)	44 (−11)	8 (+2)	1 (+1)		57.8 (+2.5)	31.9 (+1.4)	38.9 (−8.4)	21.9 (+4.4)	0 (0)	7.3 (+2.6)
Inner London	4 (+2)	19 (−4)	2 (+1)	1 (+1)		53.2 (+2.8)	23.7 (+0.8)	43.2 (−10.3)	22.7 (+5.5)	0 (0)	10.0 (+4.0)
Outer London	17 (+6)	25 (−7)	6 (+1)	0 (0)		60.4 (+2.5)	35.9 (+1.8)	36.8 (−7.6)	21.5 (+3.8)	0 (0)	5.7 (+1.9)
Rest of South East	83 (+10)	27 (−8)	7 (−1)	0 (0)		64.1 (+2.5)	43.3 (+1.8)	25.5 (−4.8)	25.5 (+1.7)	0 (0)	5.6 (+1.3)
Outer Met. Area	47 (+6)	14 (−5)	0 (−1)	0 (0)		63.9 (+3.1)	46.3 (+2.7)	26.6 (−6.4)	22.2 (+2.8)	0 (0)	4.9 (+0.8)
Other South East	36 (+4)	13 (−3)	7 (−1)	0 (0)		64.3 (+2.5)	43.4 (+1.8)	25.5 (−4.8)	25.5 (+1.7)	0 (0)	5.6 (+1.3)
South West	22 (+2)	13 (−3)	16 (+1)	0 (0)		66.3 (+1.4)	38.6 (+0.1)	22.8 (−3.4)	32.6 (+1.4)	0 (0)	6.0 (+2.0)
Devon & Cornwall	5 (+1)	3 (−1)	8 (0)	0 (0)		65.9 (+0.6)	36.1 (−0.9)	19.0 (−2.6)	36.4 (+0.5)	0 (0)	8.5 (+3.0)
Rest of S.W.	17 (+1)	10 (−2)	8 (+1)	0 (0)		66.5 (+1.8)	39.8 (+0.5)	24.6 (−3.9)	30.7 (+1.8)	0 (0)	4.9 (+1.5)

Regions *continued*

	Seats won in 2005 (change since 2001)					Share of votes cast 2001 (% change since 1997)					
	Con	Lab	Lib Dem	Nat & Other		Turnout	Con	Lab	Lib Dem	Nat	Other
East Anglia	15 (+1)	5 (−2)	2 (+1)	0 (0)	East Anglia	63.7 (+2.1)	43.3 (−0.3)	29.8 (−6.6)	21.8 (+4.4)	0 (0)	5.0 (+1.1)
East Midlands	18 (+3)	25 (−3)	1 (0)	0 (0)	East Midlands	62.4 (+1.7)	37.1 (−0.2)	39.0 (−6.1)	18.5 (+3.0)	0 (0)	5.5 (+3.2)
West Midlands	16 (+3)	39 (−4)	3 (+1)	1 (0)	West Midlands	60.4 (+1.9)	35.0 (0.0)	38.7 (−6.1)	18.6 (+3.9)	0 (0)	7.7 (+2.2)
W. Mids. Met. Co.	3 (−1)	24 (−1)	2 (+2)	0 (0)	W. Mids. Met. Co.	57.7 (+3.0)	29.5 (−1.1)	44.4 (−6.9)	18.1 (+5.0)	0 (0)	8.1 (+3.0)
Rest of W. Mids.	13 (+4)	15 (−3)	1 (−1)	1 (0)	Rest of W. Mids.	62.9 (+0.7)	39.6 (+1.0)	34.0 (−5.6)	19.0 (+3.0)	0 (0)	7.4 (+1.6)
Yorks & Humberside	9 (+2)	44 (−3)	3 (+1)	0 (0)	Yorks & Humberside	59.0 (+2.2)	29.1 (−1.1)	43.6 (−5.0)	20.7 (+3.5)	0 (0)	6.6 (+2.6)
S. Yorks Met. Co.	0 (0)	14 (0)	1 (0)	0 (0)	S. Yorks Met. Co.	54.8 (+2.1)	18.0 (−0.8)	52.7 (−6.2)	21.4 (+3.3)	0 (0)	8.0 (+3.7)
W. Yorks Met. Co.	1 (+1)	21 (−2)	1 (+1)	0 (0)	W. Yorks Met. Co.	60.0 (+3.3)	27.8 (−2.2)	45.9 (−5.6)	18.6 (+4.6)	0 (0)	7.7 (+3.2)
Rest of Yorks & Humb.	8 (+1)	9 (−1)	1 (0)	0 (0)	Rest of Yorks & Humb.	60.8 (+0.7)	38.3 (+0.1)	34.5 (−3.6)	22.7 (+2.4)	0 (0)	4.5 (+1.1)
North West	8 (+1)	57 (−3)	5 (+2)	0 (0)	North West	57.2 (+1.4)	28.7 (−0.6)	46.0 (−5.8)	21.4 (+4.6)	0 (0)	4.8 (+1.5)
Gtr. Manchr. Met. Co.	1 (0)	23 (−2)	4 (+2)	0 (0)	Gtr. Manchr. Met. Co.	54.5 (+1.6)	23.7 (−0.6)	47.2 (−6.5)	23.3 (+5.0)	0 (0)	5.8 (+2.1)
Merseyside Met. Co.	0 (0)	15 (0)	1 (0)	0 (0)	Merseyside Met. Co.	54.1 (+2.2)	19.4 (−0.7)	53.8 (−4.9)	22.9 (+5.1)	0 (0)	3.9 (+0.5)
Rest of N.W.	7 (+1)	19 (−1)	0 (0)	0 (0)	Rest of N.W.	60.3 (+0.7)	35.9 (−0.2)	41.1 (−5.5)	18.4 (+4.1)	0 (0)	4.6 (+1.5)
North	2 (−1)	32 (0)	2 (1)	0 (0)	North	58.4 (+0.9)	19.5 (−1.8)	49.8 (−6.1)	23.3 (+6.2)	0 (0)	4.3 (+1.7)
Tyne & Wear Met. Co.	0 (0)	13 (0)	0 (0)	0 (0)	Tyne & Wear Met. Co.	55.8 (+2.5)	17.4 (−0.2)	55.8 (−7.1)	23.2 (+6.6)	0 (0)	3.6 (+0.8)
Rest of Northern	2 (−1)	19 (0)	2 (+1)	0 (0)	Rest of Northern	59.8 (−0.1)	25.6 (−2.4)	46.5 (−5.7)	23.4 (+6.0)	0 (0)	4.5 (+2.1)
Wales	3 (+3)	29 (−5)	3 (+2)	4 (0)	Wales	62.4 (+1.1)	21.4 (+0.4)	42.7 (−5.9)	18.4 (+4.6)	12.6 (−1.7)	5.0 (+2.7)
Industrial S. Wales	1 (1)	21 (−3)	1 (+1)	1 (+1)	Industrial S. Wales	60.9 (+1.1)	19.3 (+1.2)	48.8 (−6.7)	17.4 (+5.0)	9.1 (−2.0)	5.5 (+2.9)
Rural Wales	2 (+2)	8 (−2)	3 (+1)	3 (−1)	Rural Wales	65.0 (+1.0)	24.8 (−0.9)	33.0 (−4.7)	20.0 (+4.0)	18.1 (−1.0)	4.1 (+2.3)
Scotland*	1 (+1)	41 (−5)	11 (+2)	6 (+2)	Scotland*	60.6 (+2.6)	15.8 (+0.3)	39.5 (−4.4)	22.6 (+6.3)	17.7 (−2.4)	4.4 (+0.2)

Notes:

The English Regions are the eight *Standard Regions*, now obsolete but used by the OPCS until the 1990s

The *Outer Metropolitan Area* comprises those seats wholly or mostly in the Outer Metropolitan Area as defined by the OPCS. It includes: the whole of Surrey and Hertfordshire; the whole of Berkshire except Newbury; and the constituencies of Arundel & South Downs; Crawley; Horsham; Mid-Sussex (West Sussex); Aldershot; Hampshire North East (Hampshire); Chatham & Aylesford; Dartford; Faversham & Mid Kent; Gillingham; Gravesham; Maidstone & The Weald; Medway; Sevenoaks; Tonbridge and Malling; Tunbridge Wells (Kent); Beaconsfield; Chesham & Amersham; Wycombe (Buckinghamshire); Bedfordshire South West; Luton North; Luton South (Bedfordshire); Basildon; Billericay; Brentwood & Ongar; Castle Point; Chelmsford West; Epping Forest; Harlow; Rayleigh; Rochford & Southend East; Southend West; Thurrock (Essex).

Industrial Wales includes Gwent, the whole of Glamorgan, and the Llanelli constituency in Dyfed.

Table A1.3 Constituency Results

This table lists the votes in each constituency in percentage terms.

The constituencies are listed alphabetically within the counties, as defined in 1974 (except that in Greater London the constituencies are listed alphabetically within each borough).

The figure in the 'Other' column is the total percentage received by all the 'Other' candidates – except the UKIP, the Green Party and Respect, which is listed separately for seats in England. In Scotland the Scottish Socialist Party's result is given in place of that of Respect.

It should be noted that all 'Other' candidates who saved their deposits (5%) are listed on p. 233.

The vote changes in Scotland are based on notional figures for what would have happened if the new boundaries had been in force in 2001. The Scottish results are not arranged within counties as too many of the constituencies crossed boundaries.

* denotes a seat won by different parties in 2001 and 2005
† denotes a seat that changed hands at a by-election between 2001 and 2005
‡ denotes the seat held by the Speaker in 2001 and 2005

Swing is given in the Conventional (or 'Butler') form – the average of the Conservative % gain and the Labour % loss (measured as % of the total poll). It is only reported for those seats where those parties occupied the top two places in 2001 and 2005. This is the practice followed by all the Nuffield studies since 1955.

ENGLAND	Turnout %	Turnout +/-	Con %	Con +/-	Lab %	Lab +/-	LD %	LD +/-	Green %	Ukip %	BNP %	Respect %	Other No. & %	Swing
Avon, Bath	69.0	+4.1	33.7	+4.6	14.8	-0.9	43.9	-6.6	5.4	1.7	-	-	(2) 0.5	-
Bristol East	61.3	+3.9	21.1	-0.7	45.9	-9.1	25.2	+8.1	3.8	2.7	-	1.3	-	+4.0
Bristol North West	61.1	+0.7	27.9	-0.9	46.7	-5.4	20.1	+4.2	-	2.4	-	-	(2) 2.9	+2.3
Bristol South	59.8	+3.2	20.0	-2.3	49.1	-7.8	22.8	+7.9	5.0	3.1	-	-	-	-
Bristol West*	70.5	+4.9	26.9	-1.9	29.4	-7.5	38.3	+9.4	3.8	0.8	-	-	(2) 0.9	-
Kingswood	66.7	+2.2	33.1	+4.7	47.0	-7.8	16.1	+1.4	-	2.6	-	-	1.2	+6.3
Northavon	72.2	+1.5	33.6	-1.1	10.6	-0.9	52.3	-0.1	1.6	1.7	-	-	0.2	-

ENGLAND	Turnout %	Turnout +/-	Con %	Con +/-	Lab %	Lab +/-	LD %	LD +/-	Green %	Ukip %	BNP %	Respect %	Other No. & %	Swing
Wansdyke	72.4	+2.5	37.0	+1.5	40.6	-6.2	19.7	+5.3	-	2.2	-	-	0.4	-
Weston-Super-Mare*	65.5	+2.7	40.3	+1.6	18.7	-1.1	36.1	-3.4	-	2.5	1.6	-	(2) 0.8	+1.3
Woodspring	72.0	+3.4	41.8	-1.9	21.8	-3.8	30.2	+5.9	2.5	2.5	1.2	-	-	+1.0
Bedfordshire, Bedford														
Bedford	59.6	-0.3	33.7	+0.9	41.7	-6.2	21.5	+5.7	-	2.4	-	-	0.7	+3.6
Bedfordshire Mid	68.3	+2.5	46.3	-1.1	22.5	-7.6	23.8	+4.0	2.6	2.7	-	-	(2) 2.1	-
Bedfordshire North East	68.0	+3.3	49.9	+0.0	25.2	-5.8	20.8	+4.5	-	4.0	-	-	-	+2.9
Bedfordshire South West	61.8	-0.2	48.3	+6.1	30.2	-10.2	16.9	+2.1	-	4.2	-	-	0.5	+8.1
Luton North	57.4	-0.5	32.1	+0.9	48.7	-8.0	15.5	+5.8	-	3.2	-	-	0.4	+4.5
Luton South	54.1	-1.0	28.2	-1.3	42.7	-12.5	22.6	+11.6	-	2.5	-	1.9	0.3	+5.6
Berkshire, Bracknell														
Bracknell	63.4	+2.7	49.7	+3.0	26.2	-6.9	19.8	+2.7	2.0	3.6	-	-	0.8	-
Maidenhead	71.7	+9.6	50.8	+5.8	9.0	-6.1	37.3	-0.2	-	1.3	1.5	-	-	-
Newbury*	72.0	+4.7	49.0	+5.5	5.9	-1.0	42.6	-5.6	-	1.6	-	-	(2) 0.9	-
Reading East*	60.3	+1.9	35.4	+3.5	34.3	-10.4	24.2	+5.7	3.5	1.9	-	-	(2) 0.6	+7.0
Reading West	61.0	+1.9	33.9	+1.8	45.0	-8.1	15.8	+3.0	2.2	2.8	-	-	0.3	+5.0
Slough	52.3	-1.1	26.1	-0.1	47.2	-11.0	15.5	+4.9	2.0	3.8	-	4.4	1.0	+5.5
Windsor	64.0	+7.0	49.5	+2.3	19.1	-5.0	26.0	-0.2	2.5	2.5	-	-	0.4	-
Wokingham	67.1	+3.1	48.1	+2.0	15.2	-2.2	32.4	0.0	-	2.2	0.8	-	(2) 1.3	-
Buckinghamshire, Aylesbury														
Beaconsfield	63.9	+3.1	55.4	+2.7	19.4	-2.4	20.4	-1.2	-	4.8	-	-	-	-
Buckingham	68.7	-0.6	57.4	+3.8	19.9	-4.3	19.7	-0.3	-	3.0	-	-	-	+4.0
Chesham & Amersham	68.0	+3.4	54.4	+3.9	14.0	-4.7	25.1	+0.8	3.5	3.0	-	-	-	+4.3
Milton Keynes North East*	64.8	+0.2	39.3	+1.2	35.9	-6.0	19.5	+1.8	2.2	2.8	-	-	-	+3.6
Milton Keynes South West	60.5	-1.8	34.6	+0.4	42.8	-6.7	16.2	+5.6	2.7	3.6	-	-	0.3	+3.6
Wycombe	62.2	+1.6	45.8	+3.4	29.9	-5.5	19.8	+2.7	-	3.9	-	-	0.7	+4.4
*Cambridgeshire, Cambridge**														
Cambridge*	62.1	+1.5	16.5	-6.4	34.0	-11.1	44.0	+18.9	2.9	1.3	-	1.1	(2) 0.3	-
Cambridgeshire North East	59.8	-0.3	47.5	-0.6	30.0	-4.8	17.1	+3.1	-	5.4	-	-	-	+2.1
Cambridgeshire North West	61.6	-0.1	45.8	-4.0	25.8	-5.6	22.9	+7.1	-	5.5	-	-	-	+0.8

Cambridgeshire South	68.4	+1.3	45.0	+0.7	19.4	-4.9	29.8	+2.9	2.9	3.0	—	—	—	—
Cambridgeshire South East	65.3	+1.7	47.0	+2.9	21.3	-5.1	31.7	+4.8	—	—	—	—	—	—
Huntingdon	62.5	+1.4	50.8	+0.9	18.7	-1.1	26.3	+2.5	—	4.1	—	—	—	—
Peterborough*	61.0	-0.3	42.1	+4.2	35.5	-9.7	16.7	+2.2	—	3.0	—	(2) 2.	—	+6.9
Cheshire, Chester, City of	64.3	+0.6	36.8	+3.7	38.9	-9.6	21.9	+7.2	—	1.7	—	0.7	—	+6.7
Congleton	64.2	+1.5	45.4	-0.9	27.7	-2.7	26.9	+5.3	—	—	—	—	—	+0.9
Crewe & Nantwich	60.0	-0.2	32.6	+2.1	48.8	-5.4	18.6	+5.1	—	—	—	—	—	+3.8
Eddisbury	63.2	-0.9	46.4	+0.1	32.8	-3.2	17.9	+2.2	—	2.9	—	—	—	+1.6
Ellesmere Port & Neston	61.6	+0.7	33.0	+3.9	48.4	-6.9	15.7	+4.1	—	2.9	—	—	—	+5.4
Halton	53.1	-1.0	20.1	+1.4	62.8	-6.4	17.2	+4.9	—	—	—	—	—	+3.9
Macclesfield	63.1	+0.8	49.6	+0.7	29.0	-4.1	19.5	+1.5	—	—	—	1.9	—	+2.4
Tatton	64.6	+1.0	51.8	+3.7	23.5	-3.8	21.8	+3.2	—	2.4	—	0.6	—	+3.7
Warrington North	55.1	+1.4	23.3	+0.5	53.5	-8.2	19.0	+5.6	—	2.7	—	1.4	—	+4.4
Warrington South	61.8	+0.6	33.0	+0.0	40.5	-8.7	23.7	+7.4	—	1.7	—	1.0	—	+4.4
Weaver Vale	57.1	-0.5	30.2	+2.3	47.6	-4.9	19.6	+5.2	—	2.6	—	—	—	+3.6
Cleveland, Hartlepool	51.5	-4.3	11.5	-9.4	51.5	-7.6	30.4	+15.4	0.8	3.5	—	(3) 2.3	—	—
Middlesbrough	48.8	-1.1	16.4	-2.8	57.8	-9.8	18.7	+8.2	—	2.4	—	(2) 2.3	—	—
Middlesbrough S. & E. Clevel'd	60.8	-0.2	31.9	-2.1	50.2	-5.1	13.8	+3.2	—	1.5	2.5	0	—	+1.5
Redcar	58.0	+1.7	17.9	-7.2	51.4	-8.9	20.2	+7.6	—	1.5	2.5	(2) 6.5	—	—
Stockton North	57.6	+2.8	20.8	-1.3	54.9	-8.5	18.9	+7.0	—	2.7	2.5	—	—	+3.6
Stockton South	63.0	+0.2	34.1	+1.7	47.8	-5.1	16.0	+2.4	—	2.1	2.7	—	—	+3.4
Cornwall, Cornwall North	64.5	+0.7	37.1	+3.3	11.9	+2.1	42.6	-9.4	—	5.5	—	(2) 3.0	—	—
Cornwall South East	66.2	+0.8	34.6	-0.9	11.4	-1.1	46.7	+0.8	—	5.0	—	(2) 2.3	—	—
Falmouth & Camborne*	67.1	+2.9	26.3	-3.6	31.0	-8.6	34.9	+10.4	—	3.8	—	(5) 4.0	—	—
St Ives	67.5	+1.1	27.7	-3.5	13.1	-0.3	50.7	-0.9	3.4	5.1	—	—	—	—
Truro & St Austell	64.2	+0.8	32.4	+0.1	13.6	-0.1	46.7	-1.6	—	5.3	—	2.1	—	—
Cumbria, Barrow & Furness	59.0	-1.3	31.0	+0.7	47.6	-8.1	16.8	+4.6	—	2.1	—	2.5	—	+4.4
Carlisle	59.5	+0.1	32.0	-2.8	48.1	-3.1	16.7	+5.0	—	2.2	—	1.0	—	+0.1
Copeland	62.3	-2.6	31.7	-5.8	50.5	-1.3	11.5	+0.8	—	2.2	—	(2) 4.1	—	-2.2
Penrith & The Border	66.1	+1.6	51.3	-3.6	19.1	+0.6	25.9	+4.1	—	2.5	—	1.2	—	—
Westmorland & Lonsdale*	71.6	+3.7	44.9	-2.0	7.6	-3.3	45.5	+5.1	—	1.3	—	0.6	—	—
Workington	64.7	+1.3	31.9	+2.3	49.2	-6.3	14.6	+2.2	—	3.3	—	1.0	—	+4.3

ENGLAND	Turnout %	Turnout +/-	Con %	Con +/-	Lab %	Lab +/-	LD %	LD +/-	Green %	Ukip %	BNP %	Respect %	Other No. & %	Swing
Derbyshire, Amber Valley	62.9	+2.6	34.4	-1.2	45.6	-6.3	13.1	+0.7	–	1.7	2.6	–	2.6	+2.6
Bolsover	57.3	+0.7	17.3	-2.2	65.2	-3.4	17.5	+5.6	–	–	–	–	–	+0.6
Chesterfield	59.6	-1.1	8.2	+0.0	40.4	-1.6	47.3	-0.5	–	2.3	–	–	1.8	–
Derby North	64.3	+6.5	35.4	+0.4	44.0	-6.9	16.5	+2.4	–	2.0	–	–	2.2	+3.6
Derby South	61.6	+5.7	18.9	-5.3	45.4	-11.1	32.3	+13.0	–	1.9	–	–	1.4	–
Derbyshire North East	61.2	+2.3	26.1	-0.4	49.3	-6.3	20.3	+2.5	–	4.3	–	–	–	+3.0
Derbyshire South	65.6	+1.7	36.4	+0.8	44.5	-6.2	13.6	+3.5	–	–	3.2	–	2.3	+3.5
Derbyshire West	69.2	+1.5	47.7	-0.3	26.6	-6.8	22.3	+6.6	–	2.6	–	–	(2) 0.8	+3.2
Erewash	64.5	+2.6	30.4	-4.5	44.5	-4.8	14.0	+2.5	–	1.9	2.6	–	(3) 6.6	+0.1
High Peak	66.4	+1.2	38.2	0.9	39.6	-7.0	20.0	+3.9	–	2.2	–	–	–	+3.9
Devon, Devon East	69.4	+0.6	46.9	-0.6	15.4	-1.2	30.7	+0.5	–	6.2	–	–	0.8	–
Devon North	68.1	-0.2	36.3	-1.8	9.0	-1.2	45.9	+1.7	3.5	5.3	–	–	–	–
Devon South West	68.6	+2.4	44.8	-2.0	23.6	-8.0	24.1	+5.7	–	7.5	–	–	–	–
Devon West & Torridge*	70.2	-0.3	42.7	+2.7	10.2	-0.5	37.2	-5.0	–	6.5	–	–	–	–
Exeter	64.8	+0.6	27.2	-0.3	41.1	-8.7	20.6	+8.2	3.4	3.4	–	–	(2) 4.4	+4.2
Plymouth Devonport	57.7	+1.0	25	-2.0	44.3	-14	19.0	+8.2	–	7.9	–	0.9	(2) 2.8	+6.0
Plymouth Sutton	56.8	-0.3	29.8	-1.7	40.6	-10.2	22.7	+8.4	–	6.3	–	–	0.6	+4.2
Teignbridge	68.7	-0.7	35.5	-3.9	11.4	-1.0	45.7	+1.2	–	6.4	–	–	1.1	–
Tiverton & Honiton	69.8	+0.6	47.9	+0.8	13.7	+1.7	28.9	-6.9	–	4.3	–	–	2.9	–
Torbay	61.9	-0.7	36.5	+0.2	14.7	+5.3	40.8	-9.6	2.4	7.9	–	–	–	–
Totnes	67.7	-0.2	41.7	-2.8	12.2	0.0	37.9	+0.7	–	7.7	–	–	0.4	–
Dorset, Bournemouth East	59.3	+1.1	45.0	+1.7	19.1	-0.7	31.1	-2.6	–	4.8	–	–	–	–
Bournemouth West	53.3	0.0	41.4	-1.4	23.1	-5.8	29.6	+4.4	–	5.9	–	–	–	–
Christchurch	69.6	+2.1	54.7	-0.4	15.6	+0.5	24.5	-3.2	–	5.2	–	–	–	–
Dorset Mid & Poole North	68.5	+2.9	36.6	-4.5	11.6	-3.9	48.7	+6.7	–	3.1	–	–	–	–
Dorset North	71.1	+4.8	44.9	-1.8	8.7	-2.5	40.7	+1.9	2.1	3.6	–	–	–	–
Dorset South	68.7	+3.2	37.9	-3.7	41.6	-0.3	15.7	+1.3	–	3.2	–	0.5	(4) 1.0	-1.7

Constituency														
Dorset West	76.4	+6.9	46.5	+1.9	7.7	−5.8	41.9	+0.1	1.8	2.0	–	–	–	+3.9
Poole	63.1	+2.4	43.4	−1.8	23.1	−3.7	28.6	+3.1	–	3.5	1.4	–	–	–
Durham, Bishop Auckland	56.5	−0.8	22.9	+0.2	50.0	−8.8	23.7	+7.9	–	3.4	–	–	–	–
Darlington	60.3	−1.7	26.0	−4.3	52.4	−3.9	18.5	+7.5	–	1.9	–	–	1.3	−0.2
Durham North	55.3	−1.6	16.8	−2.0	64.1	−3.1	19.2	+5.1	–	–	–	–	–	–
Durham North West	58.0	−0.5	16.4	−4.5	53.9	−8.6	19.9	+5.0	–	–	–	–	9.8	–
Durham, City of	62.1	+2.5	9.4	−7.9	47.2	−8.9	39.8	+16.1	–	–	–	–	3.6	–
Easington	52.1	−1.5	10.7	+0.3	71.4	−5.5	12.9	+2.5	–	–	3.3	–	1.8	–
Sedgefield	62.2	+0.2	14.4	−6.5	58.9	−6.0	11.9	+2.9	–	1.6	–	–	(11) 13.3	−0.2
East Sussex, Bexhill & Battle	67.2	+2.3	52.6	+4.5	18.1	−1.4	23.9	−0.8	–	5.5	–	–	–	–
Brighton Kemptown	60.2	+2.6	33.0	−2.2	39.9	−7.9	16.5	+6.1	7.0	1.9	–	–	1.6	+2.8
Brighton Pavilion	64.0	+5.5	23.9	−1.2	35.4	−13.3	16.5	+3.3	22.0	1.2	–	–	1.2	+6.1
Eastbourne	64.8	+5.3	43.5	−0.6	10.9	−2.4	41.1	+1.9	2.0	2.5	–	–	–	–
Hastings & Rye	59.1	+0.9	37.4	+0.8	42.1	−5.0	15.1	+4.7	2.4	2.6	–	–	(3) 0.5	+2.9
Hove	64.1	+5.2	36.5	−1.8	37.5	−8.4	17.9	+8.8	5.7	1.3	0.6	–	0.5	+3.3
Lewes	69.4	+0.9	34.2	−0.8	9.0	+1.7	52.4	−4.0	2.3	2.2	–	–	–	–
Wealden	67.7	+4.1	52.1	+2.3	16.8	−3.5	23.5	−0.3	3.9	3.8	–	–	–	–
Essex, Basildon	58.4	+3.2	36.1	+2.3	43.4	−9.3	10.4	+1.3	1.5	2.6	4.8	–	1.2	+5.8
Billericay	61.4	+3.4	52.2	+4.8	29.2	−7.2	13.2	−0.6	–	2.4	2.9	–	0.4	+6.0
Braintree*	65.9	+2.4	44.5	+3.2	37.1	−4.8	13.3	+2.0	2.5	2.2	–	–	0.4	+4.0
Brentwood & Ongar	68.4	+1.1	53.5	+15.5	14.9	+2.3	27.2	+11.6	–	4.1	–	–	0.4	+6.6
Castle Point	65.9	+7.5	48.3	+3.7	30.4	−11.7	10.3	+2.5	3.5	7.5	–	–	–	+7.7
Chelmsford West	61.9	+0.2	44.9	+2.5	25.9	−3.5	26.1	+2.8	–	3.0	–	–	–	–
Colchester	56.8	+0.7	33.1	+3.2	19.8	−5.2	47.1	+4.5	–	–	–	–	–	–
Epping Forest	61.6	+3.2	53.0	+3.9	21.0	−8.2	18.5	−0.1	–	2.3	3.9	–	1.4	+6.1
Essex North	65.7	+2.9	47.6	+0.1	24.8	−6.6	20.5	+3.0	3.6	3.5	–	–	–	+3.4
Harlow	62.6	+2.9	41.2	+6.4	41.4	−6.4	12.6	−0.8	–	2.5	–	–	2.4	+6.4
Harwich*	62.6	+0.6	42.1	+1.9	40.3	−5.3	11.7	+3.2	–	–	–	0.9	0.3	+3.6
Maldon & Chelmsford East	66.3	+3.5	51.5	+2.2	24.2	−5.9	20.1	+4.2	–	4.2	–	–	–	+4.0
Rayleigh	64.2	+3.6	55.4	+5.3	23.6	−7.2	16.0	+0.6	–	5.0	–	–	–	+6.2
Rochford & Southend East	55.8	+3.1	45.3	−8.3	31.4	−3.4	15.1	+7.7	3.4	4.8	–	–	–	−2.4

ENGLAND	Turnout %	Turnout +/-	Con %	Con +/-	Lab %	Lab +/-	LD %	LD +/-	Green %	Ukip %	BNP %	Respect %	Other No. & %	Swing
Saffron Walden	68.3	+3.1	51.4	+2.5	16.5	-6.1	26.9	+1.9	–	2.7	–	–	(2) 2.5	–
Southend West	61.9	+3.9	46.2	-0.1	22.8	-2.3	23.7	-1.2	–	3.4	–	–	(3) 3.9	–
Thurrock	54.9	+5.9	32.6	+2.9	47.2	-9.3	10.9	+0.6	–	3.4	5.8	–	–	+6.1
Gloucestershire, Cheltenham	61.0	-0.9	36.3	+1.1	11.4	-0.6	41.5	-6.2	2.1	1.4	–	–	7.3	–
Cotswold	66.7	-0.8	49.3	-1.0	17.9	-4.7	28.8	+4.6	–	3.2	–	–	0.8	–
Forest of Dean*	70.9	+3.5	40.9	+2.1	36.6	-6.8	17.2	+4.3	2.1	2.4	–	–	0.9	–
Gloucester	62.8	+3.4	36.4	-1.3	44.7	-1.1	15.1	+0.8	1.7	2.2	–	–	–	-0.1
Stroud	71.3	+1.3	39.0	+1.6	39.6	-6.9	14.1	+3.2	5.4	1.9	–	–	–	+4.3
Tewkesbury	63.0	-0.7	49.1	+3.1	20.2	-6.7	27.4	+1.1	3.3	–	–	–	–	–
Greater London														
Barking & Dag., Barking	50.1	+4.6	17.1	-5.9	47.8	-13.1	11.1	+1.4	2.1	2.8	17.0	–	(2) 2.0	+3.6
Dagenham	51.3	+4.8	25.4	-0.3	50.1	-7.1	10.1	-0.2	–	5.1	9.3	–	–	+3.4
Barnet, Chipping Barnet	64.1	+3.6	46.6	+0.2	32.5	-7.5	15.7	+2.2	2.8	2.2	–	–	0.1	+3.9
Finchley & Golders Green	61.9	+4.6	38.8	+1.0	40.5	-5.8	16.9	+4.8	2.6	1.0	–	–	0.3	+3.4
Hendon	58.3	+6.1	38.0	+3.7	44.4	-8.0	13.9	+2.4	1.8	1.5	–	–	(2) 0.3	+5.9
Bexley, Bexley Heath & Cr.*	65.5	+2.0	46.3	+6.4	35.6	-7.9	12.1	+1.0	–	3.1	2.9	–	–	+7.2
Erith & Thamesmead	52.3	+2.0	23.9	-1.9	54.4	-4.9	13.5	+2.1	–	3.9	4.3	–	–	+1.5
Old Bexley & Sidcup	65.3	+3.2	49.8	+4.4	27.5	-9.9	14.7	+1.0	–	4.5	2.8	–	0.7	+7.2
Brent, Brent East†*	55.3	+3.4	10.3	-7.9	38.8	-24.4	47.5	+36.9	2.9	–	–	–	(2) 0.5	–
Brent North	59.3	+1.6	33.0	+3.7	48.8	-10.5	15.9	+4.6	–	–	–	–	(2) 2.3	+7.1
Brent South	52.7	+1.4	15.1	+2.5	58.8	-14.5	20.7	+9.9	3.2	–	–	–	2.2	–
Bromley, Beckenham	65.5	+2.9	45.3	+0.1	28.1	-6.2	22.2	+6.1	–	2.7	–	–	1.7	+3.1
Bromley & Chislehurst	64.8	+0.5	51.1	+1.6	22.2	-6.4	20.3	+1.4	3.2	3.2	–	–	–	+4.0
Orpington	69.9	+5.4	48.8	+4.9	9.0	-1.9	39.8	-3.6	–	2.4	–	–	–	–
Camden, Hampstead & H.	55.5	+1.2	28.5	+3.9	38.3	-8.6	27.0	+6.4	5.3	0.7	–	–	0.2	+6.2
Holborn & St Pancras	50.4	+0.7	18.9	+2.0	43.2	-10.6	29.3	+11.3	8.1	–	–	–	0.4	–

Constituency														
Croydon, Croydon Central*	60.6	+1.4	40.8	+2.3	40.6	−6.5	13.0	+1.8	2.1	2.2	−	−	−	(3) 1.2	+4.4
Croydon North	52.3	−0.9	22.0	−1.2	53.7	−9.8	17.2	+6.8	2.8	1.8	−	−	−	(4) 2.4	+4.3
Croydon South	63.6	+2.2	51.8	+2.6	24.1	−5.8	20.6	+2.3	−	2.2	−	−	−	(2) 1.4	+4.2
Ealing, Acton & Shepherd's B.	56.2	+3.6	27.9	+2.8	41.8	−12.3	25.2	+8.6	5.0	−	−	−	−	−	+7.5
Ealing North	59.4	+1.4	29.9	+0.6	45.1	−10.6	19.7	+8.5	2.8	1.5	−	−	−	1.1	+5.6
Ealing Southall	56.2	−0.7	21.6	+3.3	48.8	+1.3	24.4	+14.4	4.6	−	−	−	−	0.6	−
Enfield, Edmonton	59.1	+2.8	29.9	−0.9	53.2	−5.7	12.0	+5.0	2.6	2.3	−	−	−	−	+2.4
Enfield North	61.3	+4.3	39.6	−1.1	44.3	−2.4	11.4	+2.6	−	1.8	2.5	−	−	0.4	+0.6
Enfield Southgate*	66.4	+2.8	44.6	+6.0	40.5	−11.4	11.2	+4.2	2.6	1.2	−	−	−	−	+8.7
Greenwich, Eltham	61.7	+3.0	34.3	+2.2	43.6	−9.3	16.1	+3.9	−	2.9	2.8	−	−	0.4	+5.7
Greenwich & Woolwich	55.6	+1.5	20.1	+0.8	49.2	−11.3	20.7	+5.1	4.4	2.0	−	−	−	(2) 3.6	+6.1
Hackney, Hac. N. & Stoke N.	49.6	+0.6	14.4	−0.6	48.6	−12.5	23.3	+9.0	9.9	−	−	−	−	3.9	−
Hackney South & Sh.	49.7	+2.3	14.0	+0.3	52.9	−11.3	21.2	+6.7	5.5	−	−	−	4.5	1.9	−
Hammersmith & Fulham*	62.4	+6.0	45.4	+5.6	35.2	−9.1	14.4	+2.6	3.9	1.0	−	−	−	−	+7.4
Haringey, Hornsey & Wd Gn*	61.8	+3.8	12.7	−3.0	38.3	−11.6	43.3	+17.6	5.0	0.7	−	−	−	−	−
Tottenham	47.8	−0.4	13.5	−0.4	57.9	−9.5	16.8	+7.2	4.6	−	−	−	6.4	0.8	−
Harrow, Harrow East	60.5	+2.0	36.8	+4.7	46.1	−9.2	15.2	+2.7	−	1.8	−	−	−	−	+6.9
Harrow West	64.3	+1.4	38.3	+1.8	42.5	−7.1	17.1	+4.3	−	1.2	−	−	−	0.9	+4.5
Havering, Hornchurch*	63.9	+5.6	42.8	+0.6	41.6	−4.9	7.6	−0.7	−	2.7	3.4	−	−	(2) 1.8	+2.7
Romford	62.3	+2.7	59.1	+6.1	27.3	−9.0	8.4	+0.4	−	2.2	3.0	−	−	−	+7.5
Upminster	63.0	+3.4	48.5	+3.0	31.1	−10.8	9.0	−0.4	1.6	2.0	3.4	−	−	(2) 4.4	+6.9
Hillingdon, Hayes & Harl.	56.3	0.0	25.2	+1.1	58.7	−7.0	9.8	+3.8	1.4	1.7	2.6	−	−	0.7	+4.0
Ruislip–Northwood	65.3	+4.2	47.7	−1.0	21.0	−7.5	25.3	+6.0	2.2	1.6	−	−	−	2.1	−
Uxbridge	59.4	+1.8	49.0	+1.9	31.0	−9.8	13.2	+3.0	2.1	1.6	2.2	−	−	0.8	+5.8
Hounslow, Brentford & I.	54.5	+0.8	30.2	+1.1	39.8	−12.5	22.8	+9.3	3.6	−	−	−	−	(2) 3.6	+6.8
Feltham & Heston	49.5	+0.2	29.3	+5.1	47.6	−11.6	16.6	+2.8	2.2	1.6	−	−	−	(2) 2.7	+8.3
Islington, Islington North	53.9	+5.1	11.9	+1.1	51.2	−10.7	29.9	+10.9	7.1	−	−	−	−	−	−
Islington South & Finsbury	53.6	+6.2	14.8	+1.2	39.9	−14.1	38.3	+10.2	4.8	1.5	−	−	−	(2) 0.7	+7.6
Kensington & Chelsea	50.0	+6.7	57.9	+3.4	17.6	−5.6	18.3	+2.5	4.3	1.3	−	−	−	(2) 0.7	−
Kingston & Surbiton	68.5	+0.9	33.0	+4.8	13.2	+4.4	51.0	−9.1	−	1.3	−	−	−	1.4	−
Lambeth, Streatham	51.3	+2.6	17.8	−0.1	46.7	−10.2	28.3	+10.0	5.5	1.0	−	−	−	(4) 0.7	−
Vauxhall	46.9	+2.1	14.5	+1.0	52.9	−6.3	26.1	+6.0	4.6	0.7	−	−	−	(2) 1.2	−

ENGLAND	Turnout %	Turnout +/-	Con %	Con +/-	Lab %	Lab +/-	LD %	LD +/-	Green %	Ukip %	BNP %	Respect %	Other No. & %	Swing
Lewisham, Deptford	51.5	+3.2	12.4	0.0	55.6	-9.4	16.8	+5.0	11.1	1.7	-	-	2.4	-
Lewisham East	52.6	-0.5	24.1	+0.3	45.8	-7.9	21.8	+5.4	4.0	2.2	-	-	2.0	+4.1
Lewisham West	54.7	+2.6	20.0	-2.3	52.0	-9.0	20.9	+7.5	4.6	2.4	-	-	-	+3.3
Merton, Mitcham & Morden	61.2	+3.4	24.9	+0.8	56.4	-4.0	14.0	+3.9	3.5	-	-	-	(2) 1.2	+2.4
Wimbledon*	68.1	+3.8	41.2	+4.6	35.9	-9.8	18.1	+5.1	3.2	0.9	-	-	(3) 0.7	+7.2
Newham, East Ham	50.7	-1.7	13.1	-3.5	53.9	-19.2	10.9	+3.9	-	-	-	20.7	1.5	-
West Ham	49.8	+0.9	11.7	-4.7	51.2	-18.7	10.9	+3.5	2.9	-	-	19.5	(2) 2.6	-
Redbridge, Ilford North*	60.8	+2.4	43.7	+3.1	39.8	-6.0	13.7	+2.0	-	1.3	-	-	0.7	+4.6
Ilford South	53.6	-0.7	27.2	+1.5	48.9	-10.8	20.5	+9.3	-	2.1	-	-	1.8	+6.1
Richmond, Richmond Park	72.8	+4.8	39.5	+1.9	9.3	-2.0	46.7	-1.0	2.7	1.6	-	-	(4) 0.9	-
Twickenham	71.8	+5.4	32.4	-1.0	11.4	-2.5	51.6	+2.9	2.8	0.9	-	-	(2) 0.4	-
Southwark, Camberwell & P.	52.0	+5.3	9.8	-1.1	65.3	-4.3	18.8	+5.5	4.0	1.5	-	-	(2) 0.8	-
Dulwich & West Norwood	58.1	+4.7	21.9	-0.8	45.4	-9.5	24.4	+9.2	6.5	1.2	-	-	(3) 1.1	-
Southwark North & Ber.	49.2	-0.9	12.5	+4.9	32.8	+2.0	47.1	-9.9	3.0	0.7	-	-	(2) 2.5	-
Sutton, Carshalton & W'ton	63.5	+3.2	37.8	+4.0	17.2	-1.2	40.3	-1.6	2.1	2.1	-	-	-	-
Sutton & Cheam	66.2	+3.8	40.4	+2.4	11.8	-1.4	47.1	-1.6	-	2.6	-	-	0.7	-
Tower Hamlets, Bethnal Gn*	53.6	+3.4	14.2	-10.1	34.0	-16.4	11.2	-4.3	4.4	-	-	35.9	(2) 0.2	-
Poplar & Canning Town	47.8	+3.0	21.8	+2.0	40.1	-21.1	13.9	+2.8	2.4	-	-	16.8	5.0	+11.5
Waltham Forest, Chingford	63.0	+4.5	53.2	+5.0	25.7	-7.7	17.7	+2.2	-	2.8	-	-	0.7	+6.3
Leyton & Wanstead	55.0	+0.3	22.2	+2.5	45.8	-12.2	25.2	+9.2	4.6	1.8	-	-	0.5	+7.4
Walthamstow	54.6	+1.1	18.2	+0.1	50.3	-11.9	27.1	+12.5	-	2.4	-	-	2.1	-
Wandsworth, Battersea	59.0	+4.5	40.0	+3.4	40.4	-9.9	14.6	+2.5	4.2	0.8	-	-	0.0	+6.7
Putney*	59.5	+3.0	42.4	+4.0	37.5	-8.9	16.3	+2.7	2.7	1.1	-	-	0.0	+6.5
Tooting	59.0	+4.0	30.2	+3.7	43.1	-11.0	19.5	+4.7	4.1	1.0	-	1.7	0.5	+7.4
Westminster, C. of Ldn & W'mstr	50.3	+3.0	47.3	+1.0	25.1	-8.0	20.0	+4.7	4.2	1.1	-	-	2.2	+4.5
Regent's Park & Kens'on N.	51.5	+2.7	29.7	+2.7	44.7	-9.9	18.6	+6.0	4.9	1.1	-	-	(2) 1	+6.3

Greater Manchester

Altrincham & Sale West	65.9	+5.6	46.4	+0.3	30.3	-9.2	21.7	+7.2	—	1.7	—	—	—	+4.7
Ashton under Lyne	51.3	+2.2	19.6	+0.6	57.4	-5.1	13.8	+2.0	—	2.1	5.5	—	1.5	+2.8
Bolton North East	54.8	-1.3	34.6	+1.9	45.7	-8.6	16.4	+6.1	—	1.7	—	—	(2) 1.6	+5.3
Bolton South East	50.0	-0.1	20.4	-3.8	56.9	-4.9	19.0	+7.4	—	2.6	—	—	1.1	+0.6
Bolton West	63.5	+1.1	37.4	+3.8	42.5	-4.5	17.9	-0.5	—	1.3	—	—	(2) 0.9	+4.1
Bury North	61.5	-1.5	36.5	-0.2	43.0	-8.2	14.7	+2.5	—	1.1	4	—	(2) 0.7	+4.0
Bury South	58.5	-0.2	27.7	0.8	50.4	-8.8	17.8	+3.9	—	2.7	—	—	1.4	+4.8
Cheadle	69.6	+6.4	40.4	-1.9	8.8	-5.2	48.9	+6.5	—	1.0	0.9	—	—	—
Denton & Reddish	51.9	+3.4	19.3	-0.3	57.4	-7.8	16.4	+4.0	—	3.2	3.7	—	—	+3.8
Eccles	50.2	+1.9	19.7	-1.0	56.9	-7.6	18.6	+3.7	—	4.9	—	—	—	+3.3
Hazel Grove	60.8	+1.7	29.7	-0.4	17.5	+1.3	49.5	-2.5	—	3.4	4.7	—	3.5	—
Heywood & Middleton	54.6	+1.5	21.4	-6.2	49.8	-7.9	18.6	+7.4	—	2.0	—	—	(2) 7.1	+0.9
Leigh	50.3	+0.7	16.0	-2.2	63.3	-1.2	13.6	+0.8	—	—	3.4	—	7.8	-0.5
Makerfield	51.5	+0.6	12.2	-5.4	63.2	-5.3	10.6	-0.8	—	2.7	—	—	—	-0.0
Manchester Blackley	46.4	+1.6	13.4	-1.0	62.3	-6.6	18.7	+7.3	4.4	5.6	—	—	(3) 3.4	—
Manchester Central	42.8	+3.7	8.6	-0.4	58.1	-10.6	24.7	+9.0	—	0.9	—	—	(2) 1.2	—
Manchester Gorton	45.9	+3.2	9.8	-0.2	53.2	-9.6	33.2	+11.9	—	2.7	—	—	1.2	—
Manchester Withington*	55.3	+3.3	10.5	-4.8	40.6	-14.3	42.4	+20.4	4.3	1.1	—	—	1.2	—
Oldham East & Saddleworth	57.3	-3.7	18.2	+2.1	41.4	+2.8	33.2	+0.5	—	2.0	4.9	—	0.3	+2.8
Oldham West & Royton	53.3	-4.3	21.3	+3.6	49.1	-2.0	20.0	+7.6	—	2.6	6.9	—	(2) 1.7	—
Rochdale*	58.4	+1.7	10.5	-2.9	40.0	-9.2	41.1	+6.2	1.1	1.2	4.3	—	—	—
Salford	42.4	+0.8	15.2	-0.1	57.6	-7.5	22.4	+6.2	—	4.8	4.0	—	—	+2.0
Stalybridge & Hyde	53.5	+5.1	26.0	-1.8	49.7	-5.8	15.7	+2.2	3.1	1.6	4.0	—	—	+3.5
Stockport	54.5	+1.2	24.9	-1.0	50.5	-8.1	21.9	+6.4	—	2.7	—	—	3.0	+6.7
Stretford & Urmston	61.5	+6.7	30.4	+3.3	51.0	-10.1	14.0	+4.0	—	2.2	—	2.5	—	+3.3
Wigan	53.3	+0.9	20.8	-0.0	55.1	-6.6	17.7	+2.9	—	3.4	—	—	1	+4.0
Worsley	53.1	+2.1	25.7	+1.9	51.0	-6.1	18.7	+1.2	—	4.6	—	—	(2) 2.6	+3.0
Wythenshawe & Sale East	50.4	+1.8	22.3	-1.8	52.2	-7.8	21.5	+9.1	—	3.1	—	—	0.3	—
Hampshire, Aldershot	61.3	+3.4	42.7	+0.5	20.6	-4.6	31.7	+4.0	—	2.5	—	—	—	—
Basingstoke	63.0	+2.3	41.5	-1.2	31.7	-9.1	20.7	+6.7	1.9	2.2	1.7	—	—	+3.9

ENGLAND	Turnout %	Turnout +/-	Con %	Con +/-	Lab %	Lab +/-	LD %	LD +/-	Green %	Ukip %	BNP %	Respect %	Other No. & %	Swing
Eastleigh	64.8	+1.0	37.5	+3.2	20.6	-1.3	38.6	-2.1	–	3.4	–	–	–	–
Fareham	66.9	+3.4	49.7	+2.7	25.6	-6.0	21.7	+3.0	–	2.9	–	–	–	+4.3
Gosport	60.5	+3.4	44.8	+1.1	31.5	-5.6	16.6	+1.5	2.9	4.2	–	–	–	+3.4
Hampshire East	66.6	+2.3	45.7	-1.9	16.0	-3.6	35.3	+5.4	–	3.0	–	–	–	–
Hampshire North East	64.8	+3.2	53.7	+0.5	16.1	-3.8	27.2	+4.2	–	2.9	–	–	–	–
Hampshire North West	64.3	+2.0	50.7	+0.6	20.7	-4.8	24.9	+3.6	–	3.8	–	–	–	–
Havant	60.3	+2.8	44.4	+0.5	28.7	-4.9	20.2	+1.6	2.4	2.4	1.4	–	0.5	+2.7
New Forest East	65.9	+2.7	48.6	+6.1	12.1	-9.5	34.1	+0.7	–	5.2	–	–	–	–
New Forest West	66.5	+1.4	56.4	+0.7	16.5	+1.8	18.9	-6.9	4.0	4.2	–	–	–	–
Portsmouth North	60.0	+2.6	37.8	+1.1	40.9	-9.8	17.7	+7.4	–	3.6	–	–	–	+5.5
Portsmouth South	56.9	+6.0	33.9	+4.8	21.6	-2.3	42.2	-2.4	–	2.3	–	–	–	–
Romsey	69.7	+2.5	44.4	+2.3	8.8	+0.6	44.7	-2.3	–	2.1	–	–	–	–
Southampton Itchen	54.8	+0.8	26.8	-0.6	48.3	-6.2	21.2	+6.2	–	3.8	–	–	–	+2.8
Southampton Test	57.4	+1.1	25.9	+0.4	42.7	-9.8	24.8	+6.7	3.5	3.0	–	–	–	+5.1
Winchester	71.9	-0.5	38.5	-0.7	7.8	+1.8	50.6	-3.9	–	2.1	–	–	0.9	–
Hereford & Worcester, Bromsgrove	67.6	+0.5	51.0	-0.7	29.9	-4.0	15.1	+3.2	–	4.0	–	–	–	+1.6
Hereford	65.3	+0.1	41.2	+2.5	10.2	-4.9	43.3	+2.4	2.2	2.2	–	–	0.9	–
Leominster	67.7	-1.7	52.1	+3.1	15.2	-1.6	25.0	-1.7	4.5	3.2	–	–	–	–
Redditch	62.8	+3.6	38.0	-1.0	44.7	-0.9	13.9	+3.6	–	3.4	–	–	–	-0.0
Worcester	64.1	+2.0	35.1	-0.5	41.9	-6.7	16.3	+3.7	2.0	2.4	2.1	–	0.3	+3.1
Worcestershire Mid	67.3	+5.0	51.5	+0.4	23.8	-3.6	20.4	+1.6	–	4.3	–	–	–	+2.0
Worcestershire West	70.3	+3.2	44.5	-1.4	10.5	-3.5	39.3	+5.3	2.3	3.4	–	–	–	–
Wyre Forest	64.2	-3.8	28.7	+9.7	22.8	+0.7	–	–	–	2.3	–	–	46.2	–
Hertfordshire, Broxbourne	59.7	+4.0	53.8	-0.3	25.5	-4.8	12.2	+1.3	–	3.6	4.7	–	–	+2.3
Hemel Hempstead*	64.4	+2.1	40.3	+1.9	39.3	-7.3	17.2	+4.4	–	3.2	–	–	–	+4.6
Hertford & Stortford	67.7	+5.5	50.5	+5.8	24.1	-8.7	18.4	-1.5	3.9	2.1	–	–	1.2	+7.2
Hertfordshire North East	65.6	+0.7	47.3	+3.2	28.0	-8.4	21.4	+4.2	–	3.3	–	–	–	+5.8

Constituency														
Hertfordshire South West	68.5	+3.9	46.9	+2.6	20.9	-6.1	30.0	+3.7	–	2.2	–	–	–	+7.1
Hertsmere	63.0	+2.7	53.2	+5.4	27.2	-8.8	18.4	+3.2	–	–	–	–	1.2	–
Hitchin & Harpenden	70.5	+3.7	49.9	+2.5	22.2	-10.4	25.8	+7.8	–	1.7	–	–	0.4	–
St Albans*	70.4	+4.1	37.3	+3.7	34.3	-11.2	25.4	+7.5	–	1.6	–	–	(2) 1.4	+6.6
Stevenage	62.7	+2.0	35.4	+3.7	42.9	-8.9	18.1	+4.0	–	3.1	–	–	0.4	+6.3
Watford	64.8	+3.6	29.6	-3.7	33.6	-11.7	31.2	+13.8	3.0	2.6	–	–	–	–
Welwyn Hatfield*	68.1	+4.2	49.6	+9.2	36.3	-6.9	14.1	+0.1	–	–	–	–	–	+8.0
Humberside, Beverley & H'nes	64.8	+2.8	40.7	-0.6	35.6	-4.1	19.1	+3.2	–	4.7	–	–	–	+1.7
Brigg & Goole	63.2	-0.3	38.4	-0.8	45.2	-3.6	13.4	+4.1	–	3.0	–	–	–	+1.4
Cleethorpes	61.6	-0.4	37.3	+0.9	43.3	-6.2	14.8	+2.8	–	4.6	–	–	–	+3.6
Great Grimsby	51.7	-0.5	23.8	+0.7	47.1	-10.8	19.3	+0.3	2.0	3.8	4.1	–	–	+5.8
Haltemprice & Howden	70.1	+4.3	47.5	+4.2	12.7	-3.0	36.8	-2.1	–	1.4	1.7	–	–	–
Hull East	47.6	+1.1	13.3	-0.6	56.6	-8.0	18.8	+3.9	–	–	3.3	–	(5) 8.0	–
Hull North	47.3	+1.8	12.9	-4.2	51.9	-5.2	27.1	+7.4	2.9	–	2.6	–	2.6	–
Hull West & Hessle	45.2	-0.7	20.7	+0.2	55.0	-3.4	21.0	+6.0	–	–	–	–	3.2	–
Scunthorpe	54.3	-2.4	25.7	-3.2	53.1	-6.6	17.0	+7.6	–	4.2	–	–	–	–
Yorkshire East	61.6	+1.5	45.2	-0.6	31.8	-3.2	19.3	+4.8	–	3.6	–	–	–	–
Isle of Wight, Isle of Wight	61.3	+0.5	48.9	+9.2	17.2	+1.9	29.5	-5.8	–	3.5	–	–	0.8	–
Kent, Ashford	65.0	+2.5	51.6	+4.1	25.8	-6.2	16.1	+1.0	3.4	3.1	–	–	–	+5.2
Canterbury	66.1	+5.2	44.4	+2.9	28.7	-8.2	21.1	+3.3	3.2	1.9	–	–	0.7	+5.6
Chatham & Aylesford	59.7	+2.7	38.2	+0.8	43.7	-4.6	13.7	+1.8	–	2.9	–	–	1.6	+2.7
Dartford	63.2	+1.3	41.1	+0.5	42.6	-5.4	10.8	+2.3	–	3.0	–	–	2.6	+2.9
Dover	67.6	+2.4	35.0	-2.3	45.3	-3.5	15.9	+4.5	–	2.6	–	–	1.3	+0.6
Faversham & Kent Mid	65.7	+5.3	49.7	+4.1	29.7	-5.7	16.5	+3.0	–	2.6	–	–	1.4	+4.9
Folkestone & Hythe	68.4	+4.3	53.9	+8.9	12.5	-7.7	29.9	-2.3	1.4	1.3	–	–	(4) 1.0	–
Gillingham	62.5	+3.0	40.7	+1.6	41.2	-3.3	14.9	+1.3	–	2.6	–	–	0.6	+2.4
Gravesham*	65.8	+3.0	43.7	+4.9	42.2	-7.7	10.7	+1.5	–	1.9	–	–	1.4	+6.3
Maidstone & The Weald	65.8	+4.2	52.7	+3.0	22.2	-4.8	22.2	+2.3	–	3.0	–	–	–	+3.9
Medway	61.1	+1.6	41.7	+2.5	42.2	-6.8	12.5	+3.2	–	3.6	–	–	–	+4.6
Sevenoaks	66.5	+2.6	51.8	+2.4	21.0	-4.6	21.9	+0.2	–	3.0	–	–	(2) 2.3	+3.5
Sittingbourne & Sheppey	64.8	+7.3	41.6	+5.1	41.8	-4.0	12.7	-1.4	–	2.3	–	–	(2) 1.6	+4.5

ENGLAND	Turnout %	Turnout +/-	Con %	Con +/-	Lab %	Lab +/-	LD %	LD +/-	Green %	Ukip %	BNP %	Respect %	Other No. & %	Swing
Thanet North	60.1	+1.2	49.6	-0.7	32.2	-2.2	14.4	+3.4	-	3.9	-	-	-	+0.8
Thanet South	65.0	+1.1	38.8	-2.3	40.4	-5.3	13.2	+3.8	2.2	5.0	-	-	0.5	+1.5
Tonbridge & Malling	67.3	+3.0	52.9	+3.5	23.9	-6.1	19.5	+1.6	-	3.7	-	-	-	+4.8
Tunbridge Wells	65.7	+3.4	49.6	+0.8	20.6	-2.6	26.1	+1.5	-	3.7	-	-	-	-
Lancashire, Blackburn	56.9	+1.4	22.9	-8.3	42.0	-12.1	20.6	+12.5	1.9	2.3	5.4	-	5.0	+1.9
Blackpool North & Fleetwood	57.7	+0.5	35.9	-1.4	47.6	-3.1	12.8	+3.1	-	3.6	-	-	-	+0.9
Blackpool South	52.1	-0.1	29.9	-3.1	50.5	-3.8	14.5	+3.9	-	2.2	2.9	-	-	+0.3
Burnley	59.2	+3.5	10.8	-10.1	38.5	-10.9	23.7	+7.5	-	1.0	10.3	-	(2) 15.8	-
Chorley	62.9	+0.6	35.3	+0.6	50.7	-1.6	14.0	+2.8	-	-	-	-	-	+1.1
Fylde	60.1	-0.8	53.4	+1.1	26.0	-4.8	17.0	+2.3	-	-	-	-	3.6	+2.9
Hyndburn	58.8	+1.3	31.8	-1.3	46.0	-8.7	14.1	+4.5	-	1.9	6.2	-	-	+3.7
Lancashire West	57.7	-1.1	34.0	+2.0	48.1	-6.4	14.0	+2.5	-	2.0	-	-	(2) 1.9	+4.2
Lancaster & Wyre*	64.5	-1.4	42.8	+0.6	34.8	-8.3	16.2	+6.0	-	1.9	-	-	-	+4.5
Morecambe & Lunesdale	61.4	+0.3	37.4	+0.0	48.8	-0.7	13.8	+4.6	4.4	-	-	-	-	+0.4
Pendle	63.4	+0.2	31.8	-2.1	37.1	-7.5	23.2	+9.4	-	1.8	6.2	-	-	+2.7
Preston	53.8	+4.6	22.9	-0.1	50.5	-6.5	16.7	+3.6	-	3.1	-	6.8	-	+3.2
Ribble South	63.0	+0.5	38.4	0.3	43.0	-3.4	16.1	+0.6	-	2.5	-	-	-	+1.8
Ribble Valley	65.7	-0.4	51.9	+0.4	22.0	+2.0	23.4	-5.2	-	2.7	-	-	-	-
Rossendale & Darwen	61.5	+2.8	34.6	-2.1	42.9	-5.7	15.0	+0.4	1.8	1.7	3.9	-	-	+1.8
Leicestershire, Blaby	65.5	+1.0	45.5	-0.9	29.6	-3.8	19.0	+1.6	-	2.4	3.5	-	-	+1.5
Bosworth	66.3	+1.9	42.6	-1.9	31.4	-8.0	22.2	+5.9	-	3.9	-	-	-	3.1
Charnwood	66.4	+1.9	46.6	-1.7	29.2	-3.0	17.9	+1.7	-	2.9	3.4	-	-	+0.7
Harborough	64.3	+0.9	42.9	-1.8	19.2	-0.7	34.7	+1.4	-	3.2	-	-	-	-
Leicester East	62.2	+0.2	19.7	-4.8	58.1	+0.6	17.1	+4.8	-	-	-	-	(2) 5.1	-
Leicester South†	58.7	+0.7	17.8	-5.3	39.3	-15.1	30.6	+13.4	3.3	-	-	6.4	(3) 2.6	-
Leicester West	53.3	+2.4	24.4	-0.8	51.7	-2.5	17.5	+2.2	4.7	-	-	-	1.7	+0.9
Leicestershire North West	66.8	+1.1	36.0	+2.1	45.5	-6.6	12.1	+1.7	-	3.3	3.1	-	-	+4.3
Loughborough	63.8	+0.6	37.1	+1.7	41.4	-8.4	17.9	+5.1	-	2.4	-	-	1.3	+5.0

Rutland & Melton	65.0	+0.8	51.2	+3.1	25.0	-4.8	18.6	+0.8	—	3.2	—	—	(2) 2.1	+4.0
Lincolnshire, Boston & Skeg.	58.8	+0.5	46.2	3.3	32.1	-9.6	8.7	-3.7	1.0	9.6	2.4	—	—	+6.4
Gainsborough	64.6	+0.3	43.9	-2.3	25.7	-1.4	26.4	-0.3	—	4.1	—	—	—	—
Grantham & Stamford	63.6	+2.3	46.9	+0.8	31.1	-5.2	16.6	+2.2	—	3.2	—	—	(2) 2.2	+3.0
Lincoln	56.5	+0.5	32.9	+1.7	45.4	-8.5	18.2	+5.6	—	3.5	—	—	—	+5.1
Louth & Horncastle	62.0	-0.1	46.6	-1.9	25.4	-6.1	20.3	+0.2	—	7.7	—	—	—	+2.1
Sleaford & North Hykeham	67.1	+2.2	50.3	+0.6	26.5	-5.5	18.2	+2.0	—	5.0	—	—	—	+3.0
South Holland & Deepings	62.5	+0.4	57.1	+1.7	24.4	-7.0	12.9	+2.6	—	4.0	—	—	1.5	+4.3
Merseyside, Birkenhead	48.7	+0.4	16.6	-0.1	65.0	-5.5	18.4	+5.6	—	—	—	—	—	—
Bootle	47.7	-2.0	6.2	-1.8	75.5	-2.1	11.7	+3.1	—	4.1	—	—	2.6	—
Crosby	66.7	+1.6	32.1	-0.4	48.2	-6.9	17.4	+6.3	—	1.3	—	—	(2) 1.0	+3.3
Knowsley N, Sefton E.	52.6	-0.4	13.7	-2.6	63.3	-3.4	19.4	+5.6	—	—	2.4	—	1.3	+0.4
Knowsley South	51.5	-0.2	12.3	+0.7	68.1	-3.1	19.6	6.6	—	—	—	—	—	+1.9
Liverpool Garston	54.9	+4.8	9.8	-5.7	54.0	-7.3	33.5	+10.4	—	2.2	—	—	0.5	—
Liverpool Riverside	41.5	+7.4	9.1	+0.7	57.6	-13.8	24.8	+8.1	5.5	1.5	—	—	1.6	—
Liverpool Walton	45.0	+2.1	5.9	-0.1	72.8	-5.0	15.6	+1.1	—	4.0	—	—	1.7	—
Liverpool Wavertree	50.8	+6.5	6.6	-3.0	52.4	-10.3	37.7	+13.3	—	1.9	—	—	(2) 1.3	—
Liverpool West Derby	47.2	+1.7	8.4	+0.4	62.8	-3.4	12.9	+2.0	—	1.8	—	—	(2) 14.1	—
St Helens North	55.8	+3.0	18.9	+0.1	56.9	-4.2	21.3	+3.7	—	3.0	—	—	—	—
St Helens South	53.8	+2.4	13.0	-0.9	54.5	+4.8	28.3	+5.2	—	2.4	—	—	1.8	—
Southport	61.0	+2.4	37.0	+0.6	12.8	-3.8	46.3	+2.6	—	1.8	—	—	(2) 2.0	—
Wallasey	57.5	0.0	29.9	+2.0	54.8	-6.1	13.0	+1.8	—	2.3	—	—	0.0	+4.0
Wirral South	67.5	+1.8	33.2	-1.6	42.5	-4.9	21.6	+3.8	—	1.6	—	—	1.2	+1.7
Wirral West	67.5	+2.6	39.9	+2.7	42.5	-4.7	16.1	+0.6	—	1.0	—	—	0.4	+3.7
Norfolk, Great Yarmouth	60.1	+1.7	38.2	-0.9	45.6	-4.8	11.1	+2.7	—	4.3	—	—	0.9	+2.0
Norfolk Mid	67.0	-1.1	43.1	-1.7	29.2	-6.8	23.7	+9.2	—	4.0	—	—	—	+2.6
Norfolk North	73/0	+2.8	35.5	-6.3	9.2	-4.1	53.4	+10.8	—	1.7	—	—	0.2	—
Norfolk North West	61.6	-3.4	50.3	+1.8	32.2	-9.6	13.9	+5.5	—	3.7	—	—	—	+5.7
Norfolk South	68.7	+1.0	44.8	+2.6	22.5	-2.0	29.9	-0.0	—	2.9	—	—	—	—
Norfolk South West	62.5	-0.6	46.9	-5.2	28.7	-5.8	18.5	+7.8	—	5.0	—	—	0.9	+0.3
Norwich North	61.1	+2.0	33.2	-1.3	44.9	-2.6	16.2	+1.4	2.7	2.4	—	—	0.7	+0.6
Norwich South	59.9	+0.2	22.7	-2.1	37.7	-7.8	29.0	+6.4	7.4	1.4	—	—	(3) 1.8	—

ENGLAND	Turnout %	Turnout +/-	Con %	Con +/-	Lab %	Lab +/-	LD %	LD +/-	Green %	Ukip %	BNP %	Respect %	Other No. & %	Swing
North Yorkshire, Harrogate & K.	65.3	+0.7	31.9	-2.7	8.5	+1.1	56.3	+0.7	-	2.0	1.1	-	0.3	-
Richmond (Yorks)	65.0	-2.4	59.1	+0.2	19.7	-2.2	17.7	-0.3	3.5	-	-	-	-	+1.2
Ryedale	65.1	-0.6	48.2	+1.0	20.7	+6.0	24.4	-11.6	-	3.4	-	-	3.2	-
Scarborough & Whitby*	63.6	+0.4	41.0	+1.4	38.4	-8.8	16.0	+7.6	2.6	2.0	-	-	0.0	+5.1
Selby	67.3	+2.3	42.2	+1.4	43.1	-2.0	14.8	+3.7	-	-	-	-	0.0	+1.7
Skipton & Ripon	66.1	-0.0	49.7	-2.7	18.6	+1.2	26.7	+0.6	-	4.5	-	-	0.5	-
Vale of York	66.3	+0.2	51.7	0.0	24.4	-1.4	23.9	+3.7	-	-	-	-	-	+0.7
York, City of	61.7	+2.7	24.4	+0.9	46.9	-5.4	21.8	+4.1	4.5	1.8	-	-	(3) 0.6	+3.1
Northamptonshire, Corby	65.6	+0.5	40.0	+2.7	43.1	-6.2	12.7	+2.7	-	2.6	-	-	(2) 1.6	+4.5
Daventry	68.1	+2.6	51.6	+2.4	27.3	-4.9	16.5	+0.4	-	3.2	-	-	1.4	+3.6
Kettering*	68.0	-0.1	45.6	+2.2	39.7	-5.0	12.4	+2.2	-	2.3	-	-	-	+3.6
Northampton North	56.9	+0.9	30.8	+0.4	40.2	-9.2	24.5	+6.8	-	2.5	-	-	(2) 2.0	+4.8
Northampton South*	60.7	+1.2	43.7	+2.6	35.6	-7.3	15.3	+2.8	-	1.9	-	-	3.5	+4.9
Wellingborough*	66.5	+2.4	42.8	+0.6	41.5	-5.3	11.6	+2.3	-	2.3	-	-	(2) 1.9	+3.0
Northumberland, B'wick-upon-T.	63.4	-0.4	28.9	+0.8	18.3	+0.6	52.8	+1.4	-	-	-	-	-	-
Blyth Valley	56.2	+1.5	13.9	-1.9	55.0	-4.7	31.1	+6.7	-	-	-	-	-	+1.4
Hexham	68.8	-2.2	42.4	-2.2	30.3	-8.3	25.7	+10.7	-	-	-	-	(2) 1.6	+3.1
Wansbeck	58.4	-0.9	15.0	+2.3	55.2	-2.6	26.4	+3.7	3.4	-	-	-	-	-
Nottinghamshire, Ashfield	57.3	+3.7	24.3	-0.1	48.6	-9.5	13.9	+2.6	-	-	-	-	(4) 13.2	+4.7
Bassetlaw	58.1	+1.3	29.8	-0.5	56.6	+1.3	13.6	+0.9	-	-	-	-	-	-0.9
Broxtowe	68.6	+2.1	37.2	+0.6	41.9	-6.7	16.1	+1.4	1.8	1.4	-	-	(2) 1.6	+3.6
Gedling	63.9	+0.0	37.5	-0.8	46.1	-5.0	13.8	+3.2	-	1.7	-	-	0.9	+2.1
Mansfield	55.4	+0.2	18.4	-8.8	48.1	-9.0	13.9	-1.8	-	-	-	-	(2) 19.7	+0.1
Newark	64.1	+0.6	48.0	+1.5	33.9	-3.6	15.9	+2.7	-	2.2	-	-	-	+2.6
Nottingham East	49.6	+4.1	22.7	-1.6	45.8	-13.1	22.8	+9.7	5.0	2.5	-	-	1.2	+5.8
Nottingham North	49.1	+2.4	18.7	-5.1	58.7	-5.8	17.1	+6.5	-	5.5	-	-	-	+0.3
Nottingham South	50.6	+0.4	25.9	-1.3	47.4	-7.1	22.9	+6.3	-	3.9	-	-	-	+2.9
Rushcliffe	70.5	+3.9	49.5	+2.0	26.5	-7.5	17.4	+3.8	3.0	2.4	-	-	1.1	+4.8

Constituency														
Sherwood	62.8	+2.1	34.3	+0.5	48.4	−5.8	13.5	+1.6	–	3.7	–	–	–	+3.2
Oxfordshire, Banbury	64.5	+3.4	46.9	+1.8	27.7	−7.3	17.9	+2.0	2.8	2.2	–	–	(2) 2.4	+4.5
Henley	67.9	+3.6	53.5	+7.4	14.7	−6.4	–	−1.0	3.3	2.5	–	–	–	–
Oxford East	57.9	+2.0	16.7	−2.0	36.9	−12.5	34.6	+11.1	4.3	1.7	–	–	(3) 5.8	–
Oxford West & Abingdon	65.6	+1.1	31.7	+1.6	16.6	−1.1	46.3	−1.6	4.0	1.5	–	–	–	–
Wantage	68.2	+3.7	43.0	+3.4	24.0	−4.2	27.6	−0.4	2.6	1.5	–	–	1.2	–
Witney	69.5	+3.6	49.3	+4.3	22.0	−6.8	23.0	+2.7	3.1	2.5	–	–	–	–
Shropshire, Ludlow*	72.1	+4.2	45.1	+5.7	10.7	−2.7	40.7	−2.5	1.8	1.7	–	–	–	–
Shrewsbury & Atcham	69.4	+2.8	37.7	+0.3	34.1	−10.5	22.8	+10.5	2.3	2.7	–	–	(2) 0.4	+5.1[1]
Shropshire North*	63.3	+0.2	49.6	+0.9	25.9	−9.3	19.7	+6.9	–	4.8	–	–	–	+5.7
Telford	57.7	+5.8	32.5	+5.0	48.3	−6.3	14.4	+1.5	–	4.9	–	–	–	+5.4
The Wrekin*	67.0	+3.9	41.9	+3.5	39.9	−7.2	14.7	+3.2	–	3.5	–	–	–	+2.0
Somerset, Bridgwater	63.5	−0.9	44.1	+3.7	26.5	−0.2	22.7	−7.3	2.9	3.7	–	–	–	–
Somerton & Frome	69.5	+0.2	42.4	+0.1	10.8	−0.8	43.9	+0.3	–	1.9	–	–	0.9	–
Taunton*	69.7	+2.0	42.3	+0.6	12.0	−3.0	43.3	+2.0	–	2.4	–	–	–	–
Wells	68.0	−1.1	43.6	−0.2	15.6	+0.2	37.8	−0.5	–	3.0	–	–	–	–
Yeovil	64.3	+0.1	34.3	−1.8	10.5	−4.2	51.4	+7.2	–	3.8	–	–	–	–
South Yorkshire, Barnsley C.	47.2	+1.4	13.3	+0.2	61.1	−8.6	16.6	+1.9	–	–	4.9	–	4.1	+2.5
Barnsley East & Mexboro'	49.3	−0.2	14.7	+2.3	62.9	−4.6	20.1	+4.3	–	–	–	–	2.2	+1.3
Barnsley West & Penistone	55.0	+2.1	24.6	+1.7	55.3	−3.3	20.1	+1.5	–	–	–	–	–	–
Don Valley	55.0	+0.2	29.4	+0.7	52.7	−1.9	18.0	+6.8	–	–	–	–	–	+4.2
Doncaster Central	52.3	+0.7	18.9	−4.8	51.3	−7.8	22.8	+9.8	–	3.5	3.6	–	–	+2.2
Doncaster North	51.1	+0.7	15.4	+0.8	55.5	−7.6	12.0	+1.4	–	3.0	4.8	–	(2) 9.3	–
Rother Valley	58.1	+4.9	19.4	−2.3	55.4	−6.7	15.9	+3.4	–	4.3	5.1	–	–	–
Rotherham	55.1	+4.4	16.6	−2.8	52.8	−11.1	17.2	+6.6	3.0	3.7	6.6	–	–	–
Sheffield Attercliffe	54.6	+1.7	14.4	−0.8	60.1	−7.7	17.0	+2.8	–	4.5	4.0	–	–	–
Sheffield Brightside	48.5	+1.3	9.0	−1.2	68.5	−8.4	13.1	+4.4	–	3.2	6.2	–	–	–
Sheffield Central	51.1	+1.6	10.3	−0.6	49.9	−11.6	26.3	+6.6	6.0	1.4	1.8	4.3	–	–
Sheffield Hallam	67.8	+3.0	29.8	−1.2	12.6	+0.2	51.2	−4.2	3.3	1.1	0.9	–	1.1	–
Sheffield Heeley	57.1	+2.0	14.6	+0.4	54.0	−3.0	20.6	−2.1	3.8	2.3	3.9	–	0.8	–
Sheffield Hillsborough	61.2	+3.9	10.5	−3.3	51.2	−5.7	26.7	+4.1	–	2.8	4.4	–	–	–
Wentworth	56.0	+3.3	17.3	−1.5	59.6	−7.9	13.5	+2.7	–	4.5	5.1	–	–	+3.2

ENGLAND	Turnout %	Turnout +/-	Con %	Con +/-	Lab %	Lab +/-	LD %	LD +/-	Green %	Ukip %	BNP %	Respect %	Other No. & %	Swing
Staffordshire, Burton	61.0	−0.8	38.2	−0.4	41.1	−7.9	13.0	+3.4	–	1.9	3.8	–	1.9	+3.7
Cannock Chase	57.4	+2.0	29.9	−0.1	51.3	−4.8	13.8	−0.1	–	5.0	–	–	–	+2.3
Lichfield	66.7	+0.8	48.6	−0.5	32.4	−6.1	15.6	+4.8	–	3.4	–	–	–	+2.8
Newcastle-under-Lyme	58.2	−0.7	25.0	−2.6	45.4	−8.0	18.9	+3.4	2.3	3.6	3.5	–	1.3	+2.7
Stafford	64.7	−0.6	39.0	+2.4	43.7	−4.3	14.0	+4.5	–	3.3	–	–	–	+3.3
Staffordshire Moorlands	64.0	+0.1	35.5	+0.1	41.0	−8.0	15.7	+1.8	–	7.9	–	–	–	+4.1
Staffordshire South	37.3	+23.0	52.1	+1.5	17.5	−16.6	13.8	+2.2	–	10.4	–	–	(3) 2.5	+3.7
Stoke-on-Trent Central	48.4	+1.0	17.3	−1.6	52.9	−7.7	17.9	+3.2	–	3.3	7.8	–	0.9	+3.1
Stoke-on-Trent North	52.7	+0.7	20.0	+1.2	52.6	−5.3	14.8	+2.9	–	2.3	6.9	–	(2) 3.3	+3.3
Stoke-on-Trent South	53.6	+2.1	23.9	−0.7	46.9	−6.9	15.6	+2.5	–	2.8	8.7	–	2.1	+3.1
Stone	66.9	+0.6	48.3	−0.7	29.0	−6.8	19.4	+4.3	–	3.3	–	–	–	+9.1
Tamworth	61.0	+3.2	37.1	−0.5	43.0	−6.0	14.1	+2.4	–	2.8	–	–	3.0	+2.8
Suffolk, Bury St Edmunds	66.1	+0.1	46.2	+2.8	27.4	−11.1	19.8	+5.9	3.0	3.5	–	–	–	+6.9
Ipswich	60.8	+3.8	31.1	+0.5	43.8	−7.5	20.2	+5.0	–	2.7	–	–	(2) 2.2	+4.0
Suffolk Central & Ips. N.	66.7	+3.2	43.9	−0.5	28.5	−8.6	21.1	+4.9	3.1	3.4	–	–	–	+4.0
Suffolk Coastal	67.9	+2.3	44.6	+1.2	26.1	−8.6	22.1	+3.9	3.3	3.8	–	–	–	+4.9
Suffolk South	71.8	+5.7	42.0	+0.6	24.5	−5.7	28.5	+3.5	–	5.0	–	–	–	–
Suffolk West	60.7	+0.2	49.0	+1.5	28.9	−8.6	17.1	+5.3	–	4.9	–	–	–	+5.0
Waveney	64.4	+3.6	33.4	+6.3	45.3	−5.4	15.1	+3.7	2.4	3.7	–	–	–	+3.1
Surrey, Epsom & Ewell	66.1	+3.2	54.4	+6.3	20.6	−5.9	21.4	−0.7	–	3.5	–	–	–	–
Esher & Walton	62.2	+0.3	45.7	−3.3	19.4	−4.2	29.6	+7.1	–	3.3	–	–	(2) 2.0	–
Guildford*	68.3	+5.6	43.8	+2.3	9.8	−3.9	43.1	+0.5	1.6	1.2	–	–	(2) 0.5	–
Mole Valley	72.5	+3.6	54.8	4.2	10.7	−5.9	30.5	+1.5	–	3.0	–	–	1.0	–
Reigate	64.8	+4.7	49.0	+1.2	20.9	−6.6	23.2	+2.1	–	4.5	–	–	(2) 2.4	–
Runnymede & Weybridge	58.7	+2.5	51.4	+2.7	23.0	−5.9	17.9	+1.5	2.7	3.9	–	–	(2) 1.1	+4.3
Spelthorne	62.7	+1.9	50.5	+5.4	27.3	−10.0	17.1	+2.4	–	4.6	–	–	0.6	+7.7
Surrey East	66.6	+3.3	56.2	+3.6	14.8	−4.3	23.8	−0.6	–	4.4	–	–	0.8	–

Constituency														
Surrey Heath	62.9	+3.4	51.5	+1.8	16.7	-4.7	28.8	+3.1	—	3.0	—	—	—	—
Surrey South West	71.8	+1.5	50.4	+5.1	7.9	-0.8	39.5	-4.0	—	1.8	—	—	0.3	—
Woking	63.4	+3.1	47.4	+1.4	16.3	-4.0	33.1	+2.8	—	2.9	—	—	0.3	—
Tyne and Wear, Blaydon	62.6	+5.1	8.0	-3.4	51.5	-3.3	37.9	+4.1	—	2.6	—	—	—	—
Gateshead E. & Wash. W.	56.4	+4.0	13.9	-0.9	60.6	-7.6	21.9	+7.0	—	3.7	3.9	—	—	—
Houghton & Washington E.	51.7	+2.2	13.8	-0.5	64.3	-8.9	18.0	+5.5	—	—	—	—	1.2	—
Jarrow	55.0	-0.1	14.1	-0.5	60.5	-5.6	19.6	+4.5	—	4.6	—	—	1.3	—
Newcastle-upon-Tyne Central	57.3	+6.0	16.0	-5.3	45.1	-9.8	34.0	+12.4	3.5	—	—	—	(2) 2.5	—
Newcastle-upon-Tyne E. & Wd	55.7	+2.5	11.1	-0.7	55.1	-8.0	31.2	+11.6	—	—	—	—	2.6	—
Newcastle-upon-Tyne N.	62.4	+4.9	15.7	-4.7	50.0	-10.1	31.7	+12.3	—	—	—	—	2.6	—
South Shields	50.9	+1.2	17.2	+0.4	60.5	-2.7	19.7	+2.9	—	—	3.9	—	7.1	+5.1
Sunderland North	49.7	+0.7	19.8	+1.9	54.4	-8.3	14.8	+2.7	—	—	3.8	—	0.5	+3.9
Sunderland South	49.3	+1.0	22.5	+2.5	58.6	-5.3	14.6	+2.8	—	—	4.1	1.7	—	—
Tyne Bridge	49.9	+5.1	11.2	-2.0	61.2	-9.3	21.8	+9.5	—	—	—	—	—	+5.0
Tynemouth	66.9	-0.4	37.3	+3.9	47.0	-6.2	15.7	+4.0	—	—	—	—	—	+7.1
Tyneside North	57.2	-0.6	21.2	+6.7	61.9	-7.5	16.8	+4.4	—	—	—	—	—	+6.2
Warwickshire, Nuneaton	61.7	+1.6	39.0	+4.3	44.0	-8.1	13.0	+1.9	—	3.9	—	—	1.0	+4.1
Rugby & Kenilworth*	68.3	+0.8	41.2	+1.5	38.4	-6.7	17.8	+4.0	2.3	1.6	—	—	(2) 0.0	—
Stratford-upon-Avon	68.8	+3.6	49.2	-1.1	17.4	+0.7	28.3	-0.5	2.8	2.8	—	—	—	+5.3
Warwick & Leamington	67.5	+1.7	40.1	+2.5	40.6	-8.2	14.8	+3.7	—	1.7	4.1	—	—	+2.8
Warwickshire North	62.2	+2.1	32.0	-0.4	48.1	-6.0	13.2	+1.9	—	2.7	4.1	—	—	+2.0
West Midlands, Aldridge-B'hs	64.0	+3.4	47.4	-2.8	33.5	-6.8	12.3	+3.7	3.0	2.8	—	—	—	+3.1
Birmingham Edgbaston	58.0	+2.0	37.5	+0.9	43.8	-5.3	13.8	+1.8	—	2.0	4.8	—	1.3	+1.2
Birmingham Erdington	48.9	+2.3	22.8	-1.4	53	-3.8	15.8	+4.1	—	2.3	—	—	1.8	+1.8
Birmingham Hall Green	60.4	+2.9	30.7	-3.8	47.2	-7.3	19.3	+10.5	—	2.8	5.1	—	—	—
Birmingham Hodge Hill	52.7	+4.8	13.3	-6.7	48.6	-15.2	29.5	+21.4	—	2.4	4.1	—	1.2	—
Birmingham Ladywood	46.8	+2.6	10.6	-0.7	51.9	-17.0	31.5	+23.3	—	6.0	—	—	—	—
Birmingham Northfield	56.6	+3.8	28.9	-0.7	49.6	-6.3	13.4	+2.2	—	2.1	—	—	1.9	+2.8
Birmingham Perry Barr	55.5	+2.9	16.7	-6.4	47.0	+0.4	26.5	+3.6	—	1.9	—	5.6	2.3	—
Birmingham Selly Oak	59.5	+3.2	24.9	-1.8	46.1	-6.3	23.0	+6.7	3.8	2.3	—	—	—	—
Birmingham Sparkbrook & SH	51.8	+2.5	9.1	-1.7	36.1	-21.4	20.2	+7.0	2.2	3.5	—	27.5	1.3	—

ENGLAND	Turnout %	Turnout +/-	Con %	Con +/-	Lab %	Lab +/-	LD %	LD +/-	Green %	Ukip %	BNP %	Respect %	Other No. & %	Swing
Birmingham Yardley*	57.7	+0.5	10.1	-3.0	37.3	-9.6	46.4	+8.0	–	1.1	5.2	–	–	–
Coventry North East	53.0	+2.6	18.7	-0.1	56.9	-4.1	16.5	+5.3	–	2.9	–	–	5.0	+2.0
Coventry North West	59.4	+3.9	26.8	+0.9	48.2	-3.2	18.3	+4.6	–	1.8	3.6	–	1.4	+2.1
Coventry South	59.1	+3.8	30.5	+0.9	45.8	-4.4	17.8	+3.6	–	2.0	–	–	3.9	+2.6
Dudley North	60.2	+4.3	31.1	-3.4	44.2	-7.9	10.3	+1.6	–	4.7	9.7	–	–	+2.3
Dudley South	60.2	+4.8	34.5	+3.4	45.3	-4.5	12.2	-2.7	–	3.2	4.7	–	–	+4.0
Halesowen & Rowley Regis	62.9	+3.1	36.1	+1.8	46.6	-6.4	12.6	+2.2	–	4.8	–	–	–	+4.1
Meriden	60.1	-0.3	48.2	+0.5	33.1	-6.1	15.3	+4.2	–	3.4	–	–	–	+3.3
Solihull*	68.0	+4.8	39.4	-6.0	15.4	-10.2	39.9	+14.0	–	1.9	3.3	–	–	–
Stourbridge	64.7	+2.9	40.0	+2.4	41.0	-6.2	16.4	+4.3	–	2.6	–	–	–	+4.3
Sutton Coldfield	63.5	+3.0	52.5	+2.1	26.0	-1.2	16.6	-2.4	–	4.9	–	–	–	+1.6
Walsall North	52.8	+3.9	28.0	-1.1	47.8	-10.3	12.4	+3.4	–	3.5	6.0	–	2.3	+4.6
Walsall South	58.5	+2.8	27.4	-3.1	49.9	-9.0	9.2	+2.4	–	5.2	5.0	3.2	–	+3.0
Warley	57.1	+3.0	22.8	+0.0	54.4	-6.1	13.3	+2.8	–	2.0	5.5	–	2.0	+3.0
West Bromwich East	58.6	+5.2	22.8	-3.2	55.6	-0.3	12.4	-1.4	–	1.7	6.6	–	(2) 1.0	-1.5
West Bromwich West	52.3	+4.6	23.1	-2.0	54.3	-6.5	10.3	+3.5	–	2.5	9.9	–	–	+2.2
Wolverhampton N. E.	54.4	+1.6	29.7	+1.1	54.5	-5.8	11.7	+3.7	–	4.2	–	–	–	+3.4
Wolverhampton S. E.	52.3	+1.0	22.3	+0.5	59.4	-8.0	13.0	+4.3	–	5.3	–	–	–	+4.3
Wolverhampton S. W.	62.1	+0.1	37.5	-2.3	44.4	-3.9	13.4	+5.0	–	2.5	2.4	–	–	+0.8
West Sussex, Arundel & S.D.	68.5	+3.8	49.8	-2.4	17.1	-3.6	27.1	+4.7	–	5.4	–	–	0.6	–
Bognor Regis & L'hampton	62.1	+3.9	44.6	-0.5	25.4	-5.3	21.9	+4.3	–	8.0	–	–	–	+2.4
Chichester	66.6	+2.8	48.3	+1.3	18.4	-3.1	27.6	+3.4	–	5.8	–	–	–	–
Crawley	58.4	+3.2	39.0	+6.8	39.1	-10.2	15.5	+2.8	–	2.2	3.0	–	(2) 1.1	+8.5
Horsham	67.3	+3.5	50.0	-1.5	17.1	-3.1	26.8	+2.3	–	4.7	–	–	(2) 1.4	–
Sussex Mid	68.6	+3.8	48.0	+1.9	12.7	-6.3	36.1	+5.0	–	3.2	–	–	–	–
Worthing E. & Shoreham	61.6	+1.9	43.9	+0.7	25.5	-3.4	24.3	+1.4	–	4.7	–	–	1.5	+2.1
Worthing West	62.6	+2.9	47.6	+0.1	19.2	-2.3	26.7	+0.2	–	5.3	–	–	1.2	–

West Yorkshire, Batley & Sp.	62.3	+1.7	31.1	-5.7	45.8	-4.0	14.6	+4.3	1.7	-	6.8	-	-	-0.8
Bradford North	53.3	+0.6	16.2	-7.9	42.5	-7.2	32.3	+12.5	1.6	-	6.0	1.4	-	-
Bradford South	54.2	+2.8	24.0	-4.3	49.0	-6.7	14.6	+4.0	1.9	1.5	7.8	-	1.2	+1.2
Bradford West	54.0	+0.4	31.7	-5.4	40.1	-7.9	18.2	+11.9	3.1	-	6.9	-	-	+1.3
Calder Valley	67.0	+4.0	35.7	-0.5	38.6	-4.1	18.9	+2.9	2.9	-	4.0	-	-	+1.8
Colne Valley	66.0	+2.7	32.8	+2.3	35.8	-4.5	24.2	-0.7	2.6	-	2.9	-	(2) 1.6	+3.4
Dewsbury	62.0	+3.2	29.0	-1.2	41.0	-9.6	14.6	+2.6	1.5	-	13.1	-	0.8	+4.2
Elmet	68.8	+3.2	37.6	-1.3	47.2	-0.8	12.6	+1.7	-	-	2.6	-	-	-0.3
Halifax	61.1	+3.3	33.2	-0.7	41.8	-7.2	17.9	+3.3	-	-	6.6	-	0.5	+3.3
Hemsworth	54.6	+2.8	22.1	+1.1	58.8	-6.6	15.7	+4.3	-	-	-	-	3.4	+3.9
Huddersfield	56.6	+1.6	21.7	-3.1	46.8	-6.5	22.9	+7.9	4.7	-	3.0	-	0.9	-
Keighley	67.9	+4.5	34.3	-4.7	44.7	-3.5	11.8	+0.9	-	-	9.2	-	-	-0.6
Leeds Central	46.4	+4.7	13.2	-1.0	60.0	-6.9	19.4	+6.2	-	1.7	4.1	-	(3) 1.5	-
Leeds East	55.0	+3.5	18.5	-1.0	59.2	-3.8	20.7	+7.2	-	-	-	-	1.7	-
Leeds North East	65.5	+3.5	32.2	+0.9	44.9	-4.2	20.3	+4.4	-	-	-	-	2.5	+2.6
Leeds North West*	62.4	+4.2	25.7	-3.8	33.0	-9.0	37.2	+10.2	2.5	-	-	-	(2) 1.6	-
Leeds West	53.6	+3.6	14.3	-1.3	55.5	-6.7	17.5	+7.0	7.5	1.9	3.5	-	-	-
Morley & Rothwell	58.8	+5.3	19.4	-6.2	48.4	-8.6	16.0	+1.9	-	-	5.3	-	10.8	+1.2
Normanton	57.5	+5.2	24.5	-2.5	51.2	-4.9	17.0	+2.4	-	-	5.3	-	2.1	+1.2
Pontefract & Castleford	53.3	+3.6	17.4	-0.2	63.7	-6.1	12.0	+4.6	-	-	5.6	-	1.4	+2.9
Pudsey	66.0	+2.7	33.1	-2.5	45.8	-2.3	18.4	+4.2	2.7	-	-	-	-	-0.1
Shipley*	69.7	+3.5	39.0	-1.8	38.2	-5.8	14.7	+3.9	3.5	-	4.2	-	0.4	+2.0
Wakefield	59.3	+4.9	31.5	+0.8	43.3	-6.6	16.3	+3.9	3.0	1.1	3.1	-	(3) 1.8	+3.7
Wiltshire, Devizes	65.2	+0.9	48.5	+1.3	22.3	-2.6	25.0	+3.0	4.1	-	-	-	-	-
Salisbury	68.1	+2.8	47.8	+1.2	17.4	-0.1	27.3	-2.8	2.9	4.2	-	-	0.4	-
Swindon North	61.0	-0.1	38.0	+4.3	43.7	-9.2	15.2	+3.7	-	2.2	-	-	(2) 0.9	+6.7
Swindon South	60.2	-0.9	37.2	+2.8	40.3	-11.0	16.8	+4.9	2.8	2.2	-	-	(2) 0.6	+6.9
Westbury	67.0	+0.4	44.5	+2.4	17.3	-4.1	34.9	+3.3	-	3.3	-	-	-	-
Wiltshire North	69.3	+2.0	46.9	+1.4	12.1	-2.2	37.4	-0.8	-	2.5	-	-	1.0	-

WALES	Turnout %	Turnout +/-	Con %	Con +/-	Lab %	Lab +/-	LD %	LD +/-	PC %	PC +/-	Grn %	UKI %	Other No. & %	Swing
Clwyd, Alyn & Deeside	60.2	+1.7	25.2	-1.0	48.8	-3.5	17.4	+4.4	3.7	+0.4	–	2.6	(3) 2.3	+1.2
Clwyd South	62.9	+0.5	25.7	+0.9	45.0	-6.4	15.5	+5.3	9.4	-2.4	–	2.0	(1) 2.4	+3.6
Clwyd West	64.0	-0.1	36.2	+0.7	35.9	-2.9	13.3	+1.9	10.9	-2.0	–	1.4	(2) 2.3	+1.8
Delyn	64.4	+1.2	26.2	-0.5	45.7	-5.8	17.9	+2.5	7.4	+0.9	–	1.6	(1) 1.2	+2.7
Vale of Clwyd	62.2	-1.5	31.6	-0.6	46.0	-4.0	11.8	+2.4	7.1	+0.0	–	1.2	(2) 2.3	+1.7
Wrexham	63.3	+3.7	20.0	-2.4	46.1	-7.0	23.6	+6.5	5.7	-0.2	–	–	(1) 1.6	–
Dyfed, Carmarthen E. & D.	71.6	+1.2	13.7	+0.8	28.3	-7.3	9.7	+2.3	45.9	+3.5	–	1.7	(1) 0.7	–
West & Pembrokeshire S.	67.3	+2.0	31.8	+2.5	36.9	-4.7	14.3	+5.5	14.7	-3.9	–	1.4	(3) 0.9	+3.6
Ceredigion*	67.2	+5.5	12.4	-7.1	12.1	-3.4	36.5	+9.7	35.9	-2.3	2.4	–	(1) 0.7	–
Llanelli	63.5	+1.2	13.7	+4.2	46.9	-1.6	12.9	+4.4	26.5	-4.4	–	–	–	–
Preseli Pembrokeshire*	69.5	+1.8	36.6	+3.2	35.0	-6.4	12.9	+2.3	12.3	-0.4	1.3	1.3	(1) 0.7	+4.8
Gwent, Blaenau Gwent	66.1	+6.7	2.3	-5.2	32.3	-39.7	4.3	-5.0	2.4	-8.8	–	0.5	(1) 58.2	–
Islwyn	61.0	-0.9	10.9	+2.9	63.8	+2.2	12.5	-0.7	12.8	+0.9	–	–	–	–
Monmouth*	72.4	+0.9	46.9	+4.9	37.0	-5.8	12.8	+1.4	2.2	-0.2	–	1.2	–	+5.4
Newport East	57.9	+3.2	23.4	+0.3	45.2	-9.5	23.7	+9.7	3.8	-1.0	–	3.0	(1) 0.8	–
Newport West	59.3	+0.2	29.6	+3.4	44.8	-7.9	17.9	+6.2	3.6	-3.6	1.5	2.4	(1) 0.2	+5.6
Torfaen	59.3	+1.6	15.8	-0.1	56.9	-5.2	15.8	+4.6	6.2	-1.5	–	3.2	(1) 2.1	+2.5
Gwynedd, Caernarfon	60.4	-1.7	12.4	-2.7	26.9	-5.4	12.5	+6.3	45.5	+1.1	–	2.6	–	–
Conwy	62.3	-0.6	27.9	+4.2	37.1	-4.7	20.0	+3.1	11.1	-5.4	1.5	0.9	(2) 1.5	+4.5
Meirionnydd Nant Conwy	61.7	-2.2	16.5	-2.3	19.3	-3.4	10.6	+1.7	51.3	+1.7	–	2.3	–	–
Ynys Môn	67.5	+3.8	11.0	-1.0	34.6	-0.4	6.8	-1.3	31.1	-1.5	–	1.0	(2) 15.4	–
Mid-Glamorgan, Bridgend	59.2	-1.0	26.1	+0.8	43.3	-9.1	21.0	+6.6	6.7	-0.5	1.6	1.3	–	+5.0
Caerphilly	58.6	+0.9	14.6	+3.2	56.6	-1.6	9.8	+0.4	17.4	-3.6	–	–	(1) 1.6	+2.4
Cynon Valley	58.7	+3.3	7.7	+0.2	64.1	-1.5	11.2	+1.8	14.3	-3.1	–	2.6	–	–
Merthyr Tydfil & Rhymney	54.9	-2.8	8.9	+1.8	60.5	-1.3	14.0	+6.5	9.9	-4.8	–	2.3	(2) 4.3	+1.5
Ogmore	57.8	-0.3	14.0	+2.9	60.4	-1.6	15.2	+2.4	10.4	-3.6	–	–	–	–
Pontypridd	60.9	+7.5	13.4	+0.1	52.8	-7.2	19.5	+8.7	11.2	-2.6	–	2.6	(1) 0.6	–
Rhondda	61.0	+0.4	5.6	+1.0	68.1	-0.3	10.5	+6.0	15.9	-5.2	–	–	–	–

	Turnout %	Turnout +/-	Con %	Con +/-	Lab %	Lab +/-	LD %	LD +/-	SNP %	SNP %	SSP %	Grn %	Other No. & %	Swing
Powys, Brecon & Radnorsh.	69.5	-1.0	34.6	-0.2	15.0	-6.4	44.8	+8.0	3.7	+0.2	-	1.9	-	-
Montgomeryshire	64.4	-1.2	27.4	-0.5	11.5	-0.4	51.2	+1.8	6.9	+0.1	-	3.0	-	-
South Glamorgan, Cardiff C.	59.2	+1.0	9.2	-6.7	34.3	-4.3	49.8	+13.1	3.5	-1.3	-	1.1	(3) 2.1	-
Cardiff North	70.5	+1.5	36.5	+4.9	39.0	-6.9	18.7	+3.4	4.3	-1.4	-	1.2	(2) 0.3	+5.9
Cardiff South & Penarth	56.2	-0.9	22.2	+0.4	47.3	-8.9	20.4	+7.6	5.5	-0.1	2.0	1.4	(3) 1.2	+4.7
Cardiff West	57.7	-0.7	21.9	+0.5	45.5	-9.0	17.5	+4.5	12.5	+2.8	-	2.1	(1) 0.5	+4.8
Vale of Glamorgan	68.9	+2.3	37.3	+2.3	41.2	-4.3	13.0	+0.8	5.1	-1.2	-	1.8	(2) 1.6	+3.3
West Glamorgan, Aberavon	58.9	-2.0	10.2	+2.6	60.0	-3.1	13.8	+4.0	11.8	+2.0	1.7	-	(1) 2.6	+2.8
Gower	64.9	+1.5	25.5	-2.0	42.5	-4.9	18.4	+6.4	7.8	-2.5	2.6	3.2	-	+1.4
Neath	62.2	-0.4	11.5	+2.1	52.6	-8.1	14.3	+4.7	17.1	-1.3	1.8	-	(3) 2.6	-
Swansea East	52.4	+0.1	10.1	-0.0	56.6	-8.6	20.1	+9.9	6.9	-4.6	1.6	2.2	-	-
Swansea West	57.1	+1.3	16.0	-3.0	41.8	-6.9	28.9	+12.4	6.5	-4.1	2.2	1.8	(3) 2.7	-

SCOTLAND	Turnout %	Turnout +/-	Con %	Con +/-	Lab %	Lab +/-	LD %	LD +/-	SNP %	SNP %	SSP %	Grn %	Other No. & %	Swing
Aberdeen North	55.7	-0.7	9.4	-1.0	42.5	-6.8	23.9	+11.7	22.3	-3.3	1.9	-	-	-
Aberdeen South	62.1	+2.4	17.1	-2.7	36.7	-1.4	33.5	+4.9	9.9	-2.3	1.0	1.8	-	-
Aberdeenshire West & Kincard	63.5	+2.0	28.4	-2.2	13.1	+0.9	46.3	+2.3	11.3	-0.9	0.9	-	-	-
Airdrie & Shotts	53.5	-0.7	9.9	+3.7	59.0	+0.4	11.4	+3.6	16.5	-2.6	2.1	-	1.0	-
Angus	60.5	+6.3	29.5	-2.2	18.0	-0.3	17.5	+2.7	33.7	+0.5	1.5	-	-	-
Argyll & Bute	64.2	4.1	23.5	-2.2	22.4	-0.3	36.5	3.7	15.5	-1.9	2.0	-	-	-
Ayr, Carrick & Cummock	61.3	-1.6	23.2	-1.6	45.4	-6.0	14.1	6.9	13.2	-0.5	1.2	-	3.0	+2.2
Ayrshire Central	62.5	0.9	22.1	-4.1	46.4	-2.8	16.1	9.7	11.6	-3.0	1.9	-	1.6	-0.7
Ayrshire North & Arran	59.9	-0.7	18.4	0.9	43.9	-4.4	16.4	7.7	18.0	-3.1	1.8	-	(2) 0.7	+2.7
Banff & Buchan	56.8	2.8	19.4	-2.2	12.0	-1.4	13.3	-0.5	51.2	2.3	1.1	-	(2) 3.1	-
Berwickshire, Roxburgh & Sel.	63.3	3.4	28.8	6.9	15.9	-1.0	41.8	-4.9	8.6	-2.8	1.5	-	(2) 3.3	-
Caithness, Sutherland & E.Rs	59.1	-2.1	10.2	-3.2	20.9	-3.3	50.5	11.9	13.3	-7.0	2.0	-	(1) 3.1	-
Coatbridge, Chryston & B	56.9	-3.0	7.2	2.3	64.5	-4.8	12.0	6.4	13.6	-1.2	2.7	-	-	-
Cumbernauld, Kilsyth & K.E.	60.4	1.6	7.0	1.9	51.8	-6.0	14.9	8.8	22.2	-3.8	2.9	-	(1) 1.2	-

227

SCOTLAND	Turnout %	Turnout +/-	Con %	Con +/-	Lab %	Lab +/-	LD %	LD +/-	SNP %	SNP +/-	SSP %	Grn %	Other No. & %	Swing
Dumfries & Galloway	68.5	1.5	35.4	3.3	41.1	8.8	8.4	-0.5	12.1	-12.9	1.0	1.5	(1) 0.6	-2.7
Dumfriesshire, Clydesdale & Td*	67.6	0.7	36.2	11.4	32.3	-4.6	20.3	-1.5	9.1	-5.2	1.2	–	(1) 1.0	+7.8
Dunbartonshire East*	72.1	10.1	16.5	-6.0	33.1	-0.2	41.8	14.8	5.8	-8.9	0.9	1.9	–	–
Dunbartonshire West	61.3	-2.8	6.4	1.4	51.9	-11.5	14.4	12.0	21.8	-2.2	4.1	–	(2) 0.5	–
Dundee East*	62.4	3.3	12.8	-2.5	36.2	-1.1	11.4	2.7	37.2	1.1	1.4	–	(2) 0.3	–
Dundee West	56.1	1.0	8.3	-0.6	44.6	-5.7	14.4	5.2	30.0	2.3	2.7	–	–	–
Dunfermline & Fife West	59.9	2.3	10.3	0.6	47.4	-7.0	20.2	5.9	18.9	1.1	1.6	–	–	–
East Kilbride, Strathaven & L.	63.5	1.7	10.0	0.3	48.7	-4.2	16.6	6.5	17.9	-5.8	–	3.3	(2) 3.5	–
East Lothian	64.5	+2.5	16.0	-0.1	41.5	-7.4	24.8	+7.7	13.1	-1.8	1.1	2.5	(2) 1.1	–
Edinburgh East	60.9	+8.1	10.3	-0.8	40.0	-9.7	24.4	+7.2	17.0	+0.6	2.2	5.7	(2) 0.3	–
Edinburgh North & Leith	62.4	+8.5	18.7	0.0	34.2	-7.6	29.2	+8.9	10.2	-4.2	1.9	5.8	–	–
Edinburgh South	69.4	+9.2	24.1	+1.4	33.2	-6.0	32.3	+7.0	6.2	-3.1	1.0	3.2	–	+3.7
Edinburgh South West	65.0	+6.4	23.3	-3.2	39.8	-4.6	21.1	+9.4	10.6	-2.8	1.3	3.5	–	+0.7
Edinburgh West	68.3	+4.8	19.5	-2.2	18.6	-7.8	49.5	+11.2	9.1	-1.6	1.1	2.1	–	–
Falkirk	59.6	-0.3	9.9	+1.8	50.9	-0.7	16.0	+9.5	21.4	-1.2	1.8	–	–	–
Fife North East	62.1	+5.1	19.5	-3.4	12.8	-1.6	52.1	+3.0	10.4	-0.3	1.1	2.8	–	–
Glasgow Central	43.9	+4.5	6.3	+0.1	48.2	-6.5	17.8	+8.2	14.8	-6.1	4.0	4.9	(4) 4.1	–
Glasgow East	48.2	+1.6	6.9	+0.8	60.7	-3.0	11.8	+6.1	17.0	-0.1	3.5	–	–	–
Glasgow North	50.4	+7.5	8.7	+0.5	39.4	-9.0	27.4	+8.4	12.9	-3.4	3.8	7.6	–	–
Glasgow North East‡	45.8	+1.9	–	–	53.3	-13.7	–	–	17.7	-0.5	4.9	–	(4) 24.0	–
Glasgow North West	55.2	+4.4	9.6	+0.2	49.2	-5.7	19.5	+7.9	13.7	-2.3	3.3	3.9	(1) 0.8	+3.0
Glasgow South	56.0	+3.2	12.6	-1.2	47.2	-3.2	19.0	+6.6	12.6	-4.7	3.4	4.4	(1) 0.7	–
Glasgow South West	50.1	+0.3	5.8	+0.4	60.2	-1.7	11.6	+6.1	15.4	-2.1	5.4	–	(2) 1.7	–
Glenrothes	56.1	+1.1	7.1	-0.4	51.9	-6.0	12.7	+4.8	23.4	-0.6	1.9	–	(2) 3.0	–
Gordon	61.8	+5.2	17.6	-1.3	20.2	-1.2	45.0	+6.2	16.0	-3.3	1.1	–	–	–
Inverclyde	60.9	+1.4	10.2	-0.6	50.7	+0.5	17.0	-4.2	19.6	+5.5	2.5	–	–	–
Inverness, Nairn, Badenoch & S*	63.6	+0.4	10.3	-1.9	30.9	-1.3	40.3	+10.8	13.5	-9.4	1.0	2.4	(1) 1.5	–

Kilmarnock & Loudoun	60.9	−0.3	11.3	+1.3	47.3	−7.7	11.1	+3.5	27.7	+3.2	1.9	−	−
Kirkcaldy & Cowdenbeath	58.4	+3.5	10.3	−0.3	58.1	−0.4	13.0	+3.9	14.5	−4.1	1.6	−	(4) 2.5
Lanark & Hamilton East	59.1	+0.1	12.8	+0.3	46.0	−4.5	18.6	+7.3	17.8	−4.2	1.8	−	(3) 2.9
Linlithgow & Falkirk East	60.5	+3.8	11.8	+2.0	47.7	−4.1	15.3	+5.2	23.5	−1.8	1.6	−	−
Livingston	58.1	+2.0	10.1	+2.5	51.1	−4.1	15.4	+5.5	21.6	−1.8	1.8	−	−
Midlothian	62.2	+1.0	9.4	+0.2	45.5	−5.0	26.2	+9.0	17.0	−2.2	1.9	−	−
Moray	58.4	+1.2	22.0	−0.9	20.4	−3.9	19.2	+1.3	36.6	+7.2	1.8	−	−
Motherwell & Wishaw	55.4	−0.8	9.3	−0.2	57.5	+0.7	12.0	+3.3	16.5	−4.0	2.7	−	(3) 2.0
Na h-Eileanan an Iar*	64.1	+4.0	4.4	−5.1	34.5	−10.5	7.9	+1.5	44.9	+8.0	0.7	−	(2) 7.6
Ochil & South Perthshire	66.0	+3.6	21.5	−0.6	31.4	−2.0	13.3	+2.8	29.9	−1.7	0.9	2.1	(2) 1.0
Orkney & Shetland	53.7	+1.7	13.3	−5.4	14.2	−6.4	51.5	+10.2	10.3	−4.4	5.6	−	(3) 2.7
Paisley & Renfrewshire North	64.8	+3.7	13.6	−0.1	45.7	−6.5	18.3	+10.7	18.8	−3.8	1.6	−	(2) 2.0
Paisley & Renfrewshire South	62.9	+6.0	8.4	0.0	52.6	−4.4	17.6	+8.1	17.6	−3.3	2.1	−	(3) 1.7
Perth & Perthshire North	64.8	+0.3	30.4	+5.4	18.7	−5.7	16.1	+4.0	33.7	−2.3	1.1	−	−
Renfrewshire East	72.1	+2.3	29.9	+1.1	43.9	−3.7	18.3	+5.4	6.8	−1.7	1.1	−	−	+2.4
Ross, Skye & Lochaber	64.4	+2.1	10.1	−0.2	14.9	−8.1	58.7	+14.4	9.6	−8.1	1.3	3.4	(2) 9.4
Rutherglen & Hamilton West	58.5	+3.2	8.4	−0.2	55.6	−4.1	18.4	+6.7	13.9	−1.3	2.7	−	−
Stirling	67.7	+2.8	25.1	+1.4	36.0	−7.0	20.7	+9.2	12.6	−4.5	1.0	3.0	(3) 1.6	+4.2

The vote changes in Scotland are based on notional figures for what would have happened if the new boundaries had been in force in 2001.

N. IRELAND	Turnout %	Turnout +/-	UUP %	UUP +/-	DUP %	DUP +/-	APNI %	APNI +/-	SF %	SF +/-	SDLP %	SDLP +/-	Other %
Antrim East*	59.7	+0.6	26.6	−9.8	49.6	+13.6	15.3	+2.8	2.6	+0.1	5.3	−2.0	0.5
Antrim North	65.6	+12.8	14.4	−6.5	54.8	+4.9	3.0	+0.4	15.7	+5.9	12.2	−4.7	−
Antrim South*	63.0	+8.4	29.1	−7.9	38.2	+3.4	8.6	+4.1	11.6	+2.2	12.4	+0.3	−
Belfast East	63.7	−0.2	30.1	+6.9	49.1	+6.6	12.2	−3.7	3.3	−0.0	2.7	+0.3	2.5
Belfast North	66.5	+0.9	7.1	−4.9	45.6	+6.8	1.4	+1.4	28.6	+3.4	16.2	−4.8	1.0
Belfast South*	68.9	+5.4	22.7	−22.1	28.4	+28.4	6.3	0.9	9.0	+1.4	32.3	+1.7	1.3
Belfast West	75.1	+7.6	2.3	−3.9	10.6	+4.1	−	−	70.5	+4.4	14.6	−1.4	2.1
Down North	59.1	+0.3	50.4	−5.6	35.1	+35.1	7.6	+7.6	0.6	−0.2	3.1	−0.3	3.2
Down South	70.9	−0.8	9.9	−7.7	18.3	+3.3	−	−1.3	25.8	+6.0	44.7	−1.6	−
Fermanagh & S. Tyrone	79.3	+1.3	18.2	−15.9	28.8	+28.8	−	−	36.2	+4.1	14.8	−3.9	1.3
Foyle	74.4	+4.5	2.4	−4.5	14.4	−0.8	−	−1.2	33.2	+6.7	46.3	−3.9	−
Lagan Valley*	64.8	+1.6	21.5	−35.0	54.7	+41.3	10.1	−6.5	7.5	+1.6	6.1	−1.6	3.7
Londonderry E.	65.0	+1.1	21.1	−6.3	42.9	+10.7	2.6	−1.9	16.1	+0.5	17.1	−3.7	0.2
Newry & Armagh*	76.3	+0.5	13.9	+1.6	18.4	−1.0	−	−	41.4	+10.4	25.2	−12.2	1.2
Strangford	58.1	−1.8	21.3	−19.0	56.5	+13.6	9.0	+2.3	2.6	+0.4	6.7	+0.6	3.9
Tyrone West	80.2	+0.3	6.9	−23.6	17.8	−1.9	−	−	38.9	−1.9	9.1	−19.6	27.4
Ulster Mid	78.0	−2.5	10.7	+10.7	23.5	−7.7	−	−	47.6	−3.4	17.4	+0.7	0.2
Upper Bann*	66.6	3.0	25.6	−7.9	37.5	+8.1	2.2	+2.2	20.9	−0.2	12.9	−2.0	0.8
Total NI	68.6	+0.8	17.8	−9.0	33.7	+11.2	24.3	+2.6	24.3	+2.6.	17.5	−3.5	6.7

Notes:

UUP: Ulster Unionist Party

DUP: Democratic Unionist Party

APNI: Alliance Party of Northern Ireland

SF: Sinn Fein

SDLP: Social Democratic & Labour Party

The only deposit-saving 'Other' vote was in Tyrone West (K. Deeny (Ind) 27.4%).

Table A1.4 Seats changing hands

Con Gains from Labour
Bexley Heath & C.
Braintree
Clwyd W.
Croydon C.
Dumfries+
Enfield, Southgate
Forest of Dean
Gravesham
Hammersmith & F.
Harwich
Hemel Hempstead
Hornchurch
Ilford N.
Kettering
Lancaster & W.
Milton Keynes N.E.
Monmouth
Northampton S.
Peterborough
Preseli, Pemb.
Putney
Reading E.
Rugby & K.
Scarborough & W.
Shipley
Shrewsbury & A.
St Albans
Wellingborough
Welwyn Hatfield
Wimbledon
Wrekin

Con Gains from Lib Dem
Guildford
Newbury
Ludlow
Torridge & W. Devon
Weston-Super-Mare

Lib Dem Gains from Lab
B'ham Yardley
(Brent East)
Bristol W.
Cambridge
Cardiff C.
Dunbartonshire E.
Falmouth & Camb.
Hornsey.
Inverness, Nairn, B. & S.
Leeds N.W.
Man. Withington
Rochdale

Lib Dem Gains from Con
Solihull
Taunton
Westmorland & L.

Lib Dem Gain from PC
Ceredigion

Other gains
Dundee E. *SNP from Lab*
Na h-Eilanan an Iar *SNP from Lab*
Bethnal Gn *Respect from Lab*
Blaenau Gwent *Ind from Lab*
Antrim E. *DUP from UUP*
Antrim S. *DUP from UUP*
Lagan Valley *DUP from UUP*
Upper Bann *DUP from UUP*
Belfast S. *SDLP from UUP*
Newry & Armagh *SF from SDLP*

Table A1.5   Exceptional results

Ten highest turnouts (GB) (%)
77.4 Dorset W.
73.0 Norfolk N
72.8 Richmond Park
72.5 Mole Valley
72.4 Wansdyke
72.4 Monmouth
72.2 Northavon
72.1 Dunbartonshire E
72.1 Renfrew E
72.1 Ludlow

Four highest turnouts (NI) (%)
73.5 Fermanagh & S. T.
73.2 Ulster Mid
72.7 Tyrone W
70.6 Newry & Armagh

Ten lowest turnouts (%)
(37.3 Staffordshire S.)
41.5 Liv. Riverside
42.4 Salford
42.8 Manchester C.
43.9 Glasgow C.
45.0 Liv. Walton
45.2 Hull W.
45.8 Glasgow N.E.
45.9 Man. Gorton
46.4 Leeds C.
46.4 Man. Blackley

Ten smallest majorities		*votes*	*%*
Crawley	Lab	27	0.1
Sitting bourne	Lab	79	0.2
Harlow	Lab	97	0.2
Croydon C.	Con	75	0.2
Romsey	LD	125	0.2
Battersea	Lab	163	0.4
Clwyd W.	Con	133	0.4
Solihull	LD	279	0.5
Westmorland	LD	267	0.5
Ceredigion	LD	219	0.6

Ten best Con results (% change)
+15.5 Brentwood
+11.6 Dumfries C. & T.
+9.7 Wyre Forest
+9,2 Isle of Wight
+9.2 Welwyn
+8.9 Folkestone
+7.4 Henley
+6.9 Berwickshire
+6.8 Crawley
+6.7 Tyneside N.

Ten best Lab results (% change)
+8.8 Dumfries & G.
+6.0 Ryedale
+5.3 Torbay
+4.8 St Helens S.
+4.4 Kingston
+2.6 Oldham E. & Sad.
+2.2 Brentwood & O.
+2.2 Islwyn
+2.1 Cornwall N.
+2.1 Ribble V.

Ten best Lib Dem results (% change)
+36.9 Brent E.
+23.3 B'ham Ladywood
+21.4 B'ham Hodge H.
+20.4 Man. Withington
+18.9 Cambridge
+17.6 Hornsey
+17.1 City of Durham
+15.4 Hartlepool
+14.8 Dunbarton E.
+14.4 Ealing, Southall

Ten largest SNP votes (%)
51.2 Banff & Buchan
44.9 Na h-Eilanan an Iar
37.2 Dundee East
36.6 Moray
33.7 Perth
33.7 Angus
30.0 Dundee W.
29.9 Ochil
27.7 Kilmarnock
23.5 Linlithgow

Ten largest Plaid Cymru votes (%)
51.3 Meirionnydd
45.9 Carmarthen E.
45.5 Caernarfon
35.9 Ceredigion
31.1 Ynys Mon
26.5 Llanelli
17.4 Caerphilly
17.1 Neath
15.9 Rhondda
14.7 Carmarthen W.

Ten largest Green votes (%)
21.9 B'ton Pavilion
11.1 Lewisham Deptford
9.9 Hackney N.
8.1 Holborn & St P.
7.5 Leeds W.
7.4 Norwich S.
7.1 Islington N.
7.0 B'ton Kemptown
6.5 Dulwich
6.0 Sheffield C.

Ten largest UKIP votes (%)
10.4 Staffordshire S.
9.6 Boston & Skegness
8.0 Bognor Regis
7.9 Staffs Moorlands
7.9 Ply. Devonport
7.8 Torbay
7.7 Totnes
7.7 Louth
7.5 S.W. Devon
7.5 Castle Point

Ten largest BNP votes (%)
16.9 Barking
13.1 Dewsbury
10.3 Burnley
9.9 West Bromwich W.
9.7 Dudley N.
9.3 Dagenham
9.2 Keighley
8.7 Stoke S.
7.8 Bradford S.
7.8 Stoke C.

20 Largest other votes (GB) (%)[1]
58.2 Blaenau Gwent (*Ind*)
39.9 Wyre Forest (*Ind*)
35.9 Bethnal Gn & Bow (*Respect*)
27.5 B'han Small Heath (*Respect*)
20.7 East Ham (*Respect*)
19.5 West Ham *Respect*
16.8 Poplar & Canning T. (*Respect*)
14.8 Burnley (*Ind*)
14.7 Ynys Môn (*Ind*)
14.2 Glasgow N.E. (*Soc. Lab.*)
11.8 Liv. W. Derby (*Liberal*)
11.8 Morley & R. (*Ind*)
10.2 Sedgefield (*Ind*)
9.8 N.W. Durham (*Ind*)
7.8 Makerfield (*CAP*)
7.6 Na h-Eilanan an Iar (*OCV**)
7.5 Doncaster N. (*CGRP**)
6.0 Leigh (*CAP*)
5.8 Erewash (*Veritas*)
5.0 Coventry N.E. (*SALT**)

* CAP: Community Action; OCV: Op. Christian Vote; CGRP: Community Group; SALT: Socialist Alternative.
1. For deposit saving votes between 5.0% and 7.5% won by UKIP, Greens, Respect, BNP or SSP see their columns in the table on pp. 207–29.

Major Parties' Lost Deposits (%)
4.8 Na h-Eilanan an Iar *Con*
4.3 Blaenau Gwent *Lib Dem*
2.8 Blaenau Gwent *Con*

Table A1.6   By-election results, 2001–05

	Date	Con %	Lab %	Lib Dem %	Best Other %	Rest % (no.)	Turnout %
Ipswich	2001	30.5	51.3	15.2	1.6 (UKIP)	1.3 (2)	57.6
	22.11.01	28.4	43.4	22.4	2.1 (Christian)	3.7 (6)	40.2
	2005	31.1	43.8	20.2	5.0		60.9
Ogmore	2001	11.1	62.0	12.6	14.0 (PC)	–	58.2
	14.2.02	7.5	52.0	8.8	20.8 (PC)	11.0 (5)	35.2
	2005	14.0	60.4	15.2	10.4 (PC)	–	57.4
Brent East	2001	18.2	63.2	10.6	4.7 (Grn)	8.0	51.9
Lib Dem gain	18.9.03	16.2	33.8	39.1	3.1 (Grn)	7.0 (9)	36.2
	2005	10.3	38.8	47.5	3.2 (Grn)	2.2 (3)	56.4
Leicester South	2001	23.1	54.5	17.7	2.9 (Grn)	3.4 (2)	58.0
Lib Dem gain	15.7.04	19.7	29.3	34.9	12.7 (Respect)	3.4 (7)	40.3
Lab regain	2005	17.8	39.3.	30.6	6.4 (Respect)	5.9 (4)	59.2
Birmingham,	2001	20.7	66.7	8.4	3.4 (BNP)	4.7 (4)	47.9
Hodge Hill	15.7.04	17.3	36.5	34.2	6.3 (Respect)	5.7 (3)	37.9
	2005	13.3	48.6	29.5	5.1 (BNP)	3.5 (2)	52.2
Hartlepool	2001	20.9	50.2	15.0	2.4 (Soc)	2.6 (2)	38.3
	30.9.04	9.7	40.7	34.2	10.2 (UKIP)	5.3 (10)	45.8
	2005	11.5	51.5	30.4	3.5 (UKIP)	3.1 (4)	51.3

Appendix 2: The Results Analysed

John Curtice, Stephen Fisher and Michael Steed

At first sight the result of the 2005 election looks like more of the same. Labour were re-elected for the third time in a row. While at 66 the party's overall majority was substantially less than the majorities of 179 and 167 it secured in 1997 and 2001 respectively, it could still look forward to another four or five years' dominance of the House of Commons. This does not appear to be an outcome that should be worthy of extensive analysis.

Yet this initial impression is misleading. Even the fact that Labour won yet again created a historical precedent; never before had the party managed to win three elections in a row. But more striking was the manner of its victory. It won just 36.2 per cent of the vote in Great Britain.[1] Never before had any party won an overall majority on such a low share of the overall vote. Of the four previous occasions on which no single party won as much as 40 per cent of the vote, only once (in 1923) had the electoral system produced an overall majority for the 'winner'. Despite the well-known tendency of the single-member plurality system to generate majoritarian outcomes, previous British experience did not suggest it would necessarily do so when the largest party secured such a low share of the overall vote.

Moreover, the scale of Labour's losses at the ballot box was quite remarkable. The party's share of the vote was nearly six points down on 2001, and no less than eight points lower than when it was first elected in 1997. No previous Labour Government had suffered so heavy a haemorrhage of support during its term of office. Both the Macdonald and Attlee Governments actually won a higher share of the vote when they lost office than when they were first elected. Meanwhile the defeats suffered by Harold Wilson in 1970 and Jim Callaghan in 1979 occurred after the party's tally fell by less than one point as compared with its initial victories in 1964 and February 1974 respectively.

Yet the main opposition party, the Conservatives, were largely unable to profit from the Government's evident unpopularity. At 33.2 per cent their share of the vote rose by just half a point on 2001, less than half the increase they secured in 2001 over their record poor performance in 1997. The party's share of the vote remains lower than at any time between 1857 and 1992. Meanwhile the combination of Labour's electoral reverse and the Conservatives' lack of progress meant that Britain's two main parties won just 69.4 per cent of the vote, the lowest figure since 1923.[2] The mould of Britain's two-party system appeared decidedly cracked.

Rather than the Conservatives, it was the Liberal Democrats and a range of smaller parties and independents who made an advance. While at 22.7 per cent the Liberal Democrats' share of the vote was still below the total won by the former SDP/Liberal Alliance in both 1983 (26.0 per cent) and 1987 (23.1 per cent), the party won more seats, 62, than at any time since 1923. Perhaps more importantly, the period between 1997 and 2005 was the first spell of Labour Government during which the party's share of the vote rose. While hitherto Britain's third party had appeared capable of prospering during periods of Conservative rule – the Liberal Democrats (and their predecessor parties) won more votes in 1964 than in 1951, in February 1974 than in 1970, and in 1997 than in 1979 – it had previously always fallen back while Labour Prime Ministers were in office.[3] Now for the first time ever it was capable of winning over disaffected Labour voters as well as unhappy Conservative supporters. Indeed in capturing eleven seats from Labour[4] the party gained nearly three times as many seats from Labour as it had done previously in the whole of the post-war period.

At the same time no less than 7.9 per cent voted for someone other than their local Conservative, Labour or Liberal Democrat candidate, the highest proportion since 1918. Each of the United Kingdom Independence Party, the Greens and the British National Party won a higher average vote per candidate than any of them individually had achieved previously, while a new party, Respect, a coalition of far-left groups opposed to Britain's involvement in the 2003 Iraq war, posed the most significant far-left challenge since 1945. Not only did Respect manage to win a seat, but so also did two independents; not since 1945 have so many non-nationalist others been elected to the House of Commons from constituencies in Great Britain.

All in all, in 2005 British electoral politics appeared more fractured than at any time since the last major upheaval in the party system in the years immediately following the First World War. However, the most popular party of all appeared to be 'none of the above'. Just 61.2 per cent of the registered electorate cast a vote. While this was a couple of points higher than the record low registered in 2001, it still contrasted highly unfavourably with the position at every election between 1922 and 1997, during which period turnout never fell below 70 per cent. There was little in the outcome of this election to suggest that the efforts that have been made by politicians in recent years to try and reconnect with the electorate have had much success.

The 2005 election does then throw up a number of important questions for the analyst. Why did Labour lose so much support – and yet at the same time still secure a comfortable overall majority? Why, despite Labour's losses, did the Conservatives make so little apparent progress, and why did the Liberal Democrats in contrast make such unprecedented gains at Labour's expense? What was the basis of the appeal of the significant success secured by a range of smaller parties? And why, despite the apparent plethora of choice open to them, did so many voters stay at home? In this appendix we attempt to cast as much light as possible on the answers to these questions by analysing the variation in party performance from one constituency to another.

The scale of that variation was considerable. However, considerable variation has become the norm in British elections and the figures in Table A2.1 for the standard deviation of the change in each party's share of the vote are well in line with the equivalent figures for other recent elections.[5] Indeed the variation in swing between Labour and the Conservatives was rather lower than at recent elections.[6] Most variable was the Liberal Democrat performance; the least, that of the Conservatives. Such a pattern has, however, also become the norm in British elections. In short, the country did not move as one, but in this it behaved in a manner we have come to expect.

Table A2.1 Measures of change since 2001

	Overall	Mean	Median	Standard deviation
Change in Con vote	+0.5	+0.2	+0.2	3.1
Change in Lab vote	−5.8	−5.8	−5.9	4.0
Change in Lib Dem vote	+3.8	+4.0	+3.7	4.4
Total-vote swing	+3.1	+3.0	+3.1	2.4
Two-party swing	+4.1	+3.0	+3.2	3.5
Change in turnout	+2.1	+2.0	+2.0	2.2

The table excludes the delayed election in South Staffordshire while, except in the case of change in turnout, Glasgow North East (no Conservative or Liberal Democrat candidates in either 2001 or 2005) and Wyre Forest (no Liberal Democrat candidate in 2001 and 2005) are excluded in the calculation of the mean, median, and standard deviation.

Total-vote swing is the average of the change in the Conservative share of the vote and the Labour share of the vote. Two-party swing is the change in the Conservatives share of the vote cast for Conservative and Labour only (that is, the two-party vote). In both cases, a plus sign indicates a swing to the Conservatives, a minus sign a swing to Labour.

One possible consequence of significant variation in party performance is that the average change in a party's vote might differ from the overall change in its share of the vote across the country as a whole. This will happen, for example, if a party gains ground disproportionately in smaller constituencies (when the mean change in its share of the vote across all constituencies will be higher than the change in its overall share of the vote across the country as a whole) or if it does particularly well in a small number of constituencies (when the median of all the changes in its share of the vote across all constituencies will be lower than the mean). However, with one exception, all of these possible summary measures of each party's performance are similar to each other, and thus it makes little difference which we analyse.[7] For now we should simply note that unless otherwise stated all figures quoted in this appendix for groups of constituencies are means. Apart from noting it as a Conservative victory in terms of seats won, all statistics exclude the delayed election in South Staffordshire while in the case of our analysis of Conservative, Labour and Liberal Democrat performance, the two constituencies, Glasgow North East and Wyre Forest, where one or more of these parties failed to nominate a candidate. On occasion we also further exclude the constituencies of Blaenau Gwent, Brent East and Brentwood & Ongar where the pattern of change in one or more parties' share of the vote was so exceptional, their inclusion would sometimes distort our results.

If the extent of the variation in each party's performance was considerable though unremarkable, one feature of the relationship between their performances should be noted. As Table A2.2 shows, there was little correlation between the change in the Conservative share of the vote and the change in the Labour share of the vote. In other words, it was not the case in general that where the Conservatives performed best Labour did worst (and vice versa), a pattern that in fact has not been uncommon at recent elections.[8] In contrast both the Conservatives and

Labour clearly suffered where the Liberal Democrats did best (as shown by the negative correlations in the table) and vice versa.

Table A2.2   Correlations between change in share of vote

	Level of measurement	
	Constituency	Region
Conservative and Labour	+0.06	+0.01
Conservative and Liberal Democrat	−0.42	−0.31
Labour and Liberal Democrat	−0.52	−0.69

The following constituencies are excluded in the calculation of the constituency level figure; Glasgow North East and Wyre Forest (see Table A2.1); Blaenau Gwent, Brent East and Brentwood & Ongar (exceptional change in share of vote for one or more parties).

Moreover, these statements remain true even if we look at what happened at the level of the ten principal regions (those in bold) in Table A1.2 (pp. 204–5). Here too, it was also not the case that Labour suffered worst where the Conservatives did best. Rather at this level what is most striking is the strength of the relationship between the pattern of the Labour performance and that of the Liberal Democrats; this suggests that there may have been a systematic relationship between the kinds of constituencies where the Liberal Democrats did best and those where Labour in particular performed worst. Certainly these findings suggest that there is little merit in focusing our analysis on the swing between Labour and the Conservatives, whether of the total-vote or the two-party variety; to do so would be more likely to mislead us as to the nature of the Labour and Conservative performance. Instead we focus primarily in this appendix on the change in each individual party's share of the vote.

There is, however, one small complication about measuring that change. In Scotland the election was fought on new constituency boundaries following the provisions of the Scotland Act 1998 which, in providing the legal basis for the Scottish Parliament, also paved the way for a reduction in the number of Scottish constituencies at Westminster. Following the subsequent recommendations of the Parliamentary Boundary Commission for Scotland, the former 72 Scottish constituencies were replaced by 59 new ones, only three of which were coterminus with one of the previous constituencies.[9] In order to calculate the change in each party's share of the vote in the remaining 56 new constituencies we have compared the outcome in 2005 with the estimates produced by Denver et al. of what the outcome of the 2001 election would have been if it had been fought on the new constituency boundaries.[10]

Labour and the Liberal Democrats

One feature of Labour's performance is immediately striking; the party lost support most heavily in seats it was defending. As can be seen in Table A2.3, on average Labour's share of the vote fell by seven points in those seats that it won in 2001, more than a point higher than the 5.8 points drop we have already seen it suffered across the country as a whole. We can also see from Table A2.3 that much of the damage to Labour's vote in the seats it was defending appears to have been done by the Liberal Democrats whose vote increased on average by rather more than the 4.0 points it did across the country as a whole – and especially in seats where the Liberal Democrats started off in second place to Labour.

Table A2.3   Change in share of vote by tactical situation

Winning/second party 2001	Mean change in share of vote since 2001			
	Con	Lab	Lib Dem	
Lab/Lib Dem	−1.3	−7.1	+7.8	(52)
Lab/Con	−0.1	−7.0	+4.7	(308)
Con/Lab	+1.2	−6.1	+3.0	(105)
Lib Dem/Lab	−1.0	−3.8	+6.2	(7)
Con/Lib Dem	+1.4	−2.8	+0.5	(58)
Lib Dem/Con	+0.6	−1.1	−0.6	(44)

Constituencies where a nationalist or other candidate was first or second in 2001 are excluded from this table.

In fact Labour found it particularly difficult to hold its vote in two kinds of seats. The first, as can be seen in Table A2.4, comprised those constituencies with a relatively largely Muslim population. On average Labour's vote fell more than twice as heavily in constituencies where more than 10 per cent of the population was Muslim (all of which were won by Labour in 2001) than it did in those seats where Muslims comprise less than 1 per cent. This sharp decline in Labour's vote amongst constituencies with a large Muslim constituency clearly benefited the Liberal Democrats[11] but provided no succour to the Conservatives at all; the latter actually lost ground somewhat in constituencies with the largest Muslim communities.

Table A2.4   Change in share of vote by proportion Muslim

% Muslim	Con	Lab	Lib Dem	
Up to 1%	+0.4	−4.8	+3.1	(374)
1–5%	+0.4	−6.4	+4.1	(148)
5–10%	−0.1	−8.1	+6.1	(64)
More than 10%	−1.8	−10.6	+8.8	(39)

'% Muslim' is the proportion of the population identifying themselves as Muslim in response to the 2001 Census.

The decision of the Labour Government to join in the US-led invasion of Iraq in the spring of 2003 was particularly unpopular amongst Muslims.[12] The Government's decision was supported by the Conservatives, but was opposed by the Liberal Democrats. It looks as though a significant section of the Muslim community switched from Labour to the Liberal Democrats as a means of registering their opposition to the Government's actions.

A second type of constituency where Labour generally had particular difficulty in retaining its share of the vote comprised those with relatively large numbers of students. Again votes appear to have been lost to the Liberal Democrats in particular. As Table A2.5 shows, in the typical constituency being defended by Labour with a relatively large student population, Labour's share of the vote fell by around three points more than it did elsewhere, while the Liberal Democrat vote increased by three points more. This same pattern is also evident, albeit a little less strongly, in the handful of seats with relatively large student populations being defended by the Conservatives. However, it was not evident at all in the dozen or so such seats being defended by the Liberal Democrats.

Table A2.5   Change in share of vote in seats being defended by Labour by proportion students

% Students	Mean change in share of vote since 2001			
	Con	Lab	Lib Dem	
Up to 8%	−0.2	−6.0	+4.2	(281)
More than 8%	−0.3	−8.8	+7.5	(121)

'% Students' is the proportion of adults aged between 16 and 74 classified as students in the 2001 Census.

It is likely that Labour's difficulties in seats with large student populations stemmed from another controversial decision made by the Government between 2001 and 2005, one that again was opposed by the Liberal Democrats. This was the introduction of so-called 'top-up' university fees in England, a decision made despite the fact that in its 2001 manifesto Labour had indicated that it opposed the introduction of such fees. It would appear that this decision cost Labour votes amongst those in higher education and may perhaps have contributed more generally to a perception amongst some voters that the Government in general and the Prime Minister in particular could no longer be trusted.[13] The fact that, exceptionally, Labour did not especially lose ground in seats with large numbers of students that were already in Liberal Democrat hands probably reflects the fact that the Liberal Democrats were already heavily supported by those in higher education in these particular constituencies.

The geographical pattern of Labour's losses thus provides some important apparent clues as to why Labour lost support so heavily between 2001 and 2005 and why, unusually, the Liberal Democrats have been able to advance during the tenure of Mr Blair's Government. Some of the decisions made by the 2001–05 Labour Government, such as the invasion of Iraq and the introduction of top-up fees, were decidedly unpopular with at least some former Labour voters. At the same time they were decisions where the principal opposition came from the Liberal Democrats rather than the Conservatives. As a result the Liberal Democrats were able to profit from the unpopularity of the Labour Government in a manner that had hitherto only occurred during periods of Conservative rule.

Not that all of the Government's controversial decisions cost it votes. One that apparently did not was the Government's decision to use the 1949 Parliament Act to overcome the opposition of the House of Lords to the banning of hunting with hounds, a policy strongly and vociferously opposed by supporters of hunting. At the 2001 election Labour did appear to lose support more heavily in the most rural constituencies, though whether this was occasioned specifically by Labour's promise to ban hunting as opposed to other subjects of particular concern to those living in rural areas, such as the price of petrol or the Government's handling of the 2001 foot-and-mouth crisis, was not clear.[14] In any event the fact that, as we have seen in Table A2.3, Labour lost support most heavily in seats it was defending meant that its support actually fell least in rural areas. Indeed, the difference between Labour's level of support in urban areas and that in rural areas is now less than at any time since before 1992.

The Government's decisions on Iraq and tuition fees were not only the subject of public controversy but had also caused considerable disquiet amongst Labour MPs. Both decisions occasioned substantial rebellions in the lobbies. However, the personal stance taken by individual Labour MPs on these issues did not for the most part make much difference to their electoral fortunes. There was no significant difference between the performance of those Labour MPs who voted against the war (average fall in vote 6.5 points) and those who voted in favour (down 6.7 points). Much the same can be said of the position taken by Labour MPs on two other controversial issues: the introduction of foundation hospitals and the proposed anti-terror laws debated by Parliament in the final weeks prior to the election. There is however some suggestion that, once we take into account the variety of other factors that appear to have influenced the performance of Labour candidates, those who voted against the introduction of top-up fees may on average have performed a little better, albeit by no more than three-quarters of a point. For the most part voters were holding the Government as a whole accountable for the decisions it had made over the last four years rather than casting a judgement on the stances of individual Labour MPs.

However, one group that did not appear to be particularly concerned about the performance of the Labour government over the previous four years was the so-called 'traditional' Labour voter, who, it is sometimes suggested, has been particularly unhappy at the more centrist stance taken by the Labour Party under the leadership of Tony Blair and who appears to have been more inclined to defect in 2001.[15] Labour MPs defending seats with relatively large working-class populations or with other groups who might be considered socially excluded, such as lone parents or those in poor health, did not do significantly worse than their counterparts. Indeed, on average Labour's vote fell rather less in constituencies with relatively large numbers of people in routine non-manual occupations (down 6.1 points) than it did in general in seats being defended by Labour.

The Conservatives

We have by now clearly established that across the country as a whole there is little relationship between the pattern of Labour's performance and that of the Conservatives. If the positions that had been adopted by the Liberal Democrats during the 2001–05 Parliament had enabled them to profit from Labour's unpopularity, this was evidently not true for the Conservatives. Indeed, a glance at Table A1.2 reveals that the Conservatives generally made even less progress than would seem apparent from the half-point increase in their support across the country as a whole – much of that increase was simply the result of an advance in their position in the South East of England.[16] In most of the rest of the country the party made little or no advance at all; indeed in both Yorkshire and the Northern region the party's support actually fell back by more than a percentage point.

The pattern of the improved Conservative performance in the South East is best seen if we replicate, as we do in Table A2.6, Table A2.3 for just those constituencies that lie in this part of England and then compare the results of the two tables. Within the region, the party's performance varied according to the tactical situation in much the same way as it did in the rest of the country. The party progressed least where it was lying third to Labour and the Liberal Democrats, while it advanced most in seats that it was defending or was challenging the Liberal Democrats. But in each case the party's performance is between one and two points better in the South East than it was for that kind of seat in the rest of the country.

Table A2.6   Change in share of vote in the South East by tactical situation

Winning/second party 2001	Mean change in share of vote since 2001			
	Con	Lab	Lib Dem	
Lab/Lib Dem	−0.1	−10.2	+9.9	(9)
Lab/Con	+1.3	−8.9	+4.6	(80)
Con/Lab	+2.2	−6.6	+2.4	(56)
Con/Lib Dem	+2.7	−3.8	+0.6	(29)
Lib Dem/Con	+2.5	−1.0	−2.2	(14)

The one seat in the region where the Liberal Democrats were first and Labour second (Southwark N. & Bermondsey) is excluded from this table, as are the exceptional results in Brent East and Brentwood & Ongar.

Perhaps this relative Conservative success provides some clues as to why the party was unable to make progress more generally. One possible explanation for that success might be thought to be that some voters in the South East were keener than voters elsewhere to stem the expansion of the public sector and the concomitant increase in taxation that has occurred during Labour's tenure in office because their region is less dependent on public spending than elsewhere. For such voters the Conservatives' promise to limit the growth in public spending and taxation might have been particularly attractive, even though it might have lacked resonance elsewhere. However, the proportion of people whose current or last job was in public administration, education or health and social services, all sectors of the economy that are primarily in the public sector and which have expanded under Labour, is little different in London (30 per cent) or the rest of the South East (29 per cent) than it is across Great Britain as a whole (30 per cent).[17]

Equally, it appears unlikely that the Conservatives' stance on immigration had any particular appeal in London, the most ethnically diverse and cosmopolitan part of the UK. More plausible is the possibility that the Tories' promises to cut inheritance tax and council tax may have had particular resonance in the part of the UK with the highest incomes and wealth. At the same time, another characteristic that distinguishes much of the South East from the rest of the country is that trends since 2001 in both house prices and in unemployment have been less buoyant. Between 2001 and 2004 the rate of percentage increase in house prices in the region was approximately half that in the rest of Great Britain.[18] Meanwhile, the percentage of the electorate in the region registered as unemployed increased between 2001 and 2005, whereas it fell elsewhere.[19] Perhaps the Conservatives were able to profit from economic discontent with the Labour Government in the South East, a discontent that did not exist in the rest of the country. Certainly, if we compare the figures in Table A2.6 with those in Table A2.3, we find that in most kinds of seats it is Labour rather than the Liberal Democrats who appear to have suffered from the relative Conservative success. Moreover, more formal multivariate analysis suggests that after taking into account the tactical situation Labour did perform relatively badly in areas where there had been low house-price increases and the Conservatives relatively well, while house prices made no significant difference to the Liberal Democrat performance.

At the same time, we should also bear in mind that, having performed particularly badly across most of the South East in 1997, the Conservatives may have been doing no more than recovering lost ground there this time around.[20] Nevertheless it seems possible that where voters might have had reason to be discontented with the Labour Government on the economy as opposed to Iraq or tuition fees, then the Conservatives were those who primarily profited rather than the Liberal Democrats. If so, the Conservatives' misfortune appears to have been that outside the South East at least there was too little discontent with the state of the economy to fuel any kind of Conservative advance.

Tactical voting

We have already seen in Table A2.3 that the performance of all three main parties varied markedly depending on the tactical situation. But it was a variation that was somewhat unexpected if voters who might otherwise have been expected to have voted for the third party in a constituency switched instead to one of the two leading parties locally in order to ensure the defeat of the other. Labour lost least ground in those seats where the party lay third, and this appears to be the main reason for the failure of the Liberal Democrats to make much ground in seats where they were the principal competitors with the Conservatives. This suggests that, if anything, Labour voters became less willing to make a tactical switch to the Liberal Democrats. Meanwhile, the increase in the Liberal Democrats' share of the vote in seats where they started off in third place (or worse) was little different from that across the country as a whole. From this it would seem that the Liberal Democrat vote was at least not squeezed any further in such places than it had been already.

One possible explanation for Labour's relative success in maintaining its share of the vote in seats where it was third is that its vote was already so low in many such seats, not least because it had already been squeezed tactically in favour of the Liberal Democrats at previous elections.[21] Certainly, amongst those seats where Labour were placed third or worse in 2001 but won over 20 per cent of the vote, the fall in the party's share of the vote was much greater (down 4.3 points) than was the case where the party had previously secured less than 20 per cent (down 1.2 points). On the other hand, Labour's share of the vote was still 2.1 points higher in the seats where it started off third than had been the case in 1992, suggesting that the floor in Labour support in these constituencies had not necessarily been reached.[22] So we cannot be entirely sure that some third placed Labour voters may have been more reluctant to vote tactically for the Liberal Democrats at this election than they were at the last one.

One reason why this might be the case is the fact that Labour and the Liberal Democrats were much further apart politically in 2005 than had been the case in either 1997 or 2001. At the time of the last two elections the Liberal Democrats were in 'constructive opposition' with Labour, and indicated a clear preference for a Labour government rather than a Conservative one. But as we have already noted, between 2001 and 2005 the Liberal Democrats had become the principal opponents of key planks of Government policy while some Labour spokesmen reciprocated by attacking the Liberal Democrats for being soft on terrorism and crime. But if this changed political circumstance made it less likely that Labour voters would make a tactical switch to the Liberal Democrats, it would seem that Liberal Democrat voters would also have less incentive to vote Labour in order to defeat the local Conservative, behaviour which had been one of the notable features of both the 1997 and 2001 elections.[23]

In that event we would expect the Liberal Democrats to have advanced most markedly in those seats where their votes were squeezed to Labour's advantage in 1997 and 2001. Of this, however, there is no apparent sign. As can be seen in Table A2.7, amongst those seats where the party was trailing both Labour and the Conservatives in 2001, the Liberal Democrat vote actually rose least in those seats where the party's vote was squeezed most in 2001 – that is, seats where Labour's 1997 majority over a second-placed Conservative had been less than five points – while it increased most in those where there was no immediate history of a tactical squeeze on the Liberal Democrat vote. Meanwhile, Labour's vote fell no more heavily in seats where it had benefited at the last two elections from tactical switching from the Liberal Democrats than it did elsewhere. It would appear that Liberal Democrat to Labour tactical voting failed to unwind at all despite the changed political relationships between the two parties.[24]

Table A2.7   Change in share of vote by history of tactical voting

Tactical history	Mean change in share of vote since 2001			
LD vote squeezed	Con	Lab	Lib Dem	
Heavily in 2001	+2.3	–7.0	+3.1	(18)
Somewhat in 2001	+1.3	–6.9	+4.1	(37)
1997 only	+0.7	–6.6	+3.9	(128)
Not squeezed	–0.4	–6.9	+4.6	(223)

Table confined to seats in England and Wales where Conservative and Labour shared first and second place in 2001.
'Heavily in 2001': Seats in which Lab were first in 1997, Con second, and the percentage majority was less than five points. 'Somewhat in 2001': Seats in which Lab were first in 1997, Con second and the percentage majority was between five and ten points.
'1997 only': all other seats where Con were first, Lab second in 1992.
'Not squeezed': all other seats where Con and Lab shared first and second place in 2001.

There is, however, one party whose pattern of performance does suggest a greater incidence of tactical voting. As we have already noted, the Conservatives performed worse in constituencies where the party began in third place (or worse). Moreover, it was in precisely such constituencies that the Liberal Democrats performed best. However, much of this pattern is in fact accounted for by the particular success of the Liberal Democrats in seats with relatively large Muslim and student populations, a significant number of which were seats where the Liberal Democrats were already second to Labour. Nevertheless, even if we leave these constituencies to one side the Conservative performance was on average a point worse where the party was third to Labour and the Liberal Democrats while the Liberal Democrats themselves performed a half point or so better.[25] So there may have at least been a marginally increased tendency amongst Conservative supporters to switch to the Liberal Democrats in order to try and defeat the local incumbent Labour MP. While this phenomenon was not unknown in the past, it has hitherto been relatively rare, not least because of the relative paucity of seats where Labour and the Liberal Democrats were in close contention.[26]

Minor parties

Most of the rise in support for parties other than the Conservatives, Labour and the Liberal Democrats was occasioned by the success of four parties – the British National Party (BNP), the Greens, Respect and the United Kingdom Independence Party (UKIP). Between them they won well over half of the vote won by 'Others' (including nationalists, who accounted for over a quarter) across Britain as a whole. In part their success was achieved by fighting more constituencies, but they evidently increased their support too. However, while they may all have shared in a common pattern of success, the character of their support differed considerably.

Of the four, the party that fought the most focused campaign was Respect, whose principal campaign theme, as previously noted, was opposition to the war in Iraq. It fought just 26 constituencies, far fewer than the 98 seats fought by the principal far-left group in 2001, the Socialist Alliance. But it stood primarily in constituencies with substantial Muslim populations, amongst whom, as we have already seen, the Iraq war was unpopular. The party managed on average to win no less than 6.8 per cent of the vote. Much of this success was concentrated in the heavily Muslim London boroughs of Tower Hamlets and Newham, including Bethnal Green & Bow where the party leader, George Galloway, was elected, together with Birmingham Sparkbrook & Small Heath where nearly half the population was Muslim. Elsewhere the party's average share was a more modest 2.7 per cent, and only 0.8 per cent in the four constituencies where it stood that had little or no Muslim population. Where it did secure a substantial share of the vote it appears to have done so not simply by hurting Labour (and indeed to some degree the Conservatives) but also by denying the Liberal Democrats anti-war votes that might otherwise have gone to them.[27]

Meanwhile, despite failing to progress in the 2004 European elections, the Greens achieved their best performance yet at a general election. Although they increased the number of seats they fought from 145 in 2001 to 202 this time around, the party's average vote per candidate increased from 2.8 per cent in 2001 (itself a record) to 3.4 per cent.[28] In the 108 seats the party fought in England and Wales in both 2001 and 2005, its share of the vote rose on average by 0.8 of a point.[29] As in previous elections, the party performed best in constituencies with relatively large numbers of young people, those with degrees, those who do not profess any religion and those who do not have access to a car, suggesting that the archetypal Green voter is a young well-educated professional who, living in an urban environment, eschews or cannot afford access to a car. After taking into account other influences on the pattern of party support, it would appear that where the Green vote increased on its 2001 vote Labour suffered most, but that where the Greens put up a candidate for the first time in 2005, it was the Liberal Democrats who were most affected.

The progress made by the Greens was, however, outstripped by the BNP. Despite the fact that it fought far more constituencies (119) than it did in 2001 (33), its average share of vote per candidate increased from 3.9 per cent to 4.3 per cent. This was sufficient to give it 0.7 per cent of the overall vote in Great Britain, more than the previous record high share for a far-right party of 0.6 per cent recorded by 303 candidates under the banner of the National Front in 1979. In the 22 constituencies in which the party stood in both 2001 and 2005, its share of the vote rose on average by as much as 1.7 points; however, that figure is deflated by a full percentage point by an atypical sharp drop in its vote in two Oldham constituencies where it had won more than 10 per cent of the vote in 2001. The party performed best in relatively deprived urban areas with a significant proportion of ethnic minorities, including Muslims, and may well have profited from the increased concern amongst the electorate at the time of the 2005 election about immigration and the role of Muslims. A strong BNP performance appears to have been achieved at the expense of all three main parties, albeit perhaps with the Liberal Democrats suffering least, and it seems to have stimulated a percentage point or so increase in turnout too.

The broadest challenge to the conventional party system came, however, from UKIP. It fought no fewer than 495 constituencies, an increase of 67 on 2001, while at the same time it increased its average vote share per candidate from 2.1 per cent to 2.8 per cent.[30] This improvement, which was also reflected in an average 0.8 point increase in its share of the vote in those seats it fought in 2001 and 2005,[31] was sufficient to enable the party to overtake the Scottish National Party as the fourth party in votes across Britain as a whole. The party's performance was, however, still somewhat less than that achieved by the Referendum Party in 1997, at which election that party won an average of 3.1 per cent of the vote in 547 constituencies.[32] Nevertheless, UKIP's performance confirmed the importance of the Eurosceptic mood that had been signalled by its success in coming third in the 2004 European elections.

As at other recent elections, UKIP did relatively well in constituencies with relatively large numbers of older people and self-employed, and especially so in constituencies from Lincolnshire to Cornwall on or near the coast. It secured some particularly strong advances in Devon, with which county its leader, Roger Knapman, is associated. But to this familiar pattern the party added some notable successes in a number of more urban constituencies that contain relatively low proportions of graduates, a social characteristic that previous survey research has found to be associated with support for Euroscepticism.[33] It may be that the party has now acquired a somewhat broader appeal amongst those of a Eurosceptic disposition. But at the same time it remains the case that where UKIP does best, the Conservatives suffer most.[34] For example, whereas the Conservative vote increased on average by 1.1 points in constituencies where the UKIP vote fell compared with 2001 or which the party failed to contest in 2005 after having done so in 2001, it fell by 0.6 points in seats (including those the party did not fight in 2001) where the UKIP vote was more than 2.0 points higher than in 2001, a difference of 1.7 points.[35] The equivalent difference for Labour was just 0.6 points, while the Liberal Democrats actually performed 0.3 points better where UKIP performed best.

The distinct social character of the support for these four parties suggests that their success rests not just on disillusion with Britain's more traditional parties but also on their ability to represent distinctive strands of opinion that the traditional parties are unable adequately to represent. Despite the best efforts of the Conservative party to articulate public concern about some of the forces of globalisation such as increased immigration and European integration, the BNP and UKIP have been able between them to garner high levels of support for their distinctive messages on these issues, issues that in some important respects are of concern to different kinds of people but which have in common a particular resonance for those who are less well educated. In sharp contrast the Greens appear to be increasingly successful at attracting support from a very different kind of voter – young well-educated professionals concerned about the environment. It appears that between them these three parties represent a sharp cleavage in British politics. Meanwhile, the Iraq war has opened up a fissure between the Labour party and the Muslim community that has, for the time being at least, introduced a new religious divide to British politics too.

In contrast to the advances made by the BNP, Greens, Respect and UKIP, the nationalist parties in Scotland and Wales suffered some loss of support. At 17.7 per cent, the Scottish National Party (SNP)'s share of the vote in Scotland was not only 2.4 points down on 2001, but was the lower than at any election since 1987, suggesting that the revival that the party has enjoyed since its victory in the 1988 Glasgow Govan by-election has now come to an end. The scale of the party's reverse was, however, tempered by its success in capturing from Labour, Dundee East and Na h-Eilanan an Iar (Western Isles), two constituencies that the party had previously held in the 1970s and 1980s, as well as holding the three seats it was notionally defending. Plaid Cymru's loss of support, down 1.7 points on 2001, was somewhat less than that suffered by the SNP, and at 12.6 per cent its share of the vote on Wales was in fact still higher than at any election prior to 2001. However, the party lost Ceredigion, first captured from the Liberal Democrats in 1992, and now lost to them again, not least, it seems, because of a tactical switch to the Liberal Democrats by Conservative voters.

Candidate characteristics

Previous appendices in this series have noted that MPs who are defending for the first time a seat that they captured at the last election from an opposition party often perform rather better than other candidates.[36] It would appear that such new incumbent MPs profit from a personal vote acquired as a result of their attempts to entrench themselves in their new constituency, while at the same time any personal vote held by the previous MP is lost to the party that previously held the seat. Such personal votes can help a party defend marginal seats that they might otherwise have lost, thereby limiting the impact of any adverse swing against it, and certainly the Labour party encouraged those of its MPs who were representing marginal seats to maintain a high profile in their constituency. However, at this election most Labour MPs defending marginal seats were trying to retain constituencies that they first won not at the last election, but two elections ago in 1997, and it has not been evident from previous elections that MPs defending a seat a second time around generally derive personal support additional to that which they manage to acquire first time around.

In fact, Labour MPs who were defending seats that they first won in 1997 did perform a little better than those incumbent Labour MPs who were defending seats the party had won before 1997. On average their share of the vote fell by 6.4 points, whereas their more established colleagues saw their vote fall by 7.7 points.[37] However, much of this difference of 1.3 points is accounted for by the fact that the latter were more likely to be representing constituencies with large Muslim and/or student populations.[38] For the most part it appears that Labour MPs in marginal seats were unable to insulate themselves to any greater degree than they had already from the nationwide decline in their party's support since 2001.

Still, Labour incumbents in general did better than those candidates who were defending a Labour held seat for the first time following the retirement of the previous incumbent; their vote fell on average by 8.2 points. Meanwhile, at the other end of the spectrum neither of the two Labour MPs (in Dorset South and Ynys Môn) who were defending seats they themselves gained in 2001 suffered much loss of support at all, thereby enabling Labour to save two seats they would otherwise have expected to lose. Equally, the seven Conservative MPs who were defending seats they captured from another party in 2001 also recorded an above average performance (average increase of 4.0 points).

The party for whom the personal popularity of their incumbent appeared to matter most, however, was, as in previous elections, the Liberal Democrat party. In six seats in which the incumbent MP retired, the party's vote actually fell back on average by 4.6 points, and in so doing helped at least to contribute to the loss of one seat. In contrast it rose by 3.3 points in seven seats that the incumbent captured from another party in 2001 and by no less than 5.9 points in three seats where the incumbent Liberal Democrat MP had made way for a successfully elected successor in 2001.

For the most part, once account is taken of other sources of variation in party performance, the gender of a candidate does not appear to have made a difference to their performance. But there seems to be one striking exception. Female Labour candidates defending a seat Labour won in 2001 performed less well on average than their male counterparts. Incumbent female Labour MPs (average vote down 7.6 points) lost ground more heavily than incumbent male ones (down 6.6 points). Most strikingly of all, however, in the 21 seats in England and Wales where a previous incumbent male Labour MP was replaced by a new female Labour candidate, Labour's vote fell on average by three points more than where an incumbent male Labour MP was replaced by another man.[39] Whether this reflects a more widespread opposition to the promotion of female Labour candidates than was evident in Blaenau Gwent where the male local Labour Welsh Assembly member, Peter Law, stood as an Independent and defeated the official Labour candidate selected from an all-female shortlist, is, however, uncertain.

In contrast, there does not appear to be any consistent evidence that ethnic minority Labour candidates performed any worse than their white counterparts.

Indeed, in a dozen seats in which ethnic minority candidates stood in both 2001 and in 2005, the average fall in Labour's share of the vote was, at 5.4 points, a little less than that in constituencies fought by a white candidate on both occasions (down 6.0 points).[40] Equally, in 17 seats where an ethnic minority candidate replaced a white candidate in 2001, Labour's vote fell by slightly less (5.6 points) too.[41] In contrast, ethnic minority Conservative candidates clearly performed less well than their white counterparts; 41 such candidates, a record, on average saw their vote fall by 3.2 points.[42] Attempts by the Conservative Party to create a more diverse parliamentary party evidently met some resistance from the party's electorate.

Turnout

One possible reason why the turnout was so low once more is that voters again felt that it was obvious who would win the election.[43] If voters' willingness to vote (or the parties' ability to mobilise voters) is influenced by such considerations, then we might expect to find that turnout was higher in marginal constituencies than it was elsewhere. This indeed was the case. In those marginal constituencies where the lead of the winning party over the second party was less than five points in 2001, the average turnout was 66.7 per cent; in safe seats where the 2001 lead had been more than 20 points the equivalent figure was just 57.4 per cent. Moreover, turnout increased a little more in marginal constituencies than elsewhere too; on average it increased by 2.7 points. However, around half of the seats in this group had been equally marginal in 2001, and thus here there was no additional incentive for voters to go to the polls. Indeed, it was in the remaining half of seats that newly became marginal in 2001 that the largest increases in turnout were recorded, averaging 3.2 points.[44]

However, low turnouts were not so much the preserve of safe seats in general as of safe Labour seats in particular. Indeed, in those seats being defended by the Conservatives, the turnout in safe seats was, at 65.2 per cent, not only well above the national average, but was only one point lower than in marginal Conservative seats. And even though, at 63.5 per cent the turnout in safe Liberal Democrat constituencies was 5.9 points lower than in marginal ones, it again was also above the national average. In contrast, turnout in safe Labour constituencies was just 55.7 per cent, no less than 10.2 points lower than in marginal Labour seats.

This phenomenon of low turnout in 'traditional' Labour seats is not a new one. Indeed, at 1.8 points the average increase in turnout in safe Labour constituencies was only a little below the national average. But it follows three elections in a row at which turnout has fallen more heavily in such constituencies than it has elsewhere.[45] The evidence is thus consistent with the possibility that a second factor depressing turnout at this election was a continued disproportionate reluctance on the part of some Labour voters to go to the polls,[46] a reluctance that has emerged ever since the party's drift towards the ideological centre began in 1989.[47]

Turnout was low despite the fact that anyone who wanted to could have avoided the cost of making the journey to a polling station by choosing to vote by post instead. Postal voting on demand was in fact available for the first time in the 2001 election, but as the new facility had only been established shortly beforehand, there had been relatively little time for voters to indicate to their local returning officer that they wished to vote that way. By 2005 they had had plenty of opportunity to do so. Based on data collected by the BBC for 594 of the 627 constituencies in Great Britain, it appears that just under 12 per cent of the electorate were issued with a postal ballot, three times the level for 2001.[48] However, it appears that the increase in postal voting did little to enhance the level of turnout. The increase in turnout in those constituencies where the proportion of the electorate issued with a postal ballot increased by more than ten points compared with 2001 was, at 2.2 points, only a little higher than the equivalent figure of 1.6 points in those constituencies where the increase in the proportion issued with a ballot paper was less than four points. Whatever the merits of postal voting on demand, it is evidently not a remedy for reversing the low turnout of the last two general elections.

The electoral system

Initially, it would appear as though the electoral system was rather unkind to Labour. If the overall change in each party's share of the vote across the country as a whole had been replicated in each and every constituency, Labour would have won 370 seats, 14 more than they eventually did, while the Conservatives would have won 14 fewer. Only the Liberal Democrats, with 62 seats, won as many seats as would have been expected on this basis.

In fact Labour lost more seats to both the Conservatives and the Liberal Democrats than would have happened if the change in party vote share had been uniform. The net 'additional' losses to the Liberal Democrats amounted to five seats while those to the Conservatives to no less than eight.[49] (The Liberal Democrats net gains from Labour were, however, counterbalanced by a net loss of six more seats to the Conservatives than would have been expected.) Much of Labour's extra loss to the Liberal Democrats can be accounted for by the above average drop in the Labour vote and the increase in the Liberal Democrat vote in seats where the Liberal Democrats were second to Labour in 2001 (see p. 238). The average change in party fortunes in such seats was itself enough to bring the Liberal Democrats' three gains, while a fourth is accounted for by its success in defending its by-election gain of Brent East.

Labour's higher losses to the Conservatives are, however, not so easily accounted for. At 3.5 per cent the average total-vote swing from Labour to Conservative in seats that Labour was defending against a second-placed Conservative was only a little above the national average, and is only sufficient to account for two of the Conservatives' additional gains. However, five of the eight net additional losses occurred in London and the South East (where the Conservatives performed relatively well, and Labour badly). So perhaps the higher than average swing from Labour to Conservative across the south-eastern corner of England accounts for the Conservatives' success. Indeed, if it had occurred uniformly across the South East as a whole the higher than average swing there (4.4 per cent) would (after taking into account the lower than average swing of 2.5 per cent that then occurred elsewhere) have netted the Conservatives five extra seats from Labour. That, however, still leaves us three seats short of what they actually achieved.

To understand fully why Labour lost so many seats to the Conservatives we need in fact to examine more closely how many of the seats that Labour was defending against a Conservative challenge were vulnerable for any given swing.

There were just 23 Labour seats that could be lost on a total-vote swing of 3 per cent. In contrast, there were nearly twice as many, 45, which would be lost on a swing of more than 3 per cent but less than 6 per cent (all but seven of which were vulnerable to swings of more than 4 per cent and less than 6 per cent). This meant that even if there were just random variation around the overall national swing of 3 per cent, Labour would be likely to lose more seats than it would if there were a uniform swing – more seats would be lost on swings of above 3 per cent than saved because the swing locally was less than 3 per cent. As a result the fact that not only was the swing higher than average in the South East as a whole, but (as we saw in Table A2.6 above) was also a little higher yet again in seats that Labour was defending against a Conservative (5.1 per cent, 0.7 points higher), had the potential to reap an unusually large reward (nine seats) for the Conservatives.[50]

In any event, even though Labour might have won somewhat fewer seats than it would have done if party performance had been uniform, the electoral system advantaged the party considerably. Ever since 1992 the electoral system has treated Labour more favourably than it would have done the Conservatives in similar circumstances.[51] Much of that advantage was maintained. This is illustrated in Table A2.8, which shows what the outcome would be for various hypothetical uniform total-vote swings from Labour to the Conservatives, while assuming that in all other respects the outcome was exactly as it was in 2005.

Table A2.8 Relationship between seats and votes

| | Seats (UK) | | | |
Con lead over Lab (GB) (%)	Con	Lab	Lib Dem	Other
0.0	223	334	58	31
1.0	232	324	58	32
3.0	250	307	57	32
6.4	279	279	57	31
11.8	324	236	55	31

Every row of the table illustrates the more advantageous manner in which the electoral system rewards Labour as compared with the Conservatives. If the two parties had the same share of the vote, but otherwise the outcome was as it was in 2005, Labour would still have 111 more seats than the Conservatives and enjoy an overall majority of 22.[52] Only when Labour were more than a point behind the Conservatives would they lose their overall majority. Meanwhile, if the Conservatives enjoyed the same lead over Labour as Labour actually did over the Conservatives, they would still have 57 fewer seats than Labour and the outcome would have been a hung Parliament. Only when the Conservatives are more than six points ahead of Labour would they match Labour in numbers of seats, while they would need to be nearly 12 points ahead before they enjoyed an overall majority.

Labour's ability to win an overall majority despite winning a relatively small share of the vote did not then rest on the well-known tendency of the single-member plurality electoral system to exaggerate the lead of the largest party over the second party and thereby give it an overall majority. Indeed, that tendency is actually weaker now than it once was.[53] Rather, it depended wholly on the fact that the electoral system currently treats Labour considerably more favourably than it does the Conservatives. Such a position clearly adds fuel to the debate about the merits of the continued use of the single member plurality electoral system.

Labour's advantage arose for a number of reasons. First, the average electorate in seats won by Labour was smaller than in those won by the Conservatives. At around 6,200 electors the gap was actually slightly smaller in 2005 than it was in 2001 (6,300) thanks to the reduction in the number of constituencies in Scotland.[54] However, the impact of that reduction was substantially counteracted by the pattern of population movement between 2001 and 2005 which meant that the electorate grew by 1,000 votes in the average Conservative constituency but fell by 500 in the average Labour one.[55]

Second, the turnout was lower in the typical Labour seat than in the average Conservative one. On average, 65.2 per cent voted in the average seat the Conservatives were defending, but only 58.6 per cent in the average Labour one. This gap, of 6.6 points, was even slightly larger than it was in 2001 (6.3 points). It is enough to ensure that the difference of 6,200 in the electorate of Conservative and Labour seats becomes one of nearly 8,500 when it comes to votes.[56]

Third, despite the Conservatives' success in capturing more seats than would be expected if the change in party vote share had been uniform, Labour's vote was still more efficiently distributed than that of the Conservatives. Labour wastes fewer votes piling up large majorities over their principal opponents and wins more seats by relatively small majorities. Thus, for example, if Labour and the Conservatives were to have equal shares of the vote as a result of a 1.5 point total-vote swing, Labour would win 77 seats in which they had a lead over the Conservatives of less than ten points, while the Conservatives would win only 45 where their lead over Labour was that low.

By the time of the next general election, new parliamentary constituency boundaries will be in place in England and Wales. In producing more equal sized constituencies within those two parts of the United Kingdom, this redrawing will help reduce some of Labour's advantage. (It certainly means that the figures in Table A2.8 cannot be regarded as a forecast of what will happen at the next election for any given outcome in votes.) It will not, however, eliminate it.

First of all, the work of the Boundary Commissions, the bodies responsible for drawing the new boundaries, takes no account of differences in turnout between constituencies. Their work could have some impact on how efficiently each party's vote is distributed, but is unlikely to do so to a significant degree. Meanwhile, the commissions will fail to remove all of the differences in electorate size. Wales will continue to have 40 MPs despite the fact that the average Welsh constituency, with just under 56,000 electors in 2005, was far smaller than the average English constituency, which contained over 70,000 voters.[57] At the same time, despite the reduction in the number of MPs in Scotland, the average constituency there continues to have fewer voters (65,000 electors) than its counterpart in England.[58] Meanwhile, the new boundaries themselves are being drawn up on the basis of 2001 electorates, and will thus be eight years out of date by the time of the earliest likely date for the next election, 2009. All in all, these features mean that while the difference is likely to be smaller than it was in 2005, the average Labour constituency is still likely to contain fewer voters than the average Conservative seat at the next election too.

Labour's advantage is not however the only important feature of Table A2.8. We should also note the wide range of results – anything between a Conservative lead of 1.0 point and one of 11.8 points – that would result in no single party having an overall majority. This range of nearly 11 points is greater than it has been after any previous election.[59] Its width reflects the fact that as many as one in seven MPs is now unattached to either the Conservatives or to Labour and that this figure is largely impervious to the relative popularity of the two largest parties. In eliminating some of Labour's current advantage the endpoints at which this range is located will be affected by the English and Welsh boundary review, but the range itself is unlikely to be much affected. In short, if the level and pattern of support secured by the Liberal Democrats and others in 2005 were to be maintained in future elections, the probability that one or more future elections will produce a hung Parliament would appear to be rather high.

Conclusion

Labour's ability to win an historic third term despite suffering the biggest rebuff in the ballot box ever suffered by a Labour Government rested on two foundations. First, it lost ground primarily to the Liberal Democrats who, despite performing most strongly in places where they were already second to Labour, were not anything as sufficiently well placed as the Conservatives to wrest seats from Labour's grasp. It was Labour's good fortune that it was the Liberal Democrats, rather than the Conservatives, who led the opposition to some of its most unpopular measures between 2001 and 2005 and to whom voters seem to have turned as a suitable vehicle of protest. It was perhaps even more fortunate that despite the worsening of political relations between the two parties, a significant number of potential Liberal Democrat voters still continued to vote Labour where the main challenger locally was a Conservative,

Second, even though Labour MPs in marginal seats did not secure any incumbency advantage additional to that which they had already acquired in 2001, the electoral system treated Labour in a highly advantageous fashion. That fashion, however, had little to do with the general tendency for single-member plurality to give a bonus to the largest party. Rather it arose from a bias that once more favoured Labour over the Conservatives, and which, by helping to turn what would otherwise have been a close election into a comfortable victory, may well have helped to depress turnout once again. Certainly, without it the 2005 election would have produced a hung Parliament – and the House of Commons would have been a more faithful representation of an electorate that is now more divided in its loyalties than at any time since the 1920s.

Notes

1. The outcome in Northern Ireland is not considered in this appendix, while all voting statistics exclude the delayed election in South Staffordshire. For discussion of the result in Northern Ireland see p. 197. Labour's share of the vote across the United Kingdom as a whole (35.3 per cent) was also the lowest ever won by a majority government.

2. Indeed, at 67.6 per cent their combined share of the UK vote was lower than at any time since and including the 1922 election, the first election since the partition of Ireland and the first at which Labour overtook the Liberals.
3. The party's share of the vote was 11.9 points lower in 1924 than in 1923, 6.6 points lower in 1951 than in 1945, 3.8 points lower in 1970 than in 1964, and 5.7 points lower in 1979 than in February 1974.
4. This figure excludes Brent East which was initially captured from Labour in a by-election in September 2003.
5. See the equivalent tables in J. Curtice and M. Steed, 'Appendix 2: An Analysis of the Voting', in D. Butler and D. Kavanagh, *The British General Election of 1983* (London: Macmillan, 1984), p. 334; J. Curtice and M. Steed, 'Appendix 2: Analysis', in D. Butler and D. Kavanagh, *The British General Election of 1987* (London: Macmillan, 1988), p. 317; J. Curtice and M. Steed, 'Appendix 2: The Results Analysed', in D. Butler and D. Kavanagh, *The British General Election of 1992* (London: Macmillan, 1993), p. 323; J. Curtice and M. Steed, 'Appendix 2: The Results Analysed', in D. Butler and D. Kavanagh, *The British General Election of 1997* (London: Macmillan, 1997), p. 297; J. Curtice and M. Steed, 'Appendix 2: The Results Analysed', in D. Butler and D. Kavanagh, *The British General Election of 2001* (London: Palgrave, 2001), p. 305.
6. Although lower than at any election held since (and including) 1979 on unchanged constituency boundaries, the standard deviation of two-party swing was, however, still higher than at any election prior to then.
7. The one exception is the change in two-party swing where the average (both the mean and the median) change in each party's share of the vote is markedly lower than the overall swing. This occurs because two-party swing, unlike total-vote swing, was systematically higher in constituencies with larger electorates and higher turnouts. This in turn happened because of differences in the assumptions made by the two swings about the impact of an increase in the third-party vote, such as seen at this election. Two-party swing assumes that Conservative and Labour lose votes to third parties in proportion to their respective shares of the vote whereas total-vote swing assumes they lose votes in equal proportions. As we show below, in practice Labour lost ground most heavily in seats where they were relatively strong (which seats tended to have smaller electorates and lower turnouts) while the Conservatives tended to perform best where they were already strong (where electorates and turnouts were higher). Compared with total-vote swing, two-party swing produces a relatively low figure in the former circumstance and a relatively high one in the latter.
8. For equivalent statistics at previous elections see Curtice and Steed, 'Appendix 2', in Butler and Kavanagh, *The British General Election of 1983*, pp. 334–5; Curtice and Steed, 'Appendix 2', in Butler and Kavanagh, *The British General Election of 1987*, p. 319; Curtice and Steed, 'Appendix 2', in Butler and Kavanagh, *The British General Election of 1997*, p. 298; Curtice and Steed, 'Appendix 2', in Butler and Kavanagh, *The British General Election of 2001*, p. 306.
9. *Fifth Periodical Report of the Boundary Commission for Scotland,* Cm 6427. (London: Stationery Office, 2004).
10. D. Denver, C. Rallings and M. Thrasher, *Media Guide to the New Scottish Westminster Parliamentary Constituencies* (Plymouth: Local Government Chronicle Elections Centre, 2004).

11. The most dramatic instance of this was Brent East, where 12 per cent of the population is Muslim, and which the Liberal Democrats first captured in a by-election in September 2003. Labour's vote fell by 24.7 points compared with 2001, while that of the Liberal Democrats rose by 37.0 points. But even if we exclude this constituency from the table, the average fall in Labour's vote in constituencies where more than ten per cent of the population is Mulsim is 10.3 points and the increase in Liberal Democrat support, 8.1 points.

12. See, for example, the results of an ICM poll conducted for the *Guardian* in March 2004. Details available at <www.icmresearch.co.uk/reviews/2004/guardian-muslims-march-2004.asp>.

13. J. Curtice, 'Labour's historic triumph – or rebuff?', *Politics Review*, Vol. 15, No. 1 (September 2005), pp. 2–7.

14. Curtice and Steed, 'Appendix 2', in Butler and Kavanagh, *The British General Election of 2001*, pp. 314–15.

15. Ibid., pp. 310–2; H. Clarke, D. Sanders, M. Stewart and P. Whiteley, *Political Choice in Britain* (Oxford: Oxford University Press, 2004), pp. 48–50.

16. The area of improved Conservative performance corresponds closely to the area of the former South East standard region used in Table A1.2 except that it appears to have extended to Wiltshire (part of the South West region) and Northamptonshire (part of the East Midlands), and not included a string of coastal constituencies in Sussex and East Kent.

17. Data taken from the British Social Attitudes Survey 2003. Moreover, while the same survey found rather less support in London for further increases in taxation and public spending (44 per cent in favour) than across the country as a whole (51 per cent), attitudes in the rest of the South East (52 per cent) were much the same as elsewhere.

18. Based on house price data for each county published by HBOS. See <www.hbosplc.com/economy/historicaldataspreadsheet.asp>.

19. According to unemployment data for each constituency published by the House of Commons Library. See E. Beale, I. Townsend and A. Adcock, *Unemployment by Constituency, March 2005* (London: House of Commons Library Research Paper 05/32, 2005) and J. Hough and A. Adcock, *Unemployment by Constituency, April 2001* (London: House of Commons Library Research Paper 01/53, 2001).

20. Curtice and Steed, 'Appendix 2', in Butler and Kavanagh, *The British General Election of 1997*, pp. 302–3.

21. For details of tactical voting by Labour voters to the advantage of the Liberal Democrats at recent elections see Curtice and Steed, 'Appendix 2', in Butler and Kavanagh, *The British General Election of 1997*, pp. 310–11; Curtice and Steed, 'Appendix 2', in Butler and Kavanagh, *The British General Election of 2001*, p. 321, as well as earlier appendices in the series.

22. This comparison is based on the notional results for the 1992 election as if it were fought on the 1997 boundaries, and excludes Scotland. For details of the 1992 notional results see Rallings and Thrasher, *Media Guide to the New Parliamentary Constituencies*.

23. Curtice and Steed, 'Appendix 2', in Butler and Kavanagh, *The British General Election of 1997*, pp. 309ff.; Curtice and Steed, 'Appendix 2', in Butler and Kavanagh, *The British General Election of 2001*, pp. 316ff.

24. Indeed further analysis suggests that the Liberal Democrats may well have been squeezed yet further in the most marginal Labour/Conservative seats, though if so this squeeze appears to have benefited the Conservatives to some degree as well as Labour.

25. This calculation also excludes constituencies in Scotland where the boundary review resulted in a significant number of Labour/Liberal Democrat contests where the behaviour of voters was potentially affected by their being in a new tactical situation rather than simply any change in their propensity to make a tactical switch.

26. For previous evidence on tactical switching from Conservative to the Liberal Democrats and their predecessors see M. Steed, 'Appendix 2: The Results Analysed', in D. Butler and D. Kavanagh, *The British General Election of February 1974* (London: Macmillan, 1974), pp. 317–8; M. Steed, 'Appendix 2: The Results Analysed', in D. Butler and D. Kavanagh, *The British General Election of October 1974* (London: Macmillan, 1975), pp. 339–40; J. Curtice and M. Steed, 'Appendix 2: An Analysis of the Voting', in D. Butler and D. Kavanagh, *The British General Election of 1979* (London: Macmillan, 1980), p. 407; Curtice and Steed, 'Appendix 2', in Butler and Kavanagh, *The British General Election of 1987*, p. 340; Curtice and Steed, 'Appendix 2', in Butler and Kavanagh, *The British General Election of 1992*, p. 336.

27. Respect did not contest any constituencies in Scotland where the efforts of the far left were again spearheaded by the Scottish Socialist Party (SSP), which fought 58 of the 59 Scottish constituencies. No longer lead by the charismatic Tommy Sheridan, the party won only 2.0 per cent of the Scotland wide vote, a drop of 1.2 points on its performance in 2001.

28. These figures include candidates nominated by the nominally separate Scottish Green Party.

29. This calculation excludes Scotland because the notional results for the 2001 election on the new boundaries do not provide a reliable baseline as they are not adjusted for the fact that the party may have fought part of one seat but not another.

30. UKIP faced some competition for the anti-European vote from Veritas, formed shortly before the election by Robert Kilroy-Silk who had been elected as a UKIP MEP in 2004. Veritas averaged as much as 2.2 per cent of the vote in the 16 constituencies where there was not also a UKIP candidate, but it won only 1.2 per cent in the 49 where there was a UKIP candidate. The typical UKIP performance was only 0.6 per cent worse where Veritas also stood, while UKIP ran ahead of Veritas candidates in 45 of the 49 constituencies fought by them both. UKIP thus clearly emerged from the election as the stronger of the two contenders.

31. This figure is unchanged if Scotland is excluded.

32. Curtice and Steed, 'Appendix 2', in Butler and Kavanagh, *The British General Election of 1997*, pp. 305–8.

33. See, for example, G. Evans. 'Will We Ever Vote for the Euro?', in A. Park, J. Curtice, K. Thomson, L. Jarvis and C. Bromley (eds), *British Social Attitudes: The 20th Report: Continuity and Change over Two Decades* (London: Sage, 2003).

34. Curtice and Steed, 'Appendix 2', in Butler and Kavanagh, *The British General Election of 2001*, pp. 326–7.

35. In making this calculation we have excluded all constituencies where Muslims comprise more than 5 per cent of the population or students more than 8 per cent, together with all constituencies in Scotland, Blaenau Gwent and Brentwood & Ongar.

36. Curtice and Steed, 'Appendix 2', in Butler and Kavanagh, *The British General Election of 1992* (London: Macmillan, 1993), pp. 340–1; Curtice and Steed, 'Appendix 2', in Butler and Kavanagh, *The British General Election of 1997*, p. 312; Curtice and Steed, 'Appendix 2', in Butler and Kavanagh, *The British General Election of 2001*, pp. 317–20. See also B. Cain, J. Ferejohn and M. Fiorina, *The Personal Vote: Constituency Service and Electoral Independence* (Cambridge, Mass.: Harvard University Press, 1987).

37. Constituencies in Scotland are excluded from this discussion of incumbency effects because of the redrawing of constituency boundaries there. The exceptional results in Blaenau Gwent, Brentwood & Ongar and Brent East are also excluded.

38. The gap falls to just 0.5 points once we exclude constituencies where more than 5 per cent of the population is Muslim or where more than 8 per cent are students.

39. Note that Blaenau Gwent is not included in this calculation.

40. These figures exclude Bethnal Green & Bow where the ethnic minority Labour MP, Oona King, lost to George Galloway. Scotland is excluded throughout this discussion of the ethnic minority Labour candidates.

41. These figures exclude an ethnic minority Labour candidate in Brent East.

42. These figures include ethnic minority Conservative candidates in Bethnal Green & Bow and Brent East. Their inclusion makes no material difference to our conclusion. Note that the BNP appears to have particularly profited from the presence of an ethnic minority Conservative candidate, winning around 2 per cent more of the vote where there was such a candidate.

43. C. Bromley and J. Curtice, 'Where Have All the Voters Gone?", in A. Park, J. Curtice, K. Thomson, L. Jarvis and C. Bromley (eds), *British Social Attitudes: the 19th report* (London: Sage, 2002); J. Curtice, 'Turnout: Electors Stay at Home – Again', in P. Norris and C. Wlezien (eds), *Britain Votes 2005* (Oxford: Oxford University Press, 2005).

44. Conversely, turnout increased by less than average (just 1.2 points) in those seats which had been marginal in 1997 but were not after 2001. Note that these analyses of the impact of change in marginality exclude Scotland where we do not have information on the marginality of the new constituencies in 1997.

45. Curtice and Steed, 'Appendix 2', in Butler and Kavanagh, *The British General Election of 1992*, pp. 345–6; Curtice and Steed, 'Appendix 2', in Butler and Kavanagh, *The British General Election of 1997*, p. 299; Curtice and Steed, 'Appendix 2', in Butler and Kavanagh, *The British General Election of 2001*, p. 309.

46. We should also note the possibility, however, that safe Labour constituencies contain a relatively large proportion of people who require the stimulus of a close election to be encouraged to vote. See Curtice, 'Turnout: Electors Stay at Home Again'.

47. There is, however, no evidence in the pattern of the results that the drop in Labour support between 2001 and 2005 was occasioned by further differential

abstention. If this were the case we would expect Labour's vote to have fallen least where turnout increased most. But at –0.16 the correlation between change in Labour's share of the vote and the change in turnout is actually in the opposite direction.

48. Given that at past elections those registered to vote by post have been more likely to vote this probably means that around 15 per cent of all votes cast were cast by post.

49. Labour also suffered a net loss of one extra seat to nationalists and others.

50. The figure of nine seats also takes into account the fact that, at 2.9 per cent, the average swing in seats outside the South East being defended by Labour against a Conservative challenge was almost the same as the overall national swing. In practice, as noted earlier, only a net total of five of the Conservatives' additional gains were secured in the South East while the remaining three came from the rest of the country.

51. A. Blau, 'Partsian Bias in British General Elections', *British Elections and Parties Review*, 11 (2001), 46–65; J. Curtice, 'The Hidden Surprise: The British Electoral System in 1992', *Parliamentary Affairs*, 45 (1992), 466–74; J. Curtice and M. Steed, 'Neither Representative nor Accountable; First-Past-The-Post in Britain' (paper presented at the Annual Workshops of the European Consortium for Political Research, 1998); 'The Electoral System: Biased to Blair?, *Parliamentary Affairs*, 54 (2001), 803–14; R. Johnston, C. Pattie, D. Dorling and D. Rossiter, *From Votes to Seats: The Operation of the UK Electoral System since 1945* (Manchester: Manchester University Press, 2001); R. Johnston, D. Rossiter and C. Patttie, 'Distortion Magnified: New Labour and the British Electoral System', *British Elections and Parties Review*, 12 (2001), 133–55.

52. This, however, is somewhat smaller advantage for Labour than the equivalent statistic for 2001 which put Labour no less than 140 seats ahead of the Conservatives when the two parties had the same share of the vote.

53. One indicator of this is the number of seats where the Conservative share of the two-party vote would be between 45 per cent and 55 per cent in the event of a tie in votes across the country as a whole (leaving aside seats won by a third party). The more such marginal seats there are the more likely it is that the electoral system will deliver an overall majority to a party that has only a small lead in votes. In 2005 there were 103 seats, down 11 on the equivalent statistic for 1997 and 2001. While this number is still higher than it was in 1983 when it fell to just 80 seats, it is still substantially lower than the 150 or so that was the norm up to and including 1970. See also J. Curtice, 'The British Electoral System: Fixture without Foundation', in D. Kavanagh (ed.) *Electoral Politics* (Oxford: Oxford University Press. 1992); Curtice and Steed, 'Neither Representative nor Accountable'.

54. Both these figures are based on the seats won by Labour and the Conservatives in 2001.

55. This calculation includes the new constituencies in Scotland.

56. Again these figures are based on seats won in 2001. Note that this gap is reduced to 5,370 when account is taken of the incidence of votes for parties other than Conservative and Labour, an incidence which is higher in Conservative seats (13,918) than in Labour ones (10,800). But at the same time the Conservatives are further disadvantaged by the fact that they waste more votes than Labour does in seats won by third parties. On average 12,194

votes were cast for the Conservatives in such seats, 8,151 for Labour. The Liberal Democrats' relative success in Labour territory in 2005 meant that while Labour wasted more votes than it did in 2001 in seats won by third parties the difference between Labour and Conservative seats in the number of votes cast for Conservative or Labour (4,096 in 2001) actually increased.

57. Proposals for the new constituencies published by the Boundary Commission for England to date indicate that there will be four extra constituencies in England, but this will reduce the average 2005 electorate for English seats by just 500.

58. For an explanation of why the provisions of the Scotland Act 1998 to cut the number of Scottish MPs were an inadequate means of eliminating the disparity between the size of English and Scottish constituencies see J. Curtice, 'Reinventing the Yo-Yo: A Comment on the Electoral Provisions of the Scotland Bill', *Scottish Affairs*, 23 (98), 41–53.

59. See, for example, Curtice and Steed, 'Appendix 2', in Butler and Kavanagh, *The British General Election of 1987*, p. 357; Curtice and Steed, 'Appendix 2', in Butler and Kavanagh, *The British General Election of 1992*, p. 351; Curtice and Steed, 'Appendix 2', in Butler and Kavanagh, *The British General Election of 1997*, p. 316; Curtice and Steed, 'Appendix 2', in Butler and Kavanagh, *The British General Election of 2001*, p. 331.

Select Bibliography

Books

Ball, S. and Seldon, A. (eds), *Recovering Power: The Conservatives in Opposition Since 1867* (Palgrave Macmillan, 2005).

Bower, T., *Gordon Brown* (HarperCollins, 2004).

Butler, D. and Westlake, M., *British Politics and European Elections 2004* (Palgrave Macmillan, 2004).

Childs, S., *New Labour's Women MPs* (Routledge, 2004).

Cowley, P., *Revolts and Rebellions: Parliamentary Voting Under Blair* (Politico's, 2002).

Cowley, P. and Stuart, M. 'The Conservative Parliamentary Party' in M. Garnett and P. Lynch (eds), *The Conservatives in Crisis* (Manchester University Press, 2003).

Electoral Commission, *Modernising Elections* (Electoral Commission, July 2002).

Electoral Commission, *The Shape of Elections to Come* (Electoral Commission, August 2003).

Electoral Commission, *Distribution Between Electoral Regions of UK MEPs* (Electoral Commission, 2003).

Electoral Commission, *Delivering Democracy? The Future of Postal Voting* (Electoral Commission, 2004).

Fielding, S., *The Labour Party: Continuity and Change in the Making of New Labour* (Palgrave Macmillan, 2003).

Godin, S., *Permission Marketing* (Simon & Schuster, 2002).

Gove, M., Vaizey, E. and Bowis, N. (eds), *A Blue Tomorrow* (Politico's, 2001).

Heath, A., Jowell, R. and Curtice, J. *The Rise of New Labour* (Oxford University Press, 2001).

Henig, S. and Baston, L., *Politicos Guide to the General Election 2005* (Politico's, 2005).

Henig, S. and Baston, L., *The Political Map of Britain* (Politico's, 2002).

Hutton, B., *Report of the Inquiry into the Circumstances Surrounding the Death of Dr. David Kelly* (HMSO, 2004).

Kampfner, J., *Blair's Wars* (Free Press, 2003).

Lansley, A., *Do the Right Thing* (C-Change, 2002).

Marr, A., *My Trade* (Macmillan, 2004)

Peston, R., *Brown's Britain* (Short Books, 1995).

Plant, R., Beech, M. and Hickson, K., *The Struggle for Labour's Soul: Understanding Labour's Political Thought Since 1945* (Routledge, 2004).

Quinn, T., *Modernising the Labour Party: Organisational Change Since 1983* (Palgrave Macmillan, 2004).

Richards, P., *How to Win an Election* (Politico's, 2004).

Riddell, P., *Hug Them Close: Blair, Clinton and the Special Relationship* (Politico's, 2003).

Russell, M., *Building New Labour: The Politics of Party Organisation* (Palgrave Macmillan, 2005).

Scott, D., *Off Whitehall: A View from Downing Street by Tony Blair's Adviser* (I.B. Tauris, 2004).

Seldon, A., *Blair* (Free Press, 2005).

Seldon, A. and Hickson, K., *New Labour, Old Labour: The Wilson and Callaghan Governments, 1974–79* (Routledge, 2004).

Seyd, P. and Whitley, P., *New Labour's Grass Roots: The Transformation of the Labour Party Membership* (Palgrave Macmillan, 2002).

Shepherd-Robinson, L. and Lovenduski, J., *Women and Candidate Selection in British Political Parties* (Fawcett Society, 2002).

Stuart, M. and Smith, J., *All We Ask* (Methuen, 2005).

The Times, Guide to the House of Commons 2005 (Times Books, 2005).

Toynbee, P. and Walker, D., *Better or Worse?* (Bloomsbury, 1995).

Walters, S., *Tory Wars: Conservatives in Crisis* (Politicos, 2001).

Journals

Alderman, K. and Carter, N., 'The Conservative Party Leadership Election of 2001', *Parliamentary Affairs*, July 2002.

Baker, D., Seawright, D. and Gamble, A., 'Sovereign Nations and Global Markets: Modern British Conservatism and Hyperglobalism', *British Journal of Politics and International Relations*, October 2002.

Bale, T., '"It's Labour, But Not As We Know It." Media Lesson-drawing and the Disciplining of Social Democracy: A Case Study', *British Journal of Politics and International Relations*, August 2005.

Bara, J. and Budge, I., 'Party Policy and Ideology: Still New Labour?' *Parliamentary Affairs*, October 2001.

Beetham, D., Ngan, P. and Weir, S., 'Democratic Audit: Labour's Record So Far', *Parliamentary Affairs*, April 2001.

Blau, A., 'Fairness and Electoral Reform', *British Journal of Politics and International Relations*, May 2004.

Bogdanor, V., 'The Constitution and the Party System in the Twentieth Century', *Parliamentary Affairs*, October 2004.

Borisyuk, R., Borisyuk, G., Rallings, C. and Thrasher, M., 'Forecasting the 2005 General Election: A Neural Network Approach', *British Journal of Politics and International Relations*, May 2005.

Broughton, D., 'Doomed to Defeat? Electoral Support and the Conservative Party', *Political Quarterly*, October 2004.

Bufacchi, V., 'Voting, Rationality and Reputation', *Political Studies*, September 2001.

Burch, S. and Watt, B., 'Remote Electronic Voting: Free, Fair and Secret?', *Political Quarterly*, January 2004.

Burkitt, B. and Mullen, A., 'European Integration and the Battle for British Hearts and Minds: New Labour and the Euro', *Political Quarterly*, July 2003.

Burnham, P., 'New Labour and the Politics of Depoliticisation', *British Journal of Politics and International Relations*, June 2001.

Butler, D., 'Electoral Reform', *Parliamentary Affairs*, October 2004.

Campbell, C. and Rockman, B.A., 'Third Way Leadership, Old Way Government: Blair, Clinton and the Power to Govern', *British Journal of Politics and International Relations*, April 2001.

Clark, D. F., 'When the Parties Have to Stop', *Political Quarterly*, October 2001.

Clark, G. and Kelly, S., 'Echoes of Butler? The Conservative Research Department and the Making of Conservative Policy', *Political Quarterly*, October 2004.

Coates, D., 'Capitalist Models and Social Democracy: The Case of New Labour', *British Journal of Politics and International Relations*, October 2001.

Coleman, S., 'Online Campaigning', *Parliamentary Affairs*, October 2001.

Coleman, S., 'Election Call 2001: How Politicians and the Public Interacted', *Parliamentary Affairs*, October 2002.

Collings, D. and Seldon, A., 'Conservatives in Opposition', *Parliamentary Affairs*, October 2001. Coole, D., 'Agency, Truth and Meaning: Judging the Hutton Report', *British Journal of Political Science*, July 2005.

Cowley, P. and Stuart, M., 'Parliament: Hunting for Votes', *Parliamentary Affairs*, April 2005.

Cowley, P. and Stuart, M., 'Labour in disguise? Liberal Democrat MPs, 1997–2001', *British Journal of Politics and International Relations*, August 2003.

Crewe, I., 'The Opinion Polls: Still Biased to Labour', *Parliamentary Affairs*, October 2001.

Curtice, J., 'The Electoral System: Biased to Blair?', *Parliamentary Affairs*, October 2001.

Denver, D., 'The Liberal Democrat Campaign', *Parliamentary Affairs*, October 2001.

Denver, D., Hands, G. and MacAllister, I., 'The Electoral Impact of Constituency Campaigning in Britain, 1992–2001', *Political Studies*, June 2004.

Diplock, S., Gosschalk, B., Marshall, B. and Kaur-Ballagan, K., 'Non-Voters, Political Disconnection and Parliamentary Democracy', *Parliamentary Affairs*, October 2002.

Doig, A., 'Politics and Sleaze: Conservative Ghosts and Labour's Own Brand', *Parliamentary Affairs*, April 2003.

Doig, A., '45 Minutes of Infamy? Hutton, Blair and the Invasion of Iraq', *Parliamentary Affairs*, January 2005.

Doig, A., 'Sleaze and Trust: Labour Trades Mistrust for Sleaze', *Parliamentary Affairs*, April 2005. Doig, A. and Phythian, M., 'The Hutton Inquiry: Origins and Issues', *Parliamentary Affairs*, January 2005.

Dolowitz, D.P., 'Prosperity and Fairness? Can New Labour Bring Fairness to the 21st Century by Following the Dictates of Endogenous Growth?', *British Journal of Politics and International Relations*, May 2004.

Dorey, P., 'Attention to Detail: The Conservative Policy Agenda', *Political Quarterly*, October 2004.

Dorling, D., Eyre, H., Johnston, R. and Pattie, C., 'A Good Place to Bury Bad News? Hiding the Detail in the Geography on the Labour Party's Website', *Political Quarterly*, October 2002.

Dunleavy, P., Margetts, H., Smith, T. and Weir, S., 'Constitutional Reform, New Labour in Power and Public Trust in Government', *Parliamentary Affairs*, July 2001.

Durham, M., 'The Conservative Party, New Labour and the Politics of the Family', *Parliamentary Affairs*, July 2001.

Evans, T., 'Conservative Economics and Globalisation', *Political Quarterly*, October 2004.

Fenwick, H., 'Responding to 11 September: Detention without Trial under the Anti-Terrorism, Crime and Security Act 2001', *Political Quarterly*, August 2002.

Finegold, K. and Swift, E.K., 'What Works? Competitive Strategies of Major Parties Out of Power', *British Journal of Political Science*, January 2001.

Finlayson, A., 'Elements of the Blairite Image of Leadership', *Parliamentary Affairs*, July 2002.

Fisher, J., 'Campaign Finance: Elections Under New Rules', *Parliamentary Affairs*, October 2001. Fisher, J., 'Money Matters: The Financing of the Conservative Party', *Political Quarterly*, October 2004.

Fisher, J., 'Next Step: State Funding for the Parties?', *Political Quarterly*, October 2002.

Fisher, J. and Webb, P., 'Political Participation: The Vocational Motivations of Labour Party Employees', *British Journal of Politics and International Relations*, May 2003.

Foley, M., 'Presidential Attribution as an Agency of Prime Ministerial Critique in a Parliamentary Democracy: The Case of Tony Blair', *British Journal of Politics and International Relations*, August 2004.

Fraser, D., 'Beyond the Ratchet Theory: New Labour and Policy Consolidation Strategies', *Political Quarterly*, October 2003.

Gamble, A., 'Political Memoirs', *British Journal of Politics and International Relations*, April 2002.

Garnett, M., 'The Free Economy and the Schizophrenic State: Ideology and the Conservatives', *Political Quarterly*, October 2004.

Garnett, M. and Lynch, P., 'Bandwagon Blues: The Tory Fightback Fails', *Political Quarterly*, January 2002.

Gavin, N.T. and Sanders, D., 'The Press and Its Influence on British Political Attitudes under New Labour', *Political Studies*, October 2003.

Gay, O., 'MPs Go Back to Their Constituencies', *Political Quarterly*, January 2005.

Glees, A., 'Evidence-Based Policy or Policy-Based Evidence? Hutton and the Government's Use of Secret Intelligence', *Parliamentary Affairs*, January 2005.

Grant, A., 'Party and Election Finance in Britain and America: A Comparative Analysis', *Parliamentary Affairs*, January 2005.

Hale, S., 'Professor Macmurray and Mr Blair: The Strange Case of the Communitarian Guru that Never Was', *Political Quarterly*, April 2002.

Hefferman, R., 'Beyond Euro-scepticism: Exploring the Europeanisation of the Labour Party since 1983', *Political Quarterly*, April 2001.

Henessy, P., 'Informality and Circumscription: The Blair Style of Government in War and Peace', *Political Quarterly*, January 2005.

Hennessy, P., 'Rulers and Servants of the State: The Blair Style of Government 1997–2004', *Parliamentary Affairs*, January 2005.

Higgett, P., 'Iraq: Blair's Mission Impossible', *British Journal of Politics and International Relations*, August 2005.

Hindmoor, A., 'Reading Downs: New Labour and An Economic Theory of Democracy', *British Journal of Politics and International Relations*, August 2005.

Humphreys, J., 'The Iraq Dossier and the Meaning of Spin', *Parliamentary Affairs*, January 2005.

Huntington, M. and Bale, P. 'New Labour: New Christian Democracy?', *Political Quarterly*, January 2002.

Ingle, S., 'Politics: The Year the War was Spun', *Parliamentary Affairs*, April 2004.

Jayasuriya, K., 'The New Contractualism: NeoLiberal or Democratic?', *Political Quarterly*, July 2002.

Johnston R., Propper C., Burgess S., Sarker R., Bolster, A. and Jones, K., 'Spatial Scale and the Neighbourhood Effect: Multinomial Models of Voting at Two Recent British General Elections', *British Journal of Political Science*, July 2005.

Jones, N., 'After Spin. But What about Parliament?', *Political Quarterly*, July 2004.

Jordan, A., 'Decarbonising the UK: A "Radical Agenda" from the Cabinet Office', *Political Quarterly*, July 2002.

Kelly, R., 'Conservatism Under Hague: The Fatal Dilemma', *Political Quarterly*, April 2001.

Kelly, R., 'Farewell Conference, Hello Forum: The Making of Labour and Tory Policy', *Political Quarterly*, July 2001.

Kelly, R., 'Renew and Reorganise: Party Structures and the Politics of Reinvention', *Political Quarterly*, January 2003.

Kelly, R., 'The Extra-Parliamentary Tory Party: McKenzie Revisited', *Political Quarterly*, October 2004.

Kelly, R., 'The Party Didn't Work: Conservative Reorganisation and Electoral Failure', *Political Quarterly*, January 2002.

King, A., 'The Outsider as Political Leader: The Case of Margaret Thatcher', *British Journal of Political Science*, July 2002.

Kotler-Berkowitz, L.A., 'Religion and Voting Behaviour in Great Britain: A Reassessment', *British Journal of Political Science*, July 2001.

Lambe, P., Rallings, C. and Thrasher, M., 'Elections and Public Opinion: Plus ça change …', *Parliamentary Affairs*, April 2005.

Lees-Marshment, J., 'Mis-marketing the Conservatives: The Limitations of Style over Substance', *Political Quarterly*, October 2004.

Lees-Marshment, J. and Quayle, S., 'Empowering the Members or Marketing the Party? The Conservative Reforms of 1998', *Political Quarterly*, April 2001.

Lynch, P., 'Saving the Union: Conservatives and the "Celtic Fringe"', *Political Quarterly*, October 2004.

Mullard, M., 'New Labour, New Public Expenditure: The Case of Cake Tomorrow', *Political Quarterly*, July 2001.

Newton, K. and Brynin, M., 'The National Press and Party Voting in the UK', *Political Studies*, June 2001.

Norris, P., 'Apathetic Landslide: The 2001 British General Election', *Parliamentary Affairs*, October 2001.

Norris, P., 'The Twilight of Westminster? Electoral Reform and its Consequences', *Political Studies*, September 2001.

Pattie, C. and Johnston, R., 'A Low Turnout Landslide: Abstention at the British General Election of 1997', *Political Studies*, June 2001.

Pattie, C. and Johnston, R., 'Losing the Voters' Trust: Evaluations of the Political System and Voting at the 1997 British General Election', *British Journal of Politics and International Relations*, June 2001.

Phelps, E., 'Young Citizens and Changing Electoral Turnout, 1964–2001', *Political Quarterly*, July 2004.

Phythian, M., 'Hutton and Scott: A Tale of Two Inquiries', *Parliamentary Affairs*, January 2005.

Prabhakar, R., 'Capability, Responsibility, Human Capital and the Third Way', *Political Quarterly*, January 2002.

Quinn, T., 'Electing the Leader: The British Labour Party's Electoral College', *British Journal of Politics and International Relations*, August 2004.

Rallings, C. and Thrasher, M., 'Elections and Public Opinion: The End of the Honeymoon?', *Parliamentary Affairs*, April 2001.

Rallings, C. and Thrasher, M., 'Elections and Public Opinion: Amidst the Apathy, Another Landslide', *Parliamentary Affairs*, April 2002.

Rallings, C. and Thrasher, M., 'Elections and Public Opinion: Conservative Doldrums and Continuing Apathy', *Parliamentary Affairs*, April 2003.

Rallings, C. and Thrasher, M., 'Local Electoral Participation in Britain', *Parliamentary Affairs*, October 2003.

Rallings, C. and Thrasher, M., 'Elections and Public Opinion: Leaders Under Pressure', *Parliamentary Affairs*, April 2004.

Rallings, C. and Thrasher, M., 'Explaining Split-Ticket Voting at the 1979 and 1997 General and Local Elections in England', *Political Studies*, October 2003.

Rallings, C. and Thrasher, M., 'Research Note: Measuring the Level and Direction of Split-ticket Voting at the 1979 and 1997 British General and Local Elections: a Survey-based Analysis', *Political Studies*, June 2001.

Roth, A., 'Michael Howard: The First Jewish Prime Minister?', *Political Quarterly*, October 2004. Russell, A., 'Parties and Party Systems: Realignment or Readjustment?', *Parliamentary Affairs*, April 2004.

Russell, A., 'The Party System: Deep Frozen or Gentle Thawing?', *Parliamentary Affairs*, April 2005. Russell, A., Fieldhouse, E. and MacAllister, I., 'The Anatomy of Liberal Support in Britain, 1974–1997', *British Journal of Politics and International Relations*, April 2002.

Saggar, S., 'The Race Card, Again', *Parliamentary Affairs*, October 2001.

Saggar, S., 'Immigration and the Politics of Public Opinion', *Political Quarterly*, August 2003. Sanders, D., Clarke, H., Stewart, M. and Whiteley, P., 'The Economy and Voting', *Parliamentary Affairs*, October 2001.

Sanders, D., 'Popularity Function Forecasts for the 2005 UK General Election', *British Journal of Politics and International Relations*, May 2005.

Seyd, P., 'The Labour Campaign', *Parliamentary Affairs*, October 2001.

Shaw, E., 'New Labour: New Pathways to Parliament', *Parliamentary Affairs*, January 2001.

Shaw, E., 'Britain: Left Abandoned? New Labour in Power', *Parliamentary Affairs*, January 2003.

Smith, T., '"Something Old, Something New, Something Borrowed, Something Blue": Themes of Tony Blair and his Government', *Parliamentary Affairs*, October 2003.

Snowdon, P. and Collins, P., 'Déjà vu? Conservative Problems in Historical Perspective', *Political Quarterly*, October 2004.

Stanyer, J., 'Politics and the Media: A Breakdown in Relations for New Labour', *Parliamentary Affairs*, April 2003.

Stephen, W. and Gibson, R., 'On-line and On Message? Candidate Websites in the 2001 General Election', *British Journal of Politics and International Relations*, May 2003.

Stuart, M. and Cowley, P., 'Still Causing Trouble: The Conservative Parliamentary Party', *Political Quarterly*, October 2004.

Taylor, M., 'Party Democracy and Civic Renewal', *Political Quarterly*, August 2001.

Taylor, M., 'Too Early to Say? New Labour's First Term', *Political Quarterly*, January 2001.

Tilley, J., 'Contracts, Compacts and Control: New Labour and Personal Responsibility', *Political Quarterly*, July 2005.

Webb, P., 'Parties and Party Systems: Modernisation, Regulation and Diversity', *Parliamentary Affairs*, April 2001.

Webb, P., 'Parties and Party Systems: More Continuity than Change', *Parliamentary Affairs*, April 2002.

Webb, P., 'Parties and Party System: Prospects for Realignment', *Parliamentary Affairs*, April 2003.

Whiteley, P., Clarke, H., Sanders, D. and Stewart, M., 'Turnout', *Parliamentary Affairs*, October 2001.

Whiteley, P.F., 'Forecasting Seats from Votes in British General Elections', *British Journal of Politics and International Relations*, May 2005.

Wickham-Jones, M., 'British Labour, European Social Democracy and the Reformist Trajectory: A Reply to Coates', *British Journal of Politics and International Relations*, October 2002.

Wring, D., 'Politics and the Media: The Hutton Inquiry, the Public Relations State, and Crisis at the BBC', *Parliamentary Affairs*, April 2005.

Index

24